GENDER FUTURITY, INTERSECTIONAL AUTOETHNOGRAPHY

Gender Futurity, Intersectional Autoethnography showcases a collection of narrative and autoethnographic research that unpacks the complexity of gender at its intersections, i.e. by ability, race, sexuality, religion, beauty, geography, spatiality, community, performance, politics, socio-economic status, education, and many other markers of difference.

The book focuses on gender as it is lived, chaperoned, and chaperones other social identity categories. It tells stories that reveal problematic gender binaries, promising gender futures, and everything in between—they ask us to rethink what we assume to be true, real, and normal about gender identity and expression. Each essay, written by both gender variant and cisgender scholars, explores cultural phenomena that create space for us to re-imagine, re-think, and create new ways of being.

This book will be useful for undergraduate, postgraduate, and professional degree students, particularly in the fields of gender studies, qualitative methods, and communication theory.

Amber L. Johnson is an Associate Professor of Communication and Social Justice at Saint Louis University and founder of The Justice Fleet, a mobile social justice museum fostering healing through art, dialogue, and play.

Benny LeMaster is an Assistant Professor of Critical/Cultural Communication Studies and Performance in the Hugh Downs School of Human Communication at Arizona State University. They spend most of their time in queer and trans community laughing, making art, performing, and cooking and eating, all while loving and being loved.

Writing Lives
Ethnographic Narratives
Series Editors: Arthur P. Bochner, Carolyn Ellis
and Tony E. Adams
University of South Florida and Northeastern Illinois University

For a full list of titles in this series, please visit:
https://www.routledge.com/Writing-Lives-Ethnographic-Narratives/
book-series/WLEN

GENDER FUTURITY, INTERSECTIONAL AUTOETHNOGRAPHY

Embodied Theorizing from the Margins

Edited by Amber L. Johnson
and Benny LeMaster

Routledge
Taylor & Francis Group

NEW YORK AND LONDON

First published 2020
by Routledge
52 Vanderbilt Avenue, New York, NY 10017

and by Routledge
2 Park Square, Milton Park, Abingdon, Oxon OX14 4RN

Routledge is an imprint of the Taylor & Francis Group, an informa business

British Library Cataloguing-in-Publication Data
A catalogue record for this book is available from the British Library

Library of Congress Cataloging-in-Publication Data
Names: Johnson, Amber, 1980- editor. | LeMaster, Benny, 1981- editor.
Title: Gender futurity, intersectional autoethnography : embodied
theorizing from the margins / edited by Amber Johnson and Benny
LeMaster.
Description: New York, NY : Routledge, 2020. | Series: Writing lives |
Includes bibliographical references and index. |
Identifiers: LCCN 2020001169 (print) | LCCN 2020001170 (ebook) | ISBN
9780367489618 (hardback) | ISBN 9780367489601 (paperback) | ISBN
9781003043683 (ebook)
Subjects: LCSH: Gender identity. | Group identity. | Intersectionality
(Sociology)
Classification: LCC HQ18.55 .G46 2020 (print) | LCC HQ18.55 (ebook) |
DDC 305.3--dc23
LC record available at https://lccn.loc.gov/2020001169
LC ebook record available at https://lccn.loc.gov/2020001170

ISBN: 9780367489618 (hbk)
ISBN: 9780367489601 (pbk)
ISBN: 9781003043683 (ebk)

Typeset in Bembo
by Cenveo® Publisher Services

CONTENTS

CONTRIBUTORS

Shadee Abdi is a critical cultural communication scholar whose research interests include intercultural, international, and diasporic communication; sexuality studies; family communication; performance studies; and performances of Iranian diaspora. Broadly, her work explores how conflicting discourses complicate and enhance our intersectional understandings of identity and power relative to race, culture, sexuality, gender, nationality, religion, ability, class, and family. She is specifically interested in narratives of resistance within familial and mediated contexts. She is an Assistant Professor of Communication at San Francisco State University.

Andrea Baldwin is a Lecturer at the University of Houston, Clear Lake. Baldwin received a Ph.D. from Southern Illinois University, Carbondale, in Communication Studies, and M.A. and B.A. from the University of North Texas in Communication Studies. Her research explores pedagogical experiences in spaces outside of the classroom and genealogical embodied mentoring in the academy. She has a background in Performance Studies with an interest in storytelling, adaptation, and rhetoric.

S. Donald Bellamy (Donny) is an artist and doctoral candidate in the Women and Gender Studies program in the School of Social Transformation at Arizona State University and a visiting Assistant Professor in the Gender Studies program at Skidmore College. His research explores the intersections of transgender studies, Queer of Color Critique, and masculinity studies. His most recent project, *"Tumblr Saved My Life": An Interdisciplinary Investigation of how Black Trans-Masculinity Operates through Tumblr*, uses critical and digital ethnography to explore how Black trans men articulate their racialized transgender masculinity via posts, selfies, hashtags, and reblogs on the social networking site Tumblr. As an artist and writer, Donny uses comedy and satire to explore the construction and performance of racialized gendered expressions. In both academic and creative spaces, Bellamy's work attempts to understand Black queer experiences in order to theorize subversive possibilities of being.

Wriply Marie Bennet is a proud, self-taught illustrator, actor, writer, and singer born and raised in Ohio. Her organizing work started with the Trans Women of Color Collective and expanded in Ferguson where she was a freedom rider traveling to stand with Mike Brown's family and community. Wriply's work expresses the perseverance, power, strength, resilience, grace, and beauty of trans and non-binary people. Her work sheds light on the lack of national outcry over the epidemic of Black trans women murdered each year at the hands of state sanctioned violence. Wriply's art has been used in numerous social justice flyers, and made its first film debut in MAJOR!, a documentary at the 2015 San Francisco Transgender Film Festival. She is the very talented artist of the cover artwork of this edited volume.

Gray Bowers is an independent artist and researcher with a bachelor's and master's degree in Psychological Research from California State University, Long Beach. They focus on understanding stress and trauma, as it relates to identity and its impacts on mental health and well-being. They attempt to approach their work and life with a desire for growth and promotion of well-being through personal expression in art and research.

Bernadette Marie Calafell (Ph.D., University of North Carolina) is Chair and Professor in the Department of Critical Race and Ethnic Studies at Gonzaga University. She is author of *Latina/o Communication Studies Theorizing Performance* and *Monstrosity, Performance, and Race in Contemporary Culture*, co-editor, with Michelle Holling, of *Latina/o Discourse in Vernacular Spaces: Somos de Una Voz?*, and co-editor, with Shinsuke Eguchi, of *Queer Intercultural Communication: The Intersectional Belongings in and across Difference*.

Daniel B. Coleman (he/they) is a trans feminist artist-scholar and Assistant Professor of Women's, Gender, and Sexuality Studies at the University of North Carolina at Greensboro. Daniel's research utilizes methods like Performance as Research, oral history, and critical performance ethnography to think about Black diasporic lives in the United States and Mexico, transgender embodiment practices from Black and Brown cosmologies, and critical ecological engagements with place, space, and time for TGNC people. He is currently completing his first book manuscript.

Anthony P. Cuomo (M.A., Cal State, Long Beach) is an Assistant Professor of Communication Studies and Vice Chair of the Language Arts Division at West Los Angeles College.

Shinsuke Eguchi (Ph.D., Howard University) is an Associate Professor in the Department of Communication and Journalism at the University of New Mexico.

Their research interests focus on global and transcultural studies, queer of color critique, intersectionality and racialized gender politics, Asian/Pacific/American studies, and performance studies. Their mostly recent work will appear and/ or has appeared for publication in *Journal of Homosexuality, Women Studies in Communication, China Media Research, Cultural Studies ↔ Critical Methodologies, Departures in Critical Qualitative Research, Critical Studies in Media Communication,* and *QED: A Journal in GLBTQ Worldmaking.* With Bernadette Marie Calafell, they are also the co-editor of *Queer Intercultural Communication: The Intersectional Politics of Belonging in and across Differences* released from Rowman & Littlefield (2020; Lanham, MD).

Kai M. Green is a shape-shifting Black queer feminist nerd; an Afro-Future, freedom-dreaming, rhyme slinging dragon slayer in search of a new world; a scholar, poet, facilitator, filmmaker; and an Assistant Professor of Women's, Gender, and Sexuality studies at Williams College. Dr. Green explores questions of Black sexual and gender agency, health, creativity, and resilience in the context of state and social violence. An interdisciplinary scholar, Dr. Green employs Black Feminist Theory, performance studies, and trans studies to investigate forms of self-representation and communal methods of political mobilization by Black queer folk. Dr. Green earned a Ph.D. from the Department of American Studies and Ethnicity with specializations in Gender Studies and Visual Anthropology at the University of Southern California. Kai M. Green is a former postdoctoral fellow in Sexuality Studies and African American Studies at Northwestern University and winner of the Ford Foundation Pre-Doctoral and Dissertation Fellowships. Dr. Green published and edited work in GLQ: Gay and Lesbian Quarterly, South Atlantic Quarterly, Black Camera, and TSQ: Transgender Studies Quarterly.

Kathryn Hobson (B.A., Luther College; M.A., Ph.D., University of Denver) is an Assistant Professor of Communication Studies at James Madison University. She primarily teaches courses in the cultural communication track. Her research focuses on critical intercultural communication, queer and feminist performance, and arts-based qualitative methods. She has published in *Qualitative Inquiry, Liminalities, Kaleidoscope,* and has authored and co-authored several book chapters about queer identity, femininity, and social change.

Billy Huff, Ph.D., is a Lecturer of Communication at the University of Illinois at Urbana Champaign and a Research Associate with the Unit for Institutional Change and Social Justice at the University of the Free State in Bloemfontein, South Africa.

Greg Hummel (Ph.D., Southern Illinois University, Carbondale) is an Assistant Professor of Communication Studies at SUNY Oneonta. Greg earned his doctorate at Southern Illinois University. Broadly, Greg is interested in conceptualizations of identity, voice, agency, and social justice activism globally and locally. His research is framed within critical, interpretative, and performative paradigms that center questions of power, privilege, marginalization, and oppression across various intersecting identities including race, class, gender, sexuality, disability, religion, ethnicity, nationality, and size. His latest co-authored publication focuses on queering the bully-victim dichotomy to re-narrate and implicate each of us as "bully" in hopes that we reflexively question our communicative engagement with each other differently. Greg also embraces a critical pedagogy in each of his courses. He is currently teaching Intercultural Communication, Rhetoric, Argumentation, Perspectives on Communication, and Gender and Communication.

Stacy Holman Jones is a Professor in the Centre for Theatre and Performance at Monash University. Her research focuses broadly on how performance as socially, culturally, and politically resistive and transformative activity. Over the course of a 20-year career, she has developed an international reputation for leading the development of performance, feminist and cultural studies research, gender and sexualities studies, and innovative and critical arts-based methodologies. Her performance-based and narrative research spans cultural critique and social inclusion, education and resilience building, and enhancing health and well-being among minoritarian cultures and communities. She is recognized for a collaborative and impact-focused research program that integrates theory and creative practice as a means of critique and transforming lives, relationships, ways of living, and communities. She has published or has in press more than 90 articles, book chapters, reviews, and editorials, and has authored, co-authored, and edited 14 books. She is the founding editor of *Departures in Critical Qualitative Research*, a journal dedicated to publishing innovative, experimental, aesthetic, and provocative works on the theories, practices, and possibilities of critical qualitative research.

Nora J. Klein is an independent artist and poet. Her work explores themes of embodiment, dysphoria, disillusionment, and possibility.

Meggie Mapes (Ph.D. Southern Illinois University Carbondale) is Introductory Course Director at the University of Kansas. Her research emerges at the intersections of critical pedagogy and feminist rhetoric. She's currently investigating carceral feminism and the prison industrial complex, with special emphasis on batter intervention programming. Meggie lives in Kansas City with her partner and two amazing dogs.

J. Nyla McNeill is a shape-shifting, healing being living on occupied Tongva land in California. They identify as Afrohispinxy. J. Nyla's a poet, educator, dream worker, light worker, and cultural worker. A researcher in the fields of psychology and transgender health sciences, they are interested in understanding cissexism at systemic levels. Though most likely injured due to skateboarding, they love to love, dance, and feed people good food.

Shane T. Moreman is a Professor in the Department of Communication at California State University, Fresno—the department's first tenured and promoted Latinx faculty and faculty of color. As an intercultural communication scholar, his research mainly concerns Latinx/a/o populations, but more generally it involves critical approaches to the communicative and performative aspects of all cultural identity expression and interaction. Using humanities-influenced methods, his research foci encompass mediated forms, naturalistic settings, and personal narrative. He has taught in Mexico, China, Great Britain, and Costa Rica; he has guest lectured in Colombia. An avid traveler, Dr. Moreman has visited 20% of the world's countries to date. Married to an arts journalist, he is continually the plus-one at arts events locally and wherever he travels. Despite the world's arthritic structural inequality and academia's oppressive and appropriating groupthink, he remains optimistic. Dr. Moreman believes that with the right questions and methods, art always offers the better answer.

Vin Olefer is a non-binary poet studying English Rhetoric at California State University, Long Beach. Through their writing and visual arts, they explore topics such as gender and politics while exposing the beauty and absurdity of everyday life.

Miranda Dottie Olzman is a scholar/artist/activist invested in using their body, voice, and privilege to form lasting impacts within and beyond the academy. Their research trajectory blends autoethnography, performance, and critical scholarship in a fusion of intersectional and critical inquiry around body type, body image, and mediated representations and how those entities inform the way people insert their selves and their bodies in physical and digital spaces. Miranda is a doctoral candidate at the University of Denver.

Craig Gingrich-Philbrook is a Professor of Performance Studies in the Communication Studies Department at Southern Illinois University, Carbondale. His work has appeared in such journals as *Text and Performance Quarterly*, *Communication Theory*, *The Quarterly Journal of Speech*, *The Journal of Homosexuality*, *Cultural Studies*, *Departures in Critical Qualitative Research*, *Qualitative Inquiry*, *QED: A Journal in GLBTQ Worldmaking*, *International Review of Qualitative Research*, and *Liminalities: An Online Journal of Performance Studies*. At SIUC he teaches courses in Performance Studies, Autoethnography, and Queer Theory. He has presented his autobiographical performance work at universities around the country and at performance art venues including Dixon Place and SUSHI. In 2008, he received the National Communication Association's Leslie Irene Coger Award for Outstanding Performance. He also edited *Text and Performance Quarterly* from 2019 to 2021.

Julie-Ann Scott is a Professor of Communication Studies at the University of North Carolina, Wilmington. She is the Director of UNCW Performance Studies. Dr. Scott-Pollock's research focuses on personal narrative as performance of identity in daily life, as well as on stigmatized embodiment. She is particularly interested in personal stories of bodies living with illness and disability and the intersections of disability, gender, sexuality, and whiteness. Her book *Embodied Performance as Applied Research, Art and Pedagogy* is the recipient of the 2018 Book of the Year in Ethnography for the National Communication Association.

Danny Shultz is an interdisciplinary queer scholar from Southern California who recently completed a master's degree in Psychological Research at California State University, Long Beach, and is currently creating a book of poetry about familial dislocation and gender/sexual trauma. Danny's approach to creative and scholarly work incorporates influences from critical/queer theory, social psychology, psychoanalysis, and cultural studies to examine how systems of oppression are performatively maintained and embodied. Holes fascinate Danny, and they understand many social problems in terms of troubled relationships to structural lack within the human being. Danny envisions a queer world where humans no longer rely on gender and instead fully embrace their multitudes because gender is understood to be an arcane method of social control that relies upon genital signification.

ACKNOWLEDGMENTS

With every edited volume comes a host of labors that many never witness. I thank those who labored before me. I thank those who labor beside me. I thank those who will labor after me. It is because of you that this project came to fruition and will be the fruitful imaginary we all need as we work to dismantle systems of oppression and rebuild the fantastical and free future in its wake. Robin Boylorn and Mark Orbe, thank you for paving the way with *Critical Autoethnography: Intersecting Cultural Identities in Everyday Life*. I want to acknowledge all of the queer, trans, and non-binary youth and family in my life who consistently push me to re-evaluate my own assumptions about the world, while also pushing me to love the me that I am/already becoming. Thank you Axle and Oliver. To all the contributors of this volume, thank you for your vulnerability, courage, laughter, perseverance, and persistence. Your labor shows through beautifully in the work you continue to craft. To all my activist family, thank you for your care, compassion, and dedication.

Amber L. Johnson

I am a settler working on colonized lands. As such, I would like to begin by recognizing the Akimel O'odham, Tohono O'odham, and Piipaash lands on which much of this labor was conducted. With that, I am forever indebted to the indigenous persons and communities with whom I collaborate to realize a political posture that labors toward decolonization of mind, body, and land. Thank you to the Council (Meggie Mapes, Gregory Hummel, Diana Woodhouse, and Michael Selck), my amazing(!) students, my friends and colleagues, and my fellow artists, agitators, accomplices, and abolitionists. I want to especially thank my queer and trans kith and kin near and far, now and then, imagined and material. Together, we create worlds of our own design. And we thrive because of it. And special thanks to my loves, lovers, and sweeties—I love and appreciate each of you so very much. I thrive because of your support. Now, who wants tacos?

Benny LeMaster

INTRODUCTION

Gender Futurity, Intersectional Autoethnography

Gender scholarship is ripe with contention and possibility. Standing in the nexus of past, present, and future, gender scholarship finds itself at a crossroads, needing to pay particular attention to intersectionality, new and emerging gender identities, diverse gender expressions, and the constant need to reimagine what is possible when we think of bodies as houses for gender simulation. There exists a massive need to unpack the complexity of gender as it chaperones/is chaperoned by ability, race, sexuality, religion, beauty, geography, spatiality, community, performance, politics, socio-economic status, education, and many other markers of difference. While artifacts worthy of media analysis help us understand and confront stereotypical depictions of gendered bodies and lived experiences, what is possible, complex, and promising about gender rests in the narratives tied to real people and experiences that aren't chaperoned by attractive stereotypes and bias along the path of media production. This edited volume is a compilation of narrative research that forces us to rethink everything we know about gender at the intersections, as it is lived, chaperoned, and chaperones other social identity categories.

In 2012, Drs. Robin Boylorn and Mark Orbe co-edited a foundational text for intercultural and interpersonal communication scholars studying matters of social identity by using narrative research to unpack the messy intersections of race, gender, sexuality, health, education, religion, and socio-economic status as points of contention, disruption, and possibility.[1] What their text accomplished was introducing messy processes of identity rooted in experiences that are impossible to dismiss or refute as pretentious academic analysis reaching for appraisal and accolades. The stories they curated were deeply moving, complexly problematic, strangely familiar, and expertly contextualized through Boylorn and Orbe's masterful introductory sections.

What we curated in this volume is a similar compilation of narrative research that force us to rethink everything we know about gender at the intersections as it is lived, chaperoned, and chaperones other social identity categories. The stories reveal problematic gender binaries and promising gender futures that ask us to rethink what we assume to be true, real, and normal about gender identity and expression in an effort to reimagine, rethink, and create new ways of being. This introduction offers a short discussion of gender research, how we arrived at autoethnographic inquiry in this moment, and the organization of the volume—first, a brief look at gender, intersectionality, and the importance of theorizing from the margins.

Gender

Researching gender is necessarily complex, just as is it complex to live and embody gender. The reasons for these complexities are, well, complex. At the same time, however, the reason for these complexities can be summed up thusly: Gender is not of our own design. Gender is at once subjective and relational. Given this broad framing, Benny LeMaster and Amber L. Johnson characterize gender as *ineffable, uncertain,* and *particular*.[2] Ineffable because gender is too broad a concept to generalize in any meaningfully consistent way. Uncertain because gender emerges in the space between identity and ideology. And particular because gender is rendered articulate according to intersectional hegemonic standards (cisgender, masculine/male/man, White, able-bodied, and so on) that mediate material rewards and penalties. In addition, gender is particular in the sense that it is an embodied and felt experience even if it is inarticulate from a normative vantage.[3] Said differently, the standards that render gender normatively "meaningful" are arbitrary and reflect the sensibilities of those whose understanding of gender appears to be static through time and across space. These criteria are not new nor did they emerge in a vacuum. Rather, the criteria are historically constituted and, as a result, reflect, create, and constrain cultural meaning as it pertains to gender.

In a US context, gender, race, and ability are co-constitutive forces.[4] Indeed, the United States is a colonized and settler state "founded" under the direction of Western imperial forces seeking to displace, destroy, *and* replace local and indigenous peoples, cultures, and cosmologies for the purpose of domination and expanding capital.[5] Colonialism was/is a violent capitalist venture. Its continued "success" depends on reductive notions of bodily being that work in service of capitalist development and, in turn, securing the stability of the (colonial, settler) nation-state. For instance, the stability of the nation-state is dependent, in part, upon (cisheterosexual reproductive) inheritance rituals that ensure accumulated wealth remains in the possession of a few (largely cishet-erosexual White) entities. In this regard, gender can be thought of as a colonial technology that, at least in part, makes culture "work." Gender so understood is individually experienced and lived as it is constrained by larger, historically significant, cultural expectations. To study gender is to study culture in this broader, intersectional, and historical sense. For this, we turn to María Lugones who characterizes gender as a "modern colonial imposition."[6] Lugones is not alone in her theorizing of racialized gender as a colonial technology.[7] Though, for our purposes, her critical insight provides a productive means to deconstruct gender so as to better grapple with gender meaning in a broader, intersectional, and historical sense.

Lugones' research reveals gender to be a mark of human status, distinction. She writes, "Only the civilized are men or women."[8] Though, the mark of civi-lization was reserved for (White) Western bodies. More particularly, under colo-nialism, the (White) Western "man" came to define "human" while the (White) Western "woman" was "not his compliment" but, rather, the one charged with "reproduc[ing] race and capital."[9] As a result, (White) Western women's sexual-ity was disciplined to work in service of reproducing and upholding the human (read: White, patriarchal) race. Meanwhile, (White) Western men dominated the public sphere advancing *their own* interests both locally and globally. (White) Western men, emboldened by structures of their own design, employed colo-nization as a vehicle through which to assert their global domination. In doing so, they imposed Western ideologies, including the racist means by which to distinguish humans from non-humans. Non-Western subjects were understood as "not human, as animals, as monstrously and aberrantly sexual, wild."[10] As a result, colonizers distinguished non-Western and enslaved Africans and indig-enous populations throughout the Americas on the basis of presumed sex or sexual dimorphism. "Male" and "female" were thus used as means to distin-guish reproductive capacity, and thus bodily worth, under racist capitalism. Said more directly, "gender" was used to distinguish humans while "sex" was used to distinguish animals including non-Western humans denied human status under colonial rule. As a result, the gender binary is a White supremacist project used to distinguish White notions of gender being and becoming from racialized notions of non-human embodiment.[11] In their book, *decolonizing trans/gender 101*, b. binaohan clarifies, "the binary as tool of oppression is not about legitimizing binary genders over non-binary genders, in a general sense, but about legitimiz-ing a White notion of manhood and a White notion of womanhood. And, in turn, this is inextricably tied to who is considered 'human' and who isn't" (126). Indeed, even those whom we might understand as gender non-conforming by contemporary standards, and/or as two-spirit by/in some indigenous commu-nities,[12] were violently disciplined for failure to abide by colonial standards of gender normativity. However, these violences were not particular to gender but, rather, to racialized gender specifically. Those persons who failed to embody normative colonial notions of racialized gender were met with violent ends.[13] The impacts of these historical observations remain with us today.

In this anthology, we understand gender to be a *colonial refrain*, a performative perpetuation of racialized gender normativity rooted in colonial control and domination. Under this rubric, we can better grapple with the question: Why are transgender, transsexual, and gender non-conforming people of color, and indigenous and Black trans women of color in particular, disproportionately targeted for violence? As a colonial refrain, we can understand this violence as an ongoing effect of the socio-historical dehumanization of those who fall outside of White Western criteria for "appropriate" gender performance, comportment, embodiment, and identity. To understand gender thusly requires that we *unlearn* gender with the goal of affirming and thus humanizing racialized gender difference. The essays and poems that comprise this anthology labor to perform this unlearning process by engaging gender in critical and intersectional terms.

Intersectional Autoethnography

I (Amber) remember my first introduction to autoethnography vividly. Dr. Bob Krizek, my graduate mentor and research methods professor, read aloud his famous essay, "Goodbye Old Friend: A Son's Farewell to Comiskey Park."[14] So many thoughts swirled through my mind amidst the tears, the reflection, and the wonder as my professor narrated his grief, love, and allegiance for the memories that defined his childhood and his relational self. I remember thinking, *this is the kind of research I want to do! Emotionally captivating stories teach us so much. Why am I just now learning about this? I can be a creative writer and researcher at the same time?* In that moment, I knew I would be an autoethnographer. What I did not know was that autoethnography would save my life by providing a platform to share my experiences as poetic catharsis while also creating space to digest, and eventually divest, power. In the last lines of the essay, as Dr. Krizek wiped his own tears and the rest of us students wiped ours, I realized that research can change a person, and by extension, our world. Much like the opposite of demolishing a building and breaking the bridges that connect us to our pasts, writing down these narratives generates an archive of experience that may never die; our stories, memories, and connections not only live on, but keep changing the world into one worth preserving. When I think of that archive of experience as it relates to intersectionality and gender, I think of the lack of personal narrative gender research that promotes understanding alongside a sense of obligation to right wrongs and alter future trajectories to be radically inclusive and affirming of all gender expression. As a Black, queer, non-binary, all-gender-loving person who needs to feel and be affirmed, this is that archive for me.

I (Benny) came to autoethnography through my advisor, Dr. Marc Rich, who chaired my master thesis titled "Queering Conversion: An Ethnographic Account of the Ex-Gay Movement." My choice to engage autoethnography reflected my desire to critically explore my lived experience navigating conversion discourse, space, time, and familial relations as a young queer and trans person raised Southern Baptist. I disclose in my thesis, "I was initially focused on the sexual orientation conversion process, unprepared for the embodied responses that I would experience while partaking in Christian rituals once again."[15] Autoethnography provided a narrative and poetic means by which to articulate deep-seated, complex, and difficult expressions of embodied traumas and affects. Autoethnography continues to play an important role in my exploration of embodiment, identity, culture, and ideology as a mixed-race Asian/White queer and trans person who expresses themself in creative terms that often chafe against the decorum of academe. In addition, autoethnography is conducive to performance. As a result, I turn to autoethnography for its pedagogical potential. Said differently, my autoethnographies are intended to be read *and* performed—on the page and on the stage. While traditional research can yield important insight, it is often (rightly) charged with being inaccessible due to high publisher costs, abstract disciplinary-specific language used to convey complex ideas, or any other number of important and accurate charges. A challenge in autoethnography, to me, then, includes finding ways in which to convey complex thought into narrative forms that can engage an (non-disciplinary, non-academic) audience in far more diverse and affirming ways.

★ ★ ★

Autoethnography is research, writing, storytelling, and a method that connects the autobiographical and personal to the cultural, social, political,[16] and performance.[17] Autoethnography calls for inserting the bodily flesh and its many positions as ways of (not)knowing via autopoetic narrative,[18] autocritography,[19] performance,[20] and rhetorical autoethnography.[21] Regardless of approach, the goal of an autoethnographic text is to produce a creative yet critical articulation of lived experiences in a textual performance where different perceptions and standpoints of the same experiences enter into conversation,[22] and create new memories and new experiences that foster a space for understanding and possibility.

Intersectionality is an approach to research and theory that forefronts the compounded impact of race, class, gender, sexuality, and other social identity categories on lived experiences within systems of power. An intersectional approach to research and theory requires that the researcher be cognizant of how systems of injustice affect lived experiences across multiple categories because those categories and systems of power are interdependent, complex, and inseparable. Ange-Marie Hancock defines intersectionality as "both the normative theoretical argument and an approach to conducting empirical research...that considers the interaction of race, gender, class, and other organizing structures of society a key component influencing political access, equality and the potential for any form of justice."[23] Kimberlé Crenshaw coined the term in her groundbreaking article, "Mapping the Margins: Intersectionality, Identity Politics, and Violence Against Women of Color."[24] She used the theory to delineate the qualitative differences between cisgender women's experiences with sexual assault and domestic abuse across intersections of race and class. What Crenshaw's work contributes to autoethnographic scholarship is a formula for mapping the multiple and overlapping ways bodies not only perform as political entities through discourse but endure the systematic attempts to maintain power through representation, politics, and institutions. The labels attached to our bodies mimic more than arbitrary words designed to highlight difference; they also have the ability to (re) inforce and challenge power structures as divisive systems of oppression.

Intersectionality and autoethnography together affect what stories we choose to tell, how we understand our bodies and other bodies within stories, and how we connect our bodies and stories to larger political structures and systems of power. An autoethnographer can establish intersectional praxis by addressing the four criteria for a rigorous autoethnography—narrative fidelity and cohesion, self-reflexivity, and connecting the personal to the political—via representational, structural, and political intersectionality respectively.

Narrative fidelity and narrative cohesion via representational intersectionality. Narrative fidelity and cohesion extend from Walter Fisher's narrative paradigm, which suggests that humans are natural storytellers and communicate via stories.[25] If humans see the world through stories, Fisher crafts the criteria for judging the merit and value of story via narrative cohesion and fidelity.[26] Narrative cohesion suggests that for a story to make sense, it must be consistent internally and structurally. Internal consistency means the characters are reliable and there are sufficient details. Structural consistency means the story aligns with similar narratives. Narrative fidelity points to whether a story fits *a priori* understandings, values, and ideas.[27]

Representational intersectionality refers to the rhetorical, cultural, and social constructions of representative bodies within popular and everyday cultural contexts. For instance, mediated representations of non-trans Black women are largely wrought with stereotypes, while trans and non-binary people are largely absent from mediated representation. Implementing representational intersectionality through narrative fidelity requires that the narrator give truth to power and give power to truth. The narrator does this in three ways: (1) locating their truth as one possible truth within a complex system of power and perceptions; (2) mapping the way power affects the way they understand their truth and are willing to tell it; and (3) understanding the fissures, ruptures, and mistruths in the narrative as they are connected to power. The narrator must unpack these moments for deeper meaning and value. Incorporating representational inter-sectionality through narrative cohesion requires acknowledging how power informs the storytelling process and mapping connections to the theoretical and analytical sensibilities that drive a narrative and subsequent analysis. For instance, who do the narrators cite as framing agents in their work, what theories do they point to and why, what stories do they choose to tell, how do all of these decisions mimic their own values, and what does that mimicry suggest about power structures?

Self-reflexivity and structural intersectionality. Self-reflexivity is the intentional and rhetorical process of analyzing our own research processes, biases, word choices, story choices, and analytic choices in a constant process of perception checking. As Kristi Malterud suggests, "a researcher's background and position will affect what they choose to investigate, the angle of investigation, the methods judged most adequate for this purpose, the findings considered most appropriate, and the framing and communication of conclusions."[28] When considering the subjective and deeply personal process of analyzing our own stories as research, self-reflexivity is even more imperative. Mary Weems warns us that separating intellect, imagination, reflection, and emotion is a mistake.[29] "New ideas and reflection incorporate imagination, reason, logic, and passion that drives us to pursue research, to ask questions, and to take risks. It is not possible to formulate an idea without reflection, or to develop an idea without imagination."[30] Autoethnographic research promotes the symbiotic merging of intellectual rigor and imagination through reflexive writing. "The narrative text is reflexive," Norman K. Denzin writes, "not only in its use of language but also in how it positions the writer in the text and uses the writer's experiences as both the topic of inquiry and a resource for uncovering problematic experience."[31]

Structural intersectionality refers to location, systemic injustice, and how people experience differences due to situational circumstances as they correlate to systemic power. For instance, unemployment, immigrant status, formal job training, race and gender oppression, where one lives, and/or lack of access to resources and information determine how a person responds to a specific situation. Approaching structural intersectionality from a non-binary point, we can attend to the ways in which trans women experience structural hardships at an even greater degree due to a lack of cisgender identity, often experiencing physical and discursive violence from both cismen and ciswomen.

Self-reflexivity is an exercise in unpacking structural intersectionality because pealing back the layers of systemic power and how they dictate the way we conduct research, tell our stories, and reflect back on those processes requires a keen awareness of structural power and experience. As Kristin M. Langellier reminds us:

> Identity and experience are symbiosis of performed story and the social relations in which they are materially embedded: sex, class, race, ethnicity,

sexuality, geography, religion, and so on. This is why personal narrative performance is especially crucial to those communities left out of the privileges of dominant culture, those bodies without voice in the political sense.[32]

Being self-reflexive in an autoethnographic text is a rhetorically courageous act of unpacking our own biases and linguistic choices because they connect to larger systems of structural power.

The personal is political and political intersectionality. The final criterion for establishing rigor as an autoethnographer is the connection between the personal and political. Autoethnography highlights three concerns: (1) how cultural practices shape identity, (2) how identity shapes cultural performance, and (3) how publicly responsible autoethnography addresses central issues of self, race, gender, society and democracy, through imagination, intellect, reflection, and emotion.[33] In order to pursue the body as a reflexive site of (not)knowing, one must position the body by examining the social identity categories tied to the body, and the respective systems of power that chaperone how and why bodies moves through the world. Political intersectionality is one theoretical framework for understanding systems of power as complex, intertwined, and overlapping on the single body's social identity categories and their political ramifications.

Political intersectionality refers to the ways in which people are often silenced and marginalized by contradicting political agendas like anti-racist versus anti-sexist groups. Political intersectionality points to the ways social movements compound systemic injustice by focusing on single identity issues as if they are neat, compartmentalized, and capable of being understood apart from other identity categories within the single body. As a non-binary Black person, I (Amber) cannot separate my experiences of racism from my experiences of sexism; I understand them in tandem. Unfortunately, as social groups attempt to fuse intersectional difference across race, class, and gender, those attempts are still largely targeting cisgender experience. For instance, the inaugural Women's March in 2017, attempted to be inclusive, but the pink pussy hats identified womanhood based on genitalia, and thus excluded a lot of trans women and non-binary femmes from participating. Understanding how political discourse and social movement target individual social identity categories while excluding complex understandings of human experience is crucial in connecting our bodies as political entities to discourse and the ways in which discourses attempt to silence some parts of us while uplifting other parts. The intersectional autoethnographer must tend to the political structures within and beyond the body.

When taken together, intersectional autoethnography allows authors to unpack the complex layers of power systems that chaperone experience. Intersectional autoethnography helps the narrator and reader unpack the roles patriarchy, racism, sexism, binary gender, and colonialism play in their experiences and provide complexity, nuance, and possibility for emancipation. The intersectional autoethnographies included in this manuscript tend to the aforementioned criteria in multiple ways. *Gender Futurity, Intersectional Autoethnography: Embodied Theorizing from the Margins* comprises nine poems, one script, and eleven essays divided into four themed sections: Existence as Disruption; Identity Negotiation and Internal Struggles; The Erotic as a Site for Normative Disruption; and Queering History, Imagining Futures.

Existence as Disruption section focuses on compulsory structures and how they constrain identity. With every communication act, whether in performance, verbal communication, or otherwise, humans have the opportunity to reject, reify, challenge, or generate norms attached to identity categories. Despite the potential to disrupt, some identity categories and their attached performances of acceptability are so ingrained that humans assume they are natural and normal and reiterate those performances across interactions.[34] Adrienne Rich defines these performances as compulsory because they are assumed to be natural and carry with them consequences when humans choose to deviate.[35] Toxic masculinity is one example. When aggression, anger, and toughness are connected to masculinity, failure to perform those tropes suggests deviation from masculinity and creates space to ridicule those bodies that do not adhere to those norms. We see this carried out in everyday acts of masculine violence and the direct shaming of masculine identified folks who are more feminine in performance, queer, or refuse to engage aggression, anger, and tough statures.[36] Compulsory structures include heteronormativity, able-bodiedness, femininity, and masculinity among many others. The essays and poems in this section theorize how compulsory structures constrain identity expression and the communication acts that disrupt compulsion via non-normative existence as an act of resistance. Albeit in the collegiate classroom, a dance studio, or in online interactions, each author shows how their existence is an act of disruption against compulsory norms designed to limit and control the way bodies express themselves.

Identity Negotiation and Internal Struggles section focuses on process of identity negotiation, or the internal and external communicative process of revealing, concealing, and expressing certain facets of who we are depending upon cultural context and whom we interact. Our identities are in constant states of fluctuation, rubbing against and with other identities in our bodies, and mingling with the identities of other bodies."[37] We refine and modify our identities through processes of dyadic verbal and nonverbal negotiation.[38] Identity negotiation takes place in intercultural, intracultural, and co-cultural settings where individuals and group members uncover commonalities in order to function within dominant society while validating the vast multiplicity of experiences between and among groups.[39] Regardless of the setting, identity negotiation is mediated by discursive management whereby ones cultural identities are products of scope, salience, and intensity of attributed and avowed identities through.[40]

Albeit moving through childhood and adulthood life in Texas, Iowa, California, or via queer world making, the essays, poems, and script in this section focus on moments where identity negotiation is an explicit act pushing against the internal struggles of being and becoming.

Erotic as a Site for Normative Disruption section looks to the erotic—a sense of deep satisfaction, joy, and fulfillment beyond the sexual and pornographic[41]— as a site for disrupting normative gender roles and unsettling power relations. adrienne marie brown, in her groundbreaking text *Pleasure Activism*, recognizes that pleasure is a measure of freedom.[42] She asks us to notice what makes us feel good and what we are curious about as a potential entrance point to erotic practice as a site for liberation. Her work extends from Audre Lorde's *Uses of the Erotic*, where Lorde urges her readers to not only think about what they do, but to think acutely and fully about how they feel while doing it, and to focus on that sense of satisfaction and completion.[43] brown tells us that the erotic is not frivolous, it is freedom.[44] To work from the erotic is to be fearless in reveling in our greatest capacity for joy.[45] When coupling gender and the erotic, pursuing gender from the erotic means expressing and identifying with that which pleases us and makes us feel satisfied and complete. It is not expressing gender based on norms, expectations, or shame. The poems and essays in this section use the erotic to conceptualize what it means to embody trans identity, re-humanize marginalized bodies, and be full and unapologetic in our pursuit of relational wholeness, despite trans phobia and non-binary erasure. Through the uses of the erotic, each author theorizes and performs the erotic in a way that embodies the complex potentiality of gender.

The final section, *Queering History, Imagining Futures,* uses memory and history to forge a free future via imagination. Futurity is an intervention of sorts that asks humans to think about what is possible beyond current constraints. By looking to the past to address constraints, we create the potential to begin dreaming about what can be. Futurity signals a shift in research and praxis from deconstructing systems of power to focusing on advancing liberation and creating an environment where freedom is possible. Departing from Afrofuturism and Queer Futurity, the essays in this section lean on historical and personal memory associated with systemic oppression to begin traversing resistance as a site of world-making. To resist is to imagine; to imagine is to begin the work of activism and building.

Each section begins with a short introduction that offers the theories that inform the chapters, a brief synopsis of each chapter, and a list of discussion questions to engage the depth and potential of each chapter. The book closes with an epilogue that foregrounds our ideas for the gender future rooted in pleasure. It is our hope that our dear readers will experience this text as a departure point into futurity. As our readers melt into each chapter, we hope that they will think about their own gender free futures, what potential exist within and beyond their own constraints, and how their gender moves through the world. We also hope that our readers will confront their own implicit and explicit biases around gender expression and afford space for all non-normative gender expressions to exist more freely in the world. We hope that this text will provide our readers with substance to confront trans phobia in their own lives in an effort to begin mitigating the violence aimed at trans and non-binary bodies. We hope that our readers will think deeply about their own pleasure and locate those things that bring them great joy in their body and bodily expressions. Finally, we hope that these narratives will push our readers to celebrate gender difference and uplift those bodies whose everyday existence is an act of resistance.

Notes

1 Robin Boylorn and Mark Orbe, editors. *Critical Autoethnography: Intersecting Cultural Identities in Everyday Life* (Walnut Creek, CA: Left Coast Press, 2012).
2 Benny LeMaster and Amber Johnson. "Unlearning Gender: Toward a Critical Communication Trans Pedagogy." *Communication Teacher* 33, no. 3 (2019): 189–198, doi: 10.1080/17404622.2018.1467566.
3 Trans scholars have long made this point highlighting the ways in which postmodern theories, including notably queer theories, tend to privilege theory over embodiment. See Jeanne Vaccaro. "Felt Matters." *Women and Performance* 20, no. 3 (2010): 253–266, doi: 10.1080/0740770X.2010.529245; Jay Prosser. *Second Skins: The Body Narratives of transsexuality* (New York, NY: Columbia University Press, 1998); Viviane K. Namaste, *Invisible Lives: The Erasure of Transsexual and Transgendered People* (Chicago, IL: The University of Chicago Press, 2000).
4 C. Riley Snorton. *Black on Both Sides: A Racial History of Trans Identity* (Minneapolis, MN: University of Minnesota Press, 2017).
5 See Eve Tuck and K. Wayne Yang. "Decolonization Is Not a Metaphor." *Decolonization: Indigeneity, Education, and Society* 1, no. 1 (2012): 1–40, https://jps.library.utoronto.ca/index.php/des/article/view/18630; Corey Snelgrove, Rita Kaur Dhamoon, and Jeff Corntassel, "Unsettling Settler Colonialism: The Discourse and Politics of Settlers, and Solidarity with Indigenous Nations." *Decolonization: Indigeneity, Education, and Society* 3, no. 2 (2014): 1–32, https://jps.library.utoronto.ca/index.php/des/article/view/21166.
6 María Lugones. "Methodological Notes toward a Decolonial Feminism," in *Decolonizing Epistemologies: Latina/o Theology and Philosophy*, eds. Ada Mara Isasi-Daz and Eduardo Mendieta (New York, NY: Fordham University Press, 2011), 78.
7 Diane Detournay. "The Racial Life of 'Cisgender': Reflections on Sex, Gender, and the Body." *Parallax* 25, no. 1 (2019): 58–74, doi: 10.1080/13534645.2019.1570606.
8 Lugones, 73.
9 Lugones, 73.
10 Lugones, 73.
11 b. binaohan. *decolonizing trans/gender 101* (Canada: Biyuti Publishing, 2014), 126.
12 Saylesh Wesley. "Twin-Spirited Woman: Sts'iyóya smestíyexw slhá:li." *Transgender Studies Quarterly* 1, no. 3 (2014): 338–351, doi: 10.1215/23289252-2685624.
13 Deborah A. Miranda. "Extermination of the *Joyas*: Gendercide in Spanish California." *GLQ* 16, no. 1–2 (2010): 253–284, https://www.muse.jhu.edu/article/372454.
14 Bob Krizek. "Goodbye Old Friend: A Son's Farewell to Comiskey Park," *Omega* 25, no. 2 (1992): 87–93, doi: 10.2190/P5RF-G50T-MEYY-P8KU.

15 Benjamin R. LeMaster. "Queering Conversion: An Ethnographic Account of the Ex-Gay Movement." Master's thesis, California State University Long Beach, 2010), 146–147.

16 Carolyn Ellis. *The Ethnographic I: A Methodological Novel about Autoethnography* (Walnut Creek, CA: Alta Mira, 2004), xix.

17 Dwight Conquergood. "Performing as a Moral Act: Ethical Dimensions of the Ethnography of Performance." *Literature in Performance* 2, no. 5 (1985): 1–13, doi: 10.1080/10462938509391578.

18 Bryant K. Alexander and John T. Warren. "The Materiality of Bodies: Critical Reflections on Pedagogy, Politics, and Positionality." *Communication Quarterly* 50, no. 3-4 (2002): 328–343, doi: 10.1080/01463370209385667.

19 Michael Awkward. *Scenes of Instruction: A Memoir* (Durham, NC: Duke UP, 1999).

20 Conquergood, "Performing."

21 Amber Johnson. "Doing It: A Rhetorical Autoethnography of Religious Masturbation and Identity Negotiation." *Departures in Critical Qualitative Research* 3, no. 4 (2014): 366–388, doi: 10.1525/dcqr.2014.3.4.366.

22 Conquergood, "Performing," 9.

23 Ange-Marie Hancock. "When Multiplication Doesn't Equal Quick Addition: Examining Intersectionality as a Research Paradigm." *Perspectives on Politics* 5, no. 1 (2007): 64, doi: https://doi.org/10.1017/S1537592707070065.

24 Kimberlé Crenshaw. "Mapping the Margins: Intersectionality, Identity Politics, and Violence against Women of Color." *Stanford Law Review* 43, no. 6 (1991): 1241–1299, doi: 10.2307/1229039.

25 Walter R. Fisher. "Narration as a Human Communication Paradigm: The Case of Public Moral Argument." *Communication Monographs*, 51, no. 1 (1984): 1–22, doi: 10.1080/03637758409390180.

26 Walter R. Fisher. "The Narrative Paradigm: An Elaboration." *Communication Monographs* 52, no. 4 (1985): 347–367, doi: 10.1080/03637758509376117.

27 Walter R. Fisher. *Human Communication as Narration: Toward a Philosophy of Reason, Value, and Action* (Columbia, SC: University of South Carolina Press, 1987).

28 Kristi Malterud. "Qualitative Research: Standards, Challenges and Guidelines." *The Lancet* 358 (2001): 483–484, doi: 10.1016/S0140-6736(01)05627-6.

29 M. Mary Weems. *Public Education and the Imagination-Intellect: I Speak from the Wound in My Mouth.* (New York, NY: Peter Lang, 2010).

30 Weems, 1.

31 Norman K. Denzin. *Interpretive Ethnography: Ethnographic Practices for the 21st Century* (Thousand Oaks, CA: Sage, 1997), 217.

32 Kristin M. Langellier. "Personal Narrative, Performance, Performativity: Two or Three Things I Know for Sure." *Text and Performance Quarterly,* 19, no. 2 (1999): 129, doi: 10.1080/10462939909366255.

33 Bryant Keith Alexander. "Performance Ethnography: The Reenacting and Inciting of Culture," in *The Sage Handbook of Qualitative Research*, 3rd ed., eds. Norman K. Denzin and Yvonna S. Lincoln (Los Angeles, CA: Sage, 2005), 411–442.; See also Weems.

34 Judith Butler. "Performative Acts and Gender Constitution: An Essay in Phenomenology and Feminist Theory." *Theatre Journal* 40, no 4 (1988): 519–531, doi: 10.2307/3207893.

35 Adrienne Rich. "Compulsory Heterosexuality and the Lesbian Existence." *Signs* 5, no 4 (1980): 631–660, https://www.jstor.org/stable/3173834.

36 Rich, 636.

37 Johnson, 370.

38 Stella Ting-Toomey. "Identity and Interpersonal Bondings," in *Handbook of International and Intercultural Communication*, eds. Molefi Asante and William Gudykunst (London, UK: Sage, 1989), 351.

39 K. S. Sitaram and Roy Cogdell. *Foundations of Intercultural Communication.* (New York, NY: Macmillan, 1976), 28; Mark P. Orbe. "Negotiating Multiple Identities within Multiple Frames: An Analysis of First-Generation College Students." *Communication Education* 53, no. 2 (2004): 131, doi: 10.10/03634520410001682401.
40 Mary Jane Collier and Milt Thomas. "Cultural Identity: An Interpretive Perspective," in *Theories in Intercultural Communication*, eds. Young Kim and William Gudykunst (Newbury Park, CA: Sage, 1988), 102;
41 Audre Lorde. *Sister Outsider: Essays and Speeches by Audre Lorde* (Berkeley, CA: Crossing Press, 2007), 54.
42 adrienne maree brown. *Pleasure Activism: The Politics of Feeling Good* (Oakland, CA: AK Press, 2019), 3.
43 Lorde, 55.
44 brown, 441.
45 Lorde.

Bibliography

Alexander, Bryant Keith. "Performance Ethnography: The Reenacting and Inciting of Culture." In *The Sage Handbook of Qualitative Research*, 3rd ed., 411–442. Edited by Norman K. Denzin and Yvonna S. Lincoln. Los Angeles, CA: Sage, 2005.

Alexander, Bryant K. and John T. Warren. "The Materiality of Bodies: Critical Reflections on Pedagogy, Politics, and Positionality." *Communication Quarterly* 50, no. 3–4 (2002): 328–343, doi: 10.1080/01463370209385667.

Awkward, Michael. *Scenes of Instruction: A Memoir.* Durham, NC: Duke University Press, 1999.

binaohan, b. *decolonizing trans/gender 101.* Canada: Biyuti Publishing, 2014.

Boylorn, Robin and Mark Orbe, editors. *Critical Autoethnography: Intersecting Cultural Identities in Everyday Life.* Walnut Creek, CA: Left Coast Press, 2012.

brown, adrienne maree. *Pleasure Activism: The Politics of Feeling Good.* Oakland, CA: AK Press, 2019.

Butler, Judith. "Performative Acts and Gender Constitution: An Essay in Phenomenology and Feminist Theory." *Theatre Journal* 40, no 4 (1988): 519–531, doi: 10.2307/3207893.

Collier, Mary Jane and Milt Thomas. "Cultural Identity: An Interpretive Perspective." In *Theories in Intercultural Communication*, 122. Edited by Young Kim and William Gudykunst. Newbury Park: Sage, 1988.

Conquergood, Dwight. "Performing as a Moral Act: Ethical Dimensions of the Ethnography of Performance." *Literature in Performance* 2, no. 5 (1985): 1–13, doi: 10.1080/10462938509391578.

Crenshaw, Kimberlé. "Mapping the Margins: Intersectionality, Identity Politics, and Violence against Women of Color." *Stanford Law Review* 43, no. 6 (1991): 1241–1299, doi: 10.2307/1229039.

Denzin, Norman K. *Interpretive Ethnography: Ethnographic Practices for the 21st Century.* Thousand Oaks, CA: Sage, 1997.

Detournay, Diane. "The Racial Life of 'Cisgender': Reflections on Sex, Gender, and the Body." *Parallax* 25, no. 1 (2019): 58–74, doi: 10.1080/13534645.2019.1570606.

Ellis, Carolyn. *The Ethnographic I: A Methodological Novel about Autoethnography.* Walnut Creek, CA: Alta Mira, 2004.

Fisher, Walter R. *Human Communication as Narration: Toward a Philosophy of Reason, Value, and Action.* Columbia, SC: University of South Carolina Press, 1987.

Fisher, Walter R. "Narration as a Human Communication Paradigm: The Case of Public Moral Argument." *Communication Monographs*, 51, no. 1 (1984): 1–22, doi: 10.1080/03637758409390180.

Fisher, Walter R. "The Narrative Paradigm: An Elaboration." *Communication Monographs* 52, no. 4 (1985): 347–367, doi: 10.1080/03637758509376117.

Hancock, Ange-Marie. "When Multiplication Doesn't Equal Quick Addition: Examining Intersectionality as a Research Paradigm." *Perspectives on Politics* 5, no. 1 (2007): 63–79, doi: https://doi.org/10.1017/S1537592707070065.

Johnson, Amber. "Doing *It*: A Rhetorical Autoethnography of Religious Masturbation and Identity Negotiation." *Departures in Critical Qualitative Research* 3, no. 4 (2014): 366–388, doi: 10.1525/dcqr.2014.3.4.366.

Krizek, Bob. "Goodbye Old Friend: A Son's Farewell to Comiskey Park." *Omega* 25, no. 2 (1992): 87–93, doi: 10.2190/P5RF-G50T-MEYY-P8KU.

Langellier, Kristin M. "Personal Narrative, Performance, Performativity: Two or Three Things I Know for Sure." *Text and Performance Quarterly*, 19, no. 2 (1999): 125–144, doi: 10.1080/10462939909366255.

LeMaster, Benjamin R. "Queering Conversion: An Ethnographic Account of the Ex-Gay Movement." Master's thesis, California State University Long Beach, 2010.

LeMaster, Benny and Amber Johnson. "Unlearning Gender: Toward a Critical Communication Trans Pedagogy." *Communication Teacher* 33, no. 3 (2019): 189–198, doi: 10.1080/17404622.2018.1467566.

Lorde, Audre. *Sister Outsider: Essays and Speeches by Audre Lorde*. Berkeley, CA: Crossing Press, 2007.

Lugones, María. "Methodological Notes toward a Decolonial Feminism." In *Decolonizing Epistemologies: Latina/o Theology and Philosophy*, 68–86. Edited by Ada Mara Isasi-Daz and Eduardo Mendieta. New York, NY: Fordham University Press, 2011.

Malterud, Kristi. "Qualitative Research: Standards, Challenges and Guidelines." *The Lancet* 358 (2001): 483–484, doi: 10.1016/S0140-6736(01)05627-6.

Miranda, Deborah A. "Extermination of the *Joyas*: Gendercide in Spanish California." *GLQ* 16, no. 1–2 (2010): 253–284, https://www.muse.jhu.edu/article/372454.

Namaste, Viviane K. *Invisible Lives: The Erasure of Transsexual and Transgendered People*. Chicago, IL: The University of Chicago Press, 2000.

Orbe, Mark P. "Negotiating Multiple Identities within Multiple Frames: An Analysis of First-generation College Students." *Communication Education* 53, no. 2 (2004): 131–149, doi: 10.10/03634520410001682401.

Prosser, Jay. *Second Skins: The Body Narratives of Transsexuality*. New York, NY: Columbia University Press, 1998.

Rich, Adrienne. "Compulsory Heterosexuality and the Lesbian Existence." *Signs* 5, no 4 (1980): 631–660, https://www.jstor.org/stable/3173834.

Sitaram, K. S. and Roy Cogdell. *Foundations of Intercultural Communication*. New York, NY: Macmillan, 1976.

Snelgrove, Corey, Rita Kaur Dhamoon, and Jeff Corntassel, "Unsettling Settler Colonialism: The Discourse and Politics of Settlers, and Solidarity with Indigenous Nations." *Decolonization: Indigeneity, Education, and Society* 3, no. 2 (2014): 1–32, https://jps.library.utoronto.ca/index.php/des/article/view/21166.

Snorton, C. Riley. *Black on Both Sides: A Racial History of Trans Identity*. Minneapolis, MN: University of Minnesota Press, 2017.

Ting-Toomey, Stella. "Identity and Interpersonal Bondings." In *Handbook of International and Intercultural Communication*, 351–373. Edited by Molefi Asante and William Gudykunst. London, UK: Sage, 1989.

Tuck, Eve and K. Wayne Yang. "Decolonization Is Not a Metaphor." *Decolonization: Indigeneity, Education, and Society* 1, no. 1 (2012): 1–40, https://jps.library.utoronto.ca/index.php/des/article/view/18630.

Vaccaro, Jeanne. "Felt Matters." *Women and Performance* 20, no. 3 (2010): 253–266, doi: 10.1080/0740770X.2010.529245.

Weems, Mary E. *Public Education and the Imagination-Intellect: I Speak from the Wound in My Mouth*. New York, NY: Peter Lang, 2010.

Wesley, Saylesh. "Twin-Spirited Woman: Sts'iyóya smestíyexw slhá:li." *Transgender Studies Quarterly* 1, no. 3 (2014): 338–351, doi: 10.1215/23289252-2685624.

SECTION I

Existence as Disruption

[T]he absence of choice remains the great unacknowledged reality.
—Adrienne Rich[1]

[G]ender-conforming people may find themselves quite comfortable and even successful in the gender they perform, but political consciousness should cause them to recognize the limits and constraints of this performance.
—C. L. Cole and Shannon L. C. Cate

Gender is a colonial refrain—a racialized relic; the discursive and material consequences of which have proven rewarding for some and violent and deadly for far more. By "colonial refrain," we are referring to the historical taxonomization of bodily difference, based on arbitrary standards, rooted in modernism, that privilege and reflect the aesthetic values embodied by those with the power to define and, in turn, dominate others. Racialized notions of "sex" and "gender" were effective means by which Western imperial forces exerted their force over non-Western ways of being in the world. For instance, María Lugones's sustained analysis reveals "sex" to be a colonial technology used to assess the reproductive capacity—and in turn worth—of those constituted as "non/humans" under racist capitalism.[2] This conceptualization included both the mass destruction of indigenous cultural orientations that evaded Western cisheteropatriarchy (e.g., matrilineal lineage, non-binary/two-spirit embodiment) and the enslavement of Black folks throughout the Americas. Said differently, "sex" has been used to justify the dehumanization of, and concomitant violence enacted against, Black and Brown folks, cultures, and ways of being in the world.

Conversely, "gender" is understood as a colonial technology that was used to describe and distinguish (White) human subjects. "Man" was understood as the (White) human exemplar; a normative standard against which others were/are compared. "Woman" was understood as man's opposite; a (White) inverted-human, whose task it was to reproduce the (White) human race. It would be naïve to dismiss these decolonial analyses of sex and gender as irrelevant by today's standards. Indeed, while sex and gender may look and feel different hundreds of years after the earliest invasions by colonial forces, racialized logics continue to delimit gender potentiality. As a result, people who embody non-normative sex and/or gender identities and embodiments experience increased surveillance and violence compared to those who embody sex and gender formations that more readily acquiesce to normative expectancies.[3] And while surveillance and violence against said groups is real and material, the effects are exacerbated by racist overtones leading to the increased incarceration and death of folks of color who embody non-normative sex and/or gender identities and embodiments.[4] In short, power always delimits gender potentiality. And the study of gender, in turn, requires that we attend to and engage intersecting structures of power. Doing otherwise performs a colonialist violence rooted in whiteness.

Adriene Rich[5] engages this important analytic work in her landmark essay, "Compulsory Heterosexuality and Lesbian Existence." In it, Rich implicates heterosexuality not as a sexual preference for women but, rather, as a political institution and ideology "imposed on women" that parade as a value-neutral preference or choice.[6] One way in which this structure is secured is through the systematic erasure of "lesbian possibility."[7] From this vantage, Rich characterizes heterosexuality as a "pervasive cluster of forces, ranging from physical brutality to control of consciousness" with the most violent effects landing on those who fall outside of what we now term "heteronormativity." Gust Yep characterizes heteronormativity as "the invisible center and the presumed bedrock of society... [and as] the quintessential force creating, sustaining, and perpetuating the erasure, marginalization, disempowerment, and oppression of sexual others."[8] While Yep theorizes heteronormativity more generally, Rich dedicates her analytic energies to women revealing the ways in which heterosexuality works in tandem with patriarchy to secure the oppression of women. In turn, Rich understands "lesbian existence"—historical manifestations and continued performative enactments—under heteropatriarchy, to mark the "breaking of a taboo and the rejection of a compulsory way of life."[9] Indeed, heterosexuality—as an institution—is understood as a compulsory modality that is "covered over, with the appearance of choice (sexual preference) mystifying a system in which there actually is no choice."[10] To *exist* outside of this structure's expectancies is to resist what is culturally imposed, and, in turn, to risk the violence that attends such deviations under heteropatriarchal domination.

Judy Tzu-Chun Wu cautions, however, "awareness of heterosexuality as a normative ideology does not necessitate a celebration of non-normative sexuality or intimacy without regard to other forms of social inequality and hierarchy."[11] Said differently, difference augments lesbian existence. For example, Robert McRuer proposes "compulsory able-bodiedness" as a structural approach to the cultural constitution of disability.[12] He argues compulsory heterosexuality and compulsory able-bodiedness are co-constitutive forces that work to secure a particular normative bodily formation to which all subjects are presumed to aspire: heterosexual and able-bodied.[13] Similarly, Desiree Lewis finds nationalist projects are secured through sexual violence effectively revealing the ways in which gender is undergirded by nationalism writing, "[S]exual violence can become both a weapon of war and a potent symbolic act in patriarchal ethnic cleansing and the gendered creation of nations or national pride."[14] Conversely, racialized groups navigate both compulsory heterosexuality and, what Wu terms, "compulsory sexual 'deviance'" or the racist and discriminatory notion that racialized sexual formations are deviant and, in turn, in need of control.[15] Mattie Udora Richardson finds similar ends in her analysis of African American history writing: "The process of distorting the complexities of Black women's sexuality has its roots in the discourses of Black sexual deviance that have become part of the mythology of White supremacy."[16] In this way, compulsory sexual deviance places value on White sexual formations as it devalues—through criminalization—racialized sexual formations—lesbian, heterosexual, bisexual, queer, or otherwise.

Centering transness, C. L. Cole and Shannon Cate locate the "male/female binary sex system" as the foundation under which heterosexuality is realized in Rich's original theorization.[17] In turn, they conceptualize of binary gender as a compulsory structure that delimits gender potentiality. In turn, they propose a "transgender continuum" that fosters political connections between "those whose gender is more obviously outside society's narrow frame of the 'normal'" as opposed to pre-determined categorical labels like "man" or "woman" or "male" or "female."[18] Indeed, the transgender continuum reveals ways in which feminine women may have more in common with feminine men than with masculine women. Likewise, masculine men may have more in common with masculine women than with feminine men. However, compulsory binary gender—as a structure—would suggest otherwise—that all men are homogenous and that all women are homogenous and that women and men are heterogenous. While Cole and Rich reveal binary gender to be compulsory, they fail to recognize the colonialist histories that give rise to binary sex and gender as racialized projects. b. binaohan reminds us, "the binary as tool of oppression is not about legitimizing binary genders over non-binary genders, in a general sense, but about legitimizing a White notion of manhood and a White notion of womanhood. And, in turn, this is inextricably tied to who is considered 'human' and who isn't."[19]

The larger point is this: Gender is necessarily complex precisely because it is animated in and through intersecting structures of cultural power. As a result, to exist as a gendered being is to exist in subjective terms always constrained by historically salient sense-making structures. The essays in this section theorize both the various and intersecting compulsory structures that constrain gender potentiality and the resulting performance of mundane existence in time and space. Essays by Shadee Abdi and Anthony P. Cuomo as well as by Bernadette Marie Calafell and Shinsuke Eguchi theorize gender and existence in relational terms in the context of higher education. Abdi and Cuomo take as their site the communication classroom exploring the ways in which students engage their queer bodies of color in different ways and as a result of their different genders. Likewise, Calafell and Eguchi take as their site a disciplinary leadership role showing the ways in which their very existence—as queer bodies of color— is marked and, in turn delimited, by racist notions of cisheteropatriarchy that paint each of them in ways that are different though with the same goal: to delegitimize and dehumanize. Miranda Dottie Olzman centers their fat body in the context of a dance studio where they recognize valuations of bodily size, adoration of thinness, and sizist notions of "health" as working in concert to construct a compulsory structure of gendered bodily expectation. Finally, Julie-Ann Scott turns to mediated contexts. In particular, she examines performances of compulsory able-bodiedness and cisheteropatriarchy in the public response to mediated images of her sons she shares online. Scott reveals mediated responses performing under the so-called auspice of "care" in fact shore up support for compulsory structures that delimit gender potentiality in the development of her children. Said differently, these public responses are revealed to be normative and disciplinary parameters that project meaning onto bodies.

In addition, this section features poetry by J. Nyla, and Kai M. Green. J. Nyla's poem engages the embodied limits of compulsory expectation when pressed to first categorize their non-binary gender in binary terms and, in turn, to account for the mustache their body grows. J. Nyla performs existence in light of compulsory structures responding to the inquiring mind: "This mustache is my grandmothers. Our body hair is natural." Green takes as his site the threshold of travel as a Black trans man. Crossing through machines designed to assess normative formations, Green's body "breaks the machine" for his body exists "undisciplined" as it "does not come together for their eyes nor their technologies." In this poem, technology (U.S. Transportation Security Administration body scanners) performs the role of compulsory gatekeeper determining and regulating the movement of bodies across national borders. Taken together, this section of essays and poems reveals both the structural means by which gender becomes intelligible as well as the mundane embodied ways in which existence—in terms that evade compulsory expectations—can serve as grounds for resistance.

Discussion Questions

1. What are some of the compulsory expectations that you experience in your life?

2. In what ways does your existence and embodiment of social identities resist compulsory expectations?

3. What are some ways that you challenge and perform social and cultural expectations of gender in your everyday experiences? What are the interpersonal responses you have received? How do you work with such responses?

4. What compulsory structures limit your understanding of gender? For instance, how do your race, sexuality, class, ability, religion, and/or nationality affect your gender identity and expression? Think of a time in which you performed in service of compulsory structures by projecting meaning or delimiting the potentiality in another's gender performance? How can you change that performance so as to encourage gender potentiality in the future?

5. What identity intersections are missing from the chapters in this section?

Notes

1 Adrienne Rich. "Compulsory Heterosexuality and Lesbian Existence." *Signs* 5, no. 4 (1980): 659, https://www.jstor.org/stable/3173834.

2 María Lugones. "Toward a Decolonial Feminism." *Hypatia* 25, no 4 (2010): 742–759, https://www.jstor.org/stable/40928654.

3 Toby Beauchamp. "Artful Concealment and Strategic Visibility: Transgender Bodies and U.S. State Surveillance After 9/11." *Surveillance and Society* 6, no. 4 (2009): 356–366, doi: 10.24908/ss.v6i4.3267.

4 Gayle Salamon. *The Life and Death of Latisha King: A Critical Phenomenology of Transphobia* (New York, NY: New York University Press, 2018).

5 We would be remiss if we did not make note of Rich's affiliation with cisheterosexist scholars operating under the banner of feminism including, notably, Janice Raymond. Raymond acknowledges Rich for her consultation and support in the construction of her transmisogynistic monograph *The Transsexual Empire* (Boston, MA: Beacon Press, 1979). In addition, Rich draws on Mary Daly, who characterized transness as a "necrophilic invasion" in her monograph *Gyn/Ecology* (Boston, MA: Beacon Press, 1978), 71.

6 Rich, 652.

7 Rich, 647.

8 Gust Yep. "The Violence of Heteronormativity in Communication Studies." *Journal of Homosexuality* 45, no. 2–4 (2003): 11–59, doi: 10.1300/J082v45n02_02.

9 Rich, 649.

10 Robert McRuer. "Compulsory Able-Bodiedness and Queer/Disabled Existence." In *The Disability Studies Reader*, 2nd ed. Edited by Lennard J. Davis (New York, NY: Routledge, 2006), 302.

11 Judy Tzu-Chun Wu. "Asian American History and Racialized Compulsory Deviance." *Journal of Women's History* 15, no. 3 (2003): 60, doi: 10.1353/jowh.2003.0089.

12 McRuer, 301.

13 See also Alison Kafer. "Compulsory Bodies: Reflections on Heterosexuality and Able-bodiedness." *Journal of Women's History* 15, no. 3 (2003): 77–89, doi: 10.1353/jowh.2003.0071.

14 Desiree Lewis. "Rethinking Nationalism in Relation to Foucault's *History of Sexuality* and Adrienne Rich's 'Compulsory Heterosexuality and Lesbian Existence." *Sexualities* 11, no. 1–2 (2008): 105, doi: 10.1177/13634607080110010306.

15 Wu, 59.

16 Mattie Udora Richardson. "No More Secrets, No More Lies: African American History and Compulsory Heterosexuality." *Journal of Women's History* 15, no. 3 (2003): 64, doi: 10.1353/jowh.2003.0080.

17 C. L. Cole and Shannon L. C. Cate. "Compulsory Gender and Transgender Existence: Adrienne Rich's Queer Possibility." *WSQ: Women's Studies Quarterly* 36, no. 3–4 (2008): 280, https://www.jstor.org/stable/27649802.

18 Cole and Cate, 282.

19 b. Binaohan. *decolonizing trans/gender 101* (Canada, Biyuti Publishing, 2014), 126.

Bibliography

Beauchamp, Toby. "Artful Concealment and Strategic Visibility: Transgender Bodies and U.S. State Surveillance After 9/11." *Surveillance and Society* 6, no. 4 (2009): 356–366, doi: 10.24908/ss.v6i4.3267.

binaohan, b. *decolonizing trans/gender 101*. Canada, Biyuti Publishing, 2014.

Cole, C. L. and Shannon L. C. Cate, "Compulsory Gender and Transgender Existence: Adrienne Rich's Queer Possibility." *WSQ* 36, no. 3–4 (2008): 279–287, https://www.jstor.org/stable/27649802.

Daly, Mary. *Gyn/Ecology*. Boston, MA: Beacon Press, 1978.

Kafer, Alison. "Compulsory Bodies: Reflections on Heterosexuality and Able-bodiedness." *Journal of Women's History* 15, no. 3 (2003): 77–89, doi: 10.1353/jowh.2003.0071.

Lewis, Desiree. "Rethinking Nationalism in Relation to Foucault's *History of Sexuality* and Adrienne Rich's 'Compulsory Heterosexuality and Lesbian Existence." *Sexualities* 11, no. 1–2 (2008): 104–109, doi: 10.1177/13634607080110010306.

Lugones, María. "Toward a Decolonial Feminism." *Hypatia* 25, no 4 (2010): 742–759, https://www.jstor.org/stable/40928654.

McRuer, Robert. "Compulsory Able-Bodiedness and Queer/Disabled Existence." In *The Disability Studies Reader*, 2nd ed., 301–308. Edited by Lennard J. Davis. New York, NY: Routledge, 2006.

Raymond, Janice. *The Transsexual Empire*. Boston, MA: Beacon Press, 1979.

Rich, Adrienne. "Compulsory Heterosexuality and Lesbian Existence." *Signs* 5, no. 4 (1980): 631–660, https://www.jstor.org/stable/3173834.

Richardson, Mattie Udora. "No More Secrets, No More Lies: African American History and Compulsory Heterosexuality." *Journal of Women's History* 15, no. 3 (2003): 63–76, doi: 10.1353/jowh.2003.0080.

Salamon, Gayle. *The Life and Death of Latisha King: A Critical Phenomenology of Transphobia*. New York, NY: New York University Press, 2018.

Wu, Judy Tzu-Chun. "Asian American History and Racialized Compulsory Deviance." *Journal of Women's History* 15, no. 3 (2003): 58–62, doi: 10.1353/jowh.2003.0089.

Yep, Gust. "The Violence of Heteronormativity in Communication Studies." *Journal of Homosexuality* 45, no. 2–4 (2003): 11–59, doi: 10.1300/J082v45n02_02.

are you boy or girl?

J. Nyla McNeill

"Are you a boy or a girl?" asks the snot-nosed boy,
I think *both* and *yes* and say "girl" through gapped teeth;
"Then *why* you got a *mustache*, then?" he asks,
he scrunch-faced
   he guiltless
     he perpetuated hegemony

★★★

I think of all of the things I would like to have preached
on this eight-year-old's level in... kind, generalized speech;
(we construct children "innocent," this control we teach)
And I ask myself, "Then why *do* I got a mustache, then"?
I write a letter:
Dear snot-nosed boy,
This mustache is my grand-
mothers. Our body hair is
natural. And, going by your
rules, child—according to
biology, son—before we were
all birthed—and yes, this in-
cludes you, kid—we all
technically—just technically—
begin as girls.

DISRUPTING COMPULSORY PERFORMANCES

Snapshots and Stories of Masculinity, Disability, and Parenthood in Cultural Currents of Daily Life

Julie-Ann Scott

Performing Masculinity through Social Media Photos

A photo of my family that I posted on social media received so many compliments. We took it at Easter. My sons are in matching peach shirts with plaid bow ties and pale blue pants that are the same color as my chiffon maternity dress, which complements my husband Evan's white and blue seersucker suit. Behind us is a cross covered in spring flowers, the designated spring photo spot at our church. In that photo, we "fit," successfully performing White, heteronormative, able-bodiedness for a moment in time. We are comfortable to those around us. My conservative, Evangelical Christian and Catholic family members and acquaintances find it reassuring. They tell my mother they wish I'd post more photos like those ones, that she should tell me to do so. She does. I smile and continue to post photos that emerge as we live our lives, performing who we are with others on the Southern seashore. Some photos are like that one that everyone liked. Others are not, and those pictures make some people uncomfortable. I am a mother of three boys ages 7, 4, and 2, with a fourth child on the way. Evan and I navigate White, southern, middle-class masculinity as we parent on the North Carolina coast, wading in the swirling currents of compulsory able-bodiedness, compulsory whiteness, compulsory masculinity, and compulsory heteronormativity; we follow our sons into deeper, more complicated waters as they grow.[1] This is our story, told in our encounters, social media snapshots, and the hidden messages that ensue.

A Personal Narrative as Performance Scholar's Position

I should disclose the methodological/artistic lens that produces this essay. I am a performance and personal narrative scholar. I understand identity as continually emerging through our ongoing encounters with one another.[2] As cultural members situated in ever-changing contexts, we struggle together in a forever unfinished process to collaboratively co-create who we are with others.[3] Every human interaction offers opportunities to reiterate, resist, dismantle, and re-create meanings. That which we co-create we can also resist and dismantle. While we never lose the opportunity to undo what has been done, some meanings become so deeply embedded into our daily interactions that we mistake them as the natural order of things and expect them to be reiterated across our encounters.[4] These expected performances become compulsory, with social consequences for deviation.[5] Compulsory heterosexuality, compulsory able-bodiedness, and compulsory whiteness are examples of pervasive cultural performances.

McRuer draws upon Rich's term "compulsory heterosexuality" to argue for the pervasiveness of "compulsory able-bodiedness" across dominant culture.[6] Rich asserts that to grasp heterosexuality as the "natural order of things," there needs to be a tangible embodiment of deviance, which is queerness. The center of culture cannot be defined without the margins. Queer bodies are marginalized as deviant so that the majority can indulge in the privilege of "normal" straightness. The same thing happens to disabled bodies, though perhaps even more intensely since unlike other predictable markers of identity, such as gender or race, the disabled body is solely defined as the absence of normality.[7] Compulsory whiteness emerges in tandem with compulsory heterosexuality and compulsory able-bodiedness. To be white is to be unmarked by race. The white body is positioned as a "normal" standard, with unearned privileges and advantages tied to the categorization and performance of whiteness in daily life.[8] I've explored these terms in my lived experience as a White, physically disabled, straight cisgender woman.[9] The intersections of these terms grow increasingly complex for me as I watch my sons navigate stigma surrounding disability and gender in contemporary culture.

Our Hope That Gender Performance Tides Are Shifting

At times, my husband and I are filled with hope as we witness culture opening to the fluidity of ability and gender in our sons' unique performances of self with others. The social waters feel safe, calm and inviting, allowing us to move with ease in any direction. We revel in their expansion. At other moments we feel caught in the riptides of gender and ability performance. We are swept into currents of hate and bias and are unsure how to swim against them. Those around us question our parenting decisions and warn us about the cultural consequences for deviating from normality. They say our sons need us to monitor their daily performances for their own protection. We worry that we may lose our footing and be whipped out into the waves of cultural transgressions that come with allowing our sons who can pass for "normal" openly perform deviance. The fluidity of gender, sexuality, and ability swirl around us as we struggle to bear witness to who are sons are. We embrace them fully. We are committed to loving the blood, bones, tissues, hormones, and chemicals that form the bodies they interact with others through. We enjoy watching them continually become who they are in cultural time and space. Our embrace is in warmth, love, and acceptance, but also at times of fear and worry. Loving them is easy, but at times, cultural currents are difficult to navigate. Together, we venture into the surf braced for whatever we encounter.

Normative Bodies Performing Deviance

Our sons at first glance pass for normative. Perhaps it is because of their capacity to pass that they become so jarring in their daily performances. Our family takes people by surprise. Our seemingly familiar bodies in the photo I described at the beginning of this essay open disruption of dominant performances of gender and sexuality is disconcerting to those who assume that everyone should strive to avoid the social consequences of deviance. My sons, through their seemingly normative, White bodies, could unabashedly indulge in able-bodied and heteronormative privilege, but they do not, and we do not ask them to. In the coming pages, I will introduce Tony, Vinny, and Nico, my three sons, who surface the possibilities, hopes, and dangers of childhood masculinity as they disrupt compulsory able-bodiedness, compulsory heterosexuality, and compulsory heterosexuality in daily performances.

Boy 1: Resisting the Cultural Currents of Compulsory Able-bodiedness

Tony, my oldest, with his tall, tan muscular build, bright green eyes, and floppy sandy hair looks like the children in the promotional photos of Wrightsville Beach that is an 8-minute drive from our house. Other fathers at soccer practice look at my husband with envy, remarking that Tony is "so big" as he kicks the ball across the field, towering over the other children. He is big. He's beyond the 100th percentile for height and weight with a deep voice that stands out in our church's cherub choir. His calves and shoulders ripple with defined muscles and have since he was born three weeks early. The first comment ever made about Tony was the doctor marveling to the nurses, "Look at how strong this baby is" as he held up his head for a few seconds and arched his back, balancing on his heels and shoulders just minutes after birth.

Tony is strong. He also has frontal lobe epilepsy with localized motor seizures. They started just after his second birthday. Unmedicated he can have as many as 50 seizures every day, each lasting 5–30 seconds. During his seizures he stops, tenses, and trembles as he flushes and breathes heavily. He does not lose his balance or consciousness and remains aware during these episodes. He recovers immediately and continues on with whatever he was doing before they started. His seizures are exhausting. They interrupt his sleep, causing him to move slower, become more emotional, physical and impulsive as his brain is occupied with seizing rather than analyzing his surroundings or maintaining self-control. Medication can completely suppress the seizures, but at every growth spurt—about once every four months—his body outgrows the dosages and the seizures return for several weeks or even months as we figure out what cocktail of drugs will successfully interact with his changing body chemistry to suppress them again.

Over the last five years the ebb and flow of the seizure cycles have grown familiar to us as a family. Tony is at ease with their recurrence, pushing through the fog of exhaustion that rubs his intellect and emotions raw every few months. Tony is open about the experience of his seizures. He tries to explain to his father, brothers, and me what they feel like. They start fuzzy, like the feeling of waking up after a long sleep, and then they get scary, like when all the pans fall off the shelf at once. He says that the tensing fear feels like it will go on and on, but it stops, and he feels better, until the next one. He tells his friends that he has seizures, but he's safe, and not to be scared if they see them. His friends smile and nod, touching his hand and waiting for them to stop as they read or play together. Having a strong, White body that meets normative standards for attractiveness in our southern community helps this acceptance. I sometimes wonder what would happen if his daily performance included being of color, overweight, or gender non-conforming. Seizures are his only deviation from the dominant culture's expectations for normalcy. Tony does not remember life before seizures. They are just part of his embodied experience that he navigates. He smiles when we take photos before magnetic resonance imaging (MRIs) or electroencephalograms (EEGs) and when he has successfully made it through a day of school with multiple seizures.

In my favorite EEG photo, Tony sits in his hospital bed, a large smile with his head covered with electric wires to monitor his brain activity. He asked us to post a picture to show everyone the bright yellow minion pajamas he picked out for this hospital trip. He holds a juice cup and told me to include the caption that he can have as much juice as he wants here, and it's never watered down like I do at home. The nurses will bring him any flavor, and he can open the cup's foil lid all by himself. In another favorite photo he smiles triumphantly, holding a waffle cone full of chocolate ice cream at our celebration for new medication keeping him seizure-free for 24 hours. He asks us to post the photos on social media, so he can see the "thumbs up" and "hearts" from "all of his friends." The photo comments bring him so much joy. We are relieved that he can't see the private messages. Words emerging next to the photos of people we know from our pasts and presents, hidden from public view. They tell us to hide Tony's embodied reality that defies the preferred performances of masculinity that emerge from compulsory able-bodiedness and compulsory heterosexuality. They warn us that the social consequences of disability stigma are not worth the risk. We should hide his seizures.

SOCIAL MEDIA "FRIEND": Julie, I wanted to say that it's so good to see Tony's smiling face, but maybe you should keep his seizures off social media. And if you must post it, I wouldn't call it epilepsy if I were you. People are going to get the wrong idea. He's such a big strong boy, and so smart. You don't want people to think something is wrong with him. I mean his seizures are barely noticeable. They don't disrupt anything. There is no reason to make a big deal out of them. People online don't need to know.

ME: Tony is a big, strong, smart boy. We're so proud of him. And we're proud of how resilient he is. He wants to share his experiences on social media. He likes the reactions. And his seizures are so noticeable to him and extremely disruptive to his life. They're exhausting physically, intellectually, and emotionally. It's hard to get through.

SOCIAL MEDIA "FRIEND": Yeah, but it's not like those big scary seizures where people flop around and wet themselves. People barely notice them most of the time. They didn't disrupt a thing when he was visiting. Epilepsy and seizures sound so negative. He's such a big, strong, healthy boy. I'd keep quiet about it, for his sake if I were you. People will get the wrong idea about Tony.

ME: Well, you're not me. And big, strong, healthy, smart wonderful boys can have epilepsy. It's nothing to be ashamed of or hide.

SOCIAL MEDIA "FRIEND": I didn't mean it like that.

ME: What did you mean?

The message chain stops there. This particular "friend" had no response to my final question. Cultural response to bodies enabled and constrained by discourses of race, gender and ability surfaces with concern, fleshed, and tangible through these encounters. Dominant masculinity is inescapably tied to compulsory able-bodiedness, and its tenets of strength, self-control, and stoic independence.[10] As Tony's performance of White heteronormative masculinity swirls with frontal lobe epilepsy with complex partial seizures, Tony's familiar, culturally valued gender performance grows vulnerable to reinterpretation. Our big, strong, smart boy loses control of his body. The constant trembling leading to exhaustion that compromises his capacity for intellectual and emotional control as he becomes frustrated, reduced to tears over academic and social challenges that he usually navigates with controlled determination. To watch his struggle is awkward for those who want to celebrate his large size, physical strength, and usually predictable, "easy-going temperament." Others interpret his emotional needs, his increased tendency to crumple in exhausted frustration, needing hugs, comfort, and assurance, as a feminine, not masculine performance, that should be hidden so that he does not become embarrassed.[11] Tony is not embarrassed, but witnessing the impact of atypical brain function on his daily performance of self is disconcerting to onlookers. To watch a seemingly valued, normative, White masculine body disrupt compulsory able-bodiedness upsets them. It is perhaps more disconcerting through his large 7-year-old body that is mistaken for 10–12 years old. People desire for us to conceal this cyclic performance from them. They offer to turn away, make light of it, and dismiss it. After all, disabled bodies are marginalized, punished for their deviations from and displaced to the social margins, so avoiding that label should be preferable to us.[12] It isn't.

A Cultural Encounter with Masculinity, Emotions, and Epilepsy

Recently at the beach one spring morning, Tony suddenly started to wail. We still aren't sure why. Evan and I were talking while the boys played in the sand a few feet away. Vinny later told us that it had something to do with the shovel he was using. Tony wanted the red metal one, not the blue plastic one, but Vinny insisted he had it first. What usually would have been a quiet disagreement escalated after a few exchanges. Tony began kicking the water in the hole he had been digging with his brothers. Wet sand flew in the air, landing in each boy's hair. Both Vinny and Nico backed away as Tony's choking sobs increased. I ran behind him, wrapping my arms around him and asking what was wrong. Evan gently led Vinny and Nico toward the ocean. We understand. Tony had been seizing since his birthday two months earlier. At school he was having trouble being mindful of his body, flailing his head as he struggles to pay attention through the constant seizing. He gave his best friend a bloody nose by mistake during partner reading. He was mortified. She was understanding, so were her parents and his teacher. Again, I wondered if his White body aided in their quick forgiveness. They've watched his increasing lack of attention and mindfulness as the seizures remain unsuppressed. He is able to hold together his emotions during school for the most part, and often in public places, but today, on this quiet morning at the beach, he has reached his limit. An older couple a few yards away watch me hold my very big boy. Their eyes narrow. They shake their heads. The woman says, "He's too big of a boy to be acting like that. He needs more discipline." I look back, "No, he's not. He's seven and he needs sleep." Tony is quiet now. He looks at the couple and says, "My seizures make me so tired." They stare awkwardly. Tony lets me lead him to the blanket under the umbrella. He is asleep moments later. His body shakes with a short, 5-second seizure. I sit down beside him. I brought a book so that we could sit quietly together if he needed this time.

I wasn't going to mention his seizures to the couple. I reasoned it was none of their business, but perhaps at some level I was complying with the cultural expectation to conceal disabilities when possible. Tony refuses to comply with this expectation. Epilepsy is embedded into his identity. He has no desire to conceal his seizures or their impact on his emotional response to the world when they are unsuppressed. He alerts us, his teachers, coaches, and friends when they return, and we need to figure out his dosages again. We support that decision. Together we resist the cultural expectation to perpetuate compulsory able-bodiedness and its incompatibility with masculine performance. Tony is a big, strong, smart boy who has epilepsy. One embodied, lived experience does not cancel out the other.

A few weeks later we posted a photo of Tony. He is sitting in the playroom at his grandmother's house, wearing his red, white and blue soccer uniform, and a large smile. His floppy sandy hair brushes above his eyes. He looks strong, beautiful, and uninhibited. His arms are thrown wide. The photo celebrates that after two months, he has gone 24 hours without seizures. He wanted to post a picture to celebrate. We did. There are a lot of thumbs-up and hearts. There are also some concerned private messages urging me not to mention if they start up again. I ignore those. His performance of masculinity and ability is complex, and we embrace it, openly, publicly, refusing to conceal his embodied reality. We are hopeful that if we resist the expectations of compulsory able-bodiedness, others will also grow more at ease with the vulnerability, complexity, and diversity of our inescapably mortal bodies we depend on in order to exist with others and create meaning, identity, and culture in time and space.[13] Together, we wade in the currents.

Boy 2: Resisting the Cultural Currents of Compulsory Masculinity

Vinny is 4 years old, with long legs, a wiry build, straight dark hair, bright brown eyes, and porcelain skin. About a year ago Vinny stopped mirroring Tony's love of Pokémon, Star Wars, and the color red. He announced to us that pink and purple were his favorite colors, and he needed an Elsa Queen dress to wear while he "freezes bad guys." We obliged. The Easter Bunny left a light blue dress with a sheer cape. And he never took it off, until it fell apart so we ordered a new one. We are now on our fourth Elsa dress. He also has a Rapunzel dress, a purple ball gown he picked out for Christmas, and a red, white, and blue sundress he asked for from Costco because it looked like "it would be good to twirl in." It is. He wears these dresses with either his pink sneakers, light-up purple jelly heels, purple sandals, or pink rubber water shoes. No other shoe colors are acceptable, and he needs options. He also loves barrettes with jewels, necklaces, and bracelets. He tells us he "likes to sparkle" and is excited to share his new dresses and accessories in social media pictures for our friends and family because "he looks so beautiful."

The first photo we posted of Vinny in his Elsa dress, he is standing tall in our living room, dark eyes staring intensely into the camera, a thin, determined smile, with his arms up, ready to freeze his daddy with his magic ice powers. Delighted, Evan snapped a photo. We shared it online like we had shared past photos of the boys in their ninja turtle and storm trooper costumes. Vinny asked throughout the day to see the thumbs up and hearts. We feel thankful he could not see the private messages where multiple people expressed concern. Some were worried that Vinny would be teased, others that he would be embarrassed later in life when he realized how inappropriate it was for boys to wear dresses. Others asked how Evan and I, as his parents, could let him dress like that, that it was our job to "teach him to be a boy." One of the most startling messages sent an anti-transgender propaganda video from a Christian website that argued that gender is a "natural dichotomy" that cannot be fought, and any deviation was sinful. I find all these comments disconcerting, but the following conversation struck me:

SOCIAL MEDIA "FRIEND": Julie, I just want you to know that I pray for Vinny, that he'll realize he's a boy, and stop this. And I pray that as his parents, Evan and you will realize it needs to be stopped, and that it's your job to teach him what is right. I don't know why you make him be like this. Whether he wants to be a girl or not, he's a boy.

ME: We don't "make him be like this," he just is who he is. And while we will always support him no matter how he identifies, Vinny loves being a boy. He has never identified in any other way. He's a boy who loves pink, purple, dresses, and sparkles. Vinny's fashion choices don't need your prayers. He's a happy, beautiful boy. There's no need to pray unless you're thanking God for him.

The person never responded.

Confused family, friends, and acquaintances often ask why Tony is "such a boy" and Vinny is "so different." Their questions used to confuse me, but I've had time to make sense of it over the past few years. Entangled in this question is the assumption that childhood masculinity—the desire to kick and throw balls, use powerful machinery like trucks and bulldozers, and simulating physical violence through wrestling and play involving weapons—is normative. Tony, for the most part, gravitates to this style of play. While Vinny is not entirely rejecting of these forms of play—he enjoys soccer and sword fighting in moderation just like Tony enjoys pretending to be a daddy with dolls, wearing jewelry, and periodically watching a princess movie—he is more likely to draw rainbows in his journals, carefully choose accessories, and make up to compliment his elaborate princess pretend play, and lovingly brushes his dolls' hair for hours. We never encourage our boys to gravitate in a specific direction for preferences or play. We also do not create any restrictions. Each boy moved through options. Tony cherished his pink princess necklace with floating glitter inside for a few months. Vinny went through a strong Darth Vader stage. At this moment in time, their preferences are different. They are different boys who have the same parents. People who are uncomfortable with Vinny's performance of gender want to believe as his parents, we determined it. Tony's normative masculinity challenges this explanation, reminding cultural members that gender performance is not determined by one's genitals or dictated by external influences, but fluid and continually open to deviate from cultural expectations without any obvious explanations.

A Cultural Encounter with Masculinity, Femininity, and Heteronormativity

In recent months I have had many people ask if Vinny is gay or transgender (many seem to use the two terms interchangeably illuminating the limited understandings of gender *and* sexual identity in our society). The most recent encounter stands out to me. A few weeks ago we arrived early for the boys to sing in the church children's choir. All three ran to the refreshment table covered with pastries and jugs of fruit punch. An older woman touched my arm and I turned toward her. She looked at Vinny's pink croc shoes, bracelets, and shiny necklace he paired with his hot pink polo shirt and lemon-yellow shorts.

HER: Did he pick that out himself?

ME: Yes. He's so particular about accessories.

HER: Is he gay?

ME: Um, I don't know. He's 4. I don't really know how any of my boys identify. Right now both Tony and Vinny refer to themselves as boys and express interest in girlfriends and future wives, but they are at ease with any kind of love they see. Nico can't talk enough to say one way or the other yet. Parenting is an adventure. We'll see who they become.

HER: Oh, I didn't mean Tony and Nico. Of course they're fine. And I wouldn't worry about Vinny, either. I mean it's probably just a phase. He seems so happy and sweet and healthy otherwise.

ME: I'm not worried about any of them. And Vinny may be going through a phase or may not be. He is happy, sweet and healthy. I don't know why you say "healthy otherwise." He's not sick. Loving pink and sparkly jewelry is a preference, not an illness.

HER: But he's a boy. You maybe shouldn't let him out in public like that.

ME: Yes, he's a boy. A boy who likes sparkles, pink and swirly dresses. Can you blame him? They're fun. He's our 'glitter guy.' He has nothing to hide.

At that moment the music started. I grabbed my children's hands and started toward the choir room. That woman never approached me again. I was a bit rattled after. I talked with Evan quietly before the service and then again at home while the boys napped. He reminded me that she does not matter. Her opinions come from a set of cultural beliefs that define her, not us. My chest still tightens when I remember that encounter. We've since left that church for one that embraces the fluidity of sexuality and gender. Our boys need safer cultural waters for a spiritual community.

I worry about the cultural currents. Vinny may need to continue to swim against through life. Right now, at 4 years old, with his white skin, thin build, delicate features, and longer hair that resembles Dorothy Hamilton's iconic haircut, many older adults who smile at him as he dances through life in a shining princess dress, light up jelly heels and clip on earrings, refer to him as "she," calling him "sweetheart" and "darling" as they ensure he does not bump into their carts in the grocery store with the gentle guidance of his shoulders. White, thin, middle-class privilege insulates his passing performance of femininity. He enjoys these exchanges. He smiles and doesn't correct them. Neither do we. He will tell us later in the car, "They think since I'm wearing 'girl stuff' that I'm a girl because I'm so beautiful, but I'm not, I'm a beautiful boy. I like to be pretty and sparkle." We smile and nod. Tony will take a moment to compliment his dress or pink rainbow light up shoes reassuringly.

Vinny is big for his age and grows more muscular as he ages. I wonder, if he continues to gravitate toward feminine clothes and accessories, if passing as a girl will continue to be a social luxury for much longer. I think back to the moments when he chooses shorts and a t-shirt with his earrings, tiara, and jelly heels, and how as people realize he is a boy, these accessories spur judgment around him, and us. Much like Tony's emotional reactions, people see Vinny's fluid gender performance as problematic, and expect Evan and me to discipline our boys, to call them back into safer cultural waters. During these moments, compulsory masculinity, compulsory heterosexuality and compulsory able-bodiedness resurface for me. For a moment, Vinny's sparkling accessories and Tony's seizures swirl together for me. My sons are performing cultural deviances that others feel the need to position as minor, as nothing to worry about, and certainly not something we should publicize. In fact, they urge us to take steps to conceal them. They hope that their uncomfortable daily performances of self will fade away with the changing tides of time if we just hide them long and well enough.

Vinny's daily performance of self raises questions and evokes desires for definite labels and constructed categories that interpret his gender identity as either "normal" or "abnormal." Those around us who know and like Vinny attempt to defend his "normal" label to us, even as his performance of gender makes them uncomfortable. Vinny, as he changes between clothes from the boy and girl sections, delighting in a rainbow of colors and play, defies this cultural desire for fixed labels. He's loving, growing, becoming. So is Tony. Neither seems constrained by cultural expectations for compulsory performances. I try to embrace their ease with fluidity, moving with them. Realizing that despite opposition, their ease means those around them is moving with the changing tides that disrupt compulsory performances. The social identity waters are open. To not swim is to miss opportunities to be who we are.

Person 3 and Resisting Compulsion/Embracing Fluidity

Two-year-old Nico moves in play between the two of them (as they both did at his age). Right now, as I sit in a hammock chair writing this in our backyard, he is pretending to fight the other two with his light saber, wearing a hand-me-down Batman shirt from Tony that he has accessorized with lipstick and four necklaces from earlier princess play with Vinny. His blond hair that will turn sandy like Tony's by this time next year glints in the sun. His cheeks are flushed with exertion. His brown eyes are wide with excitement. The three laugh. Tony jumps and lands with a thud on our concrete patio. Vinny twirls in his Elsa dress. His cape flies behind him. He lands on one foot, pointing his toe gracefully. He is excited to resume ballet and tap dance lessons in the fall. Suddenly Tony stops, his arms are rigid, and he grits his teeth. Vinny, aware that a slight seizure is taking place, stops and hugs him. Nico follows and does the same. It's over and they all smile. I ask if they are okay. Tony says "yes, but I'm tired." I know he is. Seizing is hard work. Later, he'll probably need to be held as he cries, exhausted by the physical and mental effort of frontal lobe epilepsy with localized motor seizures. People will stare if it happens in public and look disapprovingly as we hold him in Costco before hoisting him into a cart where he curls up to go to sleep. We'll grab a second cart for groceries and continue on. People will look at us questioningly. Some will ask if he is too old to pull tantrums or take naps. We'll say, "different bodies need different things" and continue on. We'll also smile as they look questioningly at Vinny's sparkling barrettes and princess accessories, and Nico's equally striking superhero cape, Pokémon hat, and shiny necklaces. Their gender performances, fluid and flowing like the currents of the ocean down the road, continue. Together we ride and fight the tides we encounter.

Epilogue: Continually Understanding the Fluidity of Gender Tides in Our Performance of Parenting with Baby 4

I am going to give birth to our final baby sometime in the next five weeks. (Tony and Vinny are so excited. Nico is not quite aware of what is coming but feeds off his older brothers' energy.) We were not against knowing how doctors would categorize our child's genitals, but the baby would not cooperate (legs and feet continue to obstruct the view) and not knowing is not bothersome to us. We understand that our child's chosen performance of gender and sexuality will not be revealed through an ultrasound, and while our baby will be categorized at birth as either male or female, we will not know how gender and sexuality will surface, evolve, and change over time. We do not know if this baby will be gently carried by the tides of normative cultural expectations or disrupt them, teaching us how to better navigate against the dominant currents.

I have been a professor with a concentration in gender studies the entire time I've been a parent. Despite my understanding of gender fluidity and performance, I had no trouble seven years ago, identifying Tony as a boy after I saw a penis on an ultrasound. Evan and I announced his categorization without much thought. We made a similar announcement for Vinny four and a half years ago. With Nico, we chose not to find out his sex. We actively avoided the knowledge. Two years ago, as I became more aware of the complexities of gender and the cultural assumptions surrounding how one should raise and parent boys and girls, I wanted to avoid those awkward conversations surrounding who was growing in my uterus. When I said whether our baby was a boy or a girl did not matter, I realized on a much deeper level than I had with my first two sons, that what genitals were growing had no bearing on who was coming, so there was no need to make any plans based on them. Not knowing myself helped me embrace that irrelevance as I planned for an arrival in a nursery full of white and sea green, the colors of the ocean and foam that has become my ongoing metaphor for navigating culture as a parent.

Now, as Tony and Vinny chose to add bright splashes of rainbow to that sea green nursery, Nico moves to one of our other bedrooms, and we prepare for the final baby's arrival, not knowing the baby's categorized sex is not necessary for me to embrace the fluidity and possibilities of how gender and sexuality will surface and change over the coming years. My first three children have taught me that as their parents, we must move with them, riding and fighting cultural tides as necessary to facilitate who they are. In this moment, I have three children who seem to identify as male, though in very different ways, disability, femininity, and ambiguity swirl into the privileges of whiteness and masculinity, materializing each unique performance of self with others. Evan and I are excited to see who they and their last sibling will continue to grow into. We feel fortunate to have the opportunity to navigate the cultural currents with them.

Notes

1 Peggy McIntosh. "White Privilege: Unpacking the Invisible Knapsack." *Independent School* 49, no. 2 (1990): 31–36; Robert McRuer. *Crip Theory: Cultural Signs of Queerness and the Body* (New York, NY: New York University Press, 2006); Adrienne Rich.

"Compulsory Heterosexuality and the Lesbian Existence." *Signs* 5, no. 4 (1980): 631–660, doi: https://www.jstor.org/stable/3173834.
2 Kristen Langellier and Eric Peterson. *Storytelling in Daily Life: Performing Narrative* (Philadelphia, PA: Temple University Press, 2004).
3 Judith Butler. *Bodies That Matter: On the Discursive Limits of Sex* (New York, NY: Routledge, 1993).
4 Judith Butler. "Performative Acts and Gender Constitution: An Essay in Phenomenology and Feminist Theory." *Theatre Journal* 40, no 4 (1988): 519–531, doi: 10.2307/3207893.
5 Rich.
6 McRuer; Rich.
7 Rosemarie Garland-Thomson. *Extraordinary Bodies: Figuring Physical Disability in American Culture and Literature* (New York, NY: Columbia University Press, 1997).
8 MacIntosh.
9 Julie-Ann Scott. *Embodied Performance as Applied Research, Art and Pedagogy* (London: Palgrave MacMillan, 2018); Julie-Ann Scott. "Narrative Performance Research: Co-Storying Almost-Passing." *Departures in Critical Qualitative Research* 4, no. 3 (2015): 70–91, doi: 10.1525/dcqr.2015.4.3.70; Julie-Ann Scott. "Problematizing a Researcher's Performance of 'Insider Status': An Autoethnography of 'Designer Disabled' Identity." *Qualitative Inquiry* 19, no. 2 (2013): 101–115, doi: 10.1177/1077800412462990.
10 R. W. Connell. *Masculinities*, 2nd ed. (Berkeley, CA: University of California Press 2005).
11 Connell.
12 McRuer.
13 Scott, *Embodied*.

Bibliography

Butler, Judith. *Bodies That Matter: On the Discursive Limits of Sex*. New York, NY: Routledge, 1993.
Butler, Judith. "Performative Acts and Gender Constitution: An Essay in Phenomenology and Feminist Theory." *Theatre Journal* 40, no 4 (1988): 519–531, doi: 10.2307/3207893.
Connell, R. W. *Masculinities*, 2nd ed. Berkeley, CA: University of California Press, 2005.
Garland-Thomson, Rosemarie. *Extraordinary Bodies: Figuring Physical Disability in American Culture and Literature*. New York, NY: Columbia University Press, 1997.
Langellier, Kristen and Eric Peterson. *Storytelling in Daily Life: Performing Narrative*. Philadelphia, PA: Temple University Press, 2004.
McIntosh, Peggy. "White Privilege: Unpacking the Invisible Knapsack." *Independent School* 49, no. 2 (1990): 31–36.
McRuer, Robert. *Crip Theory: Cultural Signs of Queerness and the Body*. New York, NY: New York University Press, 2006.
Rich, Adrienne. "Compulsory Heterosexuality and the Lesbian Existence." *Signs* 5, no. 4 (1980): 631–660, doi: https://www.jstor.org/stable/3173834.
Scott, Julie-Ann. *Embodied Performance as Applied Research, Art and Pedagogy*. London, UK: Palgrave MacMillan, 2018.
Scott, Julie-Ann. "Narrative Performance Research: Co-Storying Almost-Passing." *Departures in Critical Qualitative Research* 4, no. 3 (2015): 70–91, doi: 10.1525/dcqr.2015.4.3.70.
Scott, Julie-Ann. "Problematizing a Researcher's Performance of 'Insider Status': An Autoethnography of 'Designer Disabled' Identity." *Qualitative Inquiry* 19, no. 2 (2013): 101–115, doi: 10.1177/1077800412462990.

ON POSSIBILITY

Queer Relationality and Coalition-Building in the University Classroom

Shadee Abdi and Anthony P. Cuomo

I (Shadee) "came out" to my class once. Only once, and not exactly by choice. It was winter of 2014, and it was only my second quarter as a Ph.D. student at a private university with a predominantly White, affluent student body. Toward the end of the quarter, I had assigned what would later become an article about my sexual identity negotiation to my class with all identifiers removed. I simply wanted to have a discussion about intersectionality and the politics that make intersectional queer identities complicated, but I was not ready to attach my name to that work yet. About a week before we were set to discuss this article, my most promising student asked if we could have non-scheduled office hours to discuss her upcoming performance project. We met at the Starbucks adjacent to campus, and we talked about how she could share her story in front of the class. Along the way, she used my article as an example and asked me a series of questions about it, all while avoiding asking me questions about who authored the work. She was pressing, but I wouldn't budge—awkwardly avoiding any questions that might accidentally out me as the author. We left our meeting, and I felt uneasy. Did she figure me out?

A week later, we discussed the article in class. Students seemed to have enjoyed the reading, as it was the most engaged, they had been all semester. Hands consistently raised with clarifying questions, all of which I had to carefully answer out of fear that they would find out that I was the author. With 20 minutes left in class, I thought I was safe. We had an amazing discussion as a class that was winding down, and I felt a sense of relief overcome me. Until one of my students raises her hand and proceeds, "Shadee, I have an awkward question for you… is this you?" Time stands still. My breath stops, and my body tenses. I am sitting down, but had I not been, I would have surely stumbled. I smiled awkwardly and mustered up the courage of all the women who came before me, and I smiled and responded simply, "How did you figure it out?"

A sense of awkward tension fills the room that is quickly replaced with tentative ease. My students tell me that they have known for weeks, and that they were waiting for me to talk about my sexuality. I speak about the challenges of confronting my story in the classroom, because of the fear that subsumes me. I tell them that I constantly have to negotiate my identities in a variety of contexts, and that it has never felt quite safe nor necessary to discuss my sexuality in the classroom space, to be frank, it still doesn't. We laugh and stumble through a discussion about why I chose not to disclose, and they meet me with grace and understanding. I gave up a little bit of that fear that day, but not without consequence. The conversation weighed (weighs) on me heavily. I don't regret it. I don't think of it negatively. It just was what it was, and in that moment—it felt okay. It was one of those experiences, where I was able to create a teaching moment out of merely existing.

Years later, I have kept in contact with that same student I met at Starbucks. I have helped mentor her and have watched as she successfully finished a master's degree in communication. She is now in her third year of a Ph.D. program, and we regularly talk through academic issues and the struggles of graduate school. Just recently, she told me that she had something to tell me. She tried to get me to guess what she was going to say, in my heart I knew, but I kept my hunch silent. Eventually, she sent the short message, "I don't like boys." I was the first person she had told. And she said she did it because I was a safe person to share it with. I write back that I am proud of her for sharing. And I am. I left that moment reflecting on a queer relationality that was fostered by happenstance. And, while I have not been able to assign my article again, even after its subsequent publication, because it's just too hard, I think about that class and those students often. Fondly. And I let that moment, be just that … a moment. One that will be difficult to forget.

★ ★ ★

At this point, I (Anthony) had never directly talked about my sexuality with any of my students. I came out during class as an undergraduate and graduate student, but never as a faculty member. I am sure students have suspected I might be queer. And, many might have just been able to tell based on my various performances of masculinity, heterosexuality, and my ambiguous use of pronouns when disclosing examples to my students talking about my partner in the context of conversations about communication theories. But, I felt so afraid that my students might see me differently. Even teaching at a diverse urban university in a city with a gay Latino mayor, I felt like an outsider and I was afraid that my difference might be used against me.

As a mixed-race person, I feel conflicted with coming out narratives that rely on and reflect rhetorical strategies of whiteness, which casts the "coming out process as a liberatory act [and] reflects a White middle class epistemological bias that does not necessarily resonate for queer subjects marked by racial difference."[1] Outness can fail to resonate with queer people of color, especially in contexts that require individuals to maintain family, community, and work relationship, yet still identify and live as queer individuals. While coming out can be liberating for some, performing degrees of queer invisibility—where queerness may be completely hidden or, if visible, is not openly acknowledged—emerges as an agentive practice for queers of color who may various lived experiences that complicate their ability to come out.[2] Furthermore, since coming out is often a daily and regular process, how we come out and to whom we come out to is an individual choice. Before I make my decision to come out in class, I call Shadee for advice. Immediately, she gets very quiet and sad, and I can hear her choke up as she tells me about a conversation she had in a graduate seminar with a colleague who critiqued her choice for not coming out to one of her classes. I remind Shadee that self-disclosure is a choice and because of our differing intersections—specifically our cultural identity, gender, and religious intersections—that we may make different choices in the classroom and that's not only okay, but necessary.

I came out to my Communication and Gender class, and much to my surprise, my students were very supportive. In that moment, I felt relief and excitement. After coming out, other students also identified their sexuality and our conversations became more critical and reflexive. In a sense, a queer relationality was interpellated by the act of coming out and allowed for a collective identity to be called into being. While my class was mostly cisgender, White women, there were also a couple of cis White males who also seemed to show me support and opened up more about their experiences and how we can work toward challenging toxic heteronormative behavior especially among males. If Shadee came out to my class, would she have a similar experience? I think about that all the time.

Unpacking Gender and Sexuality in the Classroom

Traditional research has looked at how gender impacts and influences classroom dynamics,[3] but much of this work has yet to look at how queer of color educators can experience that classroom in distinctively divergent ways. This chapter attempts to fill some of these gaps by locating our familiarities as queer of color educators who share intersectional identities yet differ in our individual classroom experiences. This chapter provides a collaborative autoethnography that uses performative writing and draws from critical performance pedagogy[4] to examine how power and privilege operate in the classroom, particularly in relation to gender and sexuality. Moreover, we look at the ways in which we can empower ourselves as well as our students in the classroom.

In this chapter we use critical performative pedagogy and the value of collaborative autoethnography to underscore our experiences. Because we know that "our pedagogical practices must always be informed by critical reflexivity and context," we follow with sharing our stories and locating ourselves as queer of color educators.[5] We provide our shared experiences to showcase the ways in which coalition can be built between our intersectional selves, in an effort to sustain queer relationality. In the same vein, our goal has been to underscore the ways in which institutionalized/internalized sexism, racism, and homophobia create an oscillation of privilege and oppression wherein which our identities and our politics conflate/contest, because like Eguchi and Spieldenner, we understand the academy—the Ivory Tower—to be a microcosm that "sustains the status quo, and therefore multiple racialized, gendered, and class voices emerge, but faculty and students of color continue to be minimized, silenced, and/or marginalized.[6] Toward the end, we also speak of critical love as a resistive strategy that can offer queer of color educators the promise of possibility for a more holistic experience in the classroom, with each other, and within the academy.

Collaborative Autoethnography, Performative Writing, and Pedagogy

As Calafell and Gutierrez-Perez contend, "At any moment in a classroom that is centered on culture and difference, there is a possibility of conflict—it can feel like a battlefield."[7] As queer of color educators, that battlefield is as terrifying as it is ever present. It is in these moments that we are asked to forget that more often than not, the politics of our bodies can reverberate louder than our voices. We are always already gendered, sexualized, racialized, classed, and otherwise marked in the classroom.[8] As soon as we walk into any space, our bodies tell a story—whether or not we are cognizant that it is happening or know what part of ourselves others have grasped onto. However, being that we are queer of color educators, we are also hyper-aware that while our identity vectors intersect in many similar ways, the ways in which we experience those intersections in everyday life are exponentially different. This speaks of the complex interplay that makes it unreasonable to assume that an identical experience as queer educators of color is possible. Thus, it is through this collaborate autoethnography and through performative writing that we are able to express and use our embodied knowledge of our shared experiences to make sense of and understand our positionalities in the world and, in this particular case, the classroom.

While not oppositional or always intentional, the experiences of cisgender, queer women of color are going to be similar and different to cisgender queer men of color, "the situations that women in academic environments encounter differ depending on constituents such as race, ethnicity, age, class, ability, and sexual orientation."[9] Thus, it is imperative to unpack and better understand how gender, sexuality, nationality, power, and privilege, alongside our positionalities, impact and operate in these shared yet uniquely individual spaces. Our performances of culture and everyday performances of self and identities have everything to do with temporality. Where we are, how we look, how we move, how we present all directly impact the ways in which we are able to navigate the worlds in which we live.[10] Performative writing allows scholars the opportunity to unpack what has long been theoretical, giving space to share our present, our histories, our futures, and everything in between.

The shift from disengagement in academic writing has been palpable for many years, but it has become even more urgent now in the time of fake news, to understand how the politics of self-impact and influence, what and how we research, and what and how we teach. To pretend that we can separate ourselves from our works is not only disingenuous, but it also creates a tension between lived realities and the theorizations of others. Conquergood's concern with dialogic performance, blending the self with other, defied paradigmatic barriers, while giving room to those who saw little of themselves in research (or more importantly, did not) the space to engage with the important works we engage with every day.[11] The act of recognizing/(re)writing our embodied knowledge, using performative writing, gives space for us to remain accountable to the stories of ourselves, others, and how those stories come together as a means of understanding everyday lived experiences.

Eguchi and Spieldenner argue "for investigating shared realities of and critiquing essentialized and homogenized positionalities of racialized queerness in the academy."[12] To do so, we use performative writing to form our collaborative autoethnography, which also attempts "to explicate, elucidate, and elaborate how our everyday performances of identities are intersectional, and that our embodied experiences are not reducible to a single identity category in institutional and personal praxis."[13] While each of us identifies as a queer person of color, our intersectional identities challenge conflated understandings of how we are marked in the classroom. Moreover, our shared narratives as friends, colleagues, allies, and as part of a larger queer family within the communication studies discipline, we hope to highlight how writing about our lived experiences in the context of our scholarship and academic positionings can create new possibilities for challenging hegemonic interpretations of marginalized identities in the academy. Jones and Calafell write that personal narratives are concerned with tellability and "the politics of voice."[14] It is through queer relationality[15] that we are able to share our stories with each other in such a way that listening and understanding become necessary tools for survival. Our stories are different, but it is in that difference that we are able to build coalition and sustain a queer relationality. This chapter centers our stories in order to draw on what we can do as queer of color educators to support, encourage, and build/sustain coalitions with each other for the betterment of ourselves, our students, and our pedagogical commitments. Because of these intentions, like Calafell and Chuang, our stories "cannot be disentangled from our own histories and hence we share them here."[16]

(Re)Storying Our Classroom Experiences

"Ms. Abdi?" one of my more promising students raises her hand excitedly, and I (Shadee) look up, visibly perplexed. Despite having spent the better part of the semester speaking to my students about the importance of using the titles of women, queer folks, people of color, and particularly women of color, when I hear this, feelings of uncertainty jolt through my body. I look around the room, waiting (hoping) for someone to notice and correct her, so that I don't have to. I weigh my options, wait a few more seconds, and in my calmest voice, I answer her question but begin with the word "Doctor." She stares back at me, nods, and goes back to journaling. This moment wasn't big, or grand, or triggering. It was just … a moment. And yet, I find myself thinking about it often. I wonder how folks who might not share my specific intersections might have experienced similar interactions. I think about all the times I have had to calculate the emotional labor involved in correcting a student who, as far as I can tell, meant no harm, and how many times others have had to the same.

In the classroom, I am challenged more often than I am listened to or engaged with—predominantly, though not surprisingly, by my cisgender, White, male students. At first, I thought my age was the issue. Having earned a Ph.D. before the age of 30 is not something people generally expect. But then, I realized that while age certainly must play a factor, my female colleagues and my mentors continue to experience these issues all the time, every single year—not just by students, but by administration, male colleagues, and the list goes on. And so, I walk into the classroom, nervous, *all the damn time*. When I enter the classroom for the first time, with each new group of students, I struggle to find the words, tone, and affect that I think will appease my students' expectations. I try, but even in that effort, I find myself often coming short. My appearance, how I dress, my (somewhat) feminine presentation, how old I look, how tough of a teacher I should be … all enter my thoughts. I worry about which facet of my identity my students will pick up on first … my gender, my sexuality, my race, my age? I am concerned about how much of their expectations I will/can/should successfully meet. MacNell, Driscoll, and Hunt posit that "female educators are often at a crossroads, having to navigate being nurturing and supportive while simultaneously authoritative and professional."[17] I have become hyper-aware of the role that gender, sexuality, race, religion, and age play in the classroom. The unconscious bias is palatable. While gender biases are nothing new, it does not get any easier to operate in a workplace where, "men are automatically assumed to have legitimate authority, while women must prove their expertise to earn the same level of respect."[18] Each time a student mistakenly refers to me as Ms. instead of Dr., ignoring the years of hard work I put in to earning my Ph.D., I am forced to contemplate whether I even have the energy to correct them. I have to think about the labor it would take to face another look that screams, "Oh, she's a bitch." A look I have come to know too well. I have relied on the works of feminists of color, who have taught me in so many words that while it doesn't always get easier, resistance is the only possible way to survive. And so, I am terrified of what my students think of when they see me.

When I enter the classroom, I also wonder if people will notice I am queer, and it scares me. I'm not ready to be *out* in the classroom, and I'm not sure if I will ever be. *Outness* is a privilege I am not afforded in many spaces. Like LeMaster, I understand my relationship to the closet to be relational and situational.[19] I see the closet as a contextual space wherein which my ability to oscillate the idea of out/in is "riddled with relative privilege and oppression."[20] I fully acknowledge that my experiences as a queer Iranian-US American woman is fundamentally different than even that of a queer Iranian. My US American citizenship affords me leeway to be open about my sexuality with my friends, immediate family, and my colleagues … something that I do not take for granted. But in the classroom, these things do not comfort me. My queer identity weighs on my ability to breathe easy in that space. Having taught predominantly in schools in the southwest United States, I am always hyper-vigilant about the politics surrounding me, and I am unable to take those specific risks.

As queer folks of color, one of the many choices we must make is whether we can share our identities with the certain communities and in certain spaces. As a queer Iranian-US American, I have learned to perform my identity in ways that allow me to oscillate the world safely—not only for myself but for my family, both in Iran and in the United States. This point of contention is one that I am constantly reminded of. I recall my White, queer colleagues, who claim to be my allies, questioning the "authenticity" of my performance of self as a queer woman of color, "If you don't come out to your students, you're being inauthentically queer" or worse yet, "You're a danger to the queer community." These words repeat over and over again, with each new semester and with each new group of students. Year after year, the sting of what has come to feel like inadequacy burns as harshly as the first time I heard the words spoken. To those voices, my White, queer "allies," I remind you that for queer people of color, sexuality is not an isolated identity. Our experiences are our family's experiences; our safety is our family's safety. Our genders, our cultures, our nationalities, our class standings, our ages, our religions, our abilities are always already a part of the conversation. When it feels impossible for me to "come out" in that space, I don't feel like I am doing a disservice to anyone. My politics are queer. In my classroom, I take the time to never rely on tired gendered examples and strive to create an inclusive and safe space from day 1. But my own identity, my intersectional queer experience, does not solely belong to me.

All that to say that there is no universal queer experience, and to claim that there is one, or that coming out makes you "authentically" queer does a disservice to any and all queer bodies that have insofar been made to feel invisible. "Coming out" is a privilege, because for some the option doesn't exist. The language doesn't exist. As someone who has dedicated her life to the study and research on queer of color folks, I am appalled by the assertion that for many members of the LGBTQ community, outness equals authenticity. This conversation relies heavily on US ethnocentric articulations of sexuality that do a disservice to those who do not fit within this version of queerness subsumed by Western cultural normativity. Yep explains that Western cultural normativity

> creates new hierarchies (e.g., certain cultural groups that do not practice the politics of visibility, such as not coming out publicly, are judged as homophobic, "unenlightened, and "backward," which reinforces the superiority of the West), obscures culturally specific ways of negotiating nonnormativities (e.g., creation of new forms of social arrangements and relationships), and coerces "other" individuals and groups to conform to the language and meanings of the sexual systems of the West.[21]

And so, I ask for understanding and grace from these colleagues who have contributed to further internalized homophobia and the questioning of myself as a successful pedagogue. Instead, I ask that we treat all of our queer experiences as nuanced, complex, and situationally dependent, and that we respect each other's journeys and stories along the way. Anzaldúa explains that for women of color, the act of *being queer* in so many ways, symbolizes choice. "For the lesbian of color, the ultimate rebellion she can make against her native culture is through sexual behavior. She goes against two moral prohibitions: sexuality and homosexuality … It is a way of balancing, of mitigating duality."[22] As critical scholars who should be focusing on the nuance and value of individual experiences as part of a larger cultural narrative, I beg of you to consider the liminality of sexuality and support the members of your community who exist within that liminal space.

"You're a danger to the queer community"—I reflect on those words often, and still, they are in some ways worse than any criticism I have received from my heterosexual allies. To feel like you failed your own community, to be told to your face that your identity and how you have chosen to express that identity is dangerous … well, I've clearly not gotten over it. And so, it lives within me, deep inside, and on my most vulnerable days I let myself steep in it. As a US American citizen who can make some choices that other queer of color bodies often cannot, I do not pretend to have any right to tell others how to enact their queer identities, in the classroom or otherwise, particularly for those whose identities mark their bodies as dangerous, to their families and nations of origin. While I believe families of choice are necessary for queer survival, for queer people of color, our experiences are also often intrinsically linked to our families of origin. Thus, the goal of this work is to introspectively understand how our bodies function in the classroom, and how we can use queer worldmaking and queer relationality to build transnational coalition and foster more nuanced understanding of our intersections, especially in relation to gender, sexuality, and race. For queer folks of color, our identities are imbedded in the messy mixture of all our intersections, always, and that for some, "coming out" cannot act as an end-all be-all solution, because it does not just impact *us*. The false Western creation of a family of origin/family of choice binary does not neatly apply for queer folks of color, because for many of us, we do not have the option to choose one or the other. For many, sexuality is not fixed. It's not that simple. To write about sexuality as if it is one thing, as if labels hold more value and power than story, is to do a disservice to all those whose narratives continue to go untold. And so, to my White, queer allies, I beg you to remember that while our stories might not match yours, our gendered, sexual, and racial stories are in and of themselves authentic.

To make sense of so much of these complexities, I find myself relying on Anthony to be there and to listen. When I call Anthony and tell him about a certain story or anecdote about my day, more often than not he is shocked. Not because he doesn't believe me … but because he does. He tells me that he can't understand how these experiences are my normal. I tell him how uncomfortable I am when my older, White, male student who dons a shaved head, stands at least a foot taller than me, and stays after class, every class, approaches me in the stairwell. He too, means no harm, but I find myself holding onto my keys more tightly, fingers shakenly holding onto my whistle. A whistle Anthony has never had to think about carrying. And nothing happened with that student, but the possibility terrified me.

We also speak, in great detail, about our teaching evaluations. I often tell Anthony that he is one of the best teachers I know. He preps for weeks, stays up to date with the newest pedagogical tools, and his students love him—not without merit. I've sat in on his classes and have found myself just as into the material he presents, as his students. So, when he gets high scores on his evaluations, it doesn't shock me. I too work hard for my classes, I prep, I read up on pedagogical innovations, I build relationships, and even still I worry that every move I make, every grade I give, and every lesson I teach, that somehow, I will be evaluated poorly for it. Simply put, when I present things, I always do so with the fear of evaluations looming over my shoulder. The absurdity of my reality has led us to now joke about the fact that he can bring up feminism in any class and no one would flinch. Whereas I find myself having to prep for weeks just to broach the subject—even, and it pains me to say it, in *gender* classes. Even still, being able to talk to him and debrief gives me solace. He acknowledges that his presence in the classroom, despite his queer of color identity, is one that is rarely, if ever, challenged. He gives me the space to vent, he offers his support, and he always asks what he can do to be a better ally, friend, and educator. I take comfort in this.

★ ★ ★

I (Anthony) wake up on the first day of the semester nervous. I have spent the last couple of weeks talking to Shadee as I prepare to teach an upper division communication and gender class at a four-year university for the first time. I feel especially self-conscious because unlike my other colleagues teaching this course, I do not have a Ph.D. Prior to my current tenure track position, I worked as a part-time lecturer. During that time, I felt like my credibility was always in question. Like Shadee, the stress of student evaluations were always in my mind, coupled with just how much of my identity I should disclose in the classroom. Honestly, I was scared that if I disclosed my queer identity, I might receive backlash and thought that could impact my student evaluations and therefore my job could be placed at risk.

As a contingent faculty member without job security or stability, I was fearful and, at times, felt an obligation to conform to dominant expectations of the academy to secure my employment and safety in higher education. Calafell demonstrates that faculty outside of the "mainstream" may challenge traditional tenants of the academy and are often marked with stereotypes and prejudices, especially women of color.[23] As my friend Shadee often reminds me, I am well prepared to teach the class, but my positionality as a cisgender male requires me to ask more questions. I ask her to share her experiences teaching gender where she warns me that the conversations can become contentious and that I should prepare for resistance, especially from White, heterosexual men, who may not identify with some of the lived experiences discussed in the course.[24]

As a half Latino, half White male, who often performs cisgender heteronormative expressions of masculinity, I walk into the classroom with a lot of power and privilege. Even though I identify as a queer male and as a first-generation college student, from humble socio-economic beginnings, I am steeped in privilege. Parts of that privilege are visible. You can see from my standard uniform—my gold watch, tailored button up shirt and matching pants, with oxford brown shoes … my performance is a privileged one—one that has not yet been questioned in the classroom. I find myself even being careful about how I talk, dress, and walk in the classroom to protect the vulnerability of being seen as gay or queer, and I cannot help but question why I do this. Eguchi explains, "living in a heteronormative society, gay men also experience internalized heterosexism and homophobia. These become a source of conflict for gay men during their identity negotiation process."[25] Aside from internalized homophobia, internalizing racist and classist scripts continue to influence my communicative choices, especially around disclosing my queer identity.

Throughout my life, I have struggled with the fear associated with acceptance from my family and friends, all while mostly staying closeted from the larger cultural society. To achieve acceptance, I have sought to emphasize a gendered performance which reflects hegemonic masculine traits. I mask external characteristics that mark myself as non-White and perform whiteness by adhering to White beauty standards. Straightening my curly hair and wearing clothes and artifacts that communicate privilege come from an internal struggle where I seek acceptance from one community by silencing another. These practices have led to guilt, shame, and a fear that I am letting down queer people of color around me. Like Shadee, I have also been accused of being inauthentic and falling short of others' expectations. I'm not White enough and straight enough or Brown enough or queer enough. What would make me enough?

In the classroom, I often feel shame. I watch how some of my queer of color colleagues bravely challenge our heteronormative, sexist, racist institutions by just being present. La Fountain-Stokes describes how shame is used in the gay community in order to get individuals to conform to White, Euro-centric views of the gay experience.[26] Gay shame motivates those who challenge traditional views of the gay experience to be ostracized and to be seen as "others."[27] Fountain-Stokes further explains that shame can be a central "constitutive behavior of Latina/o cultures, engaged as they are with Catholic religiosity, feelings of guilt, and remorse about improper behavior, be it religious (sins) or failing of family or social obligations."[28] Shame is something many queer Latinos struggle with on a daily basis. While some of my internalized shame may come from navigating my identity as a queer Latino, I also feel shame because at times I feel less vulnerable than other colleagues of color. Because of my White, male privilege, my presence is protected and embraced in and out of the classroom. Like Gutierrez-Perez explains, the academy is a predominately White male upper/middle-class dominated institution.[29] Because of this, I have excelled in various academic institutions partly because of my identity. I am prescribed a certain amount of *ethos* from my students and some (White, male) colleagues because of how I am read in the context of who is credible and who belongs in positions of power. Yet, by embracing ambiguity and difference, I have also disrupted some of these logics. I find myself hiding my sexuality in the classroom by performing "safe" standards of masculinity.

As a queer, gay, mixed Latino man, I experience multiple intersections between various identities and cultures. These multiple intersections have provided both barriers and opportunities in the classroom. While I do receive White privilege, there are times when my White identity cannot protect me as a queer Latino. Regardless of my performance, my lived experience does not always reflect White male privilege. In fact, when communicating with faculty and students in the academy who question my identity, I am often faced with a series of micro-aggressive questioning investigating "who I go home to at night" and questioning "how much attention" I receive from cisgender heterosexual female identified students. This encourages me to reflect on my performative choices in the classroom. Who am I serving? Who I am hurting? I am reminded by Shadee that we must collectively resist and challenge internalizing the heteronormative expectations about our gender.[30]

Shadee and I have discussed how we navigate our sexuality in the classroom in ambiguous ways for similar and different reasons. While I have come out to my colleagues, friends, and strangers, I still have a few family members who do not know that I am queer. Therefore, at times, I find myself not fully out to the world, and because of my gender performance, my ambiguous queer identity performance leaves students questioning my identity. During graduate school, I did not come out to the class because I thought I might receive backlash from students, especially cisgender, heterosexual male students. This took me back to middle school, where I was desperately trying to fit in with what I thought my cisgender male performance was supposed to be. Perhaps, I was just looking for acceptance from a group of males I had not had in my life. This toxic shame prevented me from talking about my identity and self-disclosing to my students in ways that would deepen our conversation about lived experiences and identity. Eguchi explains that our society encourages men to communicate within the confines of hegemonic masculinity, and "heterosexuality is the foundation of constructing hegemonic masculinity in the United States."[31] Therefore, I am encouraged by society to express myself as heterosexual to be perceived as masculine. But, internalizing homophobia as a survival tactic intensifies my guilt and shame. I wonder how much I can continue to invest in this structure in order to protect myself and what I can do to resist in further marginalization and oppression. For me, I felt like what I needed to do was to come out to my communication and gender class.

At the end of the semester, I debrief with Shadee. As we submit grades, we talk about the progress our students made in the rigorous upper division course. I disclose that although many of my students did not receive an A or B in the course, my evaluations were high almost receiving a perfect 6/6 for several criterion. Moreover, I explained that I never received any pushback or backlash from students when discussing issues of gender, sexuality, and feminism, even though I felt that I discussed issues of masculinity, whiteness, and culture from a critical perspective. However, Shadee's experience is different. Her evaluations critique her for focusing too much on issues about gender (even in a Gender and Communication course), and that she focused too much on pushing a feminist agenda in the classroom. I actively pushed a feminist agenda in the classroom and was never questioned. Thus, while we may have similar curriculum, read the same academic articles in our classes, and teach from a critical perspective, we simply cannot ignore that although we both identify as queer people of color, my cisgender male performance affords me an *ethos* in the classroom in which students accept my lectures and arguments about gender. The irony of which escapes neither of us.

Toward Possibility and Sustained Hope

Our experiences as queer of color educators have not been easy. They have been comparable, different, disheartening, but mostly encouraging. But, with each new class, each new semester, and each new space we find ourselves in, similar challenges remain. We are lucky to have each other, a privilege in and of itself. We have each other to lean on for support, and we argue that this sense of belonging, comfort, and friendship is necessary for queer of color scholars. We suggest that there are existing tools that we can use as queer of color educators to build coalition, form bridges, and encourage community so that we can begin to see our differently similar stories as part of a larger community narrative. This requires queer relationality, critical love, and queer of color mentoring, which have all certainly opened doors for us to better understand our collectively similar/dissimilar experiences. We also consider that it is through transcending normative expectations that we may better use these tools to holistically challenge assumptions that suggest all queer stories are the same. Or, as Yep writes that to "explore the possibilities of queer worldmaking," we must understand the importance and relativity of queer relationality.[32] As Yep maintains:

> Queer relationality entails modes of recognition, systems of intelligibility, cultural expressions, affective articulations, encrypted sociality, embodied relations, forms of belonging, community formations, and collective histories of oppression that circulate outside of regimes of heteronormativity— but frequently in relation to it—characterized by potentiality and becoming as individuals inhabiting intersectional cultural nonnormativities negotiate and navigate their social worlds.[33]

Considering the affective ties that bind us, queer relationality affords us space to create and maintain community in ways that work for us. It is in feeling communal belonging, where we may begin to call on critical love as a means of transforming our queer of color experiences.[34] As Griffin explains, "This type of love recognizes the pride and pain of humanness at the intersections of complex identities; it bears witness to ignorance, pain, suffering, suspicion, distrust, and conflict, and it allows for ugly—meaning acrimonious, crazy, and cynical—discourse."[35] Further, we agree with Calafell and Gutierrez-Perez who argue that "critical love must be undergirded by a queerness that keeps it queerly accountable to intersectional power and cultural nuance."[36] It is in starting with critical love, where queer relationality can become a tangible possibility. In regard to our gendered performances, queering ourselves in the classroom, either by disclosing our identities or by queering our disclosed performance and centralizing our intersectionalities, we hope to move past non-hierarchical performances and continue to challenge power and privilege (within us and around us) to move toward a larger gendered and queer coalition. To teach and mentor from a position of critical love, we must reconsider how our lived experiences have been juxtaposed against each other and be actively reflexive about how to challenge traditional narratives around gender and sexuality in the classroom.

Much like Johnson and Bhatt as educators and scholars we are, "committed to transforming oppression, we are concerned with navigating Cartesian dualisms in ways that allow us to build alliances and move us into a space where social justice prevails."[37] Even still, when either of us walks into our respective classrooms, we do so with our own set of expectations, experiences, and ideas. It is in those lived moments where we each learn to understand our identities in fundamentally different ways. The two of us certainly walk through the world privileged. We both identify as cisgender. We both often pass through everyday encounters without the assumption of queerness. We are both relatively young, and while that can serve as a disadvantage, our educational privilege gives us room to play with how others see and read us daily. We are both fortunate to have careers, with benefits, wherein which we are afforded the opportunity to share the parts of ourselves when we feel safe—which we fully acknowledge is not the privilege of most. Most importantly, we have each other. Two queer of color assistant professors who embody critical love, who support each other through all of the emotional turbulence, and who love each other and have each other to lean on. In writing this chapter, we have engaged in an emotional labor that asked us to think about our relationship working through our own individual experiences, and in turn, we have become stronger.

As Calafell and Gutierrez-Perez argue, "critical love in the academy must be queer, and furthermore, it must be driven by a queer politics that holds it accountable to being intersectional, non-binary, and non-hierarchical."[38] We constantly keep each other accountable, even when it is hard, even when we know it might hurt the other person; we never fail to rely on the strength of our friendship. Queer relationality gives us space to move through difficult conversations and keeps us engaged through our differences. When my (Shadee) anxiety takes over about a student, or an email, or an interaction, Anthony is the first to break down all of the things that bring these emotions forward—even when it's difficult. When I (Anthony) overlook a privileged experience, Shadee offers a gentle reminder and challenges me to be reflexive in loving and empathetic ways. What we have learned through this process, through critical love, is that there is no perfect way to live/be/act gender, sexuality, age, religion, class, ability, nationality, race—there just is not enough jargon in the world to make sense of every way that every body exists, moves, and chooses to give of themselves for others. But it is through the amalgamation of ourselves, through the trust in one another, through a mutual understanding that while we might experience differently, we are always already experiencing ... we might be able to live in our own (im)perfections.

As queer of color scholars, we push back on erasure and implore research to be more cognizant of the stories that make up our radical lived existences. We must acknowledge that while we might share intersectional identity vectors, no two stories are the same, nor should they be. We agree with Calafell and Gutierrez-Perez's assertion that "our stories are not alone."[39] Thus we hope that by sharing our stories that others, especially queer of color educators, might feel free to share theirs and, in doing so, continue a dialogue toward a more open and honest way to perform gender and sexuality in the classroom. Our stories are two of many, and we look forward to adding to the larger body of work that adds to an ongoing conversation, for the sake of ourselves, our communities, and the classroom.

Notes

1 Edward Brockenbrough. "Queer of Color Agency in Educational Contexts: Analytic Frameworks from a Queer of Color Critique." *Educational Studies* 51, no. 1 (2015): 28, doi: 10.1080/00131946.2014.979929.

2 Brockenbrough, "Queer."

3 Kathlyn Kohrs Campbell. "The Communication Classroom: A Chilly Climate for Women?" *Association for Communication Administration Bulletin* 51 (1985): 68–72; Dominique M. Gendrin and Mary L. Rucker. "The Impact of Gender on Teacher Immediacy and Student Learning in the HBCU Classroom." *Communication Research Reports* 19, no. 3 (2002): 291–299, doi: 10.1080/08824090209384857.

4 Bernadette Marie Calafell and Robert Gutierrez-Perez. "(Critical) Love Is a Battlefield: Implications for a Critical Intercultural Pedagogical Approach," in *Critical Intercultural Communication Pedagogy*, eds. Ahmet Atay and Satoshi Toyosaki (London, UK: Lexington, 2018), 49–63; Bernadette Marie Calafell and Andy Kai-chun Chuang. "From Me to We: Embracing Coperformative Witnessing and Critical Love in the Classroom." *Communication Education* 67, no. 1 (2018): 109–114, doi: 10.1080/03634523.2017.1388529; Shinsuke Eguchi and Andrew Spieldenner. "The Two 'Gaysian' Junior Faculty Talking about Experience: A Collaborative Autoethnography." *QED* 2, no. 3 (2015): 125–143, https://www.muse.jhu.edu/article/602047.

5 Calafell and Chuang, 109.

6 Eguchi and Spieldenner, 126.

7 Calafell and Gutierrez-Perez, 49.

8 Bernadette Marie Calafell. "Mentoring and Love: An Open Letter." *Cultural Studies <=> Critical Methodologies* 7, no. 4 (2007): 425–441, doi: 10.1177/1532708607305123.

9 Fatima Chrifi Alaoui and Bernadette Marie Calafell. "A Story of Mentoring: From Theory to Praxis," in *Critical Examinations of Women of Color Navigating Mentoring Relationships*, eds. Keisha Edwards Tassie and Sonja M. Brown Givens (Lanham, MD: Lexington, 2016), 61–81.

10 Bryant Keith Alexander. *The Performative Sustainability of Race: Reflections on Black Culture and the Politics of Identity* (New York, NY: Peter Lang, 2012).

11 Dwight Conquergood. "Performing as a Moral Act: Ethical Dimensions of the Ethnography of Performance." *Text and Performance Quarterly* 5, no. 2 (1985): 1–13, doi: 10.1080/10462938509391578.

12 Eguchi and Spieldenner, 141.

13 Eguchi and Spieldenner, 140.

14 Richard G. Jones and Bernadette Marie Calafell. "Contesting Neoliberalism through Critical Pedagogy, Intersectional Reflexivity, and Personal Narrative: Queer Tales of Academia." *Journal of Homosexuality* 59, no. 7 (2012): 962, doi: 10.1080/00918369.2012.699835.

15 Gust A. Yep. "Further Notes on Healing from 'The Violence of Heteronormativity in Communication Studies.'" *QED* 4, no. 2 (2017): 115–122, doi: 10.14321/qed.4.2.0115.

16 Calafell and Chuang, 110.

17 Lillian MacNell, Adam Driscoll and Andrea N. Hunt. "What's in a Name: Exposing Gender Bias in Student Ratings of Teaching." *Innovative Higher Education* 40, no. 4 (2015): 294, doi: 10.1007/s10755-014-9313-4.

18 MacNell, Driscoll, and Hunt, 293.

19 Benny LeMaster. "Relationally out: A Case for and Against the Closet." *QED* 1, no. 1 (2014): 188–192, doi: https://www.muse.jhu.edu/article/537867.

20 LeMaster, 188.

21 Yep, 118.

22 Gloria E. Anzaldúa. *Borderlands: The New* Mestiza/la Frontera (San Francisco, CA: Aunt Lute, 2012), 41.

23 Bernadette Marie Calafell. "Monstrous Femininity: Constructions of Women of Color in the Academy." *Journal of Communication Inquiry* 36, no. 2 (2012): 111–130, doi: 10.1177/0196859912443382.

24 Eguchi and Spieldenner.

25 Shinsuke Eguchi. "Negotiating Hegemonic Masculinity: The Rhetorical Strategy of 'Straight-Acting' among Gay Men." *Journal of Intercultural Communication Research* 38, no. 3 (2009): 196, doi: 10.1080/17475759.2009.508892.

26 Lawrence La Fountain-Stokes. "Gay Shame, Latina- and Latino-style: A Critique of White Queer Performativity," in *Gay Latino Studies: A Critical Reader*, eds. Michael Hames-Garcia and Ernesto Javier Martínez (Durham, NC: Duke University Press, 2011), 55–79.

27 Trace Camacho. "Navigating Borderlands: Gay Latino Men in College." Doctoral dissertation, Michigan State University, 2016.

28 Fountain-Stokes, 72.

29 Robert M. Gutierrez-Perez. "Disruptive Ambiguities: The Potentiality of *Jotería* Critique in Communication Studies." *Kaleidoscope* 14, 89–100, https://opensiuc.lib.siu.edu/kaleidoscope/vol14/iss1/10/.

30 Eguchi.

31 Eguchi, 195.

32 Yep, 119.

33 Yep, 119–120.

34 Rachel Alicia Griffin. "Navigating the Politics of Identity/Identities and Exploring the Promise of Critical Love," in *Identity Research and Communication*, eds. Nilanjana Bardhan and Mark P. Orbe (Lanham, MD: Lexington, 2012), 207–222.

35 Griffin, 216.

36 Calafell and Gutierrez-Perez, 50.

37 Julia R. Johnson and Archana J. Bhatt. "Gendered and Racialized Identities and Alliances in the Classroom: Formations in/of Resistive Space." *Communication Education* 52, no. 3–4 (2003): 230, doi: 10.1080/0363452032000156217.

38 Calafell and Gutierrez-Perez, 50.

39 Calafell and Gutierrez-Perez, 53.

Bibliography

Alaoui, Fatima Chrifi and Bernadette Marie Calafell. "A Story of Mentoring: From Theory to Praxis." In *Critical Examinations of Women of Color Navigating Mentoring Relationships*, 61–81. Edited by Keisha Edwards Tassie and Sonja M. Brown Givens. Lanham, MD: Lexington, 2016.

Alexander, Bryant Keith. *The Performative Sustainability of Race: Reflections on Black Culture and the Politics of Identity*. New York, NY: Peter Lang, 2012.

Anzaldúa, Gloria E. *Borderlands: The New Mestiza/la Frontera*. San Francisco, CA: Aunt Lute, 2012.

Brockenbrough, Edward. "Queer of Color Agency in Educational Contexts: Analytic Frameworks from a Queer of Color Critique." *Educational Studies* 51, no. 1 (2015): 28–44, doi: 10.1080/00131946.2014.979929.

Calafell, Bernadette Marie. "Mentoring and Love: An Open Letter." *Cultural Studies <=> Critical Methodologies* 7, no. 4 (2007): 425–441, doi: 10.1177/1532708607305123.

Calafell, Bernadette Marie. "Monstrous Femininity: Constructions of Women of Color in the Academy." *Journal of Communication Inquiry* 36, no. 2 (2012): 111–130, doi: 10.1177/0196859912443382.

Calafell, Bernadette Marie and Andy Kai-chun Chuang. "From Me to We: Embracing Coperformative Witnessing and Critical Love in the Classroom," *Communication Education* 67, no. 1 (2018): 109–114, doi: 10.1080/03634523.2017.1388529.

Calafell, Bernadette Marie and Robert Gutierrez-Perez. "(Critical) Love Is a Battlefield: Implications for a Critical Intercultural Pedagogical Approach." In *Critical Intercultural Communication Pedagogy*, 49–63. Edited by Ahmet Atay and Satoshi Toyosaki. London, UK: Lexington, 2018.

Camacho, Trace. *Navigating Borderlands: Gay Latino Men in College*. Dissertation, Michigan State University, 2016.

Campbell, Kathlyn Kohrs. "The Communication Classroom: A Chilly Climate for Women?" *Association for Communication Administration Bulletin* 51 (1985): 68–72.

Conquergood, Dwight. "Performing as a Moral Act: Ethical Dimensions of the Ethnography of Performance." *Text and Performance Quarterly* 5, no. 2 (1985): 1–13, doi: 10.1080/10462938509391578.

Eguchi, Shinsuke. "Negotiating Hegemonic Masculinity: The Rhetorical Strategy of 'Straight-Acting' among Gay Men." *Journal of Intercultural Communication Research* 38, no. 3 (2009): 193–209, doi: 10.1080/17475759.2009.508892.

Eguchi, Shinsuke and Andrew Spieldenner. "The Two 'Gaysian' Junior Faculty Talking about Experience: A Collaborative Autoethnography." *QED* 2, no. 3 (2015): 125–143, https://www.muse.jhu.edu/article/602047.

Gendrin, Dominique M. and Mary L. Rucker. "The Impact of Gender on Teacher Immediacy and Student Learning in the HBCU Classroom." *Communication Research Reports* 19, no. 3 (2002): 291–299, doi: 10.1080/08824090209384857.

Griffin, Rachel Alicia. "Navigating the Politics of Identity/Identities and Exploring the Promise of Critical Love." In *Identity Research and Communication*, 207–222. Edited by Nilanjana Bardhan and Mark P. Orbe. Lanham, MD: Lexington, 2012.

Gutierrez-Perez, Robert M. "Disruptive Ambiguities: The Potentiality of *Jotería* Critique in Communication Studies." *Kaleidoscope* 14, 89–100, https://opensiuc.lib.siu.edu/kaleidoscope/vol14/iss1/10/.

Johnson, Julia R. and Archana J. Bhatt. "Gendered and Racialized Identities and Alliances in the Classroom: Formations in/of Resistive Space." *Communication Education* 52, no. 3–4 (2003): 230–244, doi: 10.1080/0363452032000156217.

Jones, Richard G. and Bernadette Marie Calafell. "Contesting Neoliberalism through Critical Pedagogy, Intersectional Reflexivity, and Personal Narrative: Queer Tales of Academia." *Journal of Homosexuality* 59, no. 7 (2012): 957–981, doi: 10.1080/00918369.2012.699835.

La Fountain-Stokes, Lawrence. "Gay Shame, Latina- and Latino-style: A Critique of White Queer Performativity." In *Gay Latino Studies: A Critical Reader*, 55–79. Edited by Michael Hames-Garcia and Ernesto Javier Martínez. Durham, NC: Duke University Press, 2011.

LeMaster, Benny. "Relationally Out: A Case for and Against the Closet." *QED* 1, no. 1 (2014): 188–192, doi: https://www.muse.jhu.edu/article/537867.

MacNell, Lillian, Adam Driscoll and Andrea N. Hunt. "What's in a Name: Exposing Gender Bias in Student Ratings of Teaching." *Innovative Higher Education* 40, no. 4 (2015): 291–303, doi: 10.1007/s10755-014-9313-4.

Yep, Gust A. "Further Notes on Healing from 'The Violence of Heteronormativity in Communication Studies.'" *QED* 4, no. 2 (2017): 115–122, doi: 10.14321/qed.4.2.0115.

DANCING AT THE INTERSECTIONS

Heteronormativity, Gender Normativity, and Fatness

Miranda Dottie Olzman

Grounding Theories: Performance Ethnography, Autoethnography

I suck in my stomach as I walk back-and-forth by a CrossFit box whose address matches the address on the website for "TAPS: The Adult Professional Studio"—a studio offering dance classes for adults ranging from ballet and tap to burlesque. The entire side of the CrossFit box is made of coiling doors that roll up like garage doors. They are open, exposing the incredibly muscular and sweaty bodies streaming in and out to run the block while others are vibrating the building by lifting and dropping heavy barbells with gusto. I keep peeking inside, hoping desperately the dance studio I am searching for is not somehow located inside the CrossFit box. I am desperate to get away from the box before the potential proselytizing of the CrossFit fitness religion occurs, but their running around the building is interfering with my ability to read the other addresses listed on the mailboxes.

I am nervous. The sweat dripping from my body is an indicator that I have no interest in this ethnographic project anymore and probably should run away right now. I can feel the fat straining to peek out of my 80s inspired off-the-shoulder/leggings workout outfit. I am trapped in my clothes and my own shame. Somehow I manage to spot a small sign for TAPS next to a slim and steep staircase. Despite feeling daunted, I enter hurriedly, ducking past the sweaty muscular bodies running back into the CrossFit box, and wonder if I made a huge mistake.

★ ★ ★

The dance studio enforces familiar tropes in the United States. Parents take their young (mostly) cisgender girls to learn beautiful, *feminine*, movements. Through dance, girls learn normative performances of binary and heterosexual femininity at the intersections of body type, race, and desire while boys are often excluded or discouraged from participating.[1] From pastel pink tights and slippers normalizing white skin, to long lean lines and thin body types paraded as desirable, the dance studio can double down on compulsory heterosexuality, heteronormativity, hegemonic masculinity, and femininity.[2] In addition, dance studios can reinforce negative body ideals. For instance, in some studios, dancers can be asked to leave if their bodies are not conforming to the standards of thinness.

While dance studios do not advertise the explicit and communicative ways they construct normativities via class participation, my experiences growing up in dance classes and re-entering one as an adult reinforce expectations regarding racialized, binary gender roles and body ideals in dance studios. Over a period of 10 hours a week for ten weeks, I danced at TAPS. Through autoethnography and performative writing, I explore how TAPS dance studio communicatively constructs body normativities and gender normativities through the multitudes of dance classes they offer, as well as describe the significance of TAPS's geographic location in relationship to other types of exercise spaces. I also critically analyze what it means to use dance as an exercise as a fat gender/queer person. I begin by locating autoethnographic and performative writing as method and position my experience as a fat gender/queer person in the space.

Background

I spent ten weeks at TAPS dancing as a participant-observer conducting both ethnographic and autoethnographic research. For this project, my emphasis is on autoethnography. It was in the movement that I began to understand the ways in which norms are bred and enforced. It was through my flesh that I felt people's expectations shatter and my own shame expand. I use performative writing as a way to translate interpersonal interactions. Through this, the writing becomes its own performance.[3]

★ ★ ★

I am marked by the BMI as morbidly obese. In the beginning moments of my first jazz dance class at TAPS, I can feel each of my 260 pounds. It is as though they ooze through the workout clothes that are constructed to confine them—constructed to create the illusion of thinness as much as possible. In this moment, each of these pounds whispers to me that this is not a space for me. They whisper to me that my genetics make my death inevitable. They whisper to me to run—or, at least to back out slowly. It is as though all of the research I have done of Health at Every Size leaks out of my body and I am 16 again—terrified of who is seeing me at my fattest. And I have to spend 10 hours a week observing a place for my graduate course on qualitative methods so I choose a place where

I can dance because I love to dance. But my body is not a body expected to do dance. As a fat feminine person, it seems that most would prefer I follow the whispers of my fatness and die. I am concerned about being disciplined for my weight. I fear being asked to leave. I fear being told I must to stand in the back. I fear that I am not feminine enough for dance—that somehow dance is owned by femininity. These fears race through my body creating the feeling of cold blood, even though I somehow still continue feeling my heart race and the heat in my face. Despite my fears, I enter the studio and start my first dance class. I am relieved when my fears do not materialize. I experience joy at moving my body without thinking about weight loss. I am feeling good in my body and in my skin when I see the instructor approach me. She asks, "When would you like to discuss how nutrition can affect your weight loss goals? Oh! And I was thinking, you might like to join my husband's gym next door." The joy I was feeling slowly leaks out like the fat compressed in my spandex. I am deflated.

★ ★ ★

For some who have never experienced the shame that can come with fatness, it may come as a shock that one might be asked to leave. However, this fear is real and predicated on my experience searching for a place to do this ethnography. I began by researching pole fitness classes.[4] Each studio I called told me the weight limits of their poles would not allow me to participate. Their limits ranged from 215 to 225 pounds. Later, a friend who was a regular at various pole institutions told me that most pole fitness studios have limits between 300 and 500 pounds. I never called the studios to double-check her statement. I felt too ashamed in my own feelings, making the educated assumption that they would not want fatness to encroach their spaces designed to lure people in with promises of thinness. A simple Google search of pole studios proved my friend right. There are poles that can hold multiple people at over 500 pounds if the studio invests in sturdy poles and takes the time to have them professionally installed using bolts to the floor and ceiling. The studios in my area chose not to invest in a body-positive environment, further making me feel undesirable, unwelcome, and inappropriate. The way our bodies are read and move always affect the space we are in, and the communication we participate in. They affect the spaces that we are seen in and what those spaces are perceived to be doing. While I will never know the answer, perhaps my body in this studio would lead others interested to believe that they were not teaching enough "real" fitness.

LeBesco calls for queering fat bodies/politics by stating, "But if we think of *revolting* in terms of overthrowing authority, rebelling, protesting, and rejecting, then corpulence carries a whole new weight as a subversive cultural practice that calls into question received notions about health, beauty, and nature."[5] Through this, I am making a political move by stepping into the dance studio. While it might be a small political move, I am still taking up space that is not traditionally welcoming to fat bodies. As a participant observer, I experienced what it was to be apart from, and a part of, this community and that adds to the depth of my research. According to Angrosino and Rosenberg,

> But the ways in which we are researchers negotiate the shifting sands of interactions, if we are careful to observe and analyze them, are important clues to the ways in which societies and culture form, maintain themselves, and eventually dissolve. In other words, the contexts may be evanescent, but the ways in which those contexts come to be may well represent enduring processes of human interaction.[6]

TAPS was not in place 50 years ago and may not be in place 50 years from now, yet my observations and our communicative acts help me explore themes that can last beyond the physical presence of the research. Conquergood reminds us, "Instead of endeavoring to rescue the *said* from the *saying*, a performance paradigm struggles to recuperate the *saying* from the *said*, to put mobility, action, and agency back into play."[7] Meanings are co-created and affected by my presence in a space. My performance of self matters as much as what I am observing. Therefore, if I am not willing to participate, then I am not willing to observe, even if that means my discomfort in a space that does not cater to me. My body is on the line.

TAPS, Day 1

After ducking through the crossfitters and swinging the metal industrial doors open, I walk up metal industrial stairs to the second story. The studio walls are painted dark purple and gray with "TAPS" written out in swirling gold letters. A metal air duct wrapped in twinkling white lights hovers just below the ceiling. During burlesque, instructors turn off the overhead light and use the twinkle lights for atmosphere. Barres wait in the corner for the next ballet class, and the pillars in the dance studio are home to outlines of comical, thin women dancing. There are no men painted on the pillars. While one might assume they are thin in order to fit on the pillars, other stereotypes suggest this move was subconscious and rooted in normativity. There are different styles of dance represented by their bodies ranging from tap to ballet, but they are all thin with long flowing hair. It is clear from the pillars that cisgender men and fat women are not the studios target audience or identity. Dangling from the ceiling in the upper left corner is a mobile that features each of the instructors in their most flattering poses. Their physiques are shown off in a way that advertises why people might want to join the studio—the unobtainable dancer's physique. Each instructor is in a different position that shows off a part of their lean and muscular bodies. Finally, as a person enters the space, they pass a chalk-painted wall that says, "Before I die, I want to _____." People fill in the blank line with their goals. I dub this the "Goals Wall" and notice that each week it changes. One night I write, "I want to perform in front of thousands." While no one saw me, writing this on the wall feels like marking my body in this place of athleticism. I feel vulnerable and alert.

Students usually chat with one another upon entering a class session. Most wear yoga pants or shorts with a tank top or loose t-shirt. I observe TAPS as a dance studio for fitness and not for professional dancers because the usual leg warmers, leotards, and layers are missing. Most people do not wear shoes (unless it is hip-hop), whereas in a professional dance studio, dancers will have shoes that reflect the genre of dance they do. The easiest way to identify the instructor in the space is to look for the one who shows the most skin or, conversely, who wears the most layers. They use layers to keep warm in between the classes, and then they remove layers during the class. The instructor's dress is particular to a given class. For example, on Monday nights in the ballet class, the instructor usually has on tights and a leotard—sometimes shorts before she warms up (to keep her hips warm). In hip-hop, the male instructor wears giant sweat pants and t-shirts that make it nearly impossible to see how his body moves. In opposition to that, BUTI yoga—a combination of vinyasa yoga, dance, and plyometrics—is completely different. The BUTI yoga instructor is always in tiny shorts that are almost like underwear, a cut-off shirt or tank top, and the occasional leg warmers. In her class, the emphasis is on core and hips, so she wears an outfit that shows off what her workout is expected to give her while still keeping her ankles warm.

The studio schedules classes in a disorganized format where one ends at 7:00, and the next begins at 7:00. This creates a sense of confusion for the dancers. No one knows who is going and coming, or what class is currently happening. During this time, the instructors often discuss with each other what their schedules are like, and what the studio is lacking. In terms of lack, the studio struggles to keep clients coming, but they also do not do a good job of advertising. The instructors mention this. In addition, I wonder if this lack of a clear schedule frustrates others as much as it does me. As everyone is leaving the class, people tend to converse about what other classes they plan on doing that week, but the conversation is usually minimal. It seems as though most people come to dance by themselves.

★ ★ ★

The stairs are a struggle for the second day of dance. I am sore as if I have not worked out in years. My thighs protest the steep incline. I do not feel like having another interaction like yesterday. Thinking about being confronted about my weight invites social anxiety to seep into my normally extroverted self. I do not want to make friends in this class. I do not want others to stare at me. I wonder if I am arrogant. That perhaps no one sees me the way I see myself. I have others who have protested that I call myself fat. But in these moments where physical ability is judged by your waistline, I fail miserably. I fail.

I am failing. My fat is my failing. It hurts when I enter the dance studio. I am even slow to open the door.

Body Normativities

Despite fearing my own fat body failures, I climb the TAPS stairs excited to dance, I am not free from damaging behaviors that trigger my body dysphoria. I continue to compare myself to other present people for three reasons. (1) I have been trained to compare my body to other bodies my entire life. (2) I have been approached in multiple classes by teachers assuming I have a weight loss goal. The teachers consistently ask me how much weight I want to lose or offer nutrition advice. To be trans parent, I struggle with the complexities of my body changing. My body is stronger and slighter leaned when I am active. But I don't enter spaces desiring bodily change explicitly. (3) Each time I climb the stairs and see what I dubbed the "Goals Wall" full of new goals, I notice that only two are not about weight loss. This makes me slide down the question rabbit hole. I question if weight loss should be my goal. I question not wanting to lose weight. I question my physical and academic goals as well. This questioning is an experience my body knows well. As soon as I am insecure about my body, I slowly spiral into becoming insecure about everything. And because my research centers fatness, I wonder if this research is creating more problems than it is solving. Internalized fatphobia is a dangerous beast.

Each time I walk through this space, I see my body as a site of failure. I fail to conform at every turn. My continued acceptance of my fat body does not fit this space—I know that I am supposed to be creating goals about weight loss and I feel as though I am a failure. This is not failure with a sense of possibility. It is a feeling that my body is wrong or that I cannot find health at *this* size.

My fears and questions are confirmed by the owner of the studio. While taking her yoga class, she pushes a diet on me. Her yoga class emphasizes that I do not fit the dancing mold. There are multiple women and men in the class showing off their low body fat percentage in small clothing. Running shorts and tank tops are standard wear for the men, while most of the women wear yoga pants and tiny tank tops. To be clear, these clothes may serve vanity but also serve a pragmatic purpose. It is much easier to move through a yoga flow if you do not have excess material getting in the way. My baggy shirt over ill-fitting yoga pants stand out. I choose not to wear small clothes because they make me uncomfortable. But now, potential stares are making me uncomfortable. I am worried about judgments. It is clear what bodies belong, and conversely, what bodies do not. Mine does not.

At the end of the class people are receiving raffle tickets. When I ask the instructor about the raffle, she tells me they are doing a challenge where students receive a raffle ticket for each fitness class they take. The instructor and her husband own the dance studio and Element 3 studio next door (a fitness program that claims to include nutrition, health, and fitness planning). I am not eligible to participate because I am not yet a member of TAPS or Element 3. Their membership prices are out of my budget. Assuming the conversation is over, I prepare to leave, but the teacher continues. She suggests I try out Element 3 because "it would help [me] understand nutrition and weight loss better."

★ ★ ★

I have a history of disordered eating that threatens to resurface when fitness studios that "focus" on nutrition try to lure me in. It is threatening to resurface now. In my mind I am running through what I have eaten that day, counting the calories and thinking about if I have consumed enough protein. I even pause to contemplate not eating for a few days to give my body a dieting head start. Somehow, I am suddenly 19 again training for Collegiate Nationals in Judo. I have been training to get down a weight class, losing 28 pounds in a little over a month. When I finish my first match of Nationals, my coach looks at me and says, "it would help to drop another weight class. You have an Olympian in your weight class and she will be too hard to beat." I pause and accept that I would just need to do that. I do not know how to do this though. I was already working out 40 hours a week and eating 500–1,000 calories a day. I was slow when I fought. I felt like I was disappearing.

★ ★ ★

I take a breath and ask her to not discuss nutrition with me because it tends to trigger my disordered eating. I tell her that I do not have weight loss goals—I'm just here to dance. The way she responds would lead one to think that this was our first time having this conversation. It is not. But she still stares at me in confusion and says, "Nutrition is common sense. Some foods are bad, and some are good." I do not know how to explain to her that I have tried to rid myself of the moralizing of food. I watch her as she tries to disconnect my fat body from the goal of loss. I wonder if I can. I simultaneously feel hyper-invisible.[8] My body has become a problem to be fixed—a site that is up for discussion while my voice is silenced. They don't see me as a whole person; they see me as a fat person who could benefit from nutrition and exercise as if I have never attempted to lose weight. I am inclined to cut and run in these moments. But I do not. I am concerned that she will lump me with fat folks who do not want to move. I am concerned she will slide more stereotypes onto my body and they will fit. I am the lazy fat person. My own internalized fat phobia is showing. I am nauseated. She continues to push me to join in the following weeks even though I ask her to stop. It is hard to feel angry at fat phobia cloaked in concern.

★ ★ ★

Weight loss talk and diet culture are ingrained into fitness culture. The triggering element of diet culture discourse can come out of nowhere. I can recall having wonderful conversations about the joys of dance when people overshare unrelated facts about why a plie is the best way to lose weight. For example, before burlesque class at TAPS, I am standing outside the door stretching when a woman I met in a different class arrives with a friend. I immediately notice her friend's beautiful, swirling tattoos as we begin talking. They are in their mid-fifties and giggling like teenagers, which I find refreshing. The tattooed woman tells me pole classes are also fun. I explain that I wanted to try them, but when I inquired about weight limits, I chose not to attend because I knew I was too heavy. She tells me that is "fucking bullshit" and begins to ask about all the studios. I try to explain that I had already spoken to the studios and they told me their limits. She continues to talk over me. I want to argue but feel the fear of being perceived as too aggressive. I am always perceived as being too aggressive. I am never sure if this is because of my size, my volume, my perceived racial ambiguity, or something else. I just know I have always been told that I am too aggressive. So instead I remain calm and non-confrontational. Her dismissiveness is exhausting. I just want this conversation to end but have no idea how to do so without being rude. I retreat into my own head and wonder what it would be like to be accepted anywhere and have a space to workout. To feel worry free traversing the exercise world. Her friend interrupts her and asks me, "do you want to lose weight?" I am momentarily relieved as most people just assume that is my goal. However, when I respond with "no," she adds, "Oh because if you did, I have the best nutritionist, I've lost eight pounds in a week." After this comment, she begins to explain her diet down to the number of raw almonds (5) she ate. Concern masks disgust for fatness. And to interrupt concern is to risk being perceived as rude. The intersection of White femininity and diet culture is thick—perhaps so thick, it has always been one and the same. Through their continued talk they demonstrate that they believe they have the information I need. They see me as lacking—as though my intelligence is lessened through my fatness. They continue to explain ways to lose weight, talking over each other as my presence ceases to matter.

★ ★ ★

Conversations about weight loss and folks' struggles with their bodies are as foundational to the dance studio as music. I often drink smoothies during class as I find them to be good fuel. During ballet, my teacher asked me what was in it. My explanation of spinach, Greek yogurt, and raw almonds prompted her to tell me all about what works for her body and what does not. Further into ballet class, the instructor continued to tell me her own tales of struggling with weight loss as a dancer. I did not ask about her struggles. She began sharing after I told her I believed I was having trouble with my relevé—a movement that involves rising up on one's toes—because of my weight. From there she told me that my weight was no excuse, and then spent the rest of the class on her own struggles with weight. The major difference, she has what a doctor might call 10 "extra" pounds. In her world though, because it is dance, those 10 pounds can make an extreme difference, especially in the eyes of others. I grow more uncomfortable in this space. I am comparing myself to others again. If she finds disgust with her body, then she must be super disgusted with mine. I am at least two of her. In my head I giggle at this measurement of weight. I am two ballet teachers. The giggle is a short reprieve from the humiliation I feel. I am angry at myself for always blaming my body, always being mad at it. I do not consider other possibilities for why I am struggling—it is always fatnesses' fault.

TAPS, Weeks in and Beyond

The comments about my body started when I started dancing at TAPS. Outside of the dance studio, my body is garnering more attention than it has in a while. As soon as people notice that I have lost weight or am shaped differently than I was ten weeks ago, they ask what I am doing to lose weight. People ask to go to the studio with me so that they can lose weight too. Instead of shifting toward a different body politic, I reify the old. I am torn between understanding my individual needs and the ways in which my body is inherently political. I move because I love it. But when I am consistent in movement, the aesthetic of my body always shifts. My body has always responded well to exercise. I somehow forget that my body loves movement and training, despite the fact that they used to carry much shame for me. Trainers often marked my body as masculine because of my body's ability to build muscle. Multiple trainers said to me, "You put on muscle like a man." Having large muscles manifested into shame and being told I was ugly growing up. I spent a lot of time concerned that men would not find me beautiful. Despite loving how strong I was, I bore internal shame about not being feminine enough. I still bear the shame, and it is magnified by my fatness. A little fat in what society considers the right places can accentuate curves and femininity. But "too much" fat and curves are erased, breasts blend with stomachs, and my body is unreadable in its femininity. I am not supposed to take up this much space.

My mom mentions over Skype, after being asked not to comment on my body an exhausting amount of times in the past, that she is excited because she can see my waistline again. She sounds much more excited than when I told her I was accepted to multiple doctoral programs. And although her enthusiasm stings, I struggle to be angry with her. She is part of this culture that places so much of our worth on thinness cloaked in the guise of health. This theme of the body being the utmost important measure of success rings in my ears. My dance instructors comment that my hips are looser and I am stronger and more flexible. I love the comments about my abilities, but people are also beginning to comment on my body in terms of loss. The loss of my girth creates a loss of comfort.

While I have tried to shift this space and observe it by inserting my body into it, I fear that I am recreating more than revolting. I am in a constant state of struggle where I never know if I am doing enough to shift our world. I never know if I am doing enough to take care of me. The line of just living my life has never been clear. And when I lose weight, it virtually disappears. Instead of being told about nutrition, I am being asked by people what types of foods I eat. Instead of being told what workout someone is doing, I am being asked about mine. I cannot decide if this is purposeful assimilation, or accidental.

★ ★ ★

Losing weight not only affects how people discuss food with me; it shifts gazes around me. I notice that as my body size reduces, the male gaze becomes more prevalent. The loss of weight affects how people perceive my sexuality. The assumption of queerness seems to shrink along with my body size. Yep reminds us that, "Heteronormativity is so powerful that its regulation and enforcement are carried out by the individuals themselves through socially endorsed and culturally accepted forms of soul murder."[9] Heteronormativity is so accepted that it is like the air we breathe, making it difficult to cut through and explain the regularly occurring examples of heteronormativity. However, it gives us a much more complex way to analyze how sexuality and gender are treated within particular locations and contexts. In this case, heteronormativity and gender normativities trend as themes within the dance studio albeit in different forms. In burlesque, instructors emphasize becoming hyper-feminine to increase attraction and the male gaze. She uses language that suggests the dancers in the studio are pandering to their male partners. In hip-hop class, instructors ask dancers to bring out their anger and strength—two traits associated with masculinity. It is impossible to de-link heteronormativity and gender normativities because they feed into and prop each other up. At TAPS, the implicit nature of both heteronormativity and gender roles are made clear within the dance studio. The colors on the wall and the décor of the studio strongly resemble an updated baby shower for a baby assigned female at birth. Other than the hip-hop and tap instructor, none of the instructors are cisgender men, marking a delineation in what forms of dance are appropriate for cisgender men and women teachers. The vast majority of the women present—whether instructors or students—embody socially accepted feminine norms. White, physically able, slim women with long hair run this space—metaphorically and literally. Others are (almost) welcomed. And as the next segment illustrates, sexuality is almost always assumed to be straight.

★ ★ ★

The opening of the burlesque class feels uncomfortable. The teacher asks us to do a "sexy walk" across the floor and tells us all to let our hair down. All of the women in the class pull off their pony-tail holders. I watch as long, voluminous hair tumbles out of its confines. I run my hand uncomfortably over my shaved sides and 3-inch-tall hair on top. I wonder if I can be sexy without hair. I try to shake the 3 inches I have on top, but it is a tad pathetic as I look as though I am shaking water from my ears after a day at the pool. The instructor shouts, "think about crawling towards your man like this, BUT NAKED." The third time she shouts at us to crawl toward our man, I stage whisper, "Not all of us date men in here." She doesn't hear me. She shouts to crawl again and look for our man. I say once again that "not all of us date men." The dance class participants turn and look at me with suspicion. I am not sure if they are suspicious of my non-conforming gender queer fat body, or if they are suspicious that in my queerness I am searching for prey.

★ ★ ★

It is in burlesque where I find the strictest conformity to societal gender norms. Our bodies are referenced as sexy and assumed to please men. Although the studio says all are welcomed, I do not feel safe in this space. In burlesque class, many of the women wear their long flowing hair down, sports bras, and yoga pants. We have a different burlesque teacher every three weeks. Each teacher, in her own way, teaches that burlesque is intended to entice an audience so we should find a man (or imagine one) in any audience we connect to. When my instructor meets Katie, my partner of seven years, she is flushed. The next week she shouts at us to, "find your significant other in the crowd." I feel slightly please. However, quickly after, she reverts to telling us to search for a man. Heteronormativity is hard to break. It is also clear that the expectation on women's bodies is that being sexy is needed to please the men that are in our lives. And being sexy is only seen through the lens of normative femininity. This space does not welcome bodies that break these norms whether that be through hair or body size. The checklist of normative feminine bodies and expectations is long. Burlesque makes apparent that body size and sexuality are inextricably linked.

One night we are doing a dance that involves a folding chair. I protest. I know the chairs are not intended to hold my weight. The teacher dismisses my plea. When I spin on the chair, I hear the creak and feel it cave in the center. I broke the chair. I am fighting back tears over the humiliation of my body breaking a chair. I am also furious at myself for not being adamant about knowing the chair would not hold my weight. I also know that I do not speak up because I am worried about being seen as a problem. I want to be accommodating. I want to be like the other women in this class. I want to blend in. But, between my short hair and crushing a chair, my body does not fit in this space. I run out of the class that night without a word, leaving the chair discarded on the floor feeling guilt and humiliation at how my body takes up space. In this moment, I am not pleasing anyone "properly."

★ ★ ★

The yoga classes I participate in also have clear lines based on gender. Men come to the traditional yoga class but do not partake in BUTI yoga for the most part. BUTI yoga has an emphasis on wiggling hips and general jiggling. One night I brought a friend who is an awesome dancer. The teacher perked up when he was there and asked him to come again. The next week he did not join me again because the schedule did not work for him. In his absence, the instructor shared with me that she enjoyed having a man in the class. The instructor went on to explain to me that men are usually too shy to do BUTI yoga. She said they feel that it is not manly enough, or feel incapable of moving their bodies in jiggly and wiggly ways. Her assumptions regarding essentialism and dance are clear—men cannot move the way women do. Our abilities to dance are set in gender essentialism.

Closing Thoughts

During my time at TAPS I had the opportunity to push my body and mind in ways that were quite unexpected. Much of the time I spent at TAPS was filled with understanding how internalized fatphobia has continued to affect the ways that I move through the world. I entered this project with the assumption I would spend the ten weeks at TAPS thinking only about weight. Yet, as I moved through the space, it became clear how much fatness is connected to gender and heterosexual normativities. Prior to this experience, I had not spent enough time, examining the ways that fitness is deeply connected to sexuality and gender norms. Through this project, I want to express some of the ways working out and the ways in which we do it are gendered—both celebrated and disciplined. Gender normativities hold the potential to choose how and where we work out.

TAPS provided a solid base to begin researching the intersections of fatness, heteronormativity, and gender normativities within fitness. This project has only increased my interest in writing about fat, fitness, and femininity. The diet and fitness culture within the United States constructs a space where companies stand to make millions if they find a formula that works for the perception of health. The vast majority of companies are based through the lens of weight loss. I hope that sharing these narratives will change how fat bodies participate in fitness and eventually shift the narrative of movement for loss to movement for gain.

Notes

1 Claire Englemann. "Hey Ballet Dress Code... Let's talk about Queerness." *Dance Major Journal* 5 (2017), https://escholarship.org/uc/item/8975h498; Tracey Owens Patton. "Final I Just Want to Get My Groove On: An African American Experience with Race, Racism, and the White Aesthetic in Dance." *The Journal of Pan*

African Studies 4, no. 6 (2011): 104–125, https://jpanafrican.org/docs/vol4no6/4.6-7IJustWant.pdf; Mark Edward. "Stop Prancing about: Boys, Dance, and the Reflective Glance." *Equality, Diversity, and Inclusion* 33, no. 5 (2014): 470–479, doi: 10.1108/EDI-03-2014-0018; Doug Risner. "Rehearsing Masculinity: Challenging the 'Boy Code' in Dance Education." *Research in Dance Education* 8, no. 2 (2007): 139–153, doi: 10.1080/14647890701706107; Carolyn Hebert. "Mini & Macho, Small & Sexy: The Perpetuation of Heteronormativity, Hegemonic Masculinity, and Femininity within the Culture of Competitive (Jazz and Hip-Hop) Dance." *Congress on Research in Dance Conference Proceedings* 2016 (2016), 208–216.

2 Hebert, 208.

3 Della Pollock. "Performing Writing," in *The Ends of Performance*, eds. Peggy Phelan and Jill Lane (New York, NY: New York University Press, 1998), 73–103.

4 Pole fitness involves exercises that stem from stripper performances and fitness routines.

5 Kathleen LeBesco. "Queering Fat Bodies/Politics," in *Bodies out of Bounds*, eds. Kathleen LeBesco and Jana Evans Braziel (Berkeley, CA: University of California Press, 2001), 75.

6 Michael Angrosino and Judith Rosenberg. "Observations on Observation: Continuities and Challenges," in *Collecting and Interpreting Qualitative Materials*, 4th ed., eds. Norman K. Denzin and Yvonna S. Lincoln (Thousand Oaks, CA: Sage, 2013), 158.

7 Dwight Conquergood. "Beyond the Text: Toward a Performative Cultural Politics," in *Cultural Studies: Performance, Ethnography, Praxis*, ed. E. Patrick Johnson (Ann Arbor, MI: The University of Michigan Press, 2016), 55.

8 Amber Johnson. "Straight Outta Erasure: Black Girl Magic Claps back to the Hyperinvisibility of Black Women in Straight Outta Compton." *National Political Science Review* 19, no. 2 (2018): 13.

9 Gust A. Yep. "The Violence of Heteronormativity in Communication Studies: Notes on Injury, Healing, and Queer World-making." *Journal of Homosexuality* 45, no. 2–4 (2003): 22, doi: 10.1300/J082v45n02_02.

Bibliography

Angrosino, Michael and Judith Rosenberg. "Observations on Observation: Continuities and Challenges." In *Collecting and Interpreting Qualitative Materials*, 4th ed., 151–176. Edited by Norman K. Denzin and Yvonna S. Lincoln. Thousand Oaks, CA: Sage, 2013.

Conquergood, Dwight. "Beyond the Text: Toward a Performative Cultural Politics." In *Cultural Studies: Performance, Ethnography, Praxis*, 47–64. Edited by E. Patrick Johnson. Ann Arbor, MI: The University of Michigan Press, 2016.

Edward, Mark. "Stop Prancing about: Boys, Dance, and the Reflective Glance." *Equality, Diversity, and Inclusion* 33, no. 5 (2014): 470–479, doi: 10.1108/EDI-03-2014-0018.

Englemann, Claire. "Hey Ballet Dress Code… Let's talk about Queerness." *Dance Major Journal* 5 (2017), https://escholarship.org/uc/item/8975h498.

Hebert, Carolyn. "Mini & Macho, Small & Sexy: The Perpetuation of Heteronormativity, Hegemonic Masculinity, and Femininity within the Culture of Competitive (Jazz and Hip-Hop) Dance." *Congress on Research in Dance Conference Proceedings* 2016 (2016), 208–216.

Johnson, Amber. "Straight Outta Erasure: Black Girl Magic Claps back to the Hyperinvisibility of Black Women in Straight Outta Compton." *National Political Science Review* 19, no. 2 (2018): 13.

LeBesco, Kathleen. "Queering Fat Bodies/Politics." In *Bodies out of Bounds*, 74–90. Edited by Kathleen LeBesco and Jana Evans Braziel. Berkeley, CA: University of California Press, 2001.

Patton, Tracey Owens. "Final I Just Want to Get My Groove On: An African American Experience with Race, Racism, and the White Aesthetic in Dance." *The Journal of Pan African Studies* 4, no. 6 (2011): 104–125, https://jpanafrican.org/docs/vol4no6/4.6-7IJustWant.pdf

Pollock, Della. "Performing Writing." In *The Ends of Performance*, 73–103. Edited by Peggy Phelan and Jill Lane. New York, NY: New York University Press, 1998.

Risner, Doug. "Rehearsing Masculinity: Challenging the 'Boy Code' in Dance Education." *Research in Dance Education* 8, no. 2 (2007): 139–153, doi: 10.1080/14647890701706107.

Yep, Gust A. "The Violence of Heteronormativity in Communication Studies: Notes on Injury, Healing, and Queer World-making." *Journal of Homosexuality* 45, no. 2–4 (2003): 22, doi: 10.1300/J082v45n02_02.

ARE WE QUEER YET?

Queerness on the Horizon in Academia

Bernadette Marie Calafell and Shinsuke Eguchi

As queers of color we find ourselves consistently under the microscope, or what José Esteban Muñoz terms, being subjected to the burden of liveness.[1] Our bodies are always expected to be live or at the service of others. We are consistently called to perform. Defying these expectations or performing the wrong kind of liveness has its consequences. This we know as queers of color in the academy, especially as we try to remake the academy, and its few queer spaces in particular, more hospitable.

We are not the only ones who have looked for spaces of possibility as marginalized people in the academy. For example, González narrates the emergence and formation of what are now the Latina/o Communication Studies Division and La Raza Caucus of the National Communication Association, marking important moments in the history of the field of Communication Studies.[2] It's a history he has a stake in as he helped create it. Inspired by González, we follow suit and use autoethnography to narrate our own stakes and performances in moving toward queerness in our involvement as queers of color in the Gay, Lesbian, Bisexual, Transgender, and Queer (GLBTQ) Communication Division of the National Communication Association. We show how our raced, gendered, sexualized, and classed performances disrupt normative expectations as we push for a more inclusive and radical queerness and gender futurity that exists on the horizon. We work to unsettle the ironically normative or hegemonic expectations that play out in everyday acts or micro-aggressions. As neither of us performs the "ideal queer," who is subservient, passive, and ideologically aligned with whiteness, we argue that this construct has held us as a community back from creating radical spaces of queerness in our disciplinary formations. Our ability to perform ideal queerness is mitigated by our race, nationality, class, and performances of gender.

Our gender performances are informed by the desire to be queer—a queerness driven by an intersectional gender futurity that we have not yet reached. Allen echoes our sentiments: "Apparently, the larger project of queer theory is currently experiencing an existential crisis, brought on by its limited archives, lack of engagement with on-the-ground movement, and turning away from radical feminist rhizomes that sought intersectional approaches."[3] We are inspired by Ahmed's question, "How does it feel to inhabit a body that fails to reproduce an ideal?"[4] While Ahmed raises this question in regards to bodies that fail to reproduce heteronormativity, we ask this question in regards to bodies that fail to reproduce homonormativity. How might centering these narratives and performances shift us to a more inclusive queerness and gender futurity?

Queerness on the Horizon

Muñoz writes, "Queerness is not yet here. Queerness is an ideality. Put another way, we are not yet queer."[5] No more do Muñoz's words ring true in academia where queerness as an idea is hastily welcomed, whiteness or those who perform whiteness including people of color, queer homonormative, cisgender bodies are invited, and gender queer, trans, and many queers of color who resist or don't embody the ideal are relegated to the periphery. We recognize like Enke that,

> First, binary gender norms and gender hierarchies are established and maintained through violence against those who visibly deviate from them; second, many humans—in their gender identities and/or gender expressions—do not conform to conventional gender expectations or moral judgments about what kinds of gender 'go with' what kind of body; and third, this gender variation itself is intensely valuable as one facet of the creative diversities essential to wise and flourishing societies.[6]

Transfeminism opens up new ways for us to think about gender, but it must also be intersectional.[7] We strive for not only queerness on the horizon but gender possibilities on the horizon.

Alexander explores his own ambivalence around the word *queer* because of its historically negative meanings, as well as his personal experiences as a Black gay man.[8] He wants something more. Similarly, Ahmed addresses the everyday experience of making feminism a way of life by writing, "To live a feminist life is to make everything into something that is questionable."[9] In thinking about remaking feminism, Ahmed desires something more:

> If we become feminists because of the inequality and injustice in the world, because of what the world is not, then what kind of world are we building? To build feminist dwellings, we need to dismantle what has

already been assembled; we need to ask what it is we are against, what it is that we are for, knowing full well that this *we* is not a foundation but what we are working toward.[10]

Just as Ahmed wants a different way of being feminist, we desire a different way of being and performing queer. Alexander and Ahmed's desires echo Muñoz's words.[11]

Muñoz's vision of queerness on the horizon is decidedly intersectional and built on the backs of queer, feminists of color. It is a queerness that fights back against the idea that there is no hope for us queers, as it is fueled by an educated hope.[12] Muñoz argues that:

> Feeling Revolutionary is feeling that our current situation is not enough, that something is indeed missing and we cannot live without it. Feeling revolutionary opens up the space to imagine a collective escape, an exodus, a "going-off script" together. Practicing educated hope, participating in a mode of revolutionary consciousness, is not simply conforming to one group's doxa at the expense of another's. Practicing educated hope is the enactment of a critique function. It is not about announcing the way things ought to be, but, instead, imagining what things could be. It is thinking beyond the narrative of what stands for the world today by seeing it as not enough.[13]

This educated hope is fueled by a desire for something more, something better. Some misconstrue our hope or talking back as simply unproductive anger as a way to dismiss us and not hold themselves accountable. Those who perform queer and femme of color affects always already read as threatening or hostile. Ahmed recognizes the revolutionary potential of hope as she states,

> Hope is not at the expense of a struggle but animates struggle; hope gives is a sense that there is a point to working things out, working things through. Hope does not only or always point toward the future, but carries us through when the terrain is difficult, when the path we follow makes it harder to proceed. Hope is behind us when we have to work for something to be possible.[14]

Hope is political as it drives our desire to reimagine and reanimate queerness. We continually strive for a critical, radical, and intersectional queerness.

Critical Autoethnography/Autohistoria-teoría

In thinking through other ways of being and narrating our stories, we follow Stacy Holman Jones' approach to autoethnography as it "works to hold self and culture together."[15] For us, autoethnography is critical[16] and also intersectional.[17] Critical autoethnography is about placing our voices in conversation with larger cultural, social, political, and economic contexts.[18] Our stories speak beyond the self to reverberate to larger structures and histories of power.[19] In this they reveal how the individual is implicated in, affected by, and performing with or against larger structures of power. As Spry reminds us, "The purpose of performative autoethnography is to better understand who we are in relation to others in culture."[20] In telling our stories we understand the importance of intersectional reflexivity, which compels us to be attendant to the multiplicities of our identities and the privileges and oppressions that they entail.[21] It requires that we do more than scratch the surface and go deep in our vulnerability and reflection.[22] It requires at times that we hurt.[23] Intersectional reflexivity asks us to write intersectionally and critically about our lives, by not simply focusing on one aspect of our identities as we tell our stories by considering how they work together to shape our experiences.[24]

In telling these stories, it is important that we note that what is now termed *autoethnography* has long been utilized by queer women of color, such as Cherríe Moraga and Gloria Anzaldúa, who understand the importance of listening to the body or the theories in our flesh.[25] For example, Anzaldúa's *autohistoria-teoría* is a decolonial process, which is, "More than writing self into existence, a move made by many minoritized scholars, autohistoria-teoría represents a hybridized space of creativity and bridge building, in which we use our life stories to develop deep critical, spiritual, and analytical insights, to boldly theorize experiences and insights against the broader landscape of specific sociocultural discourses."[26] We draw on our theories in the flesh to narrate our critical autoethnographies of our participation in shaping a disciplinary space for queers of color.

To do so, each of us writes our embodied narratives from different standpoints. So, we recognize that our critical autoethnographies of queerness are transnational and transcultural products of collaboration in and across race, ethnicity, gender, sexuality, class, and the body. Accordingly, we approach our collaboration as a political and intellectual space of efforts and possibilities in which we, as queers of color, productively work with differences within differences. As Puar has suggested, the common failure of queer politics is to unintentionally reproduce and reconstitute an essentialist boundary between queerness and heteronorms.[27] In order to avoid such unintentionality, we explicate how our differential performances of queerness, revealing ongoing negotiations of structural variables, produce and reproduce particular experiences for each of us. Consequently, our collaboration is meant to showcase the complexity, fluidity, and multiplicity of queerness performed across differences. Queerness is never singular, stable, and essentialized. Now, we move to showcase our critical autoethnographies of such queerness.

Looking for Queerness or Looking for the Horizon

Reading an email laced with insinuations of wrongdoing, questioning my choice of reviewers, and suggesting I have an agenda, I see that it's easier for this White gay cisgender man to believe that I am unethical as a program planner rather than his paper is not good enough. I repeat this over and over again in my head. *I knew this would not be easy.* My performance as a queer femme Chicana in what has been a space that gives authority to White gay men renders me less than credible and, at times, suspect.

Over the approximately 20 years that I have been a member of the National Communication Association, I have cycled through the leadership of the Latina/o Communication Studies Division/La Raza Caucus (LCSD), the Gay, Lesbian, Bisexual, Transgender, and Queer (GLBTQ) Communication Studies Division, and the Rhetorical and Communication Theory (RCT) Division. In only one case have I ever truly felt at home or welcomed—in the LCSD. This is not to make any kind of essentialist argument; rather, it *feels* familiar and welcoming. My entrance into the leadership of the GLBTQ Communication Studies Division did not come organically. Instead, I felt like an outside con-tractor who was invited in to help renovate a stuffy, out-of-date office space. I was invited by the Nominating Committee of the Division to run for a leader-ship position. Though my work certainly connected to each of the areas, I had never attended the business meetings. I didn't *feel* welcome. I mean feel quite literally. My body felt out of place. Like many spaces in the academy, "diverse" bodies are desired as long as they don't disrupt the status quo. Reed articulates this well: "Race as theoretical fetish satisfies an institutional need for multi-cultural representation and theoretical diversity, while perpetuating colorblind logics that foreclose possibilities for justice by denying the existence of White supremacy."[28] Reed further suggests that there is a "spectacular absence"—a lack of discussion of systematic racism and race in mainstream queer theory while a desire to still appropriate the trauma of queer people of color.[29] This desire to appropriate the trauma, experiences, and bodies of people of color was quite apparent to me in the overwhelming whiteness of the membership of the divi-sion, the performance of advocacy, as well as the scholarship they honored, and scholars who were held in high esteem. All of this made me feel out of place.

Despite my trepidation, I pursued a leadership position in the GLBTQ Division, and to my surprise, I won the election. My plan was to infiltrate the organization and force it to diversify. I expected resistance, but it still hurt and often led to me feeling miserable. Whether it was the crossed arms, bored, unfriendly looks as I led the meeting, or assurances from a more senior queer scholar of color that what I was experiencing was not imagined, I often cursed myself for taking on the position. I heard familiar refrains of, "I don't under-stand why they don't come..." or "People in the past signed up for stuff but didn't follow through…" These words would be decoded for me by the queer of color elder who shared the other side of the story: people of color didn't feel welcomed or accepted; as a result, they dropped out. I get it. *I feel it.* The critique of the whiteness of queerness is not new. Scholars like Gloria Anzaldúa, E. Patrick Johnson, Hiram Pérez, and José Esteban Muñoz have raised this critique.[30] However, it's more than that. It's the anti-fat, anti-femme, bi-phobia, the excesses and inadequacies of my class performance that undergird my hesitance. My embodied raced, classed, and gendered performance of queerness is read as unintelligible. My performance is in line with a vision of gender futurity that honors others.

We Are Not Yet Queer

I stayed because I could. I had/have a great deal of privilege as someone who is tenured and now holds the rank of professor. I also experience the privileges that come along with having white skin and being cisgender. I take none of this for granted and, when possible, use it as a weapon or means to fight back. Women of color are expected to take a great deal of pain because we are seen as excessively strong. This assumed strength and tolerance for pain meets my performance of femme in an interesting space because even my performance of femme is fraught with insecurities. I feel femme, but my fat, working class, and Chicana femme performance often misses the mark. Do I believe this because I have internalized images of what femme is supposed to be rather than being okay with remaking and shifting it? I consistently resist the urge to doubt myself.

I'm taken back to every moment I haven't felt quite queer enough. I'm not sure what that means, but I know who controls the meaning. As someone who identifies as a cisgender Chicana bisexual femme, I have always felt suspect.[31] Part of this is connected to larger cultural discourses that frame both bisexuals and femmes as suspect, untrustworthy, or not really queer within queer communities.[32] Certainly my working class identity, my fatness, and my Chicanisma also don't make me the ideal queer. My body, my gender performance (as awkward as I feel it is), and my so-called lack of civility were all out of place in the sea of White queerness that centered thin, White, gay, cisgender, male bodies. If I had any doubt about my place, I was reminded of it when I was introduced to a prominent White male queer studies scholar in the bar at a meeting of the annual National Communication Association convention, and his first words to me were, "Oh, you're the one." All this occurred in the midst of officially fighting racialized sexual harassment at the university where I worked at the time. He made my place clear. We shared no queer relationality. I did not fit. I was the "one" who was causing all the problems. My performance of femme resistance and activism against patriarchal violence was quickly rejected. While he was the ideal queer, he made it clear that I was not.

Rinse and repeat: *We are not yet queer.*

And so I return to where I started. A White gay cisgender man finds it more believable that I and the anonymous reviewers are unethical and uniformed, than his paper didn't make the cut on its own merit. He accuses me of having an agenda (*I do. I want to make others feel like they are included. I want us to move toward queerness.*), and heavy handedly threatens to raise it as an issue at the business meeting of our next convention. I must produce "proof"; all the raw data reviewers submitted about his paper to placate him for a while.

Rinse and repeat: *We are not yet queer.*

Will We Ever Be?

In each of these instances I experience cognitive dissonance. *I have always been queer.* One of the first academics who showed me critical love and who brought me into the fold was a White queer cisgender man. *He has always been queer. But as a whole, are we queer yet?*

★ ★ ★

We are not yet queer! I resonate with this statement that Bernadette has just showcased. At the same time, I must recognize and work with the ways in which my orientation to the idea—*we are not yet queer*—is quite different from hers. I critique that my mid-30s East Asian/Japanese male able-body, as an intersectional site of theorizing about, researching of, and living with queerness and gender futurity, makes and remakes such differential orientation. My transnational mobility, global north citizenship, and cultural and economic capital operate as privileges in which I repeatedly engage in the western sexual cultural representation of "gaysian fabulosity."[33] That is, a queer Asian male subject who aims to self-fashion and perform a White gay male lifestyle visualized through the Western/US American popular media. Consequently, I am easily read as an *almost White* feminine queer male who is unintelligent, superficial, and incomplete. Thus, I ironically overcompensate such markings of my gendered, racialized, and classed queerness by performing "extra," which has led some people to name me as a *bougie Asian bitch.* However, from this social and performative space of gender, sexuality, and the body, I am committed to embodying what I envision is intersectional queer politics disrupting hegemonic, heteronormative, and homonormative circulations of power, discourse, and knowledge in the academy. Still, my vision of intersectional queer politics is never perfect and complete. In fact, I recognize that I am ideologically forced to internalize and go along with the status quo. I am a part of the majoritarian belonging as it is always already reinforced through our everyday interactions, relationships, and contexts. Accordingly, my intersectional queer politics often operate as the gendered reality of a failure that "is something queers do and have always done exceptionally well."[34] Therefore, I am always trying and trying again to become and be queer. *How can I be a queer, gender queer, and be happy in the present colonized by the heteropatriarchal times and spaces?*

During 2017's International Communication Association (ICA)'s conference in San Diego, a colleague asks me, "How is queer studies overall different from critical/cultural studies?" I immediately feel "hot!!!" because I find such a question illustrates the hetero-colonialist logics of color-blindness erasing, marginalizing, and ignoring how White queer and queer of color. Communication Studies scholars have been dedicated to fighting against heteronormativity and patriarchy for so long in the discipline(s). While queer studies is apparently situated in the tenets of critical/cultural studies, it explicitly centralizes sexuality and gender as a main site of knowledge to destabilize, dismantle, and shift taken-for-granted states of ideas and social relations. So, times and spaces of queer possibilities through which differences are equalized are made and remade. Eng, Halberstam, and Muñoz assert, "Sexuality is intersectional, not extraneous to other modes of difference, and calibrated to a firm understanding of queer as a political metaphor without a fixed referent."[35] Thus, the production of queer studies is indeed the intellectual and political movement in the discipline(s).[36] So, as I try my best to hide my "bitchyness," I reply to my colleague's question by saying "Queer studies locates sexuality and gender as a major paradigm in doing critical/cultural studies."

Simultaneously, my answer to the aforementioned question reminds me of an ethnographic observation I have been making in the discipline(s). Under the current political climate, topics and issues related to lesbian-gay-bisexual-transgender-queer (LGBTQ) people are "timely," "cool," and/or "sexy" in and across local, national, and global contexts. Consequently, many communication scholars are increasingly interested in identifying with queer studies. Such intellectual movement is politically beneficial to establish and reestablish the field's visibility across the discipline(s). At the same time, I also remain concerned of such movement. I worry that strategic normalizations of queer studies into Communication Studies may re-center and re-secure the hetero-patriarchal colonialist dominations of White, middle/upper-class, able-bodied, and cis-gendered heterosexuality as invisible and universal power.

As the 2017 program planner and a regular reviewer of NCA's GLBTQ Communication Studies Division, I have come across a number of queer studies identified work that approach sexuality as a variable in and across multiple social positionings, such as race, ethnicity, gender, nationality, class, and the body. While sexuality is intersectional, Yep, Lovaas, and Elia have already advocated that queerness is about a political identity interrogating and critiquing the institutional norms, practices and discourses regulating sexual, gender, and cultural experiences.[37] Queerness should never be depoliticized for the sake of inclusivity of sexual and gender identity as a variable in the research. In fact, queerness is everything we, as queers, gender queers, do. However, *we are not queer yet.* We collectively fail to politicize and historicize our critical dissatisfactions with cis-hetero-patriarchal colonialist maps of the present time. Instead, we, as queers, are consciously and unconsciously seeking for assimilations into the mainstream. Being a part of such problem, I feel that the radicality of queerness begins to be obfuscated.

Simultaneously, I critique my own vision of intersectional queer politics requiring the acts of speaking up and standing up. As an able-bodied person of color having recently achieved tenure, I am extremely privileged to openly and frankly perform my racialized, gendered, and classed queerness of *gaysian fabulosity* through theorizing, researching, and living. For example, even when I write close readings of media texts that are not autoethnographic works, I unapologetically situate my body as a referring point to theorize about and research racialized same-sex sexual desires. If editors and reviewers of my work despise my methodological orientation, I speak back to them because my tenure or job security gives me such privilege to do so. In addition, with my fashion style, I am always *out* about my racialized same-sex sexual desires in my everyday social interactions. By pushing the political elements of my desire, I do not shy away from arguing with people when they say and do something against intersectional queer politics. I violate the politics of respectability that organize and govern interpersonal interactions. Accordingly, such performative mode authenticates me as alternative queer voice according to the hetero-patriarchal colonialist logics of power rooted in whiteness. Yet, this embodied performance of forefronting my racialized same-sex sexual desires in and across the personal and academic lives are taking place in the Western sexual knowledge of coming out of the closet. As scholars such as Eguchi, Files-Thompson, Calafell, McCune, and Snorton have argued before, the paradigm of coming out restores the Western cultural myth of individual agency and sexual freedom ignoring the historical and structural constraints for queers of color who remain discreet about their sexualities through gender performances.[38] Everyone is not equally situated to speak up about and stand up for their queerness. Thus, I am in need of fighting against my privileges of *outness* to find ways to revise and expand my intersectional queer politics further. *How do I work with my privileges to incorporate differential visions of intersectional queer politics that are much more ambiguous and nuanced than I know into what I do as a scholar?* Here, I feel I am not queer, gender queer yet. I feel that I am just an *extra* gaysian.

In the meantime, along with Bernadette, I am fully committed to create and recreate an intellectual and academic space through which we move to become queers and gender queers for the future. What I can do now with the material limitations of my intersectional queer politics is that I continue to speak up about and stand up for queerness, intersecting with race, ethnicity, gender, nationality, class, and the body, as the political and intellectual movement. For example, I will continue to challenge people who say and do something against intersectional queer politics. I will use my privilege of being out about my racialized same-sex desires to do so. At the same time, I cannot victimize myself when others neither easily agree with my politics nor respect who I am and what I do. Such pushback is a part of being queer in the present occupied by the logics of cisheterosexism. I need to constantly remind of myself that I can never give up moving toward queerness even when I am in a situation through which I am an only one person who speaks up from a paradigm of intersectional queer politics. I need to try and try again to shift away from victimizing myself because I can be easily trapped in that space. I have been already framed as a (foreign/transnational Asian male queer) villain who threatens White hetero-civility as a sign of modernity and progressivity rooted in US American imperialism. So, I might as well embrace such framing to become and be queer. Simultaneously, I remain seeking a space in which we as a whole will become and be queer one day. Still, queerness is hopelessly a multiple, fluid, and temporal production of ideality in the present time.

★ ★ ★

Queerness and Gender Futurity beyond the Ideality

We've laid bare our journeys toward queerness, particularly as they intersect with our movement in and through the disciplinary formation of queer Communication Studies. These journeys are highly colored through the simultaneous technology of our gender intersecting with race, class, nationality, and sexual performance. Our performative modes of queerness, which largely remain invisible, are almost always translated through how we correctly and incorrectly perform gender. Thus, we hope that through sharing our journeys to become and be queer, we can jump-start a larger disciplinary move toward gender futurity on the horizon. Only when we begin to center differences in meaningful ways, such as having queer, gender queer, and trans people of color who are committed to social justice at the forefront of our movements and organizations, can we move toward queerness, then toward gender futurity.

If we are going to embrace and perform gender futurity, it requires that we find new ways of speaking and creating knowledge. It requires us to be intersectionally reflexive about who we are, what we do, and how we make sense of what we do. Our bodies are always already implicated by cultural memory, power, and history. Thus, we politicize that our autoethnographic writing and performative sharing of stories is the first step in our move toward queerness and then toward gender futurity. Together our collaborative narratives reflect and refract from one another new meanings and how we are implicated by one another's experiences in larger structural systems of power. Gender futurity requires us to consider who we see our queerness in kinship with. In order to become and be queer, we must think about gender differently. Queerness on the horizon means the potential for gender queer future. An intellectual and political move toward queerness and gender futurity and its possibilities is needed if we are going to move the field of queer Communication Studies into actually being queer and gender queer.

Thus, we end this essay by arguing that gender futurity requires us to move beyond hegemonic meanings associated with different bodies. This move not only requires us to intellectually and politically reframe our "failed" gendered performances. Bernadette's fat cisgender, Chicana body doesn't necessarily have to be read as failure or excess. Instead, we suggest reading her body in terms of gender futurity and within the possibility of queerness on the horizon. At the same time, Shinsuke's femme bitchyness may be also a queer potentiality of gender futurity. Yet, the narrow definition of gay masculinity rooted in whiteness almost always contains and disciplines Shinsuke's racialized queerness. However, incorporating Big Sean's Song "I Don't Fuck with You," we as queers of color together should be able to rap, "I don't give a fuck, I don't give a fuck, I don't, I don't, I don't give a fuck!" Why do we need to care about the normative tastes? We must start ourselves to move beyond or queer the normative gender. But also, this move requires that we reflexively consider how we as queer, trans, and gender queer people consider the ways that we have been complicit in upholding rigid gender binaries against others. This means that we need to challenge often invisible assumptions we make about performances of "bitchyness," anger, and femme. What would it mean to reclaim femme from White thin bodies, homonormativity, and heteronormativity? A desire for gender futurity pushes us to reconsider the judgments we make about others' forms of activism. We embrace Gloria Anzaldúa's assertation that the borderlands are a queer space occupied by the freakish. Together we take a step toward the horizon like those that Muñoz and Anzaldúa offer us. *Will you join us?*

Notes

1 Muñoz.
2 Alberto González. "Listening to Our Voices: Latina/os and the Communities They Speak," in *Latina/o Discourse in Vernacular Spaces: Somos de Una Voz?*, eds. Michelle A. Holling and Bernadette M. Calafell (Boulder, CO: Lexington Press, 2011), 3–16.
3 Jafari S. Allen. "Black/Queer Rhizomatics: Train up a Child in the Way Ze Should Grow…," in *No Tea, No Shade: New Writings in Black Queer Studies*, ed. E. Patrick Johnson (Durham, NC: Duke University Press, 2016), 35.
4 Sara Ahmed. "Queer Feelings," in *The Routledge Queer Studies Reader*, eds. Donald E. Hall and Annamarie Jagose (New York, NY: Routledge, 2012), 424.
5 Muñoz, 1.

6 A. Finn Enke. "Introduction: Transfeminist Perspectives," in *Transfeminist Perspectives in and beyond Transgender and Gender Studies*, ed. A. Finn Enke (Philadelphia, PA: Temple University Press, 2012), 4–5.

7 Jack Halberstam. *Trans★: A Quick and Quirky Account of Gender Variability* (Berkeley, CA: University of California Press, 2018).

8 Bryant Keith Alexander. "Queer/Quare Theory Worldmaking and Methodologies," in *The Sage Handbook of Qualitative Research*, 5th ed., eds. Norman K. Denzin and Yvonna S. Lincoln (Thousand Oaks, CA: Sage, 2018), 275–307.

9 Sara Ahmed. *Living a Feminist Life* (Durham, NC: Duke University, 2017), 2.

10 Ahmed, *Living*, 2.

11 Alexander; Ahmed, *Living*; Muñoz.

12 Lisa Duggan and José Esteban Muñoz. "Hope and Hopelessness: A Dialogue." *Women and Performance* 19, no. 2 (2009): 275–283, doi: 10.1080/07407700903064946.

13 Duggan and Muñoz, 278.

14 Ahmed, *Living*, 2.

15 Stacy Holman Jones. "Autoethnography: Making the Personal Political," in *The Sage Handbook of Qualitative Research*, 3rd ed., eds. Norman K. Denzin and Yvonna S. Lincoln (Thousand Oaks, CA: Sage, 2005), 764.

16 Bernadette Marie Calafell. "(I)dentities: Considering Accountability, Reflexivity, and Intersectionality in the I and the We." *Liminalities* 9, no. 2 (2013), http://liminalities.net/9-2/calafell.pdf; Shinsuke Eguchi and Mary Jane Collier. "Critical Intercultural Mentoring and Allying: A Continuing Struggle for Change in the Academy." *Departures in Critical Qualitative Research* 7, no. 2 (2018): 49–71, doi: 10.1525/dcqr.2018.7.2.49.

17 Richard G. Jones Jr. "Putting Privilege into Practice through 'Intersectional Reflexivity': Ruminations, Interventions, and Possibilities." *Reflections: Narratives of Professional Helping* 16, no. 1 (2010): 122–125; Richard G. Jones Jr. and Bernadette Marie Calafell. "Contesting Neoliberalism through Critical Pedagogy, Intersectional Reflexivity, and Personal Narrative: Queer Tales of Academia." *Journal of Homosexuality* 59, no. 7 (2012): 957–981, doi: 10.1080/00918369.2012.699835; Calafell, "(I)dentities"; Shinsuke Eguchi. "Queer Intercultural Relationality: An Autoethnography of Asian-Black (Dis)connections in White Gay America." *Journal of International and Intercultural Communication* 8, no. 1 (2015): 27–43, doi: 10.1080/17513057.2015.991077; Amber Johnson. "Negotiating More, (Mis)Labeling the Body: A Tale of Intersectionality," in *Critical Autoethnography: Intersecting Cultural Identities in Everyday Life*, eds. Robin Boylorn and Marc P. Orbe (Walnut Creek, CA: Left Coast Press, 2013), 81–95; Benny LeMaster. "Telling Multiracial Tales: An Autoethnography of Coming out Home." *Qualitative Inquiry* 20, no. 1 (2014): 51–60, doi: 10.1177/1077800413508532.

18 Calafell, "(I)dentities."

19 Calafell, "(I)dentities."

20 Tami Spry. *Body, Paper, Stage: Writing and Performing Autoethnography* (Walnut Creek, CA: Left Coast Press, 2011), 51.

21 Jones, "Putting."

22 Jones, "Putting."

23 Jones, "Putting."

24 Calafell, "(I)dentities"; Jones, "Putting."

25 Cherríe Moraga and Gloria Anzaldúa, editors. *This Bridge Called My Back: Writings by Radical Women of Color* (Watertown, MA: Persephone Press, 1981).

26 Kakali Bhattacharya and AnaLouise Keating. "Expanding Beyond Public and Private Realities: Evoking Anzaldúan Autohistoria-teoría in Two Voices." *Qualitative Inquiry* 24, no. 5 (2018): 345–354, doi: 10.1177/1077800417741976.

27 Jasbir Puar. *Terrorist Assemblages: Homonationalism in Queer Times* (Durham, NC: Duke University Press, 2007).

28 Alison Reed. "The Whiter the Bread, the Quicker you're Dead: Spectacular Absence and Post-racialized Blackness in (White) Queer Theory," in *No Tea, No Shade: New Writings in Black Queer Studies*, ed. E. Patrick Johnson (Durham, NC: Duke University Press, 2016), 49.

29 Reed.

30 Gloria Anzaldúa. *Borderlands/la Frontera: The New Mestiza*, 4th ed. (San Francisco, CA: Aunt Lute Books, 2012); E. Patrick Johnson. *Appropriating Blackness: Performance and the Politics of Authenticity* (Durham, NC: Duke University Press, 2003); José Esteban Muñoz. *Disidentifications: Queers of Color and the Performance of Politics* (Minneapolis, MN: University of Minnesota Press, 1999); Hiram Pérez. *A Taste for Brown Bodies: Gay Modernity and Cosmopolitan Desire* (New York, NY: New York University Press, 2015).

31 Jessica A. Johnson and Bernadette Marie Calafell. "Disrupting Public Pedagogies of Bisexuality," in *Queer Communication Pedagogy*, eds. Ahmet Atay and Sandra Pensoneau-Conway (New York, NY: Routledge, 2020), 62–72.

32 Shadee Abdi and Bernadette Marie Calafell. "Em*[Race]*ing Visi(bi)lity: An Analysis of Callie Torres' and the (Im)Perfect Operation of Bisexual Identity on *Grey's Anatomy*," in *Identity Politics and the Power of Representation: Adventures in Shondaland*, eds. Rachel Alicia Griffin and Michaela D. E. Meyer (New Brunswick, NJ: Rutgers University Press, 2018), 120–137; Lisa Duggan and Kathleen McHugh. "A Fem(me)inist Manifesto." *Women and Performance* 8, no. 2 (1996): 153–159, doi: 10.1080/07407709608571236; Kathleen M. Hertlein, Erica E. Hartwell, and Marshara E. Munns. "Attitudes toward Bisexuality According to Sexual Orientation and Gender." *Journal of Bisexuality* 16, no. 3 (2016): 339–360, doi: 10.1080/15299716.2016.1200510; Kathryn Hobson. "Sue Sylvester, Coach Beiste, Santana Lopez, and Unique Adams," in *Glee and New Directions for Social Change*, eds. Brian C. Johnson and Daniel K. Faill (New Milford, CT: Sense Publishers, 2015), 95–107; Stacy Holman Jones and Anne Harris. "Monsters, Desire, and the Queer Creative Body." *Continuum* 38, no. 5 (2016): 518–530, doi: 10.1080/10304312.2016.1210748.

33 Eng-Beng Lim. *Brown Boys and Rice Queens* (New York, NY: New York University Press, 2014), xiii.

34 Jack Halberstam. *The Queer Art of Failure* (Durham, NC: Duke University Press, 2011), 3.

35 David L. Eng, Jack Halberstam, and José Esteban Muñoz. "Introduction: What's Queer about Queer Studies Now?" *Social Text* 23, no. 3–4 (2005): 1, doi: 10.1215/01642472-23-3-4_84-85-1.

36 Gust A. Yep. "The Violence of Heteronormativity in Communication Studies: Notes on Injury, Healing, and Queer World-making," in *Queer Theory and Communication: From Disciplining Queers to Queering the Discipline(s)*, eds. Gust A. Yep, Karen E. Lovaas, and John P. Elia (Binghamton, NY: Harrington Park Press, 2003), 11–59.

37 Gust A. Yep, Karen E. Lovaas, and John P. Elia. "Introduction: Queering Communication: Starting the Conversation," in *Queer Theory and Communication: From Disciplining Queers to Queering the Discipline(s)*, eds. Gust A. Yep, Karen E. Lovaas, and John P. Elia (Binghamton, NY: Harrington Park Press, 2003), 1–10.

38 Shinsuke Eguchi, Nicole Files-Thompson, and Bernadette Marie Calafell. "Queer (of Color) Aesthetics: Fleeting Moments of Transgression in VH1's *Love & Hip-Hop: Hollywood Season 2*." *Critical Studies in Media Communication* 35, no. 2 (2018): 180–193, doi: 10.1080/15295036.2017.1385822; Jeffrey Q. McCune Jr. *Sexual Discretion: Black Masculinity and the Politics of Passing* (Chicago, IL: University of Chicago Press, 2014); C. Riley Snorton. *Nobody Is Supposed to Know: Black Sexuality on the Down Low* (Minneapolis, MN: University of Minnesota Press, 2014).

Bibliography

Abdi, Shadee and Bernadette Marie Calafell. "Em*[Race]*ing Visi(bi)lity: An Analysis of Callie Torres' and the (Im)Perfect Operation of Bisexual Identity on *Grey's Anatomy*." In *Identity Politics and the Power of Representation: Adventures in Shondaland*, 120–137. Edited by Rachel Alicia Griffin and Michaela D. E. Meyer. New Brunswick, NJ: Rutgers University Press, 2018.

Ahmed, Sara. *Living a Feminist Life*, 2. Durham, NC: Duke University, 2017, 2.

Ahmed, Sara. "Queer Feelings." In *The Routledge Queer Studies Reader*, 424. Edited by Donald E. Hall and Annamarie Jagose. New York, NY: Routledge, 2012.

Alexander, Bryant Keith. "Queer/Quare Theory Worldmaking and Methodologies." In *The Sage Handbook of Qualitative Research*, 5th ed., 275–307. Edited by Norman K. Denzin and Yvonna S. Lincoln. Thousand Oaks, CA: Sage, 2018.

Allen, Jafari S. Black/Queer Rhizomatics: Train up a Child in the Way Ze Should Grow…" In *No Tea, No Shade: New Writings in Black Queer Studies*, 35. Edited by E. Patrick Johnson. Durham, NC: Duke University Press, 2016.

Anzaldúa, Gloria. *Borderlands/la Frontera: The New Mestiza*, 4th ed. San Francisco, CA: Aunt Lute Books, 2012; E. Patrick Johnson. *Appropriating Blackness: Performance and the Politics of Authenticity*. Durham, NC: Duke University Press, 2003.

Bhattacharya, Kakali and AnaLouise Keating. "Expanding Beyond Public and Private Realities: Evoking Anzaldúan Autohistoria-teoría in Two Voices." *Qualitative Inquiry* 24, no. 5 (2018): 345–354, doi: 10.1177/1077800417741976.

Calafell, Bernadette Marie. "(I)dentities: Considering Accountability, Reflexivity, and Intersectionality in the I and the We." *Liminalities* 9, no. 2 (2013), http://liminalities.net/9-2/calafell.pdf

Duggan, Lisa and José Esteban Muñoz. "Hope and Hopelessness: A Dialogue." *Women and Performance* 19, no. 2 (2009): 275–283, doi: 10.1080/07407700903064946.

Duggan, Lisa and Kathleen McHugh. "A Fem(me)inist Manifesto." *Women and Performance* 8, no. 2 (1996): 153–159, doi: 10.1080/07407709608571236.

Eguchi, Shinsuke. "Queer Intercultural Relationality: An Autoethnography of Asian-Black (Dis)connections in White Gay America." *Journal of International and Intercultural Communication* 8, no. 1 (2015): 27–43, doi: 10.1080/17513057.2015.991077.

Eguchi, Shinsuke and Mary Jane Collier. "Critical Intercultural Mentoring and Allying: A Continuing Struggle for Change in the Academy." *Departures in Critical Qualitative Research* 7, no. 2 (2018): 49–71, doi: 10.1525/dcqr.2018.7.2.49.

Eguchi, Shinsuke, Nicole Files-Thompson, and Bernadette Marie Calafell. "Queer (of Color) Aesthetics: Fleeting Moments of Transgression in VH1's *Love & Hip-Hop: Hollywood Season 2*." *Critical Studies in Media Communication* 35, no. 2 (2018): 180–193, doi: 10.1080/15295036.2017.1385822.

Eng, David L., Jack Halberstam, and José Esteban Muñoz. "Introduction: What's Queer about Queer Studies Now?" *Social Text* 23, no. 3–4 (2005): 1, doi: 10.1215/01642472-23-3-4_84-85-1.

Enke, A. Finn. "Introduction: Transfeminist Perspectives." In *Transfeminist Perspectives in and Beyond Transgender and Gender Studies*, 4–5. Edited by A. Finn Enke. Philadelphia, PA: Temple University Press, 2012.

González, Alberto. "Listening to Our Voices: Latina/os and the Communities they Speak." In *Latina/o Discourse in Vernacular Spaces: Somos de Una Voz?*, 3–16. Edited by Michelle A. Holling and Bernadette M. Calafell. Boulder, CO: Lexington Press, 2011.

Halberstam, Jack. *The Queer Art of Failure*, 3. Durham, NC: Duke University Press, 2011.

Halberstam, Jack. *Trans*: A Quick and Quirky Account of Gender Variability*. Berkeley, CA: University of California Press, 2018.

Hertlein, Kathleen M., Erica E. Hartwell, and Marshara E. Munns. "Attitudes toward Bisexuality According to Sexual Orientation and Gender." *Journal of Bisexuality* 16, no. 3 (2016): 339–360, doi: 10.1080/15299716.2016.1200510

Hobson, Kathryn. "Sue Sylvester, Coach Beiste, Santana Lopez, and Unique Adams." In *Glee and New Directions for Social Change*, 95–107. Edited by Brian C. Johnson and Daniel K. Faill. New Milford, CT: Sense Publishers, 2015.

Johnson, Amber. "Negotiating More, (Mis)Labeling the Body: A Tale of Intersectionality." In *Critical Autoethnography: Intersecting Cultural Identities in Everyday Life*, 81–95. Edited by Robin Boylorn and Marc P. Orbe. Walnut Creek, CA: Left Coast Press, 2013.

Johnson, Jessica A. and Bernadette Marie Calafell. "Disrupting Public Pedagogies of Bisexuality." In *Queer Communication Pedagogy*, 62–72. Edited by Ahmet Atay and Sandra Pensoneau-Conway. New York, NY: Routledge, 2020.

Jones, Stacy Holman. "Autoethnography: Making the Personal Political." In *The Sage Handbook of Qualitative Research*, 3rd ed., 764. Edited by Norman K. Denzin and Yvonna S. Lincoln. Thousand Oaks, CA: Sage, 2005.

Jones, Stacy Holman and Anne Harris. "Monsters, Desire, and the Queer Creative Body." *Continuum* 38, no. 5 (2016): 518–530, doi: 10.1080/10304312.2016.1210748.

Jones Jr., Richard G. "Putting Privilege into Practice through 'Intersectional Reflexivity': Ruminations, Interventions, and Possibilities." *Reflections: Narratives of Professional Helping* 16, no. 1 (2010): 122–125.

Jones Jr., Richard G. and Bernadette Marie Calafell. "Contesting Neoliberalism through Critical Pedagogy, Intersectional Reflexivity, and Personal Narrative: Queer Tales of Academia." *Journal of Homosexuality* 59, no. 7 (2012): 957–981, doi: 10.1080/00918369.2012.699835.

LeMaster, Benny. "Telling Multiracial Tales: An Autoethnography of Coming out Home." *Qualitative Inquiry* 20, no. 1 (2014): 51–60, doi: 10.1177/1077800413508532.

Lim, Eng-Beng. *Brown Boys and Rice Queens*, xiii. New York, NY: New York University Press, 2014.

McCune Jr., Jeffrey Q. *Sexual Discretion: Black Masculinity and the Politics of Passing*. Chicago, IL: University of Chicago Press, 2014.

Moraga, Cherríe and Gloria Anzaldúa, editors. *This Bridge Called My Back: Writings by Radical Women of Color*. Watertown, MA: Persephone Press, 1981.

Muñoz, Jose Esteban. *Cruising Utopia: The Then and There of Queer Futurity*. New York: NY: New York University, 2009.

Muñoz, José Esteban. *Disidentifications: Queers of Color and the Performance of Politics*. Minneapolis, MN: University of Minnesota Press, 1999.

Pérez, Hiram. *A Taste for Brown Bodies: Gay Modernity and Cosmopolitan Desire*. (New York, NY: New York University Press, 2015.

Puar, Jasbir. *Terrorist Assemblages: Homonationalism in Queer Times*. Durham, NC: Duke University Press, 2007.

Reed, Alison. "The Whiter the Bread, the Quicker You're Dead: Spectacular Absence and Post-racialized Blackness in (White) Queer Theory." In *No Tea, No Shade: New Writings in Black Queer Studies*, 49. Edited by E. Patrick Johnson. Durham, NC: Duke University Press, 2016.

Snorton, C. Riley. *Nobody Is Supposed to Know: Black Sexuality on the Down Low*. Minneapolis, MN: University of Minnesota Press, 2014.

Spry, Tami. *Body, Paper, Stage: Writing and Performing Autoethnography*, 51. Walnut Creek: CA: Left Coast Press, 2011.

Yep, Gust A. "The Violence of Heteronormativity in Communication Studies: Notes on Injury, Healing, and Queer World-making." In *Queer Theory and Communication: From Disciplining Queers to Queering the Discipline(s)*, 11–59. Edited by Gust A. Yep, Karen E. Lovaas, and John P. Elia. Binghamton, NY: Harrington Park Press, 2003.

Yep, Gust A., Karen E. Lovaas, and John P. Elia. "Introduction: Queering Communication: Starting the Conversation." In *Queer Theory and Communication: From Disciplining Queers to Queering the Discipline(s)*, 1–10. Edited by Gust A. Yep, Karen E. Lovaas, and John P. Elia. Binghamton, NY: Harrington Park Press, 2003.

Black. Queer. Fly.

Kai M. Green

She walk through airport security lines/ Tall, Black, and fine/ Smile so bright and Black joy/ Marley locs hang and wrap around head/ Blue jeans become altar where hips be hugged /And I say, "Yes, Goddess, Black thighs do matter!"/ She walk like Black love groove/ Foot workin'/ Muhammad Ali smooth/ She fly and float/ She provoke security's compulsory desire to search and scan her body just a little bit mo'/ TSA[1] wonder how it is possible she put herself together this way/ She (TSA) casually motions her (Black queer femme) out of the machine that seeks to see and seeks to know, not just where, but how it is her Black magic move and how it grow/ "You know what's coming next."(TSA) / Yes, we do./ Smile not returned/ I watch her turn to face this Woman (TSA) she don't know/ Pat locs down/ But she (TSA) don't find a thing she's looking for/ Maya Angelou "Phenomenal Woman" stanzas start to moonwalk through my mind as I watch my Black lover stand still and be touched by not a lover's hand nor heart/

"...The span of her hips...The stride of her step...The curl of her lips...They try so much...But they can't touch...Her inner mystery... "

I follow her/ Me, Black transman/ I step out of the unseeing machine/ "You'rem crotch area is setting off the machine... "/ TSA agent reaches out to touch me Black/ "I will have to pat your breasts area... "/ "I do not have that...breasts," I respond/ She quickly pulls her hands off of my chest, realizing she should not be touching this body/ This Black (trans) man's body/ Baffled, she tells me to go through the machine again/ I obey, but my body does not submit/ It breaks the machine/ My body does not come together for their eyes nor their technologies/ My body is undisciplined/ But I walk through again, nonetheless/ I stand/ Pose/ Hands up/ Feet facing forward/ They scan/ I exit the machine and face the TSA agent/ I'm forced to look away from the machine which (un) clearly reveals something, something that I do not wish to explain/ They tell me, "That's better!"/ "What's better?" I wonder/ What do they see when they look at the machine body me?/ A body scan don't reveal Black, but clumsily stumbles upon queer, unable to process/ This Black/ But they don't need the machine to tell them that/ Black queer femme and Black transman long to take flight/ And they do, despite the surveillance/ They use their words like sage to cleanse their Black beings after this unwanted touch/ They hold each other and whisper in ears/ Black spells, prayers, love, release/ They affirm their Black magic is, was, and always be—

Note

1 TSA stands for Transportation Security Administration and is the organization responsible for airport security at all airports operating in the United States of America.

SECTION II

Identity Negotiation and Internal Struggles

Scholars define identity in several ways. Some scholars agree that identity is an inherently communicative process and should be understood as a transaction where messages are exchanged.[1] Other theorists extend beyond this idea of identity as a transaction and focus on identity as a social process.[2] This process entails the "the manner in which individuals, groups, communities, cultures, and institutions define themselves."[3] Thus, identities have individual, social, and communal properties,[4] are embedded in multiple layers and social ties, and are interdependent.[5]

Identity negotiation is rooted in communication, performance, and relationality. Mary Jane Collier and Milt Thomas contend that identity negotiation is mediated by discursive management whereby one's cultural identities are products of scope, salience, and intensity of attributed and avowed identities.[6] Stella Ting-Toomey further adds that identity is refined and modified through processes of dyadic verbal and non-verbal negotiation.[7] We are constantly in a state of negotiating who we are based on who we are talking with (*Hello cisgender, White man*), the identities we avow (*I'm a Black trans woman*), and the manner in which that individual attributes identities to our bodies (*you are a non-binary Korean immigrant*). While Ting-Toomey's theories emphasized intercultural communication, identity negotiation takes places in intracultural,[8] and co-cultural settings where group members uncover commonalities in order to function within dominant society while validating the vast multiplicity of experiences between and among groups.[9]

Michael Hecht's communication theory of identity constructs identity as a social process, rooted not only in the individual and society but as relational, communal, and enacted as well.[10] There are four layers proposed in the theory—personal, communal, relational, and enactment—and they emphasize the interdependency of identity.

Personal identity is a "characteristic of the individual stored as self-cognitions, feelings about self, and/or a spiritual sense of self-being."[11] From this perspective, identity is a process of self-definition, exposing the "direct relationship between identity and one's ability to self-define."[12] According to Hecht, there are three assumptions of personal identity: "(1) identities are hierarchically ordered meanings attributed to the self as an object in a social situation; (2) identities are meanings ascribed to the self by others in the social world; (3) identities are sources of expectations and motivations."[13]

Identity as enactment assumes that "identities are enacted in social interaction through communication and may be defined as those messages."[14] Even though all messages are not about identity, identity is a part of all messages and may be expressed as a part of a message or as the central significance. Peter J. Burke and Donald C. Reitzes understand the link between identity and performance through meanings: "The meanings of self are established and assessed in terms of the meanings of the performances generated by that self within the culture of the interactional situation."[15] Judith Butler situates identity in performance as well, suggesting that identities are not static understandings or facts, but instead are rooted in, performed, and disciplined through everyday practices.[16] In order for an identity to exist, or for someone to claim an identity, that identity must be performed.

The *identity-as-relational* layer suggests that communication has both content and relationship dimensions, and that identities emerge in relationships to other people and are enacted in relationships. What occurs in these relationships is primarily identity negotiation and building.[17] "Identity is mutually constructed in social interaction and emerges as the property of that relationship because it is jointly negotiated."[18] Several scholars have taken to the study of identity negotiation.[19] According to these scholars, there are two types of negotiations: they can be contractual[20] or they can be based in conflict resolution.[21]

Simon Frith contends that the reason for identity negotiation occurs in performance.[22] When people perform their identities, it is the aesthetics of that performance anchored in the situation, organization, and/or context, where conflict arises between the society, the group, and the individual. It is through performance that the process of negotiation takes place. It is deciding what sounds right, feels right, and looks right that people both express (them)selves and lose (them)selves in an act of participation.[23] While processes of negation are relevant to the relational frame, identity can also be seen to exist as a *communal frame*. Identity can be studied as communal when the group's members identify with something that bonds the group together.[24] In the communal frame, identity is situated in the group instead of the individual or interaction, and identities are jointly held, remembered, and taught to new members.

The stories told in this section focus on the moment where identity negotiation becomes a clear performance pushing against the internal struggles of being and becoming. As a non-normative body living in a system designed to be binary, our bodies are constantly doing the work of assessing situations and relationships for safety or lack thereof, locating home, and critiquing discomfort within and beyond the body due to other people's assumptions about normative approaches to gender.

Nora J. Klein's poem, "I Was the First to Tie My Laces," takes on a playful and often times painful journey through childhood where she is becoming and negotiating what it means to be a trans girl surrounded by a lack of acceptance and celebration of her identity. In "Lone Star Feminist: An Autoethnographic Explanation of Identity and Regionality," Andrea Baldwin uses thunder and lightning as metaphors to invite the reader on an intersectional journey through Texas via race, gender, feminism, and performance. Greg Hummel's essay "My Gender Struggle: Attempts at Storying Queer Worldmaking" use a process of articulation—disarticulation—rearticulation to grapple with what it means to be seen as masculine and male bodied, but identify as a differently gendered body, and the queer world-making necessary to thrive despite the constraints on gender identity. In "Beauty in the Intersections: Reflections on Quiet Suffering," Amber L. Johnson troubles boundaries of binary labels attached to class, beauty, and sexuality in addition to race, and the ways in which markers of authenticity, desire, and positionality influence our perceptions of self in a constant state of negotiation. In "Your Memories Are Not Your Own," Meggie Mapes uses a series of second-person narratives beginning with growing up a girl in Small Iowa to render the reader, "you," as the situated "I" of the story grappling with gender, invincibility, the strange, and the familiar. Finally, J. Nyla's poem "Dysphoria/Y'all Know What I Mean?" takes us on a journey of explaining and exploring gender dysphoria as it manifests in/on/with the body.

Discussion Questions

1. Do you struggle with your gender? How often do you think about your gender? If you have never thought about your gender before, what does it mean to have to think about it now? What does it mean for you to process through your relative privilege for never having to think about your gender? What other identities have you not had to think about regarding race, sexuality, ability, nationality, ethnicity, religion, size, and beauty?
2. How do you understand and enact femininity, masculinity, *and* androgyny in the everyday?
3. Do you find your experiences with and expression of gender shifting depending upon whom you are talking to, where you are talking, or the various social identity categories of the people involved? For instance, do you enact

masculinity, femininity, and/or androgyny differently when at a religious function, versus a family gathering, versus a quiet evening with close friends?

4. Human beings are constantly evolving and changing, which means old memories may not ring true eternally. How do you interact with memories that push you to negotiate your identity with yourself? How do the authors grapple with memories that force them to rearticulate their gender and other social identities?

5. Each of the chapters in this section pulls the reader into the experience. What connections do you feel between "you" as the potential reader, speaker, author, and "you" as yourself? Does the use of "you" in the stories reveal anything about yourself—a memory, a moment—that you hadn't previously considered?

Notes

1 Peter J. Burke and Donald C. Reitzes, "The Link between Identity and Role Performance." *Social Psychology Quarterly* 44, no. 2 (1981): 83–92, doi: 10.2307/3033704; Mary Jane Collier and Milt Thomas, "Cultural Identity: An Interpretive Perspective," in *Theories of Intercultural Communication*, eds. Young Yun Kim and William B. Gudykunst (Newbury Park, CA: Sage, 1988), 99–122; Kenneth J. Gergen and John Shotter, *Texts of Identity* (London, UK: Sage, 1989).

2 Alessandro Pizzorno, "Political Science and Collective Identity in Industrial Conflict," in *Resurgence of Class Conflict in Western Europe since 1968*, eds. Colin Crouch and Alessandro Pizzorno (New York, NY: Holmes and Meier, 1978), 277–298; Alberto Melucci, *Nomads of the Present: Social Movement and Individual Needs in Contemporary Society* (London, UK: Hutchinson Radius, 1989); Michael L. Hecht, Mary Jane Collier, and Sidney A. Ribeau, *African American Communication: Ethnic Identity and Cultural Interpretation* (Newbury Park, CA: Sage, 2003).

3 Ronald L. Jackson, *The Negotiation of Cultural Identity* (Westport, CT: Praeger Press, 1999), xiii.

4 Doug McAdam and Ronnelle Paulsen, "Specifying the Relationship between Social Ties and Activism." *American Journal of Sociology* 99, no. 3 (1993): 640–667, https://www.jstor.org/stable/2781286.

5 Sheldon Stryker and Peter J. Burke, "The Past, Present, and Future of an Identity Theory." *Social Psychology Quarterly* 63, no. 4 (2000), 284–297, doi: 10.2307/2695840; Sheldon Stryker, "Identity Competition: Key to Differential Social Movement Participation?" in *Self, Identity, and Social Movements*, eds. Sheldon Stryker, Timothy J. Owens, and Robert W. White (Minneapolis, MN: University of Minnesota Press, 2000), 21–40; Peggy A. Thoits and Lauren K. Virshup, "Me's and We's: Forms and Functions of Social Identities," in *Self and Identity Fundamental Issues*, eds. Richard D. Ashmore and Lee Jussim (New York, NY: Oxford University Press, 1995), 106–135.

6 Collier and Thomas, 102.

7 Stella Ting-Toomey, *Communicating Across Cultures* (New York, NY: Guilford, 1999).

8 K. S. Sitaram and Roy T. Cogdell, *Foundations of Intercultural Communication* (Columbus, OH: C. E. Merrill, 1976), 28.

9 Mark P. Orbe, "Negotiating Multiple Identities within Multiple Frames: An Analysis of First-Generation College Students." *Communication Education* 53, no. 2 (2004): 131, doi: 10.10/03634520410001682401.

10 Michael L. Hecht, "2002—A Research Odyssey: Toward the Development of a Communication Theory of Identity," *Communication Monographs* 60, no. 1 (1993), 76–82, doi: 10.1080/03637759309376297.

11 Hecht, 79.

12 Jackson, *Negotiation*, 9.

13 Hecht, 79.

14 Hecht, 79.

15 Burke and Rietzes, 85.

16 Judith Butler, *Bodies that Matter* (New York, NY: Routledge, 1993); Judith Butler, "Burning Acts: Injurious Speech," in *Performativity and Performance*, eds. Andrew Parker and Eve Kosofsky Sedgwick (New York, NY: Routledge, 1995).

17 Paul Watzlawick, Janet Beavin Bavelas, and Don. D. Jackson, *The Pragmatics of Human Communication* (New York, NY: Norton, 1967).

18 Hecht, 79.

19 Stella Ting-Toomey, "Intercultural Conflict Styles: A Face Negotiation Theory," in *Theories in Intercultural Communication*, eds. Young Yun Kim and William B. Gudykunst (Newbury Park, CA: Sage, 1988), 213–235; Nancy Whittier, *Feminist Generations: The Persistence of the Radical Women's Movement* (Philadelphia, PA: Temple University Press, 1995); Nancy Whittier, "Political Generation, Micro-Cohorts, and the Transformation of Social Movements." *American Sociological Review* 62, no. 5 (1997): 760–778, https://www.jstor.org/stable/2657359; Catherine Tinsley, "Models of Conflict Resolution in Japanese, German, and American Cultures." *Journal of Applied Psychology* 83, no. 2 (1998): 316–323, doi: 10.1037/0021-9010.83.2.316; Donatella Della Porta and Mario Diani, *Social Movements: An Introduction* (Malden, MA: Blackwell Publishing, 1999); Jeanne M. Brett, "Culture and Negotiation," *International Journal of Psychology* 35, no. 2 (2000): 97–104, doi: 10.1080/002075900399385; William B. Gudykunst and Young Yun Kim, *Communicating with Strangers: An Approach to Intercultural Communication*, 4th ed. (New York, NY: McGraw-Hill, 2003); Jackson, *Negotiation*; Ronald L. Jackson, "Cultural Contracts Theory: Toward an Understanding of Identity Negotiation." *Communication Quarterly* 50, no. 3–4 (2002): 359–367, doi: 10.1080/01463370209385672; Ronald L. Jackson, "Exploring African American Identity Negotiation in the Academy: Toward a Transformative Vision of African American Communication Scholarship." *Howard Journal of Communications* 13, no. 1 (2002): 43–57, doi: 10.1080/106461702753555030.

20 Ronald L. Jackson, "Cultural Contracts Theory: Toward a Critical-Rhetorical Identity Negotiation Paradigm," in *New Approaches to Rhetoric*, eds. Patricia A. Sullivan and Steven R. Goldzwig (Thousand Oaks, CA: Sage, 2004), 89–107.

21 Peter J. Carnevale and Dean G. Pruitt, "Negotiation and Mediation," *Annual Review of Psychology* 43 (1992): 531–582, doi: 10.1146/annurev.ps.43.020192.002531.

22 Simon Frith, "Music and Identity," in *Questions of Cultural Identity*, eds. Stuart Hall and Paul du Gay (London: Sage), 108–127.

23 Frith.

24 Pizzorno, "Political Science"; Melucci, *Nomads*; Jean L. Cohen, "Strategy of Identity: New Theoretical Paradigms and Contemporary Social Movements." *Social Research* 52, no. 4 (1985): 663–716, https://www.jstor.org/stable/40970395; Gerry Philipsen, "The Prospect for Cultural Communication," in *Communication Theory: Eastern and Western Perspectives*, ed. D. Lawrence Kincaid (San Diego, CA: Academic Press, 1987), 245–254; David Middleton and Derek Edwards, *Collective Remembering* (London: Sage, 1990).

Bibliography

Brett, Jeanne M. "Culture and Negotiation." *International Journal of Psychology* 35, no. 2 (2000): 97–104, doi: 10.1080/002075900399385.

Burke, Peter J. and Donald C. Reitzes. "The Link Between Identity and Role Performance." *Social Psychology Quarterly* 44, no. 2 (1981): 83–92, doi: 10.2307/3033704.

Butler, Judith. *Bodies That Matter*. New York, NY: Routledge, 1993.

Butler, Judith. "Burning Acts: Injurious Speech." In *Performativity and Performance*, 197–227. Edited by Andrew Parker and Eve Kosofsky Sedgwick. New York, NY: Routledge, 1995.

Carnevale, Peter J. and Dean G. Pruitt. "Negotiation and Mediation." *Annual Review of Psychology* 43 (1992): 531–582, doi: 10.1146/annurev.ps.43.020192.002531.

Cohen, Jean L. "Strategy of Identity: New Theoretical Paradigms and Contemporary Social Movements." *Social Research* 52, no. 4 (1985): 663–716, https://www.jstor.org/stable/40970395.

Collier, Mary Jane and Milt Thomas. "Cultural Identity: An Interpretive Perspective." In *Theories of Intercultural Communication*, 99–122. Edited by Young Yun Kim and William B. Gudykunst. Newbury Park, CA: Sage, 1988.

Della Porta, Donatella and Mario Diani. *Social Movements*. Malden, MA: Blackwell Publishing, 1999.

Frith, Simon. "Music and Identity." In *Questions of Cultural Identity*, 108–127. Edited by Stuart Hall and Paul du Gay. London, UK: Sage, 1996.

Gergen, Kenneth J. and John Shotter. *Texts of Identity*. London, UK: Sage, 1989.

Gudykunst, William B. and Young Yun Kim. *Communicating with Strangers: An Approach to Intercultural Communication*, 4th ed., New York, NY: McGraw-Hill, 2003.

Hecht, Michael L. "2002—A Research Odyssey: Toward the Development of a Communication Theory of Identity." *Communication Monographs* 60, no. 1 (1993): 76–82, doi: 10.1080/03637759309376297.

Hecht, Michael L., Mary Jane Collier, and Sidney A. Ribeau. *African American Communication: Ethnic Identity and Cultural Interpretation*. Newbury Park, CA: Sage, 2003.

Jackson, Ronald L. "Cultural Contracts Theory: Toward a Critical-Rhetorical Identity Negotiation Paradigm." In *New Approaches to Rhetoric*, 89–107. Edited by Patricia A. Sullivan and Steven R. Goldzwig. Thousand Oaks, CA: Sage, 2004.

Jackson, Ronald L. "Cultural Contracts Theory: Toward an Understanding of Identity Negotiation." *Communication Quarterly* 50, no. 3–4 (2002): 359–367, doi: 10.1080/01463370209385672.

Jackson, Ronald L. "Exploring African American Identity Negotiation in the Academy: Toward a Transformative Vision of African American Communication Scholarship." *Howard Journal of Communications* 13, no. 1 (2002): 43–57, doi: 10.1080/106461702753555030.

Jackson, Ronald L. *The Negotiation of Cultural Identity*. Westport, CT: Praeger, 1999.

McAdam, Doug and Ronnelle Paulsen. "Specifying the Relationship Between Social Ties and Activism." *American Journal of Sociology* 99, no. 3 (1993): 640–667, https://www.jstor.org/stable/2781286.

Melucci, Alberto. *Nomads of the Present: Social Movement and Individual Needs in Contemporary Society*. London, UK: Hutchinson Radius, 1989.

Middleton, David and Derek Edwards. *Collective Remembering*. London, UK: Sage, 1990.

Orbe, Mark P. "Negotiating Multiple Identities Within Multiple Frames: An Analysis of First-Generation College Students," *Communication Education* 53, no. 2 (2004): 131–149, doi: 10.10/03634520410001682401.

Philipsen, Gerry. "The Prospect for Cultural Communication." In *Communication Theory: Eastern and Western Perspectives*, 245–254. Edited by D. Lawrence Kincaid. San Diego, CA: Academic Press, 1987.

Pizzorno, Alessandro. "Political Science and Collective Identity in Industrial Conflict." In *Resurgence of Class Conflict in Western Europe since 1968*, 277–298. Edited by Colin Crouch and Alessandro Pizzorno. New York, NY: Holmes and Meier, 1978.

Sitaram, K. S. and Roy T. Cogdell. *Foundations of Intercultural Communication*. Columbus, OH: C. E. Merrill, 1976.

Stryker, Sheldon, "Identity Competition: Key to Differential Social Movement Participation?" In *Self, Identity, and Social Movements*, 21–40. Edited by Sheldon Stryker, Timothy J. Owens, and Robert W. White. Minneapolis, MN: University of Minnesota Press, 2000.

Stryker, Sheldon and Peter J. Burke. "The Past, Present, and Future of an Identity Theory." *Social Psychology Quarterly* 63, no. 4 (2000): 284–297, doi: 10.2307/2695840.

Thoits, Peggy A. and Lauren K. Virshup. "Me's and We's: Forms and Functions of Social Identities." In *Self and Identity Fundamental Issues*, 106–135. Edited by Richard D. Ashmore and Lee Jussim. New York, NY: Oxford University Press, 1995.

Ting-Toomey, Stella. *Communicating Across Cultures*. New York, NY: Guilford, 1999.

Ting-Toomey, Stella. "Intercultural Conflict Styles: A Face Negotiation Theory." In *Theories in Intercultural Communication*, 213–235. Edited by Young Yun Kim and William B. Gudykunst. Newbury Park, CA: Sage, 1988.

Tinsley, Catherine. "Models of Conflict Resolution in Japanese, German, and American Cultures." *Journal of Applied Psychology* 83, no. 2 (1998): 316–323, doi: 10.1037/0021-9010.83.2.316.

Watzlawick, Paul, Janet Beavin Bavelas, and Don D. Jackson. *The Pragmatics of Human Communication*. New York, NY: Norton, 1967.

Whittier, Nancy. *Feminist Generations: The Persistence of the Radical Women's Movement*. Philadelphia, PA: Temple University Press, 1995.

Whittier, Nancy. "Political Generation, Micro-Cohorts, and the Transformation of Social Movements," *American Sociological Review* 62, no. 5 (1997): 760–778, https://www.jstor.org/stable/2657359.

I Was the First to Tie My Laces.

Nora J. Klein

I was the first to tie my laces.

Rarely quick on my feet
Adults called it weakness.

too sensitive soft touches cuddles under silk streams,
freckled baby dolls parts,
mermaid Barbies
shiny scales reflect the sea.

A vandalized painting won't ever
sit straight, walk right, nor smile like it could.
If my body is a puzzle
My pieces
Are not fitting.
I take a deep breath
Go back
To a beginning

You know who you are not,
my voice changing
tightens
the knots.
Impossible to shift this trajectory
Transgender princess masked effectively.

I like boys when I'm not with them
rather stare from afar
imagine kissing him,
take me to a castle and
adorn me with stereotypes.

Clean feet skipping under the spiral of mutual symbols
Synergy splashing the satellites.
Kingdoms get invaded, the heart is stolen. So I disguise my fantasies
because I'm young and broken.

Coax me to come out,
Then my house burnt down.
Precious things beneath the brick
lost in the wreckage
and never found.

Nobody hears me in the playground,
I misplaced my sound.
Can't find me in the ball pit,
When I need to be felt.
Nor speak to me if convinced
what's expected of me.
This is my history
I should say something but
like faeries
you don't believe I'm existing.

I don't fit in so I'll quiet my senses
make fun of how I wore my clothes,
I hate them too
Yes, my mother picked out these shoes.

DANCING WITH MY GENDER STRUGGLE

Attempts at Storying Queer Worldmaking

Greg Hummel

As I sit here attempting to engage the painstaking (for me) writing process required by my profession, I feel every square inch of fabric pressed tight against my breasts. Resting atop my furry belly, lazily hanging away from my core, my nipples begin to say hello. Areola slowly activating like the spinning rainbow wheel of doom on my iMac, my nipples come to attention, flooding with the energy and imagery of milky mammalian life juice ready and wanting to nourish the next generation of genderqueer people thirsty to be seen. To be heard. To be recognized. Perhaps it's a projection of my own thirst to be seen, to be heard, to be recognized. My tits begin to tighten as if to transform into tear drops that I've learned through media's misogynistically sculpted lenses is supposedly the ideal female form. Before long, I'm transformed and transported to a dance floor in nothing but glittery nipple covers, kitty heels, bikini bottoms, and long luscious waves of silky-smooth hair rooted deep in my skull; the crowd is screaming, waving their dollar bills, and the smell of stale beer, fog machine, cologne, and musk fills my cavities. They're living for me, and I for them. They see me. I feel them. I pop down into a deep squat with legs spread eagle; every inch of their energy feeding my lycra-covered undercarriage. There's magic happening in my imaginary moment, even as my breasts begin to slump once more and my breath brings me back to the page as my critical awareness recognizes that my imaginary body is as normative as Barbie.

These imaginings are not new to me. I've been playing with them since before I first made friends with celestial stars around the age of 5.[1] While much of my mental musings continues to center around gender—my gender(s)—the images of gender's futurity continue to change. Over the last six years, I've continued to learn a process of what Richard Jones calls *intersectional reflexivity*.[2]

That is, I continue to work hard to process through both my privileged and disadvantaged identities in relational contexts, focusing on the material, discursive, and performative effects this dialectical tension has on both myself and the people and communities with whom I interact in the everyday across varying identity vectors and multiverses. Performing a pedagogy that centers intersectional reflexivity in my classrooms, I ask students to grapple with not only the social constructions of gender, race, ability, ethnicity, sexuality, nationality, religion, size, and beauty, but also the ways in which these identity categories are marked on the body, contested on and through the body, serving as much needed resistance toward cisheterosexist, racist, colonialist, patriarchal, able-bodied, Christo-capitalism, and its much-needed resistance. In learning how to see, feel, and identify these systems in our bodies and the bodies of our peers, my goal is to lead students on a journey of self-implicature whereby we all come to work through the privilege-disadvantage dialectical tension[3] that simultaneously recognizes the need for social justice activism in everyday life and the everyday enactments and shifts in bodily performances that can lead to social justice activism. Indeed, I ask my students to work through Kathryn Sorrells' model of intercultural praxis to envision a different world only available through the marking of the systems that bind us—privileged and disadvantaged—together in a dance for resources to which 99% of us have little or no access.[4] This process of intersectional reflexivity, indubitably, changes me each and every time, if only momentarily allowing me to interject into what John T. Warren marked as opportune moments to shift the performative repetitions of identity.[5] Jones's process of intersectional reflexivity also requires that I call myself into being and becoming differently, even in my mental musings that undoubtedly house some of the most unconscious inscriptions of hegemonic ideologies needing to be unhinged, unearthed, and purged to make space for gender sans colonial inscriptions of White supremacist, capitalist, cisheteropatriarchy; even as I recognize that this desire to purge gender from the grips of colonial inscriptions is, in and of itself, an embodied musing, for we must reconcile with the persistent presence of colonialism and its White supremacist, capitalist, ableist, cisheteropatriarchial structures. Intersectional reflexivity offers us this potentiality as we center self-implicature within the flows of these systemic power structures.

In this chapter, I use a process of articulation—disarticulation—rearticulation that Benny LeMaster and I developed in a response essay for *Communication Education*[6] to autoethnographically-engage my dances with genders. I begin with a storied interaction with my then-romantic partner as a way to *articulate* my struggles with being ascribed male/man/masculine/boy in this hirsute bag of bones I inhabit. I then follow with a narrative surrounding an interaction I had with one of my students as I work to *disarticulate* my gender. I finish with a brief ode to the queer people in my life who have helped and continue to help me *rearticulate* a gender narrative that dances somewhere in-between, around, outside of, next to, and away from the gender binary. At the core of these stories are the queer relationships and the queer bonds that call me in to being and becoming differently-gendered.

Naming the Systems That Bind Me: Articulating My Struggle to Name My Gender

I looked at him in earnest as he sipped his drink, my voice quivering as my tongue found every possible hedge. With each drag of a cigarette, I tried harder to find my words as we stood in front of each other, in our underwear, in his bedroom, anticipating sexual escapades. "Because, ya know, I don't know what my gender is really. Like who does? I don't know. I swing from masculine to extreme forms of feminine and back to masculine again. Like, I don't know how to … or how I, uh, feel about my penis some daaa … ." He cuts me off in an anxiety-driven panic.

"Oh my god. Please just be a boy. Be a boy. I like your penis. I like penises. I'm gay. You're gay. Just be a boy." My heart sinks into my stomach and my throat swells as I watch my then-boyfriend flamboyantly beg me to avow to a normative, infantilizing binary sex category (boy) that has little to do with my attempts to articulate where I am in terms of gender. His collapse of my body speaks of the normative scripts we have for gender in contemporary mainstream US-America and much of the postcolonial world. Gender seems to disappear under the sexed scriptures of genitalia. I realize, in this moment, that he will never be able to touch my body in ways that affirm me beyond the pornographic scripts for male-male(?) sexual entanglements. He will never comfortably cup my breasts in ways that I imagine affirm their feminine form, even as they remain coated in dark mammalian proteinoid-based hair. He will never reach his hands down my stomach and over my briefs curving his two middle fingers up and into my genital cavity to caress the parts of me that the genetic roll of the dice missed. He will never do as my stalker did, leaning into my ear as he caressed my body, whispering:

"Oh right, you like it like the girl you are."

I snap back into the moment with my then-boyfriend as I realize I'm mentally dancing with the affirmations from a man who created a fake social media profile to follow me for four years before working his way back into my bed after that hook-up so many years earlier. By now, my then-boyfriend is chastising me for my masculine passing privilege in ways that do not speak to how I understand Martin and Nakayama's privilege—disadvantage dialectic.[7] Somehow, my masculine passing privilege is now being collapsed into my pretty privilege that undoubtedly, to him, marks him as feminine, flamboyant, and ugly in everyday life. Somehow, my marking of my gender uncertainty triggered him in a tailspin of a future unknown to both of us. I finally cut him off: "You think you're more feminine presenting than you are and our White bodies save us in this White supremacist system. Even so, your fear of presenting femme is a mark of your issues with toxic masculinity and internalized sexism. Let's not make this about me."

We went to bed that night without touching each other. Sleep escaped me. I couldn't help but swirl through my own fears of presenting more feminine than I do. Beyond occasional fashion choices and performances of movement, I lay there caught in the tension between his assertions and my inner turmoil. I am masculine passing much of the time, even as I descend stairwells in imaginary ball gowns and figure-molding, body-damaging, breathtaking corsets. My limp wrists and pointed pinkie fingers sometimes wink to my students, even as my beard serves as a beard to my breasts. I lay there wondering, problematically, about who would make love to a 6′2″ (188 cm), fat, hairy, highly-educated, working-class person who has been working hard to simultaneously embrace the body that I have and the body that I want. "Just be a boy" echoes through my skull and shivers through my body as I tearfully feign an existence where I can be embraced for who I am becoming while maintaining the body that I live in. Sometimes man. Sometimes woman. Much of the time somewhere in-between, around, outside of, next to, away from, and beyond the binary in ways that resist the reification of the binary with cultural scripts that scream: "You're a boy. Be a boy." And, "You're only other option is to transition." Even now, a year-and-a-half later, newly-coupled in central New York, I want both/and. Even now, I wonder how much of my desire for the both/and is a mark of my fear to transition away my masculine passing privilege in a cisheterosexist world. Even now, I battle with my own internalized transphobia while searching for ways to embrace non-normativity. Even now, undoubtedly, my white skin protects me. And with the social embrace of the "dad bod," my hirsute body protects me. And with the title of "Doctor," my new assumed-class protects me. Combined, they make me appear nearly-impenetrable in a cisheterosexist, misogynist, racist, classist USAmerica. "Be a boy" still makes me sick to my stomach.

Naming the Relations That Bind Us: Disarticulating My Gender Dysphoria

She
Can't yet
Avow
to her
fully.　　　　　　*She*
says,

　　　　　Call me whatever.

She arrives at my office door during finals week, face wrapped in aviator sunglasses and a heavy black winter scarf on this unusually warm May day. I'm exhausted from grading and administrative work at the close of my first year on the tenure-track, and all I can see are her bloodshot and teary eyes struggling to lift her heavy brown eyelids. We've been here before, on a number of occasions this semester, all of them involving her experiences with transphobia, all of them involving an extension on an assignment. But given the institutional constraints within which I work (i.e., faculty must submit final grades 48-hours following the commencement of the final exam), there is no more time. I'm also driven by a deadline to finish my semester early, as I have a then-boyfriend to pick up at the airport in St. Louis before heading to my own graduation. I need to be in the car in less than 24 hours, and I just can't. I don't want to let her in. Not right now.

My head slouches in my hand as a meme of Audre Lorde on my desktop background meets my side-eye. Right forefinger and thumb gripping her chin, eyes slightly gazing above the tip of her nose, Audre Lorde's words come into focus: "There is no such thing as a single-issue struggle because we do not live single-issue lives."[8] I exhale as I hear Lorde's call to intersectionality, resilience, and resistance in her Malcolm X Weekend talk at Harvard University in the winter of 1982. I inhale as I look up again to see my student standing in my doorway. I know my student, and she knows me. I am still her "prafessa," in her best Bronxian latinx tongue. She is still my queer sibling, the only student to ever ask my pronouns and gleefully squeak at the opportunity to call me "gurl." Our similarities in queerness and class build bridges across our differences in race and age, leading us to what AnaLouise Keating theorized as "commonalities"[9] and "interrelatedness"[10] in a "metaphysics of interconnectivity"[11] from her work with Cherríe Moraga and Gloria Anzaldúa's, *This Bridge Called My Back*.[12] I wasn't ready, in this moment, for the third component of Keating's call: "listening with raw openness."[13] But my student needed to be heard. And I needed time and space to do what I came to my office to do. Instead of being compassionate, I responded curtly, exhaustedly, almost blatantly annoyed: "You have five minutes."

She collapses her body in half, noting her gratitude, as she enters and closes the door. I'm immediately uncomfortable and ask if this needs to be a close-doored meeting. For my own protection, I never like the door closed when a student is in the room. She pleads with me to keep it closed. I nod, maintaining a firm and almost-emotionless posture; a masculine power-move to be certain. The clock is ticking as she slowly removes her scarf, revealing a slightly darkened yet thick shadow of facial hair across her chin. My gaze softens, my body relaxes, and my breath returns as she gestures toward her face. "This. This is me. This is all of me. And it's killing me." My heart breaks for her, and for my own, hirsute body, as the clock ticks are replaced with heart beats and shared tears.

Deep breaths. I say, "What's going on, gurl?"

She struggles to find breath and voice in between her gasps for air. We breathe together; just long enough for her to tell me that her transphobic uncle—her transphobic cisgender gay uncle—refuses to come to graduation if she shows up as her authentic self. She finds the words between her erupting cries to tell me that her transphobic cisgender gay uncle is using her accepting-grandmother as a guilting mechanism, proclaiming that her grandmother will die if she sees her in all her first-generation, mixed race, transgender woman authentic glory. She finds the strength to bear her fears between the now-flood of tears to say:

> "And to top it all off, I have to let this fuck of a beard grow out so I can wax it for graduation. And these fucks on campus don't fucking get it. A friend of mine told me, 'You look like a terrorist.' Yeah, I know I look like a fucking terrorist. Like, what the fuck? I don't trust these fuckers to see me like this. So great, I look like a terrorist."

I'd be remiss if I didn't write that I had the same reaction when I first saw her, a perspective that has taken on a differently acute awareness since moving to the state of New York. Her appearance was far more Unabomber sheik, a caricature of a terrorist, rather than a xenophobic and Islamophobic stereotype of Muslim people. But, of course, due to years of studying critical intercultural communication, I had more wherewithal to say this and I have more experience with reflexivity to know that she is not intentionally mocking or attempting to invoke a stereotype of Muslim people. I also, thankfully, had the reflexive moment to check my own perceptions of what "terrorist" looks like; checking my pre-conceived, stereotypical, xenophobic, and racist assumptions. That is, western USAmerican whiteness was framing my perceptions and western USAmerican whiteness was trying its best to frame my response. It was a messy few seconds in my mind. If this were any other student, we likely would have had a conversation about what she was attempting to do with her attire. But not here, not now. I knew what she was doing, and she knew what she was doing. She was covering up her body the best way she knew how in the moment, her gendered terror horrific-enough for her to risk performing terrorist, dismissing the racial and religious implications Muslims experience across the United States. The conversation called for a different response:

> "Your gay uncle is being transphobic as fuck. And how dare he use your grandmother as a scapegoat for his transphobia. You deserve better than this. You worked hard for this week. For this day. Damnit, you deserve to be you and praised for the goddess you've become and applauded as you walk that graduation in your sickest heels."

Her entire body shifts—her entire energy shifts—as she muscles out a tongue pop between her congested sinuses.

I continue to think back on that day, months later, wondering what I could have done differently to meet her where she was. I think back on that day worried about how close I came to being one of the many mostly-White mostly-male faculty members across the nation who our students of color complain about for not giving them the time of day. I think back to that day knowing that marginalized faculty members are almost-required to shoulder the burden of the neoliberal academy that continues to cut resources to our most underrepresented and underserved students and faculty as a way to maintain a bloated administrative structure in the wake of decreasing governmental assistance that makes calling our public institutions of higher education "public" a sad joke; this affective labor undoubtedly marked by Audrey Williams June in their essay, "The Invisible Labor of Minority Professors," in *The Chronical of Higher Education* as a labor that falls inequitably and inevitably on the shoulders of marginalized faculty in an academy that demands faculty fulfill the roles of teacher, mentor, and therapist as we continue to cut programs specifically designed to assist our most vulnerable siblings.[14] I think back to that day when I almost dismissed my first-generation, working-class, mixed-race, trans-woman student of color because I was tired. Tired. Tired, frustrated, and angry knowing that students and faculty both locally and globally do not have enough institutional support to help our students and faculty with her/our trans-specific health needs, nor do we have enough institutional support to keep us, marginalized faculty members, from being affectively overworked and over-serviced as we continue to serve as teacher, mentor, and therapist both for their needs and our own. I think back to that day breathing into the exhaustion of working within a neoliberal academic structure, breathing into the fine lines between exploitation and queer relational intimacy so well documented by Bernadette Calafell[15] and her students/mentees/colleagues.[16] I think back to that day, fondly, knowing that I finally had the reflexive and critical integrity to listen into the space created between our hearts and bodies over the last 15 weeks, almost ignoring the ways that I needed her support as much as she needed mine, months later finally recognizing that as a genderqueer, gender non-conforming professor that I have so very few people to turn to who can hear me beyond the binary in ways that don't collapse my everyday into their guilt for their ignorance or their pride for their ability to quote statistics in an attempt to prove their alliance. I think back to that day, angry that I don't have someone here who I can feel as comfortable with, for the people I thought I could hear me served plates of apologies at best, bowls of transphobic and homophobic gaslighting at worst. I think back to that day, embarrassed that I struggled with the institutional power that I had "over" my student that almost prevented a much-needed queer bonding moment, rather than recognizing the complicated power structures at play; a move sociologist Jonathan Hearn might distinguish as a power "with" my queer-as-fuck sibling.[17] I think back to that day, grateful that she affirmed me in ways that busted a dichotomous power structure, in ways that stripped through my mostly-masculine exterior. I think back to that day, grateful that I had access to Keating's framework, access to trans-specific issues with dysmorphia and the body and the social and cultural systems that deny the most vulnerable of our queer siblings life and breath; grateful that I saw her through her moment of terror; grateful that she saw me through my moments of exhaustion; grateful for all of the forces in the universe that pushed me say, "You have five minutes," and grateful for all of the forces in the universe that compelled her to come to my door on this unusually warm May day.

Our 5 minutes turned into at least an hour. She talked more openly about her grandmother and their mutual love and respect for one another. We talked about her sadness for her cisgender gay uncle who could never quite let loose, living in fears he has made his own but are fears that are not his to bear. As we talked, I sat in silent mourning for my own difficulties with "letting loose" from the confines of the gender I've been ascribed, reflecting on my own fears that should not be mine to bear. We talked about our toxic family members and their propensity to project. Tears and sniffles slowly transformed in smiles and giggles, while tea and shade danced with each other from her cup to mine and back again. In our time together, I found the affirmation of my struggles through her stories, affirmations that my then-boyfriend inevitably invalidated in the past and would come to invalidate once more in the week that would follow.

As it was clear she was feeling better and ready to return to her room, I finally asked her: "What do you think about these for graduation?" I showed her a picture of my 5-inch white MaryJane platform heels and a picture of my maroon and black doctoral regalia, a fabulous pairing that would never come to fruition as I caved and conformed to my then-boyfriend's discomfort at the sight of the queer combination. Her excitement activated me, and her questions hugged me. We shared in the affective labor that cisheterosexist systems seek to destroy. I then showed her several more pictures of me in various forms of my gender-queerness, including some staged and impromptu drag. This moment was a first for me in my nearly ten years of teaching in higher education, as this moment queered the traditional scope of the professor-student relational bond in ways I've never experienced; in this moment, I'm reminded of the question Calafell, a prolific queer woman of color in the academy, writes to her student of color: "Do you know how important your presence has become to me in making this university a place I could live?"[18] In this moment, I breathe into her presence in my life and the ways that her queerness breathes into the genders I work to become. Grounded, for the moment, we finished our conversation with mutual demands for emailed selfies from our respective graduations being held at the same time, a thousand miles apart. Months later, I long for the queer relationality that she and I created together in those moments and the weeks that led to her disruption to my neoliberal flow that day.

I still think back to that day, and the last semester, wondering how different her experience in my intercultural communication class would have been had she had access to me in this way 15 weeks prior. And then I remind myself to stop with the "what ifs" and to stop with the broken scripts that demand my body be something other than what I want it to be, when I want it to be. I remind myself to resist shouldering the burdens of thousands of years of cisheterosexist ideologies both in and outside of the academy that disallow professors from divulging any sense of non-normative self beyond the binary for fear of "ruining" the educational experiences of our students, while simultaneously reflecting on the ways in which I must continue the process of implicating my own internalized cisheterosexist ideologies that dismiss these moments of queer intimacies as something other than what Craig Gingrich-Philbrook writes as "natural, normal, neutral, or necessary."[19] I remind myself that her journey is not my journey, and that I can cheer her on from my position in the world, that I can use my institutional power to assist her in as many ways as I can, and that I can utilize—in the ways that I continue to manifest—my masculine- and class-passing privileges and my White privilege to push my students and colleagues into spaces of discomfort around identity and body politics in ways that many of my women-identified and colleagues of color cannot without being denigrated as complainers, in ways that will have little institutional recourse on my White hirsute body. I remind myself to continue the process of affirmation for our ourselves and our most vulnerable students and colleagues, as affirming transness and blackness and brownness and femmeness and disabledness and working-classness in this cisheterosexist White supremacist ableist Christo-capitalist patriarchy is a labor of resistance and love that has the power to envision a gender futurity so many of us desperately need to survive and thrive in these marginalizing structures. And I remind myself that affirmative resistance may not shift the material realities for my student in this moment, but that affirmative resistance could serve as a one response to bell hook's claim that "profound changes in the way we think and act must take place if we are to create a loving culture"[20]—a culture that cultivates a vast array of affirmative dances that most accurately represent the multiverses of genders, races, sexualities, classes, ethnicities, disabilities, nationalities, religions, sizes, and beauties that our bodies inhabit and perform in the most mundane ways every day.

Naming Queerness That Animates Me: Rearticulating My Gender Dysphoria as Queer Worldmaking

Writing elsewhere, Benny LeMaster and I draw on Gust Yep to conceptualize queer relationality. We write, citing Yep,

[Q]ueer relationality provides the foundation for queer worldmaking through affirming "modes of recognition" characterized by "potentiality and becoming" where the individual crafts a self-determined futurity in the present.[21] ... According to Yep, queer relationality privileges non-normative means of relating within "spheres of intimacy" that range from "fleeting to enduring" and across "spheres of desire" that range from "internally held to externally articulated."[22] ... These spheres help to nuance relational dynamics that emerge in and through the intersubjective constitution of self and/as other in the context of [in that case] bullying across intersectional difference across space-time. The work of queer worldmaking begins by listening with raw openness to the complexity of these queer relational ties while embracing the difficulty of implication.[23]

For me, these spheres of desire have led to a confluence of queer relationalities in a process of queer worldmaking that affirm the affective ties that bind us, processes that have been happening long before I knew the phrase "families of choice."

Queer worldmaking, in my world, happened when my mixed-race trans-sibling processed openly with me about their gender while inviting me to do the same. On countless occasions. Queer worldmaking, in my world, happened when they verbalized their affirmation for my struggle, when they verbalized their affirmation of my departure from normative scripts of gender performativity, when they verbalized that they saw me. And I, them. For me, queer worldmaking happens when my trans-siblings and I sit together, in silence, knowing each other's existence and stories and lives bear the weight of colonial, cisheterosexist, racist, dis/ableist, sizeist, xenophobic, Christo-capitalist structures while our bodies are similarly-implicated and marked as always-already privileged. Queer worldmaking happens, for me, in heart strings that vibrate when they say, "Oh, Miss Greeeeg," and when they shift the Dr. to Dx.

Queer worldmaking, in my world, happened when my queer-identified second-cousin used the phrasing, "I'm as close to a boy as you can get without HRT [Hormone Replacement Therapy]," while lovingly laughing when I respond that we must have stolen each other's genders during a diaper change when we were young. Queer worldmaking happened when we both said, "if only it were that easy," followed by a solid minute of laughter that was filled with the soon-to-be-spoken memories of when, while gaming, I always needed to be Princess Toadstool and she always needed to play as Luigi. Queer worldmaking, for me, happened when she came out as a lesbian; it happened when she went back into the closet because her homophobic mother threatened to disown her; it happened when she came out, three children later, as bisexual in spite of her mother's dwindled control. Queer worldmaking, for me, seems to happen in the knowing look we give each other in those rare moments when we see each other.

Queer worldmaking, in my world, happened when my White trans-sister of affluent origins asked me if I was trans. And it happens when she unexpectedly flips the script between calling me "big sister" and "big brother."

Queer worldmaking, in my world, happens when my genderqueer friend and mentor of color openly expresses their genderqueerness in their social media. And it happens every time someone dismisses my White working-class gender-queer sibling's genderqueerness. And it happens every time I correct myself or someone else regarding their respective pronouns.

Queer worldmaking, in my world, happened when my queer colleague of color expressed to me their messy and contested relationship with gender. And it happens every time I can see the intentional messy in their words.

Queer worldmaking, in my world, happened when my queer crush said he would eat my pussy in the lunch room of an international conference. And it happens every time I think about his brazen acceptance of my messy gender.

Queer worldmaking, in my world, happened when my lesbian sibling called me out for unquestioningly thinking that I could openly and without impunity touch women's breasts, a script taught to me by many White gay men. And it happens every time that moment comes into consciousness for me, and especially when a friend with breasts asks me to touch them.

Queer worldmaking, in my world, happened when an international queer professor asked me if I was queer yet. And it happened when I became upset that I did not understand her question or her intentions. And it happens when I think back to her query. And it happens every time a queer sibling balks against the term queer.

Queer worldmaking, in my world, happens when my queer students see me and I see them. When they feel me and I feel them. When one of us needs affirmation, and one of us is able and willing to deliver. When one of us needs support, and one of us is able and willing to listen with raw openness.

Queer worldmaking happens when any of us fails to meet each other where we are, an occurrence most of us have in common. Queer worldmaking happens when we acknowledge these failings as productive points of departure from normative expectations, when we are willing to implicate ourselves and be implicated by others, when and where we find ourselves willing to listen openly with rawness.

When does queer worldmaking happen for you?

With whom do you have relationships that can foster a sense of commonality, where you can recognize and acknowledge your interrelatedness, and where you can listen to each other with raw openness?

Students, what does it mean for you to know that a professor of yours—could be any one of your professors—struggles with their gender? Professor, what does it mean to you know that some of your students are undoubtedly struggling with their gender? What does it mean for you to think about anyone in your life struggling with their gender, socially and/or culturally?

In what ways do you struggle with your gender? And if you have never thought about your gender before, what does it mean to have to think about it now? What does it mean for you to process through your relative privilege for never having to think about your gender? What other identities have you not had to think about regarding race, sexuality, ability, nationality, ethnicity, religion, size, and beauty?

Dancing with My Gender Struggles: Who Takes the Lead?

For me, queer worldmaking is necessary every time a trans-woman of color is murdered in this world, every time a White trans-woman takes her own life, and every time these two ideas are presented as mutually exclusive ways that our most vulnerable trans-siblings' lives are lost to us. Queer worldmaking is necessary in the minutes, hours, days, weeks, and years leading up to one of their deaths, and it is necessary in the minutes, hours, days, weeks, and years that follow. Queer worldmaking is necessary across time-space in our colonial, racist, cisheterosexist, abilist, sizist, nationalitist, xenophobic, classist, Christian, capitalist patriarchy.

As I sit here, dancing with the myriad of confusing and messy mental musings on my supposed genders, I nod to the Barbie in my body—the Barbie that is big and beautiful and hairy and marked by what most of society deems masculine. I hug her chubby belly deeply, breathing into the anxiety that these words on these pages may one day haunt me, knowing that this very anxiety and fear is bred of a common experience for many queer, trans, and genderqueer people around the world. And so I pull my imaginary hair up into a tight pony tail atop my "male-patterned" baldness, and I take a deep breath in hopes that my struggles with genders will continue to contribute to dislodging and disrupting normative structures and institutions that necessitate the making of queerer worlds.

Notes

1 Gregory Sean Hummel. "Dancing in/out/around/about the Closet: Narrating Autoethnographic Agency from [a] Marginalized Voice." (Master's thesis, Colorado State University, Fort Collins, 2010).

2 Richard G. Jones Jr. "Putting Privilege into Practice through 'intersectional Reflexivity': Ruminations, Interventions, and Possibilities." *Reflections* 10, no. 1 (2010): 122–125.

3 Judith N. Martin and Thomas K. Nakayama. "Thinking Dialectically about Culture and Communication." *Communication Theory* 9, no. 1 (1999): 1–23, doi: 10.1111/j.1468-2885.1999.tb00160.x; Judith N. Martin and Thomas K. Nakayama. "Intercultural Communication and Dialectics Revisited," in *The Handbook of Critical Intercultural Communication*, eds. Thomas K. Nakayama and Rona T. Halualani (Malden, MA: Wiley-Blackwell, 2010), 69–83. The privilege-disadvantage dialectic asks us to recognize that we can be both privileged and disadvantaged simultaneously, relative to the identities we embody in relation to the people and contexts within which we communicate. In that,

"hierarchies and power differentials are not always clear. Individuals may be simultaneously privileged and disadvantaged, or privileged in some contexts and disadvantaged in others" (Martin and Nakayama, "Thinking," 17-18).

4 Kathryn Sorrells. *Intercultural Communication: Globalization and Social Justice*, 2nd ed. (Thousand Oaks, CA: Sage, 2016).

5 John T. Warren. "Performing Difference: Repetition in Context." *Journal of International and Intercultural Communication* 1, no. 4 (2008): 290–308, doi: 10.1080/17513050802344654.

6 Benny LeMaster and Greg Hummel. "We, Bully: On Politicizing Compulsory Bullying." *Communication Education* 67, no. 4 (2018): 520–527, doi: 10.1080/03634523.2018.1506138.

7 Martin and Nakayama, "Thinking"; Martin and Nakayama, "Intercultural."

8 Audre Lorde. *Sister Outsider: Essays and Speeches by Audre Lorde* (Berkeley, CA: Crossing Press, 1984/2007), 138.

9 AnaLouise Keating. *Transformation Now!* (Urbana, IL: University of Illinois Press, 2013), 36.

10 Keating, 49.

11 Keating, 30.

12 Cherríe Moraga and Gloria Anzaldúa, editors. *This Bridge called My Back: Writings by Radical Women of Color* (Watertown, MA: Persephone Press, 1981).

13 Keating, 52.

14 Audrey Williams June, "The Invisible Labor of Minority Professors." *The Chronical of Higher Education* 11 (2015): 11, 32, https://www.chronicle.com/article/The-Invisible-Labor-of/234098.

15 Bernadette Marie Calafell. "Mentoring and Love: An Open Letter." *Critical Studies <=> Critical Methodologies* 7, no. 4 (2007): 425–441, doi: 10.1177/1532708607305123.

16 Haneen Ghabra and Bernadette Marie Calafell. "From Failure and Allyship to Feminist Solidarities: Negotiating Our Privileges and Oppressions across Borders." *Text and Performance Quarterly* 38, no. 1–2 (2018): 38–54, doi: 10.1080/10462937.2018.1457173; Richard G. Jones Jr. and Bernadette Marie Calafell. "Contesting Neoliberalism through Critical Pedagogy, Intersectional Reflexivity, and Personal Narrative: Queer Tales of Academia." *Journal of Homosexuality* 59, no. 7 (2012): 957–981. doi: 10.1080/00918369.2012.699835; Krishna Pattisapu and Bernadette Marie Calafell. "(Academic) Families of Choice: Queer Relationality, Mentoring, and Critical Communication Pedagogy," in *Identity Research and Communication: Intercultural Reflections and Future Directions*, eds. Nilanjana Bardhan and Marc P. Orbe (Lanham, MD: Lexington, 2012), 51–67.

17 Jonathan Hearn. *Theorizing Power* (New York, NY: Palgrave Macmillan, 2012).

18 Calafell, 426.

19 Craig Gingrich-Philbrook. "Removed, and Making Do." *Text and Performance Quarterly* 30, no. 4 (2010): 455, doi: 10.1080/10462937.2010.509449.

20 bell hooks. *All about Love: New Visions* (New York, NY: Harper Perennial, 2000), xxiv.

21 Gust A. Yep. "Further Notes on Healing from 'The Violence of Heteronormativity in Communication Studies.'" *QED* 4, no. 2 (2017): 120.

22 Yep, 120.

23 LeMaster and Hummel, 525.

Bibliography

Calafell, Bernadette Marie. "Mentoring and Love: An Open Letter." *Critical Studies <=> Critical Methodologies* 7, no. 4 (2007): 425–441, doi: 10.1177/1532708607305123.

Ghabra, Haneen and Bernadette Marie Calafell. "From Failure and Allyship to Feminist Solidarities: Negotiating Our Privileges and Oppressions across Borders." *Text and Performance Quarterly* 38, no. 1–2 (2018): 38–54, doi: 10.1080/10462937.2018.1457173.

Gingrich-Philbrook, Craig. "Removed, and Making Do." *Text and Performance Quarterly* 30, no. 4 (2010): 453–455, doi: 10.1080/10462937.2010.509449.

Hearn, Jonathan. *Theorizing Power.* New York, NY: Palgrave Macmillan, 2012.

hooks, bell. *All about Love: New Visions.* New York, NY: Harper Perennial, 2000.

Hummel, Gregory Sean. "Dancing in/out/around/about the Closet: Narrating Autoethnographic Agency from [a] Marginalized Voice." Master's thesis, Colorado State University, Fort Collins, 2010.

Jones Jr., Richard G. "Putting Privilege into Practice through 'intersectional Reflexivity': Ruminations, Interventions, and Possibilities." *Reflections* 10, no. 1 (2010): 122–125. http://thekeep.eiu.edu/commstudies_fac/3.

Jones Jr., Richard G. and Bernadette Marie Calafell. "Contesting Neoliberalism through Critical Pedagogy, Intersectional Reflexivity, and Personal Narrative: Queer Tales of Academia." *Journal of Homosexuality* 59, no. 7 (2012): 957–981. doi: 10.1080/00918369.2012.699835.

June, Audrey Williams. "The Invisible Labor of Minority Professors." *The Chronical of Higher Education* 11 (2015), https://www.chronicle.com/article/The-Invisible-Labor-of/234098.

Keating, AnaLouise. *Transformation Now!* Urbana, IL: University of Illinois Press, 2013.

LeMaster, Benny and Greg Hummel. "We, Bully: On Politicizing Compulsory Bullying." *Communication Education* 67, no. 4 (2018): 520–527, doi: 10.1080/03634523.2018.1506138.

Lorde, Audre. *Sister Outsider: Essays and Speeches by Audre Lorde.* Berkeley, CA: Crossing Press, 1984/2007.

Martin, Judith N. and Thomas K. Nakayama. "Intercultural Communication and Dialectics Revisited." In *The Handbook of Critical Intercultural Communication*, 69–83. Edited by Thomas K. Nakayama and Rona T. Halualani. Malden, MA: Wiley-Blackwell, 2010.

Martin, Judith N. and Thomas K. Nakayama. "Thinking Dialectically about Culture and Communication." *Communication Theory* 9, no. 1 (1999): 1–23, doi: 10.1111/j.1468-2885.1999.tb00160.x.

Moraga, Cherríe and Gloria Anzaldúa, editors. *This Bridge Called My Back: Writings by Radical Women of Color.* Watertown, MA: Persephone Press, 1981.

Pattisapu, Krishna and Bernadette Marie Calafell. "(Academic) Families of Choice: Queer Relationality, Mentoring, and Critical Communication Pedagogy." In *Identity Research and Communication: Intercultural Reflections and Future Directions*, 51–67. Edited by Nilanjana Bardhan and Marc P. Orbe. Lanham, MD: Lexington, 2012.

Sorrells, Kathryn. *Intercultural Communication: Globalization and Social Justice,* 2nd ed. Thousand Oaks, CA: Sage, 2016.

Warren, John T. "Performing Difference: Repetition in Context." *Journal of International and Intercultural Communication* 1, no. 4 (2008): 290–308, doi: 10.1080/17513050802344654.

Yep, Gust A. "Further Notes on Healing from 'The Violence of Heteronormativity in Communication Studies.'" *QED* 4, no. 2 (2017): 120.

BEAUTY IN THE INTERSECTIONS

Reflections on Quiet Suffering

Amber L. Johnson

Mud

"It is often dirty work, this digging into the rich soil of humanity. Digging into our humanity, we cannot keep the soil out from under our nails, the clay off our faces, and the sand away from the folds of our skin. We write with humility about that which makes us remember our humanity, that which makes us human."[1]

Research is supposed to be Clean
        Formulaic
    Scientific.
Washed White as Snow
Pure
        Signifying Truth
           on a sheet of 60 lb card stock white as the hands that wrote It.
research is not supposed to be dirty.
      black.
make you cry.
      feel pain.
drag you through muddy waters and plop your ass
        on the side of a subway train with no directions for return.

there is no return from autoethnography.
        only the movement forward
           with a knowledge designed to procreate,
      should it desire to do so.

I think about the moments of childhood where beauty was thrown at my face. Like a punching bag I was expected to take those throws. Shadowboxer. A champ, I was beautiful. I didn't have the harsh experiences of the chocolate girls being called monkeys, tar and test tube babies. I didn't have the desire to wash the black off my face or use skin lightening cream. Didn't matter I was disinterested in matching hair bobbles and new fashion. Didn't matter that I wanted to bake mud pies or preferred eating my boogers in solitude. I wasn't interested in beauty from an US American standard perspective. And at 32 years old, I find myself in the same place. With a bright pink mohawk, missing toe nails from mud races, and a bag full of athletic gear.

Small sparrow studs in my ears, the desire to be a bird, and fly against the current.

Perhaps because despite being beautiful, I was still bullied. Still hurt. Still ashamed. I remember girls teasing me, accusing me of wanting to be White. Calling me names. Accusations of not being Black enough. Too light to be an Oreo, I was just the cream in the middle. Fake. Too good. Thought my shit smelled like Reece's Peanut butter cups. There were many nights I wished I could wash the beauty off my face and just blend in. Many nights I wished for darker skin so I could be a friend to the chocolate girls. Many nights I wondered why those same chocolate girls who I sought approval from hated me so much because I was born with ugly pale skin. Summers I spent in the sun trying to darken my body. But no matter how many times I tanned, winter washed away the color like a hose of purification. So I resorted to making mud pies. Watching my hands darken against the squishy substance, wishing it was permanent. It is no wonder autoethnography chose me.[2] Autoethnography likes people who aren't afraid of their own dirt.

Dark

> You are beauty personified
> A refracted sun ray at midnight
> Peach nectar after dark
> Heavy syrup dripping from rain clouds
> Dark chocolate staining my tongue
> Sincere as the wind kissing my cheek on a summer evening
> Rain cleanses
> So does honest reflection
> However dark it may begin
> And however dark it may remain

★ ★ ★

Intersectionality stems from a desire to acknowledge the ways multiple identities overlap, transect, and interact within social, personal, economic, and political structures. As a Black woman, race is always there, but perhaps not as important or visible as other facets of my identity in a particular moment. Intersectionality studies allow researchers to embrace salience and multiplicity as fluid responses to stimulation and experience, resulting in more empathy, more compassion, less generalization, and, thus, sometimes messy, unkempt, unresolved epistemological embodiments.

Performative autoethnography calls for inserting the bodily flesh and its many positions as ways of knowing. Engaging what Alexander and Warren term *autopoietic*[3] narratives, I summon a creative yet critical articulation of my lived experiences in a textual performance where different perceptions and standpoints of beauty enter conversation,[4] and create new memories and new experiences, that, in this case, foster a space for understanding and possibility. Following Boylorn's successful plan to trouble boundaries of race, marking them as incessant and in constant negotiation,[5] I wish to trouble boundaries of binary labels attached to class, beauty, and sexuality in addition to race, and the ways in which markers of authenticity, desire, and positionality influence our perceptions of self.

Through performative and poetic storytelling, I share memories attached to beauty and how the aesthetics of perfection dance in the intersections with gender, race, class, and geography. Beauty is a contentious frame, not always settled comfortably in the eye of the beholder, not always a disappointment, but something complex, laced with tension, and personally and politically connected to systems designed to flatline the value of the marginalized bodies. I struggle with these stories, wondering whether they are just as meaningful as other stories I have published and shared privately. Wondering whether they have a place in this volume. I don't find answers. Only the capacity to dig deep inside, purging my past in an attempt to help someone else's ability to deal with their own shit. These are my stories. Our stories. And I think they matter even though I have moments where I want to delete them, wipe them clear, leave them out. I put them here to expose the parts of my life where I experience some of the most privilege because of my light skin, big eyes, bright smile, tall, mesomorph, able body that dwells in spaces where those things matter. To expose is to accept. These are my acceptance speeches. They are not pretty, ironically, but they are mine.

Beauty: First Memories

My first memories of being beautiful follow my body back into pre-adolescence. I grew up on a street of all boys. And while some of those boys were friendly, some of them were not so silly, but rather threatening. The one I had a crush on told me I was cute as he spun me in the middle of streets. He was like a bigger big brother. Likely a pre-teen or tween at the time, he sported a loose, curly afro, and had skin the color of butter scotch. His thick-framed glasses may or may not have been held together by white tape across the bridge of the nose. He made me feel special in that beautiful, innocent memory kind of way.

But the teenage boy up the street was not the same. He was a Brown boy with a football-shaped head and close fade. He lived in the biggest house on the street, the one we were never allowed to go into. He told me I was beautiful as he lured me deep into his backyard for a game of hide and seek. He sat on an old, weather worn, dingy, piss-stained mattress and began to take his pants off while I asked shyly, where is everyone else? Hiding? He told me I was beautiful when I sensed something was wrong and thought to run. He told me I was beautiful when he grabbed me by the ankles, forcing me to trip and face plant into the dirt. My Brown, dirt-stained face was still beautiful when he let my ankle go so he could stand up and get better footing to grab me. I wasn't so beautiful when I was too quick for his clumsy ascend, and I ran as fast as my feet could carry me. I was six years old. Beauty has been my thorn for a long time.

Writing about beauty as a person who has been told by strangers and loved ones alike that she is beautiful her entire life feels blasphemous. Like the blond-haired, blue-eyed White girl attempting to plead her case of reverse racism. What am I trying to accomplish here? To purge my own feelings of doubt, fear, and shame associated with wanting to be desired? I want to think my stories are similar to other women identified folks. I reckon my struggle with beauty is a universal one. Regardless of the angle/position along the intersectional continuum of attractiveness, or the types of experiences, women folk are subjected to the harsh realities of pressure placed upon our bodies to present beautifully, be perfect, perform as ideal women, as sexual objects, as flesh created to be desired. My definitions of beauty were so narrow, so defined by heteronormative sexualities, that I, too, manipulated who and what I was to fit standard definitions. However, I understand my body moves through the world with the privilege to fit standard definitions of beauty easier than others, and that my perceived cis gender identity prevents me from experiencing particular types of violence. It isn't just the body that defines us. It isn't just the shape of the noses, the color of the eyes, the length and texture of the hair, the size of the pores, the perkiness of the breasts, the roundness of the ass, or the definition in the legs and biceps; it is about the way lingering eyes consume those body parts, take them in, digest them, speak about them to us, for us. Those lingering eyes don't just belong to them, they belong to us too. It is also about the way those eyes turn violent when they perceived our bodies or behaviors to be violations of their expectations. Gender is ugly in many ways. And in my privileged body, I tend to suffer silently.

The Talent Agency, Age 7, Beverly Hills, CA

I was discovered by a talent agency when I was seven years old. I was a part of an after-school program and Cunningham modeling agency came to recruit fresh faces for their Beverly Hills office. They chose me, the bright skinned, big eyed, girl. My look was palatable to them. My body was skinny like Olive Oyl. My hair was long and "manageable." I was articulate in a "you talk like a White girl" kind of way. I was perfect enough to land national commercial gigs like "Get Urkelized with Urkel O's," Jaleel White's short-lasting cereal career. During the filming of his commercial, I was pretty enough for him to say to me, "Your face is flawless." I told him to "shut up." I thought he was making fun of me. I was perfect enough to win beauty pageants and be cast as Dorothy in *The Wiz*, but not perfect enough to be cast for Barbie. For five years, Cunningham Talent Agency sent me on auditions for Barbie commercials. Each time I was sent to audition, I would quietly walk into a room alone, my body on display in front of a panel of four to six White men requesting that I move, dance, laugh, talk, and play with the Barbies on the table. Nevermind that I didn't play with Barbies and was rather afraid of dolls, this was work and I was being judged by those men watching with piercing eyes, deciding who would play with Barbie on the big screen. They never booked me. Countless auditions, never a job. Those long car rides home from Hollywood to Inglewood were always painful. My mother would attempt to console me by saying:

"I don't know why they keep sending you on those auditions, you never book them. They always cast them funny looking White girls. You're prettier than Barbie."

Imagine hearing that for five years. Five years. My young mind interpreted her statements as such:

"I don't know why they keep sending you on those auditions, you never book them."

Interpretation: inadequacy

"They always hire them funny-looking White girls"

Interpretation: Mommy makes White girls look bad because she knows my beauty is not equal to White beauty, even though I pass as a bi-racial child.

"You're prettier than Barbie"

Interpretation: Back-handed compliment, kind of like the qualifier: "I have Black friends" after using the word "nigga."

Desire and the Other, Ages 17, 12, and 33, St Louis, MO

After I graduated high school at 17, I moved to St Louis, Missouri to pursue my undergraduate education. After 17 years of fitting the standard definitions of beauty for a young Cali girl (tall, thin, light skin, long hair, sharp and small facial features), I found myself all of sudden othered by my native St. Louis classmates. My butt was way too small, my skin was way too light, my hair was way too natural, and my accent was way too proper. They labeled me, White, almost as it if was an accusation. But I was also an anomaly. I performed bohemian ethnic

Black girl blues to perfection. Headwraps in extravagant west African prints, distinctive fashion that blended a mix of styles from various South East Asian and West African countries, sage and nag champa incense, and a chill vibe only the state of California coupled with nice Midwestern parents could bread. I confused my classmates. They called me Oreo, told me I was weird. Eventually, I started to shroud my beauty in oversized clothing to avoid the naming. But like clockwork my mother would highlight my visibility and say,

"I love when White men look at you with desire, but can't have you."

My mother spoke from a position of empowerment and took ownership over something that those in power could not have. But that empowerment did not translate. I felt abused. I felt dirty. Every time a White man looked at me, I scowled. My mother brought to my attention a reality I spent a decade of my life trying to run from. Ironically, I, the model, was cast as spectacle in various commercial and television projects. Intuitively, I, the 12-year-old intellectual, chose to stop modeling. I did not like the way my friends began treating me. I did not like the way they projected their jealousy into my body. Instead of finding new friends who accepted me for who I was, I chose to stop modeling. I didn't want to be on display, and I didn't want to lose my friends. Yet my mother put me back in my place. Not as an aggressor, but just by making a simple statement. I remember my stepfather saying out loud, "children are to be seen and not heard." His words and my mothers' words meshed together to form a refrain that forced me to tread a back alley of my identity and negotiate someone else's gaze.

Fast forward to Summer 2013. I am invited to be a research fellow in New York. My first presentation centers on a story about learning and then unlearning I was Puerto Rican. The performance is set to music. My body wants to dance as the music fills the room and my words pulsate to a rhythmic cha cha cha. But I refuse to move. I refuse to dance. I am looking at the dozen White men sitting around the table, starring at my Brown body, waiting for me to move *it*. I know my presentation will not be as dynamic, but I am too sensitive to dance for *them*. I remember my mother's statement. She may feel empowered by coveting something, but I, the coveted, do not.

On the final night of the symposium, we all celebrate with dinner. One of my colleagues, an older White man, drinks excessively and gets a little cheeky. I make a comment about his appearance. He is round with a white beard. I think he resembles Santa Clause if he had a summer home in the Hamptons. His response, well why don't you come sit on my lap. He then laughs a big bellied laugh, and continues along the line of *its not like I wasn't thinking it, might as well be honest*. I wasn't surprised, but I was caught off guard. I didn't know how to respond. I felt verbally assaulted. Coveted. Put back in my place as a thing to be desired by *them*. While a different White male colleague began to tell him his behavior was inappropriate, I packed my things and left. I had had enough.

Story 3: Daddy Issues, Los Angeles, CA

My parents divorced when I was two
I never knew my father as a toddler.
Met him when I was 6.
In the world of heteropatriarchy, he took to me
because I was his smart, beautiful, baby girl.
His trophy. He showed me off.
Like a brand new Rolex, a technological gadget,
he'd recite my specs as if he had anything to do with it.
A laundry list of my childhood accomplishments rolled off his tongue like chocolate.
He is a performance artist of the perfect U.S. American Daddy.
And to this day, the anxiety I harbor anytime I'm performing
is because I don't like people looking at me.

After 18 years, I was honest with my father.
I realized he tried to be there.
He did the best he could.
I forgave both of my parents,
but that intersection took 18 years to build.
The memory of its history I cannot delete in one performance.

So I navigate these streets carefully, recognizing the role my perception plays in the development of this story from inception. Finding that my body yearns to perform, to dance, to sing, to move. But my mind throws shade from a cloud called circumstance.
I am a product of these stories.

I Am Not My Hair, Age 21, Los Angeles, CA

For my 21st birthday, I wanted to match my mamma. She had beautiful long locks. Walked around telling people the Queen has been freed from hair slavery. I wanted to taste that freedom. To feel beautiful about my hair and the way it coiled and attached to itself, forming a strong rope like twine.

I understood my mother's fight for freedom. She told me stories of her mother calling her hair nappy. Straightening it with a hotcomb. Burnt ears and grease spread thick across her hairline.

I experienced it decades later. Sitting in the same chair, same kitchen as my mamma. Grandma making me beautiful.

Straightening my hair so I would look more like the other girls with "good" hair.

I also remember my grandmother telling my mother she had snakes growing out of her head. She hated my mother's locks. But something about my mother locking her hair freed her from the negative comments. And I knew it would free me too. So at 21, instead of enjoying my freedom to finally drink and party, my mother and I celebrated for 16 hours while I locked my hair. A bonding experience with three Black women pouring our souls out over hair-stories.

Free queens together. Connected to our hair. Twined together in story.

That moment was beautiful, even though it extended from a not so beautiful sentiment rooted in normative notions of "good" hair.

These next moments are not all beautiful.

Sometimes, beauty is pain. Pain on the inside. Pain on the outside. Pain.

We don't realize the fragility of beauty until beauty is taken away from us, painfully at times, on purpose at times. Fragile and complicated regardless.

Fat, Bald, Black, and Pregnant, Age 26, Los Angeles, CA

I was one month pregnant when I cut my locks off. Glowing from pregnancy. Happy. My then husband helped me. Each lock falling to the floor felt like a release from an energy I no longer wanted or needed. Waste length locks that flowed in the wind and followed me into rooms. Locks that commanded attention and compliments. Lock that lay on the floor in pieces of unremarkable fuzz that would turn into regret.

I was one month pregnant and still living in my mesomorph body. Tall, thin, in shape. Fine as some would call it. And cutting my locks off did nothing to change that summation. Until I began growing the baby in my womb, and the belly, hips, nose, and thighs surrounding it.

I was growing, and growing fast. I told myself I would be one of those power moms who ate raw and vegan, did pushups in maternity work out pants, and moved gracefully like a swollen gazelle through the city streets. Instead, I ate. I ate everything I wanted to because I had a visible excuse. French fries oozing the grease from chili and cheese. Fat, green, sour-pickles with now n' later candy juices pouring down the sides. Molten hot chocolate lava cake and vanilla bean ice cream. You name it, I craved it; you made it, I ate it. It felt good to indulge and blame it on the baby growing inside of me. I was finally able to eat without my consciousness telling me I was killing myself. Making myself *fat* as if *fat* was a bad, ugly, damaging word. The borderline anorexia I experienced as a college student vanished.

I was eating and growing at a rapid weight. I began to miss my hair. Missed the thing that marked me as distinctly feminine and pretty. Missed the thing that could rival my growing nose and hide it from onlookers.

I never realized how my hair and self-esteem were connected, or the fragility of my self-esteem until I gave birth. For some reason, I assumed that when I pushed the baby out, the fat would follow and the baby would replace my baldness like a new accessory.

The fat did not slide out.
> The hair did not grow back.
>> The baby did not mask my flaws.

I was fat, Black, bald-headed and no longer pregnant.

I was dying inside.

To be Black in US America is ugly enough.
> To be fat is ugly enough.
>> To be fat and Black? Damn.
>>> To be fat, Black, and bald headed, disaster.

Stripped of my femininity,
> grace,
>> beauty,
>>> intelligence,
>>> worth,
>>>> the
>>>> list
>>>> goes
>>>> on.

I grew very conscious of my lack of hair and my post-mortem tiger striped skin and squishy belly dangling over my pant closure like a deflated whoopee cushion filled with stale water and painted with stretch marks.

When people would ask me when I was due, despite the newborn baby cooing softly in my arms, I fantasized about slitting their throats so they could no longer speak.

And when they would continue to let words spill out of their mouths, words like "for just having had a baby, you sure look great." I wanted to feed them their tongues and watch them choke.

The Transition or Finding Myself in My Body, Age 32, Houston, TX

It happened over a two-year period. It started with me building muscle and changing my body. I lost over 50 pounds and built biceps my shallow mind deemed worthy of a squeeze. Then I cut my hair, *again,* after growing it out for four years. Jarring. I forgot how to love myself. I felt ugly. I could feel the femininity washing away from my body with every change I made, but it was the feminine that I had been taught to love about myself for so many years. It was the pretty privilege that taught me I was worthy. And here I was, sabotaging my pretty privilege. The compliments stopped. The staring stopped. I became invisible. I wanted the invisibility in theory, but I had no idea how inadequate it would make me feel as a human being who was taught that the complimentary gaze was what made you valuable as a woman. After I cut my hair, I had to fall in love with myself all over again. And it proved to be a difficult process. I think of the transition narratives I have read and the way they must skip over the part that illustrates just how scary it is to craft these changes and grow beyond everything you were taught was right and diving head first into a very confused can of worms who are also searching for something stable just like you. I started buying new clothes. First straight cut slacks and simple button-ups from the women's department that were labeled "boyfriend cut." Then accessories. A big watch, bowties, neckties, fedoras. Then tattoos. Lots of tattoos. I stopped wearing make-up. Eventually, I built the courage to start shopping in the men's section. I found that the cut of the pants fit my androgynous body better. I was beginning to love my new self. I got more tattoos. My wardrobe almost completely shifted, and the complimentary gaze began to return, only from a different audience. New wardrobe, new hair, new muscles, new acceptance of my more androgynous body that once caused me shame but was now welcome, new appreciation for small breast that can flatten with a sports bra, new love for a straight waist and small butt that can be easily hidden in trousers and slacks, an acknowledgement of the self-hate I went through when I began to shift in all manners of my life. I learned how to wear make-up again without feeling *wrong*. I developed a new appreciation for arriving in a place closer to freedom replete with self-love, new relationships, romantic love, and family dynamics that constantly push me to ask these questions and be thankful. I also began to see very clearly that I gave up one set of rules for a new set of rules. In the beginning, I had to learn the rules. Now I have fun breaking them. I am different now. But I am not done.

Relapse. Or Finding Myself in a New Body, Age 37

I am definitely not done. At age 34, I stop training and learn to paint seriously. My life changes. I find pleasure and purpose in paint strokes designed to interrogate oppression more deeply, render justice more visually. Painting takes over my free time, resulting in the direct neglect of my physical health. I have re-imagined my purpose only to relapse back into body image and gender dysphoria. You see, there are moments. Moments of becoming and dismantling. Sometimes long moments, sometimes short moments, sometimes fleeting moments, sometimes a lingering too long moment like house guests I wish would depart. Moments where I doubt my value, my worth, my ability, my growth. Moments where I wonder why I do any of the things I do. Moments where imposter syndrome flanks me on both sides, whispering, "Who do you think you are?" Moments when I give into the belief that my squishy coming back is somehow a failure. That my softened muscles and loss of brute strength over the past three years when I decided to paint instead of train my body are somehow a failure. Moments where I can't stand to touch myself, or grow angry when I misgender myself, or wonder if I ever was what I thought I was. There are moments. I am not done. Just in a constant state of growing, transforming, learning, relapsing, and loving again.

Epilogue, Age 37.5, New York, NY

I have a tattoo on my forearm of an Ouroboros dragon. The Ourboros dragon signifies transformation by eating its own tail in a circulatory formation of renewal. As it consumes, so it grows, changing both its form and the form to come. Our transitions echo the Ouroboros dragon when we treat them as sites of self-reflexive knowledge with the specific intention to create new stories and new ways of understanding and bettering our world. If the Ouroboros dragon only deconstructed the world, it would eat its own structural waste. I don't want to live in a world that eats its waste. I want to live in a world where our fruitful knowledge creation bears new beginnings. A world that plants seeds for new life. That is the point of our stories. That makes us significant as we transition beyond strict definitions of gender. Our stories must be a form of knowledge that feeds off its own fruitful creation. The Ouroboros dragon must generate a new body in order to eat their own tail. We are a part of the assembly line of transformation, using our words and performance to change the very nature of our bodies, our communities, and our world. We are the rebuilders. And that matters.

It is in the moments of recovering from the assaulting eyes upon my skin that I learn to accept my body for what it is. I begin embracing other parts of me that are beautiful in an effort to regenerate my confidence. It wasn't until I began writing these stories that I started to understand my history. Understand the ways in which each comment, each gaze, defined a part of who I am. I had to dig deep and confront the ways racism, colorism, body image, hair, class, beauty, geography, and other identity markers intersected on and in my body. I had to learn to love me from the inside out, not outside in. How we read and appropriate beauty, normalcy, rightness and wrongness directly affect the way we see and understand our bodies, the way we see and understand other's bodies, and the way we perform and use our bodies. Beauty is pain. And the reflection looking back in the mirror when we fail to see beauty staring back at us is pain. Learning to love myself from the inside out took many painful poems, journal entries, conversations, and my own brand of therapy. But now, when I rock my funky colored flat top and gender neutral clothes, I do not think twice about someone defining my beauty based on the length of my hair, the color of skin, or the curves of my waist. I have learned to define beauty by the relationships I foster and my desire to give of myself freely. Sometimes it is easy. Sometimes it is hard. But it is always worthy.

Notes

1 Lesa Lockford. "Talking Dirty and Laying Low: A Humble Homage to Humanity," in *The Green Window: Proceedings of the Giant City Conference on Performative Writing, April 26–29, 2001*, eds. L. C. Miller and R. J. Pelias (Carbondale, IL: Southern Illinois University Press, 2001), 118.
2 Keith Berry. "The Ethnographic Choice: Why Ethnographers do Ethnography." *Cultural Studies Critical Methodologies* 11, no. 2 (2011): 165–177, doi: 10.1177/1532708611401335.
3 Bryant Keith Alexander and John T. Warren. "The Materiality of Bodies: Critical Reflections on Pedagogy, Politics, and Positionality." *Communication Quarterly* 50, no. 3–4 (2002): 328–343, doi: 10.1080/01463370209385667.
4 Dwight Conquergood. "Performing as a Moral Act: Ethical Dimensions of the Ethnography of Performance." *Literature in Performance* 2, no. 5 (1985): 9, doi: 10.1080/10462938509391578.
5 Robin Boylorn. "Gray or For Colored Girls Who Are Tired of Chasing Rainbows: Race and Reflexivity." *Cultural Studies <=> Critical Methodologies* 11, no. 2 (2011): 178–186, doi: 10.1177/1532708611401336.

Bibliography

Alexander, Bryant Keith and John T. Warren. "The Materiality of Bodies: Critical Reflections on Pedagogy, Politics, and Positionality." *Communication Quarterly* 50, no. 3–4 (2002): 328–343, doi: 10.1080/01463370209385667.

Berry, Keith. "The Ethnographic Choice: Why Ethnographers Do Ethnography." *Cultural Studies ⇔ Critical Methodologies* 11, no. 2 (2011): 165–177, doi: 10.1177/1532708611401335.

Boylorn, Robin. "Gray or For Colored Girls Who Are Tired of Chasing Rainbows: Race and Reflexivity." *Cultural Studies <=> Critical Methodologies* 11, no. 2 (2011): 178–186, doi: 10.1177/1532708611401336.

Conquergood, Dwight. "Performing as a Moral Act: Ethical Dimensions of the Ethnography of Performance." *Literature in Performance* 2, no. 5 (1985): 9, doi: 10.1080/10462938509391578.

Lockford, Lesa. "Talking Dirty and Laying Low: A Humble Homage to Humanity." In *The Green Window: Proceedings of the Giant City Conference on Performative Writing, April 26–29, 2001*, 113–121. Edited by L. C. Miller and R. J. Pelias. Carbondale, IL: Southern Illinois University Press, 2001.

YOUR MEMORIES AND MASCULINITIES' MANTRAS

Meggie Mapes

[Your] body is a cultural billboard advertising the effects of selves/others/contexts interacting with and upon it.[1]

'Hegemonic masculinity' is not a fixed character type, always and everywhere the same. It is, rather, the masculinity that occupies the hegemonic position in a given pattern of gender relations, a position always contestable.[2]

In this autoethnographic rendering, you, the reader, are situated as the "I," positioned as the key perspective in the stories. The following essay unfolds through a series of second-person narratives, beginning when you were a young, invincible girl growing up in a small Iowa town where you oscillate between the familiar and the strange, between invincibility and doom.

★ ★ ★

It feels so early, but you slip out of bed and place your bare feet on the carpet of your single-wide Iowa trailer. Stretching, you can hear the rat terrier barking outside and quickly realize that your nap has planted you firmly in dinner time territory. It's not so early after all.

You have to get ready: a classic cornfield party—the type of Midwestern party that you are sadly accustomed. You regularly joke with friends that you grew up alongside the corn stalks. Your eyes roll.

In anticipation, you glance at the dresser mirror, slowly moving focus from your pale white skin to your mid-length blonde hair, never staring directly into your eyes. You try to remember when you chose to look this way but, overall, you feel Ok about your womanness; about the woman that you're becoming.

"I guess it wasn't that hard," you joke to yourself, sarcastically. Secretly it's no secret that you have no idea what you're doing. Does anyone? You remember that, as a young girl, your mother cut your hair into a bowl cut, resulting in numerous folks inquiring about your gender.

"I look like a woman *now*," you surmise.

You want to look like a woman—a desirable woman—but, the "young feminist" pin on the dresser reminds you that you struggle to perform a passive femininity that mark your regular encounters with other women your age. Instead, your single-mother's mantra rings in your ear like a hamster wheel:

> *You do not need a man for happiness.*
> *You can do anything that a man can do.*
> *Stand up for yourself. You are strong.*

You believe those things. You don't yet realize the trail of heteronormativity in your independence mantra. In fact, your young feminist enactments were guilty of only examining "women's relationship to male supremacy,"[3] and while you commonly discuss "the patriarchy" and "male supremacy" with mother, you are not afraid of men.

No way.

You know that you are the same as men.
You are equal.
You will perform equal.

Your feminism makes you feel invincible, an epistemic rendering of theory in your small Iowa body. Feminism, for you, is "a movement that aims to make women the social equals of men."[4] Feminism, for you, feels like a superhero cape granting personal freedom to assimilate toward equality. You can do anything that any man can do.

You remember cracking the code; after all, for your life's duration, you've continuously witnessed and observed a seemingly infallible character trait that guaranteed access to equality: masculinity. Masculinity has, after all, always been an instrument and reward for men's power "and as central to the maintenance of patriarchy and women's subordination."[5] You, too, often conflate masculinity with men and all men with the White men surrounding you.

You laugh, thinking, "I can do that, too"—the mantra slowly playing in the background like subtle elevator music. You fight to laugh.

You are now ready for the summer party and head out with a group of close friends.

You arrive and whiteness grants you entry.

Time passes at the party, and you find yourself living in a familiar feeling. You find yourself fighting.

You try to remember the moment that solidified the fight. You try to remember when you decided to fight—when you decoded the situational symbols to intervene—when fighting became the communicative proof of your power—when your feminism required fighting to stifle your failed femininity.

You feel the sensation where familiarity meets the strange; you know that you have been here before—a feeling of normality that sits just on the tip of your tongue. You cannot name that time and place, though, and the new and strange circumstances pull your knowing to the back of your throat. The strange pulls you back to now.

You are fighting men—pushing, swinging, pulsating toward them—after stepping in to a circle of heteropatriarchy forming firmly around your friend as they taunt him.

"Fag!" they chant.

You push the man with the loudest voice, pushing him squarely in the chest as your feet stay firmly planted in the gravel below.

For much of your life you will play this part of "protector"—a White masculine savior in the name of social justice—a display of toxic masculinity under the guise of honorable protection. Do you feel regret?

For now, you push. You feel invincible. Masculinity pulses through your veins—a materialization of your feminist enactments—an epistemic materialism. Somehow, you operationalize feminism as fighting—fighting that both encompasses and antagonizes masculinity.

"I am equal," you believe.

Only later will you realize that "male supremacist ideology encourages women to believe [you] are valueless and obtain value only by relating to or bonding with men."[6]

Breathing in the Iowa dust in the humid night, you relate. "I can feel it," you think. "Would my body ever lie?"

You began counting your breath;

(1)

   In......

    Out.......

  (2)

   In.......

    Out.......

Time, though, wraps you in a chokehold so tight that you may never breathe again.

You become an olive in a martini glass, unsure if you will float to the top or sink to the bottom. Sunken while soaking in masculine toxicity; a toxin so readily available, sought out, and desired.

You desire it, too.

But he will not push you back, and you resent the perception of fragility. You breathe, finally, and your friends move to leave.

The drive is silent.

As the car pulls into the lot where you live, you hold your breath out of habit. Despite the strength of your demeanor, you resent your socioeconomic status. You live in a trailer, after all, a sort-of local white trash. At the time, though, you don't yet realize the depth your whiteness.

Slowly blinking, memory plays back the night like an unpredictable dream. Holding tight to the story, you exit the car with a now-smashed window—a casualty of leaving the party before White masculinities' grace.

Inside, you open the fridge to scan for anything but Diet Coke—a staple of your mother's type 1 diabetes. No luck, so you grab a glass of water, drinking it in a slow yet militant pace to wash down the dusty remains of the evening. As you look into the night's darkness, you see the familiar medium-length blonde-hair and fair skin reflecting, making eye contact.

"It's Ok," your eyes say in harmony. "What were you supposed to do? You had to fight." You continue staring, convincing yourself that you are not a phony, convincing yourself that you are strong, convincing yourself that others will see your strength and power, too. You feel like you are living praxis.

"The world needs disruptive women. This is the only way."

You play back the mantra as you walk the short hallway to your room:

> *You do not need a man for happiness.*
> *You can do anything that a man can do.*
> *Stand up for yourself. You are strong.*

At the time, you don't yet realize your feminism is contextually grounded—the theoretical strands band in moments of geographic upbringing—your upbringing marked by whiteness in a small Iowa town. Gender was binary for you; a knowledge epistemically rooted in context.

Time passes.

You become older, and you think intently and confidently on how much you have grown and who you have become. You are a strong woman. "You are invincible," you think, pushing out memories of the week.

As you glance out your office window, the dusk kisses the inside of the enclosed glass, hinting at the looming darkness.

"He leaned her over a table." You wince as your memory re-plays despite your resistance. "He had, for months, been finding ways to lean up against her, and he wouldn't stop saying that he loved her smile," she whispered to you. Even now, the story drains you.

"What should we do?" she asks. "He runs the anti-oppression group, too. He has been advocating for sexual assault awareness pins to distribute." You wince again.

"What should we do? How do we fight?" she asks, again. They ask you again and again and again. You feel tired and exhausted, and you are unable to fully grasp the simplicity of words sitting on the tip of your tongue: you don't know what to do. For you, fighting feels different these days—it feels institutionalized—an institution that grants you access through your whiteness. For you, fighting is an emotional battle to show up; a psychic commitment to labor for and with others. Fighting, now, often feels futile. You often miss the feel of your fighting fists. You often feel like a hamster on a wheel, running in circles while every win is clouded by the stormy reality of materialism. You feel doomed.

Before leaving, you quickly glance through your calendar, realizing that tomorrow marks another meeting for a larger discussion on gender-inclusive restrooms. You remember the fight.

"I'm not disagreeing with the idea," she says as another member of the committee. "But as a victim of sexual assault, it makes me nervous."

This is all she says, but you look up quickly, scanning the room. A sea of predominantly White faces shifts their gaze to hers, nodding in a slow sign of support as if to say, "We hear you. Thank you for sharing."

"I'm sorry, what makes you nervous?" you ask. You try not to shake as your memory replays, "it makes me nervous"—the beginning lines of a narrative used to sustain separate restrooms. Your brain is screaming and your words shake.

"As a feminist, I think you'd understand that sometimes it's important to listen to stories of victims," a third person intervenes. You wonder when all feminisms became yours.

You began counting your breath;

(1)
   In......
     Out.......
   (2)
   In.......
     Out.......

"What should I do?" you ask yourself as infinite outcomes play in your mind like a matinee. Fighting feels different these days; fighting feels internalized. You are always fighting yourself, fighting with and toward a consciousness of critical. You worry that your masculinity is showing. Does it belong there?

You blink your way back to the office, trying to forget the verbal fight. As you look into the now dark night, you make eye contact with the eyes of the familiar short, dirty blonde-hair and fair skin reflected in the window. "I can't do this right now," you tell her.

You check your watch to verify what the absent sun has made clear: it is time to go. Grabbing the recently delivered books on feminist theory, you pack your bags and flip off the light.

Walking out into the Midwestern summer night, you curse softly, realizing that you should have moved your car closer to the building. You shake off the nerves as undue paranoia, though you're unsure if the goosebumps from the cool night breeze are a sign of distress or comfort. Standing under a lamplight, your manta rings in your ear like a hamster wheel:

> *Pepper spray is on your person.*
> *Hold your key between your finger.*
> *Look under the car once you arrive.*

The mantra continues like elevator music, and you try to remember when you learned those notes, searching for a direct memory. Somehow, the mantra, like memory, "operates as both quotation and invention, an improvisation on borrowed themes, with claims on the future as well as the past."[7]

You take solace, though, in the familiar walk to the parking lot, noting the light-up blue box positioned nearby for emergencies. It makes you feel invincible. It does, right? You wonder briefly why the light-up blue box didn't help the woman from the story. You wonder how pushing the button would have helped. You wonder if the woman looked under her car. You wonder why there are more light-up blue boxes than inclusive restrooms. You remember that being afraid is futile, that you are equal to any enemy, that you are a fighter.

On the drive home, immense guilt swells throughout your body, and you wonder, "How can I be both a feminist mentor—a place to go for help and a bad feminist, all in a few days?" "How can my feminism lead to the perception of my invincibility to somehow fix a system and simultaneously doom me to inaction?" You have made it about you, again.

The next morning, when you wake, the muscles in your throat contract as you look anxiously around the room for water. You are sick.

You head two blocks to the grocery store where you are a regular customer. Someone is standing outside. "Hello," and you respond with a similar greeting.

"Want to go out sometime?"

"No, thanks, but have a good day," you say while briefly providing a staple Midwestern nod.

You get groceries.

As you exit, you notice that the someone is still standing outside.

"Are you sure I can't take you out? We'd have a great time."

You slightly tilt your head down and shake, "no." For hours, you will scrutinize that moment of passivity; for days, you will wonder where your strength went; for years, you will replay the memory with direct eye contact. Forever, you tell yourself, "I am invincible."

"Bitch," the someone says.

You revel in the word momentarily, almost laughing at the predictability of the language; almost laughing at the ease in which it slipped off of the someone's tongue. You try to remember when "bitch" became part of your mantra—a word you felt feminism would opt to adopt. You try to remember the first time that you were called a bitch and laugh again at your failure. "A memory" seems too specific to reference interactions of repetition.

You wonder how to fight the situation, but instead, you tremble, resentful for feeling weak, for feeling powerless despite the story that you've tried to build around you. You can't remember what fighting means; you can't conjure the correct move so quickly. "I am a bitch. Leave me the fuck alone," you whisper to yourself, slowly oscillating between invincibility and doom.

Once home, you quickly walk into your kitchen and unload the few groceries. Opening the tab of vitamin C, you shake the cold water until the tablet appears fully dissolved. The cool and orange flavored drink provides temporary relief for your swollen throat.

You cry, ashamed of who you were and who you are. You cry tears of pride, too. You were/are a fighter. As you look up, the short, dirty-blonde and pale skinned friend appears in the dark reflection of the microwave.

Making eye contact, you realize that, during many of your life's stories, your enactments of masculinity were situational: White, middle-class, masculinities. You try to remember when you first had this thought—a moment that you're unable to grasp, like a dream that sits on the tip of your tongue. You feel categorically trapped, knowing that, for years, you used masculinity to gender assimilate, viewing masculinity as the key embodiment in opposition to the weakness of femininity. You bought it, giving-in to the constructed categorization of femininity as somehow lesser than, resenting when others viewed your femininity as weakness. You made it all too simple, too categorical.

Placing the now-empty glass on the counter, the small remains of vitamin C leave a grimy taste in your mouth. You try to remember when you first had this feeling—when your lips first had this taste. Your mouth tastes like Iowa dust.

You remember telling the Iowa fight story and a friend responding angrily, later texting you that masculine behavior and roles are antithetical to the women's liberation movement.[8]

"All masculinities?" you think before feeling the obvious ramification of their rhetoric: you are a bad feminist. You are a bad woman. You wonder why your friend assumes that only women should be liberated. You wonder what kind of women they mean.

Time passes.

You are standing inside the conference lobby. Feeling confident and invincible, you scan the open corridor for any sign of coffee; you aren't thirsty and don't need caffeine, but you need something to do. Upon your return, the panel moderator introduces you to the two other male participants: one is a librarian and one is a political science professor. You shake their hands and provide a slight Midwestern nod, asking them general questions about their research and background. They ask you nothing.

You feel anxious to get seated. You want to look at your notes. You feel small, young, too feminine.

Finally, while seated, you inhale the remaining coffee.

You began counting your breath;

(1)
    In......
      Out.......
(2)
    In.......
      Out.......

You shake off the nerves as undue paranoia, though you're unsure if the goosebumps from cool room air are a sign of distress or comfort. Slowly, you trust your labor as your body remembers hours of work. "Just like riding a bike," you think.

Moments before the panel begins, the moderator convenes a quick huddle to consider the participants' speaking order and, as she leads the discussion, your masculine-oriented co-panelists take out a fresh, clean sheet of paper—a paper so white that the audience is reflected.

"That must be for questions," your mind considers, and your face burns with anxiety. "Why didn't you bring extra paper?" you scream, tilting your head down in a gesture of self-doubt. They must be more experienced; they must be more credible and more prepared.

The panel begins, and the moderator introduces each participant: "Dr. A, Dr. B., and Dr. C." You are scheduled to speak last. As introductions unfold, you sit in the middle of Dr's A and B—two men—soon realizing that the clean white paper is their script; an illusion of labor as they spin their unopened pens while they present.

As you speak, you feel powerful in your position, staring down at the sea of eager faces as they peer up into your expertise. You feel masculine in your knowledge. You feel like you belong.

As the panel concludes, audience members ask a flurry of questions to each panelist.

"Dr. A," they begin.

"Oh, Dr. B," they inquire.

Excitement fills your body until a familiar sound is called: your first name. The familiarity catches you off guard in the strangeness of the space. You look around and realize, "Yes: you. They are asking you a question." You answer. You are, after all, a good, feminine, Midwestern girl.

As you drive home, guilt fills your body.

Later, your failure is confirmed as you share the encounter online like a good feminist.

"Didn't you correct them? Didn't you tell them 'it's Dr'?"

"I would have beat them down."

"That's so typical. How did you respond?"

You feel like you didn't fight. Every day is a feminist fight—a fight toward some unknown; a fight amidst the intersections. You consider the ease in which your labor becomes invisible wondering, "wasn't my masculinity enough?" You are tired and replay the day like a bad movie over and over in your mind, asking, "what was the correct response? Why wasn't my body enough?"

Feeling doomed, you lay on your queen-sized bed, slowly petting your wrinkly dog that cuddles you for support. Slightly hysteric, you giggle to yourself at the absurdity that you are, in fact, a Ph.D.

"People really are supposed to call me Dr.!" you laugh out loud and your pup looks up, bewildered. Laughter dulls the feelings of fragility and failure. You remember feeling invincible as a doctoral student, as though the degree would somehow create a protective new layer.

You wonder if you'll ever stop chasing the invincibility cape.

You doze off, remembering the fight story. It wasn't your fight, but the memory plays like the plot of a bad romance comedy: inevitable despite its predictability.

"I almost got in a fight," he bragged to you.

"The someone in the bar was purposefully rubbing up against her. I had to stand up to him. He stopped, but we almost fought," he finished; the tale told through a serious smile. He was pleased with himself. He was waiting for you to be pleased with him, too.

At first, you laugh to yourself, thinking, "I can do that, too." You feel envious as your mantra plays in the background like subtle elevator music:

> You can do anything that a man can do.
> Stand up for yourself. You are strong.

Quickly, though, your body fills with a numb disbelief and confusion as new sounds push their way into your consciousness:

> Pepper spray is on your person.
> Hold your key between your finger

The subtle songs overlay, and you began counting your breath;

(1)

In......

Out.......

(2)

    In.......

    Out.......

Time, though, wraps you in a chokehold so tight that you may never breath again.

You become an olive in a martini glass, unsure if you will float to the top or sink to the bottom. Sunken while soaking in masculine toxicity; a toxin so readily available, sought out, and desired.

You desire it too, but are afraid.

Time passes. You awake, but you're unsure if the awake is reality or dream's mythic screen. You arrive at an unfamiliar street near a park and you park the car, sliding out into the humid Midwestern night. As you walk, someone passes you in the road. As they pass, something drops and bounces off the hot summer concrete.

"Uh, excuse me," you say. "You've dropped something," handing them the fallen item.

The someone takes the item and they outstretch their free hand, as if to offer you a handshake of thanks. Instead, though, your hand is greeted with intent, and you are pulled into the someone's body as they plant a kiss on your cheek.

You feel doomed. You try to fight, pushing the someone while masculinity pulses through your veins—an epistemic materialism. Somehow, fighting becomes both antagonistic to and encompassing of masculinity. You feel invincible.

Panting, you walk quickly to your car. In the driver's seat, you push the lock button and peer into the rear-view mirror.

"[You] believe [you] exist somewhere amid the sociopolitical narratives written on [your] body; you however, duck, and dodge to resist a reifying surface/ body politic" as a daughter, White, Midwesterner.[9] Although you resist, you know, too, that you reify. You are forever invincible, and forever doomed.

Looking at the short, purple-hair and pale skinned reflection, you wonder, what now? Where do we go from here? You try to remember when you first had this thought but the objective memory fades to black.

You drive home.

Notes

1 Tami Spry, "Tattoo Stories: A Postscript to Skins." *Text and Performance Quarterly* 20, no. 1 (2000): 84, doi: 10.1080/10462930009366285.
2 Raewyn Connell. "The Social Organization of Masculinity," in *Feminist Theory Reader: Local and Global Perspectives*, eds. Carole R. MacVann and Seung-Kyung Kim (New York, NY: Taylor & Francis, 2005), 292.
3 bell hooks. *Feminist Theory: From Margin to Center* (New York, NY: Routledge, 2015), 27.
4 hooks, 19.

5 Athena Nguyen, "Patriarchy, Power, and Female Masculinity." *Journal of Homosexuality* 55, no. 4 (2008): 668, doi: 10.1080/00918360802498625.
6 hooks, 43.
7 Joseph R. Roach. *Cities of the Dead* (New York, NY: Columbia University Press, 1996), 33.
8 Judith Kegan Gardiner. "Introduction," in *Masculinity Studies and Feminist Theory: New Directions* (New York, NY: Columbia University Press, 2002), 1–29.
9 Spry, 84.

Bibliography

Spry, Tami. "Tattoo Stories: A Postscript to Skins." *Text and Performance Quarterly* 20, no. 1 (2000): 84–96, doi: 10.1080/10462930009366285.

Connell, Raewyn. "The Social Organization of Masculinity," in *Feminist Theory Reader: Local and Global Perspectives*, eds. Carole R. MacVann and Seung-Kyung Kim (New York, NY: Taylor & Francis, 2005), 252–264.

hooks, bell. *Feminist Theory: From Margin to Center.* New York, NY: Routledge, 2015.

Nguyen, Athena. "Patriarchy, Power, and Female Masculinity." *Journal of Homosexuality* 55, no. 4 (2008): 665–683, doi: 10.1080/00918360802498625.

Roach, Joseph R. *Cities of the Dead.* New York, NY: Columbia University Press, 1996.

Gardiner, Judith Kegan. "Introduction," In *Masculinity Studies and Feminist Theory: New Directions.* New York, NY: Columbia University Press, 2002, 1–29.

LONE STAR FEMINIST

Storming through Autoethnographic Performance

Andrea Baldwin

Scene 1: Pressure Shifts

Setting: (Booker, Texas digital video one [Video of west Texas storm clouds]. One chair down stage left.)

[Lights come up on ME, cue: Henrietta slow mo 1]

ME: Petrichor—the beginning. Petrichor is the word for the smell of rain. Actually, the scent of when rain first meets the soil. I can smell the storm coming. Sometimes, but not always, the universe gives us signs of the shift. Whether we choose to see them or not is always contextual. A lot of the time, we don't notice until its right up on us, and we have to survive on the fly. And only in retrospect, we can see the signs pointing to the shift. Experience teaches me that … and I can smell the storm coming.[1]

In Texas, thunderstorms come in the spring, the mix of cool and warm of atmospheric pressure that changes leaves us privy to flash floods and tornados. Growing up, I knew that from February to May I should mark the signs … the air, which normally smells dry and warm, suddenly has a tiny hint of cool in it. My senses get tingly and my head feels foggy from shifting pressures in the atmosphere, as if to warn me to "be alert" for the change to come. Then the sky … sometimes clear, sometimes overcast, moves and shifts, as if it's uncomfortable too. The wind picks up, forcing you to confront the inevitable, and then … the rumble in the distance, the flicker of lightning in the farthest direction of vision. The storm has arrived, and there is nothing you can do but be present and allow it to pass.

My life was, like many Texans, peppered with knowing that we were proud of our state and who we are. Texans lead with just that … Pride first. I still know the Texas flag pledge and every word to the state song. By. Heart. I didn't even look up these facts to check, I just know them.

STATE PLEDGE "HONOR THE TEXAS FLAG, I PLEDGE ALLEGANCE TO THEE, TEXAS ONE AND INDIVISIBLE." State Bird? Mockingbird. State Flower? Bluebonnet. State Tree? Pecan. State Food? BBQ but was changed to Tacos. State Motto? Friendship.

STATE SONG "TEXAS OUR TEXAS, ALL HAIL THE MIGHTY STATE! TEXAS OUR TEXAS, SO WONDERFUL SO GREAT! BOLDEST AND GRANDEST, WITHSTANDING EVERY TEST, O EMPIRE WIDE AND GLORIOUS, YOU STAND SUPREMELY BEST! GOD BLESS YOU TEXAS, AND KEEP YOU GREAT AND STRONG, SO YOU CAN GROW IN POWER AND WORTH, THROUGHOUT THE AGES LONG"

When I left the state to get my Ph.D., I was annoyed at my colleagues from the Midwest and California who did not share their own state pride or know these facts. It seems foreign to me, just as much as I seemed foreign to them. The pride instilled in Texans leaves us with an effervescent confidence that intimidates some and captivates others. We are resolute in it, which leads to great victory or great embarrassment. Sometimes, Pride can operate with fearless abandon.

Everything is bigger here, the hair, the racism, the hospitality, the hatred, the sky, the shady politics, the love, and the disgust. It all weaves a beautiful, painful tapestry that is the foundation of my identity. I gladly came home after living in the Midwest for years—I missed Texas so much. I defended it even when I didn't live here.

My experience is both familiar and unfamiliar. On or about my first years in college, I first identified myself as a feminist; I said it casually in conversation over drinks with other students in Denton, Texas. The action, of calling myself something, altered my identity. Now both Texan and feminist brought on a new energy of self. The pride of both budding in all aspects of my life. This, now capped with the obvious identity marker of my race. I am a biracial Black woman, so my politic, my skin, my existence is both welcome and a threat to many. I learned at an early age this painful lesson. The song says, "Texas, our Texas" but some days, it's not my Texas … it's someone else's. Someone who doesn't want me to be here, or someone who is envious. But it's my home, and while the slumlord is enduring, they can be cruel at times.

This artistic adventure you chose to watch is my ugly explanation of that. And its ugly, make no mistake, its fucking unpolished, the seams are uneven, its makeup smeared, and the curls are starting to fall and frizz. This explanation is not winning any beauty pageants or getting drinks paid for at the bar. But this explanation is doing its best to look its best … aren't we all though? This explanation of self knows itself, and that it is imperfect. It doesn't mind eating alone in public and or going to events solo. Just like you, it's trying real hard, in a world/state that demands so much of its citizens. It's an experiment in embracing identity, enduring the storm, even when it's a hot mess.

My feminism is messy, it fails sometimes. I always thought that to be a feminist, you needed to be all things feminist. Once someone goes public as a feminist, we expect them to be the embodiment of the entire movement. No one wants to talk about what happened before they called themselves feminist. The times they got called out by other feminists, the times they followed along even when they didn't agree, the times they felt the identity not worth it.

I am not, all things, all of the time. I have, for the sake of friendships and conflicts, felt not worth it, toned down my feminist or Texan rants. I've overlooked misogynist language; I've actively avoided coming to my home region of west Texas for YEARS. I negated who I was on both fronts before I became them.

I realize that a part of calling myself a Texan feminist means that I have to truly embrace the ugly of what both identities mean.

To be a Texan means I love where I'm from, truly, madly, deeply, but that others will hate it just as much. That for every push for political progression, there are national embarrassments that feed the non-Texan haters. And y'all are out there, I know. That for each time I y'all, or say hello to a stranger or smile, someone will think I am a creep. For each part of my life as a Texan that comes naturally, will be a part that is absolutely, and aggressively foreign to others.

To be a feminist, is to embrace the powers of my woman identity, to know the body I have has the potential to give life if I choose or take it away if I choose. But knowing that ability is desperately under fire to be government regulated. That the movement against patriarchy and misogyny is a long, tenacious war, that may not be solved in my lifetime, but I'm going to choose to fight it anyway. That my choice as a feminist to include all genders and even all races and classes does not agree with others, and that as a feminist there are true battles within ourselves.

All this, laced with the fact that I am also Black and Japanese. The melanin in my skin does not, nor has ever allowed me to hide. The struggle is always real (isn't it real for everybody?), but with all this the road is a little more complex. Black women who are activists are often on the front lines of the movement, and get no credit for it, and are often hated by Black men. By this principle, the fact that I am Texan, Black, and feminist means no one fucking likes me. And yet, here I am.

This show is a journey to realize the ever-evolving self, a self that is always in turmoil ... but knowing the turmoil marks a shift. A self I've loved and tried to love all my life. It's about the public figures that I found connection to, that help in that love and evolution and in the need to see our likeness somewhere even in small bids. The storm within ourselves—of three big identity markers, rooted in love and care, to discover and proclaim the obvious—I love Texas, I love being a feminist, and I love being a woman of color.

END SCENE 1

Scene 2: White Lightning and Thunder (Ann and Wendy and Dixie Chicks)

(Pre-Scene: 45 second mashup of Ann and Wendy's "Speeches" laced with lightning and the Dixie Chicks's "Wide open Spaces" [Instrumental]) (Cue Texas lightning video).

On a Friday night, my mom, who was a nurse at Hendrick Hospital in Abilene Texas, was leaving a shift at the hospital to go to a high school football game, she had intentions to stop at the Dairy Queen (DQ) to get a blizzard and pick up my older sister. Until her water broke. She then simply closed her station, called the janitor to clean up, then walked downstairs to labor and delivery and told her friend, a nurse working the desk at Labor and Delivery, to call my father and my grandmother, and then to go to the DQ and get ice cream for her. 6 hours later, I was born. My father was aghast at my mother's chill, my grandmother was furious there was no fuss and that she was not the first called. However, my mother simply requested that no photos be taken of her and her second daughter until she had some lipstick and earrings on. If that's not bad ass, I don't know what else is. Friday night football, DQ, looking good, and handling shit like a boss … it's the Texan way. I would hear that story once a year on or around my birthday and it served as a reminder of how awesome my mom was, and no action, even the miracle of childbirth could not be documented unless we look our best.

When you see lightning, count the seconds … then wait for the sound of thunder. Each second that occurs marks the miles away the lightning or the storm is … or so tall tales tell me. Lightning is the electrostatic discharge that comes from a result of pressure shifts. Light travels faster than sound—but the rumble of the thunder is the true show of power. Sometimes, you only see a tiny crack of lightning that yields a gentle rumble of thunder. Sometimes, the light splits the sky in half with a bright white light … then the thunder rattles the house, shakes your insides and flickers the electricity in the house.

It is a wonder … we see the lightning, and feel the thunder.

Ann Richards is everything you'd expect out of a Texas figure. Tall white hair styled to the sky, she rode Harley and went hunting. She drank too much and had killer one-liners. She was an iron fist in the velvet glove. The second female governor of the state and a lifelong Democrat. She had an "East Texas" accent … which sounds more Southern than Western. Long o's and u's calmly putting her male counterparts in their place.

I was in Elementary school when we got to mock vote for Governor. I am learning that most states don't aggressively teach state history like we do, but I remember her, through my mother. As a small child, I did not know the power of Richards running for office, but I could see the interest in my teachers, who were women, and my mother and her friends. I understood in their voices that something was important to Ann, not just her policies ... but because she was a woman. **We see the lightning, but feel the thunder.**

Because I am a feminist, am I expected to support every woman who goes up for office? Because we identify, am I automatically required to support? The answer at 8 years old was easy, but as an adult, I struggle.

Ann, was my first real vision of Woman power as a kid, and I bathed in the electricity of her campaign and election. I recognized her cool articulation of words when delivering her one-liners, as it came with my Teachers and other Texas women in my life. I imagined being in her presence. I wondered what it would be like to stand next to her. (Pause to smell the air)

I bet she smelled like Mary Kay perfume and baby powder. She looked like every old White lady I knew, but just slightly beyond them ... almost unattainable.

She is the first voice of the older generation of feminists, and is as second wave as they come. She'd march with us if she were alive, pussy hat in tow, but she was not inclusive. She passed quiet anti-LGBT laws during a time when inclusion was just a far-fetched idea. Her daughters pick up the torch where she left off, extending their feminism where Ann's ended.

We'd "yes ma'am, no ma'am ... yes sir, no sir" any and everyone who was older than you. It was a sign of respect. But if we respect our elders, can we honestly critique them? In the way that we can look at an older generation for not knowing current trends, we blame them for these trends too. Before we allow gratitude to come forward to them for building the bridge for activism, sometimes we are quick to critique how they built the bridge ... period. It is a slippery slope, to hold the hand loosely of someone who may snuff the extension of the work we do.

Where Ann was unattainable, Wendy Davis was within my reach. Her famous 2013 filibuster put her on the map, pink tennis shoes and chic Chanel business suit, she read the narratives of women who would be affected. Here, stood a politician who was about the action—and like many other Texan Feminists, that spoke to me. I pull from my Facebook post the morning after:

It takes tenacity to make change.

Yesterday, while I went about my daily actions, I kept a close ear to Austin, Texas where Wendy Davis was proving just that. I think of other notable Texas women, Barbara Jordan, Ann Richards and Molly Ivins who, like her, stood up and remained tenacious against a government that the rest of the world believes cannot be moved. I think of the folks in the spectators' booths, in the galleries of the state capitol, and on the streets outside the building, cheering so loudly the last ten minutes, resulting in killing the vote. I think of the constant refreshing of my twitter page, getting updates from friends and prominent blogs about what's going on.

All this, reminds me it takes tenacity to make change. This morning, as always, I woke up proud to be a Texan. Proud to be born and raised in a state where as a woman of color, I was always against the grain. When one fights all their life, you learn to pick your battles (and your weaponry, so to speak) wisely, and once you have chosen, you never let up. I am proud to watch history as it happened, and proud to say that I am a woman from Texas. Things do not change overnight (well in this case it did, seeing that I woke up to the news that the legislation didn't pass), there's still a lot of work to do, but when you are tenacious and passionate, you can and will accomplish.

We see the lightning, but we feel the thunder...

I wrote that when I was on fire. I was lit up by her power and bravery. She ran for governor off the fire of that action, and lost to Greg Abbott—a deeply conservative man with aggressive Republican views. I was able to work with her when I headed up the campaign to bring her to my alma mater to speak for Women's History Month in 2015. She was a calm and quiet woman, the opposite of Ann's seemingly high energy. But she was gracious, all the way.

I felt like a superhuman, being next to her, I was excited to be in her energy and was hoping that I was getting some super feminist superpower from being around her. She still fights to this day, as tenacity takes little to no breaks off. She wore a pussy hat and marched in January 2016, she is more inclusive than Ann, but also ran a severely ablest commercial against her opponent (who is in a wheelchair) she admits it was a mistake, but the damage was done.

Because we identify, am I supposed to automatically support? I see what Ann and Wendy did for women in Texas, I won't doubt that. However, I do not see me, and in some ways, they don't quite see me either. Ann didn't see the harm of her anti-LGBT laws, and Wendy at the time did not see the harm of her ablest advertisements.

Lightning is lightning but lightning is white. History won't forget them; history will bow to their efforts and turn away from their shortcomings. Privilege in activism is a luxury that is exclusively White. Their Pussy hats fit easily on their White lady heads and snug over their white hair. Whiteness reminds me my hat might struggle to fit on my head. I know this—I try not to fault them for it, but it leaves me with a feeling of frustration and longing that I do not know how to process.

When I was 3, my mom enrolled me in Ballet classes. In every activity I was the "raisin in the white rice" easy to find. A sea of blond White girls next to her little copper skinned baby with an afro bun. Through the observation mirror, other mothers would ask who their daughters were, and when they asked my mom, she played along, describing me based on my outfit and avoiding other distinguishable characteristics. I could see her nonverbals in the mirror and if she could say what she wanted to say I imagine she would have turned and said, "Bitch … the Black one."

I did my best, to look my best. But I remain unseen. And my story is common, the stories of White feminism are paramount, and we go to great strides to keep it that way it seems. When I think of Ann and Wendy, I must think of them as imperfect, and that is hard to do, we want our heroes to be absolute perfection, the symbol of hope. However, Light means we also create shadows, and after all, even the creation of lightning is imperfect—the mix of positive and negative electro neurons happen all the time, only when the right mix happens, when the right—white—circumstances occur … that is when lightning strikes.

The lightning makes the storm and is a part of the whole, we see the lightning but we feel the thunder.

END SCENE 2

Scene 3: All Hail and Reign (Barbara Jordan and Leticia Van De Putte)

(45-second mashup of Barbra and Leticia speeches. Barbara from the Democratic National Convention and Leticia from the night of the filibuster. Then Cue "Hail storm videos on slow mo")

The sound comes after the sight … and on occasion, the storm brings intense precipitation. Thunder and Hail bring emotion out of me based on the sound. I've never been outside when hail has erupted but the sound, on rooftops, on car roofs is terrifying, even when it's pea sized, you wonder if the sheer amount of it all will cave your shelter. Thunder claps most intense with my memory, I recall the sights of lightning, but the feeling of thunder in my body—the way it makes my hair stand on end, the way I feel it in my heart—connects me and makes me aware and pay attention.

I first heard of Barbra Jordan when I was 17. I lived my life knowing of Texas history, the White men who were once "immigrants" [Air quotes made with sarcasm] to Texas who fought to settle and colonize the land I now reside in. The stories of White women like Susanna Dickinson who held down the fort at the Alamo and Lady Bird Johnson with her gardens. I knew them in songs as a child and in picture books. I didn't know Barbara Jordan until I was in high school for a special "Black History Month" event where I was picked from the handful of Black students to participate. Isn't this always the way of history? Unless we are White or male we stumble upon ourselves, our story. I remember being asked to read from a card for the announcements about her. Isn't that always the way? As people of color we stumble upon our history, stumble upon ourselves. I didn't know how much I needed Barbara Jordan until I was 17.

She was a successful Lawyer who grew up in Houston's 4th ward, a prominent Black community, she grew up poor, became a powerful leader in civil rights and lead the impeachment hearings for President Nixon. To this day, that's all I knew about her. Prior to doing research for this show ... that still remains what I know about her.

I grappled with this as I wrote this show ... do I educate you on this woman, or am I honest about my knowledge? Am I a bad Black feminist for not educating you? Even worse, am I a bad Texan feminist for leaving her story short?

Bad Black feminist ... maybe. Black feminist stories are always sold short. Feminism can be many things, but not intersectional. We stay saving White feminists from themselves, much like Barbara Jordan did for Ann Richards and the countless lives who are better for the work she did. She was not flashy or radical like Rosa Parks or Angela Davis, she stayed in her lane, and worked the system to her benefit. In history's eyes, if history chooses to remember her, she is unremarkable.

If well-behaved women rarely make history, Ms. Jordan is the proof of that. She is the rumble of the storm, the soft murmur of thunder in the distance. The smattering of pea sized hail in the storm. Effective in warning, does its job, but no cause for alarm. This is what it's like every day as an activist. Black activism is sometimes invisible labor. That for every Angela Davis, there are at least 50 Barbara Jordan types that exist. Feminism sometimes is about timing and action. Many of us do the work not for the notoriety, and yet sometimes get angry if we are not seen. WE, Black bodies, are not seen in a lot of spaces, and I am no angel here ... In the scene to follow you will see me wax deep poetic about another Black body from the same hood.

I am imperfect. This is an elder I should honor, and yet, I do not know much more about her than what I've given you. The sound becomes before the light. I am in a lot of ways invisible labor, in the way that she is. WE do the work beyond knowing if we will get the acknowledgment because if not me, then who?

Right time right place? Impact is all about timing. The circumstances need to be just right, the alignment to the stars just so, the timing precise. Good Feminism is about timing, right?

It's not feminism unless it's documented, that selfie at the march with you and your girls has to be posted with the hashtag feminism or it's not feminism!

Every comment on social media fighting patriarchy has to happen there and not in quiet ephemeral conversation or it's not feminism.

I need to tell you, and you and you and you that I am a feminist every time and every chance I get because it's not feminism if it's not documented.

IF I don't proclaim it, you will forget and I will miss my cue, my timing, my position in the world ... and I am a Fucking Feminist! Your invisible labor does not count here!

I don't blame the rhetoric. I don't blame the need. I don't blame the ones who hit the timing right. If you do the work every day, one day, you will strike true.

Everyone just wants to strike true, right? Leticia Van De Putte had the timing just right. She's Mexican American, and ran with Wendy Davis for Lt Gov. of Texas in 2013. Prior to this, she was like Jordan, and invisible person-of-color political worker who stayed in her lane, did the work as an advocate for other Mexican Americans in Texas and did not raise much fuss, but 2013 changed many lives in Texas. On the day of Wendy's 11-hour filibuster, Van De Putte was burying her father in San Antonio, one hour away from the capital. At 11:30 pm, after the funeral, she arrived to the capital to speak and vote for her district. When a male counterpart refused to let her speak and cast her vote multiple times, she said "at what point must a female senator raise her hand or her voice to be recognized over the male colleagues in the room?" which was met with thunderous cheers and applause, and launched her into the limelight next to then Senator Davis.

I think about her words, a woman, grief stricken from the loss of her father, fatigued by what that kind of pain does to the body, still remaining civil but firm against adversity. The sound comes before the light … her words shaking the state into a sonic boom of solidarity. Invisible no more, the room and the world had a new feminist star. It takes a story and a well-placed well-documented statement. We see the lightning, but we feel the thunder. I erupted in front of my laptop as I watched this happen live that day, adding my voice to the cacophony of thunder that swept over me and my friends.

The thunder makes me move, it activates me. I can't help it. I feel it deep in my soul and relate to it. Invisible or earth shattering, it activates me. Barbara is my base line, the everyday small conversations I have with my students about how to make things better and working with conservative students one conversation at a time. Invisible feminist work is the equivalent of the soft rumbles in the distance, you kind of expect it, but it is not a true motivator, but the more those small actions, small rumbles build, the more change can be made … then suddenly the sonic boom that shakes the house arrives. We know from lighting and thunder that you cannot have one without the other and that the thunder strikes the most emotion.

This is to say, that vibrations are the motivator, lights can dazzle, but the feeling is activating. And I mean this from a personal standpoint, they motivate me … the way that hospitality motivates me to connect with people, to defend a state that would and still does shitty things to its women and nonwhite constituents. The Thunder and hail are the true signs of the storm.

END SCENE 3

Note

1 During this solo performance, the sole character ("Me") has little documentation to stage cues. During the performance, the performer has the freedom to gesture and move as the texts inspires them to do so.

Dysphoria/Y'all Know What I Mean?

J. Nyla McNeill

I never know what to say
when someone's eyes ask,
What
       was
           your
              gender
                   dysphoria
                    like?
COMMAND-F'ing my body for answers
I searched for my whole life.

But I guess I could say—
"well, shit—I can feel it in my fucking *gait*,
the way each step feels like an approximation
of what I believed I was *supposed* to walk like/
talk like when *supposed to* doesn't really exist,
and it sure as hell *definitely* ain't me!"

I kinda want to say—
"well, it feels like fitting an F into an M shaped hole—
but I don't want to use that metaphor—
sex and gender, in fact, being metaphors,
because I don't identify much with either/or
or the concept of gender at all—"

It sorta feels like—
"Do you understand when
I say 'F' and 'M' and how they don't
really exist—
how they are metaphors—
concepts?
Not 'me'?"

Y'all know what I mean?

SECTION III

The Erotic as a Site for Normative Disruption

She did not have a language nor a vocabulary to talk about the body, about making love. The clit, her serpent's tongue, her sexual tongue had been silenced. Or because of disuse, she had forgotten to speak its language, how to move its tongue.

She was not allowed, nor had she allowed herself, to express who she was sexually. She had abnegated the responsibility to be who she was, to act out who she really was.

—Gloria E. Anzaldúa[1]

Who would have thought mention of sex would make distinguished professors so nervous?

—Thomas K. Nakayama and Frederick C. Corey[2]

What is at stake in the erotic? In a word: everything.

—Aimee Carrillo Rowe[3]

The erotic holds within it the capacity to unsettle power relations. And suppression of the erotic marks a cornerstone performance of cultural violence under racist cisheteropatriarchy. The erotic has been theorized in a number of ways and for our critical purposes, we begin with Audre Lorde. Lorde theorizes the erotic as a "measure between the beginnings of our sense of self and the chaos of our strongest feelings. It is an internal sense of satisfaction to which, once we have experienced it, we know we can aspire. For having experienced the fullness of this depth of feeling and recognizing its power, in honor and self-respect we can require no less of ourselves."[4] As a measure, the erotic gestures at what is and what can be by highlighting structural constraints stifling satisfaction, possibility. In turn, the erotic drives us to live satisfying lives and to note and resist—as one is able and equipped to do so—that which emerges as hegemonic constraints delimiting said satisfaction; and to those constraints that are beyond one's immediate control, we turn to sustained and committed activism, which labors against intersecting structural oppressions enabling those constraints.

In the context of gender, the erotic highlights the space between what currently is based on structural constraints and what can be with the removal of those constraints. Said differently, the erotic presses us to explore the potentiality of our many, many genders including the capacity to experience satisfaction in/with our gendered sense of self in light of those structural barriers. Trans and gender non-conforming (GNC) people are well acquainted with the structural barriers restricting gender potentiality. Dean Spade advances "administrative violence" as "an area of control and legal codification" that may be more violent toward trans and GNC subjects due to its regulation of gender based on normative criteria.[5] Administrative apparatuses are especially violent because they "often appear 'neutral,' especially when discrimination has been framed as a problem of individuals with bad intentions who need to be prohibited from their bad acts by law."[6] Even though administrative means may appear neutral, their violent effects are far greater—particularly for those trans subjects who embody multiple marginalized identities—than that found in individualized interpersonal enactments of violence. In this regard, gender is regulated at the structural level via administrative means as well as at the individual level through the regulation of gender via interpersonal violence and the erotic reveals constraints as they emerge at both individual and structural levels.

Clearly, the path toward one's gender subjectivity is never easy, and the erotic highlights the path toward subjective gender potentiality. Kate Bornstein uses the metaphor of "splattering" to draw attention to the various, often contradictory, cultural means constraining gender potentiality.[7] In a thought experiment, Bornstein implores us to envision ten relational dynamics in which each dynamic demands a different enactment of y/our gender self/selves. For instance, your gender with your workplace manager, with one or more of your (a)romantic and/or (a)sexual partners, with a teacher or mentor, with your neighbor, with your crush down at the local craft store, with a religious leader, with a teammate, and so on. Now, what would happen if you hosted a dinner party where you invited all ten people and where, as a result, you embody all ten variations of your gender simultaneously to/with all ten guests. This thought experiment draws our attention to the subtle ways in which we self-regulate our genders across relational contexts, just as it highlights the variability of gender in one body across space and through time. Conversely, Bornstein writes, "It's when we splatter consciously, I think, that we expand our ability to stretch our genders, let ourselves go, lose a sense of who or what we might 'really' be, and we're simply there."[8] This is erotic energy. Though, while this thought experiment in erotic energy does not dissolve structural barriers, it gestures at what is possible and, in turn, enables the mapping of a different sort of relating. This different sort of relating draws our attention to the structural barriers delimiting gender subjectivity, which encourages us to transform those barriers so that we might be "simply there."[9]

Feminist women have long understood the premise that gender is constrained under racist cisheteropatriarchy. And, Lorde adds, "women so empowered are dangerous."[10] Why? Because the erotic highlights the ways in which cultural enactments of power (e.g., racist cisheteropatriarchy) stifle agency. Given this framing, the embodiment of the erotic can be felt in the twirl of every young Black trans femme and in the swirl of every fat Latinx single parent and in the whirl of every disabled cis queer man of color each navigating intersecting structures of domination including White supremacy, cisheterosexism, and ableism, for instance. To be clear, rather than focusing on a particular act or action, the erotic draws our attention to "how acutely and fully we can feel in the doing," for instance, of the twirl, of the swirl, and of the whirl, in the face of structural domination.[11] In practical terms, the erotic provides "the power which comes from sharing deeply any pursuit with another person" and, in turn, underlines the "capacity for joy" in relation with self and/as other.[12] Erotic knowledge is thus onto-epistemic in its capacity to empower us as it provides a "lens through which we scrutinize all aspects of our existence, forcing us to evaluate those aspects honestly in terms of their relative meaning within our lives" and in relation with others.[13]

While the erotic references the "conscious endeavor to reclaim the full potentiality of our creative force," it is notably regulated in cultural performances of sex and sexuality with different effects attached to different gendered bodies.[14] Gloria Anzaldúa captures this tension—between uninhibited and suppressed erotic energy in the context of sex—in the opening epigraph. For Anzaldúa, sexuality, like spirituality, serves as an ontological conduit by which she is equipped to integrate what she understands as fractured selves. She clarifies: "When I'm there being sexual, sensual, erotic, it's like all the Glorias are there; none are absent. They've all been gathered to this one point …: Gloria who's compassionate, Gloria who's jealous, Gloria who's a freak, Gloria who's lazy. It's ok to be me. In both the sexual and the spiritual act, all the 'you's' are there, and it's a tremendous amount of energy."[15] This energy is erotic energy. It is also explicitly sexual in this context. It is erotic to the degree that Anzaldúa was alienated from her own body (an effect of the marginalization she experienced due to violent responses to her embodied difference) and, as a result, sought to learn the contours of her bodily capacity through sexual and spiritual exploration/introspection. For Anzaldúa, the sexual ("… like during orgasm: I disappear and am just this great pleasurable wave, like I'm uniting with myself in a way I have not been."[16]) and the spiritual ("When I'm meditating... there's a connection with the source."[17]) serve as means toward realizing wholeness in oneself. And in this subsection of poems and essays, both the spiritual (see Daniel B. Coleman's essay) and the sexual (see Billy Huff's as well as Benny LeMaster and S. Donny Bellamy's essays) are conjured as erotic means toward realizing "gender." In Gray Bowers untitled poem, the embodied tension of being silenced under the pressing gaze of binary expectancies, as a non-binary subject in intimate relational contexts, is performed as an erotic space disallowing a sense of self to emerge on one's own terms. Conversely, Danny Shultz's untitled poem explicitly highlights the erotic space between a gender sense of self and cultural ideologies resulting in affective disarray in the form of gender dysphoria.

In their essay, Daniel B. Coleman conceptualizes of the erotic as "a driving force in the lifelong struggle for [the] existence and re-humanization" of/as Black people. To accomplish this, Coleman unhinges "rigor" from post-positivist articulations advocating, instead, for an "intimate decolonial walking" that affirms the temporal complexity of colonized life histories. Taken together, rigor is reconceptualized less as a colonizing research instrument functioning under the guise of "neutrality" (i.e., as administrative apparatus) and objectivity and, rather, as an embodied recuperation of complex (colonized) histories that enables a more whole present and future self, understood as an erotic embodiment, to emerge. While the erotic and the sexual are not synonymous, it is worth focusing our energies on sexuality as a specifically regulated space, particularly in academe.

Thomas Lindlof and Bryan Taylor write, "academics—at least in Communication—seem most likely to tolerate sexuality in their journals if its depiction is muted, heteronormative, and moralized (e.g., with clearly identified villains and victims). Narratives that vex this code by celebrating bodily pleasure, by exposing complicity of participants in sexualized encounters risk provoking controversy."[18] As such, this subsection of essays can be conceptualized as controversial from the vantage of those who more closely embody the "charmed circle" of normativity.[19] And to such charges we say: Good. We are disinterested in flirting with moralistic charges as they serve the purpose of reifying normativity as a self-evident fact, which we reject. Following Fredrick Corey and Thomas Nakayama, we understand epistemology to be "mobile" and, as a result, "we need to push ourselves to think of new ways of knowing, grounded in experience."[20] And for our purposes, we encourage readers to explore the constitution of gender through the erotic as it emerges across a variety of intersectional, embodied, and affective realms including that of the sexual.

Elizabeth Bell shows us, "Exploring sex acts is one route to interrogate" gender as a multitude of "utopian constructions that move beyond binaries *and* as material realities that regulate and control" marginalized genders.[21] With that, we consider essays by Billy Huff and Benny LeMaster and S. Donald Bellamy who each draw on sexual storytelling to theorize gender embodiment as trans subjects. These authors can be conceptualized of as, in Fredrick Corey and Thomas Nakayama's theorization, "fulcrum subjects" who are writing between "the language of academia" and "the language of sex."[22] In their (in)famous[23] essay, "Sextext," Corey and Nakayama add, "To swing into the fulcrum is to challenge the fact/fiction binary, to discover the truth of fiction, to factualize the plot of my imagination."[24] Huff swings into the fulcrum as he writes against the stigmatization of fetishization as a trans masculine subject navigating gay (cisgender male) sexual politics. For Huff, existence and the felt sense of embodied pleasure depends on the interrogation of, and defense of, the fetishization of transness. In this regard, Huff assumes a decidedly non-normative position and calls on his audience to consider the ways in which respectability serves as a discursive wedge disallowing his erotic embodiment as a gay trans man. LeMaster and Bellamy swing into the fulcrum when they explore critical erotica as a narrative and performative means to explore gender through sexual encounters and scenes that are both "experienced and imagined." The larger goal is to narrate unstoried and embodied experiences that work against the racist cisheteronormative hegemony delimiting what sex and sexuality can be. In the end, this collection of poems and essays theorize and perform the erotic as an embodied means to understand the potentiality of gender in more complex ways.

Discussion Questions

1. The erotic is understood as a measure between what is and what can be. If we theorized our gender in erotic terms, what are the structural barriers that disallow a fully realized gender sense of self to emerge?
2. How do normativities hinder your erotic sense of gender? For instance, how do racism, religion, ableism, and immigration status inform your erotic sense of gender performance?
3. Can you name a time when you were objectified, but it was constructive, productive, and consensual?
4. Across these chapters, authors highlight a tension between the need for belonging and the recognition of individual desires. In what ways are the two sides of this tension incompatible with each other? In what ways might they be reconciled? How does an intersectional lens complicate your response?

Notes

1 Gloria E. Anzaldúa, "Dream of the Double-Faced Woman," in *The Gloria Anzaldúa Reader*, ed. AnaLouise Keating (Durham, NC: Duke University Press, 2009), 71.
2 Thomas K. Nakayama and Frederick C. Corey, "Nextext," *Journal of Homosexuality* 45, no. 2–4 (2003): 319–334, doi: 10.1300/J082v45n02_15.

3 Aimee Carrillo Rowe, "The Sacred and the Profane: Uses of the Erotic in *Banging the Bishop*," *Text and Performance Quarterly* 27, no. 3 (2007): 270, doi: 10.1080/10462930701412395.
4 Audre Lorde, *Sister Outsider: Essays and Speeches by Audre Lorde* (Berkeley, CA: Crossing Press, 2007), 54.
5 Dean Spade, "*Normal Life: Administrative Violence, Critical Trans Politics, and the Limits of Law* (Durham, NC: Duke University Press, 2015), 86. See also p. 16, where administrative systems include any structural apparatuses that regulate gender through a lens of normative intelligibility including, for instance, "public benefits and housing programs, work eligibility verification programs, criminal and immigration enforcement systems, and health care programs that purport to distribute life chances through neutral and standard criteria."
6 Spade, 16.
7 Kate Bornstein, *My New Gender Workbook* (New York, NY: Routledge, 2013), 116.
8 Bornstein, 120.
9 Bornstein, 120.
10 Lorde, 55.
11 Lorde, 54.
12 Lorde, 56.
13 Lorde, 57.
14 Carrillo Rowe, 266.
15 Anzaldúa, "Spirituality," 85.
16 Anzaldúa, "Spirituality," 85.
17 Anzaldúa, "Spirituality," 85.
18 Thomas R. Lindlof and Bryan C. Taylor, *Qualitative Communication Research Methods*, 2nd ed. (Thousand Oaks, CA: Sage, 2002), 290.
19 Gayle S. Rubin, *Deviations: A Gayle Rubin Reader* (Durham, NC: Duke University Press, 2011), 152.
20 Frederick C. Corey and Thomas K. Nakayama, "deathTEXT," *Western Journal of Communication* 76, no. 1 (2012): 21, doi: 10.1080/10570314.2012.637542; see also Tami Spry, "Performing Autoethnography: An Embodied Methodological Praxis," *Qualitative Inquiry* 7, no. 6 (2001): 726, doi: 10.1177/107780040100700605.
21 Elizabeth Bell, "Sex Acts Beyond Boundaries and Binaries: A Feminist Challenge for Self Care in Performance Studies," *Text and Performance Quarterly* 25, no. 3 (2005): 204, doi: 10.1080/10462930500271752; see also Kristen C. Blinne, "Auto(erotic)ethnography," *Sexualities* 15, no. 8 (2012): 971, doi: 10.1177/1363460712459153.
22 Frederick C. Corey and Thomas K. Nakayama, "Sextext," *Text and Performance Quarterly* 17, no. 1 (1997): 59, doi: 10.1080/10462939709366169.
23 For an analysis of the disciplinary impact of this essay, see Thomas W. Benson, "A Scandal in Academia: Sextext and CRTNET," *Western Journal of Communication*, 76, no. 1 (2012): 2–16, doi: 10.1080/10570314.2012.637464.
24 Corey and Nakayama, 66.

Bibliography

Anzaldúa, Gloria E. "Dream of the Double-Faced Woman." In *The Gloria Anzaldúa Reader*, 70–71. Edited by AnaLouise Keating. Durham, NC: Duke University Press, 2009.
Bell, Elizabeth. "Sex Acts Beyond Boundaries and Binaries: A Feminist Challenge for Self Care in Performance Studies," *Text and Performance Quarterly* 25, no. 3 (2005): 187–219, doi: 10.1080/10462930500271752.
Benson, Thomas W. "A Scandal in Academia: Sextext and CRTNET," *Western Journal of Communication* 76, no. 1 (2012): 2–16, doi: 10.1080/10570314.2012.637464.

Blinne, Kristen C. "Auto(erotic)ethnography," *Sexualities* 15, no. 8 (2012): 953–977, doi: 10.1177/1363460712459153.

Bornstein, Kate. *My New Gender Workbook*. New York, NY: Routledge, 2013.

Corey, Frederick C. and Thomas K. Nakayama. "deathTEXT," *Western Journal of Communication* 76, no. 1 (2012): 17–23, doi: 10.1080/10570314.2012.637542.

Corey, Frederick C. and Thomas K. Nakayama. "Sextext." *Text and Performance Quarterly* 17, no. 1 (1997): 58–68, doi: 10.1080/10462939709366169.

Lindlof, Thomas R. and Bryan C. Taylor. *Qualitative Communication Research Methods*, 2nd ed. Thousand Oaks, CA: Sage, 2002.

Lorde, Audre. *Sister Outsider: Essays and Speeches by Audre Lorde*. Berkeley, CA: Crossing Press, 2007.

Nakayama, Thomas K. and Frederick C. Corey. "Nextext," *Journal of Homosexuality* 45, no. 2–4 (2003): 319–334, doi: 10.1300/J082v45n02_15.

Rowe, Aimee Carrillo. "The Sacred and the Profane: Uses of the Erotic in *Banging the Bishop*," *Text and Performance Quarterly* 27, no. 3 (2007): 266–272, doi: 10.1080/10462930701412395.

Rubin, Gayle S. *Deviations: A Gayle Rubin Reader*. Durham, NC: Duke University Press, 2011.

Spade, Dean. "*Normal Life: Administrative Violence, Critical Trans Politics, and the Limits of Law*." Durham, NC: Duke University Press, 2015.

Spry, Tami. "Performing Autoethnography: An Embodied Methodological Praxis," *Qualitative Inquiry* 7, no. 6 (2001): 706–732, doi: 10.1177/107780040100700605.

Untitled

Gray Bowers

My then partner:
"Are you only still with me 'cause it'd be too hard to explain all your...
stuff to someone new?"
Silence
What?! I burst
Are you serious... all my "stuff," is it really so "weird" or "shameful" or
"awkward" that I can't share my "stuff" with other people?
Because that's what you've just made clear
That's how you feel, that what you think of me, and apparently any one
nonbinary...
I scream in my head
Silence still
"No, of course not" I mumble

IF RIGOR IS OUR DREAM

Theorizing Black Transmasculine Futures through Ancestral Erotics

Daniel B. Coleman

Womb

When I decided to live in and with the fullness of my non-binary transmasculine personhood, I crawled back into my own womb and re-birthed myself.[1] I mother, nurture, and tend to this body and this form from the creative energy that this corporeal geography provides. I am not alone. This is not solitude, nor singularity. This is collective and ancestral justice. When my head full of dry curls began to crown, I reached down to pull her out, but larger forces flung my hands upward, palms open—***the ancestors were my midwives***.[2] My body and my life are theirs and only through them am I my own person. I collectively negotiate the terms of my existence by remaining vigilantly in-relation with and sensing of them. I became a fugitive when I disidentified from scientific rationalizations of embodied life and all that is posed as its other.[3] Now I am home.

Seven generations behind me and seven generations before me, our footsteps mesh into one another's toenails. Manifold and multiplying historical back aches live in the S-curve in my spine. As new muscles form alongside the vertebrae, historical tensions are able to compensate. I learn how to re-member each time my back bleeds; every time I choose to open my skin in performance. I am inventing a body worthy of both the porosity and encasement of the ancestors— I enter into a cultural field they left behind. She, this body, will always be in the process of becoming. She is bigger than all the violence she has held and that we have held. We hold these together.

I hold my right hand over my heart and under my breast as my left hand is held by the skin that gathers life force at the matrix beginning three fingers below my navel. I close my eyes and find breath. I am. We are. I pledge allegiance to Turtle

Island, to Oshun, to Olodumare, to Abya Yala, to Yóok'ol Kaab… Here I share a love story for my ancestors who walk with me and who have never given up, even as they have waited patiently for my arrival at deep listening. I had to learn how to seek them. I had to learn that they were always just a call away. Without the divine feminine and the energies beyond occidental binaries, I am nothing and I would not be able to feel them. I would/we would cease to exist. I call to my mother-father and s/he responds.

Brown Girl, Purple Room

Nannie Coleman gave me a Black baby doll at age 4. Honoring my grandmother and her insistence on my entry into play through Blackness and Blackness through play, I named her Nannie. Since she was a plastic doll with a hole in both her mouth and cavernous stomach, I would pour cow's milk into her from a plastic bottle with a pink nipple. When I haphazardly threw her over my shoulder, I could not understand why the milk came back out of her, through the same hole I was using to nurture her. She was ridding herself of the whiteness. The first lesson.

Around age 10, the walls of my childhood room went purple. Mama and I painted them together—a deep lavender oasis. The throw adorning my bed was a replica of a Degas painting—pinks and purples to match the new environment. A plastic storage bin began accumulating the pointe shoes that made my tender new feet go raw time and again, getting rougher and more worn with time. Obedient, quiet, soft-spoken, impeccably neat and clean—a quintessentially feminine child and an easy person to discipline, I gave myself over to be molded and shaped by teachers, choreographers, and other authority figures. I learned all of what was appropriate and expected and resided there, without question or rebellion. Strength is not gendered and sometimes obedience precedes freedom. These were the second lessons.

Staccato

I was not a tomboy. I have never played a group sport. I was not friends with boys at all. My father had feminist praxis. My mother was the deeply nurturing provider; the rebel bread winner. I have never been in a physical fight and no one has ever tried to fight me. I cannot be psychoanalyzed along sexed and gendered lines and given a diagnosis from the DSM. Alongside these affirmative truths, I was met with the advisories: In professional ballet training, I was warned about the problems of my **Black** buttocks, my **Black** feet, my **Black** legs, my **Black** muscles. I have never known what it is to have a body that is not hailed by racialization, by sexism, and by exotification. [Being trans hasn't necessarily made any of that go away.] I wanted to be the perfect European ballerina. I forgot that I am earth, I am soil, I am Blackness, or perhaps it was simply that none of these locations and enunciations had been ignited in me yet. I had not yet become historical. I cannot separate my race from my gender nor my gender from my race. These are the lasting lessons.

I was a stereotypical little girl that now asks to be called he and they, inter-changeably. I confess I am not sure masculinity is even the right word. But, neither is femininity. Neither is male nor female. This is not a biological or psychological fact. Neither is my body. My embodiment is a both, *and*... This is part of a life project. I am not talking about dysphoria. I was not born in the wrong body. This is not desiring to occupy a space of power cum gender, nor an association with patriarchy, violence, imperialism, war, heteronormativity, coloniality, or marriage, nor can this be collapsed into or defined as a rebellion against these forces of normalization. Esto es *un camino otro*. This is *ancestral*. This is *legacy*. This is a call to live to carry out the embodiments of ancestral memories that brought me to this life. This. Is. Not all marginalized identities are patho-logically constituted. The lessons made in echoes.

If Rigor Is Our Dream[4]

If rigor is our dream, canonical forces cannot make us blind and pedagogical lessons must be listened to from every experience on this embodied journey. If rigor is our dream, our horizons must reach back in order to reach forward and we must learn to move as serpentine subjects and leave behind the histori-cally trapping lie of linearity. If rigor is our dream, we need to redefine rigor to include channels and experiences purposefully excluded from the cultural texts that do not give us language for our lives and realities. Rigor must be rede-fined in order to meet the challenges of ancestral, psychic, spiritual, existential, material, intellectual, and other modes of survival—"submerged perspectives."[5] Rigor is not the standardization or normalization of our referents but rather an intimate decolonial walking-with the fullness of our past as our present and future selves. Rigor is aligning ourselves with this walk through deep listening upon entering into this work and the vigilance to continue on the path. Rigor must always be re-defined and rigor remains rigorous as long as it is slippery. Rigor is erotic.[6]

In my desires for rigor, I call upon Black feminist brilliance to lead the way, honoring that most of my life journey thus far has been as a mixed-Black woman.[7] This always requires that I honor the complex ancestry I walk with in genealogical and spiritual reckonings of my African American family's history of enslavement and resistance in the US South. I feel a spiritual-existential require-ment to honor the sacred feminine in me, throughout. Having lived the majority of my life up to this point as a woman of color now living with transmasculine becoming, it is not my desire to deny or to erase this lived history and all of the ancestral echoes of Black womanhood. I bring these two tensions together here on a spiritual plane.

I choose to begin by calling upon Audre Lorde:

> The erotic is a measure between the beginnings of our sense of self and the chaos of our strongest feelings. It is an internal sense of satisfaction to which, once we have experienced it, we know we can aspire. For having experienced the fullness of this depth of feeling and recognizing its power, in honor and self-respect we can require no less of ourselves.[8]

The erotic, as Lorde contends, is a form of measurement. It allows us to bear witness to ourselves and to determine our degree of satisfaction within and beyond affective immediacies: it is to tune in with our feel-thinking selves, *longue durée*. By aligning with our erotic, what we put our trust in inevitably shifts. The erotic is an internal source of power—one no one can touch or violate. Once we access its power, in self-respect, we hold ourselves to and even demand its constant presence. It becomes the root from which we live—a requirement for full existence.

In the ongoing dehumanization of Black people where the pornographic as a White cis male heteronormative colonial morbid gaze reigns, the erotic, I contend, is a tool for recovering our personhood. I would also argue that were Lorde alive today, the erotic would not be limited to cisgender women, identifying with their designation at birth, only. Rigor allows for access to the erotic to also be an invitation for trans and gender non-conforming people and their/our bodies.[9] Rigor, then, as a recuperation of a sense of being fully embodied by nurturing the erotic's power, is an erotic production of knowledge. The amount of ways we and our people can be and have been violated are innumerable. The longevity of these violations is outside of comprehension and even, always hovers over us lingering in a shadow threshold of total despair and pessimism. The erotic is also an antidote to eternal reaction and defense in the face of this historical despair, and a driving force in the lifelong struggle for existence and re-humanization in the forms we determine to be in alignment with our fullest selves. What point of departure might we then call upon?

Presa—Prey

At age 13, when training with what was, at the time, The School of San José Cleveland Ballet in San José, California, I caught the eye of a Venezuelan choreographer who was also one of our ballet masters. He was branching into contemporary and modern dance choreography and saw the untapped "wild" within me. One rehearsal afternoon, he threw out one of his primary dancers for her mouthiness and called me to the center of the room. We were, of course, to never speak unless spoken to because this was the nature of professional training. The piece, "Presa," required us to have our hair (in my case, my large curly mane) completely released in order for us to embody "predators" and "prey." The taller young women were the predators and those of us who were smaller were the prey. I remember every rehearsal he watched and molded me voraciously— providing the first space, within the containment of precise technique and musicality, for me to let everything out. I learned that certain structures provide the greatest freedom.

As a contemporary dance piece, we were barefoot, with full-body deep green and brown unitards designed for the earthy nature of the choreography. They showed every budding curvature of our bodies. The lighting was dark with sporadic shadows across the stage and the music was an ominous struggle meant to create a scene of the nature of violence and resistance. Physically and musically, the piece built in a passionate crescendo as the long-limbed predators tried to devour their prey. In the end, only one escapes. I run up to downstage right where the music stops, and the stage goes black except for a spotlight and the limb-jolting sound of a beating heart. I gaze out into the dark horizon, grounded in the gravitas of my muscles, inhaling and exhaling with each heartbeat and with such fervor that the last audience member can hear me. Simultaneously, I measuredly flap my wings like the dying swan in Swan Lake, in the ecstasy of the initiation of my fugitivity; the first memory I have of tasting full erotic freedom. Its mark is fused into every pore of my being. Flight.

My auntie, of White descendance, who had been at the performance, expressed the difficult feelings that arose and comingled in her chest: the beauty and power of my movement and the discomfort at seeing her young niece moving in such an "animalistic," sensual and earth-driven way. "Nice job kiddo," she says, a face full of mixed emotions. She followed up immediately with: "And it was hard to see my niece *like that*." I felt repulsed at such a response and confused as to where to locate it in my body. I tried not to show it in my face but the feeling of deep disappointment in not being seen seemed to rise out of my skin. Nothing in me desired to feel that tasting my fugitive possibilities would be met with affective and corporeal censorship. Even at that age, I knew. This lesson on alienation meant I needed to absorb and immediately deflect so as to continue to allow my fugitive nature to guide my flight and my erotics. Power.

My first language was movement. I learned to communicate mostly fluently through physical expression before any other language. It is my sense of gravity and molecular insulation. It was a language I learned within the rigidity of militaristic training but whose freedom was incited within me like the fire of a meteoroid, that, upon hitting the ground, burns for all of time. The cognitive dissonance I experienced in this moment of performance response, opened up a channel for knowing beyond the seeming immediacy and kinship of the nuclear. Upon realizing that my body could be policed by someone with whom I shared a bit of DNA and whose racial structure differed from mine up-shored ancestral pain—I knew that if I did not protect myself, a loss of my creative fire would be possible. Shortly after, in an attempt to hold myself too rigidly, I experienced my first major back injury and I knew something was wrong, off, astray. I started to leave my body, physically and spiritually—protection from the potential of taking from me; better to take from myself. I began to travel on planes and in movement, trying to come back to this home space, but only landing further away. It would take some time to turn inward...

Blackness, Fugitivity, and Transness

Synchronizing with Alexis Pauline Gumbs's[10] work with fugitivity and poetry in *spill*, in response to Hortense Spiller's[11] intellectual legacy, I call upon both of them to articulate a *Spirit-filled Black ancestrality*. In so doing, I map a historical terrain for the emergence of a particular Black trans subjectivity, one that allows ancestors to show us the path—a path of escape and of freedom.

In *spill: scenes of Black feminist fugitivity*, Gumbs uses poetry to *speak with* some of Spillers' major works. In this particular poem,[12] Gumbs comes into conversation with Spillers'[13] "Mama's Baby, Papa's Maybe [...],"

> because she was a cave. papyrus. she was inventing a language. herself. she was lighting up the darkness. her skin. however dull, the person who holds the tool can say *i am not an animal*. can she? can say there is control. there is reason in what she feels. cannot. say that and be heard. she is not. an animal. so she brights it in the darkness. her skin. so she spells it in the tomb. her covered arms. her battered womb. she makes a place to right her walls again. she tilts and wields it expertly. her pain. the spell she scratches in her skin. her name.[14]

Gumbs, in this poetic dialogue with Spillers, responds to a number of contentions. I hear one connection point being drawn along the lines of Spillers' conversation with Meillassoux, where Spillers, articulates,

> [...] "femininity loses its sacredness in slavery" [64], then so does "motherhood" as female blood-rite/right. To that extent, the captive female body locates precisely a moment of converging political and social vectors that mark the flesh as a prime commodity of exchange.[15]

If the flesh is the site of commodification and dehumanization, it is fugitivity that allows Black women, in the obscenity of the conditions of slavery's confinement, to become embodied subjects. This is also where, as Snorton reads Spillers, the Black woman's child comes into the world as flesh since its only purpose was to be sold off to enslavement to the highest bidder.[16] Gumbs's response is a poetic rendering of personhood.[17] But, before getting that far, what happens when the material conditions for flight, in the desire for full humanity, are not present? And what is the relationship between essentialist femininity equating womanhood to womb and biological reproduction, that both Gumbs and Spillers are challenging, alongside the sociopolitical and historical conditions of enslavement?

Spillers, as Riley has argued, lays the terrain for the historical conditions of possibility for a trans non-binary space of being vis-à-vis enslaved blackness, saying that "dispossession" is "the *loss* of gender."[18] Then, Gumbs works through the conditions of these dispossessions and their responses: "she invented a language. herself." "Herself," I read here, is the invention of words/embodiment for naming that exist outside of discursive formations, often times not attuned to these racialized histories of dispossession. *Inventing herself* is a birthing of self— not in biological terms, nor in terms existing only-in-relation to women's subordination in the face of those designated male at birth. In fact, here we experience a complete inversion and rupture with the binary logic of gender roles, since the historical conditions of enslavement created a different site of gendered materiality for African American men and women. Agreeing with Spillers and Riley, and holding tight to Gumbs's poetry, African American men did not exist as superior to, but rather could only come into existence as fully human through a reclamation of Black womanhood and motherhood, acknowledging legacies of orphanhood that haunt historical memory.

Spillers continues:

> Therefore, the female, in this order of things, breaks in upon the imagination with a forcefulness that marks both denial and an "illegitimacy." Because of this peculiar American denial, the Black American male embodies the *only* American community of males which has had the specific occasion to learn *who* the female is within itself, the infant child who bears the life against the could-be fatal gamble, against the odds of pulverization and murder, including her own. It is through the heritage of the *mother* that the African American male must regain an aspect of his own personhood—the power of "yes" to the "female" within.[19]

The "yes" Spillers is referring to walks in time with Lorde's erotic "yes." Can the Black man and can Black masculine-identified people learn to mother ourselves? Black transmasculinity, I insist, particularly transmasculinity that exists outside of the binary and/or that centers anti-patriarchal embodiment as its core, has a unique opportunity to re-write a grammatical and historical script of masculinity that has been complicit with White supremacy and patriarchy, vis-à-vis not knowing how to reckon with its dispossession. By acknowledging the woman within ourselves and doing the work of our own mothering, can we heal multiple generations of toxic masculinity and its birthparent: enslavement? All we gotta do is say "yes."[20] It is with this we must contend.

Circling back through Gumbs's work, I want to highlight her poetic emphasis on re-humanization: "she is not. an animal. so she brights it in the darkness. her skin. so she spells it in the tomb. her covered arms. her battered womb." A haunting of death encircles these lines. The womb is a force that is damaged. I read this as the colonial battering of Black womanhood—a factor of legitimization that was too often claimed through force and violation—removal of the child as commodity exchange whether through chosen or forced pregnancy, with similar childless endings accompanied by the law of partus sequitir ventrem. Here, I would like to offer that Black transmasculine folk who identify with African American masculinity stemming from genealogies and legacies of enslavement, must birth ourselves through the reimagination of Black women's resistance as a worldmaking project, in order to break free of colonial legacies of masculinist and racial violence.[21] I would like to emphasize that this is in *sharp* contrast to asking or requiring that femmes and Black women do any sort of labor for us, but rather that we do the labor (in all of its physical and birthing connotations) of honoring the Black women in our lines and in our own bodies that, quite literally, made our existence possible. Can we also honor the Black women's bodies that we were born in and designated to and birth our transmasculine forms *from* them as the he's and they's we are, inviting a sacred healing of Black trans mothering and childhoods in the process? I think we MUST.

The African American male, according to Spillers, is the *only* site of maleness within this historical reading that can learn who Black women are by learning this within themselves. In fact, this is *required* to have access to full humanity. We are drawn back to an earlier claim of Spillers in this same piece. She says, "At a time when current critical discourses appear to compel us more and more decidedly toward gender 'undecidability' it would appear reactionary, if not dumb, to insist on the integrity of the female/male gender."[22] Binary absolutisms must be suspended in the approximation of full subjecthood. Binaries, in conversation with Spillers, can sometimes approximate a rigid form of White supremacist naming practices. The erotic offers an alternative way of walking in a pluriversal universe where historical contingencies of race and gender are offered in their plenitude as corporeal realities.

Contextualizing the time of "Mama's Baby, Papa's Maybe," we must remember that thirty-three years have passed since the first publication. The present relevancy of this work to the current moment responds both to the circularity of history and to the necessity of claiming that "Black lives matter" in order to simply render these lives legible, with the most mediatized brutality of Black bodies shown to be against the Black man. Spillers's claims are neither incongruent nor dated. I would like to hold space for what Spillers' arguments could mean in relation to a Black transmasculinity formed in and interdependent of Black womanhood, held within the purview of histories of enslavement and "freedom." That is to say, I would like to invite Black transmasculinities to birth their forms and ways of walking in the world from ancestral reckonings with and loving of the historical position of the Black woman.[23]

Interlude: Forms and Figures

I always felt so masculine. I was not quite sure what this meant but I just knew that this is what I felt. As the estrogen began to course through my body, I ate more and with all of the ballet and modern dance training, combined with my African American genes, I gained muscle very fast. I was very strong. I could jump high and for days. I had a lot of endurance and was always pushing my physical capacity to the next thresholds. My body started to come into what it meant to shift the fat and muscle content around and what shapes felt right alongside its muscles and bones. In training intensives, I realized I no longer had a little girl's body. I would sweat profusely and feel my muscles ripping and tearing at my bones as they sought their place beneath my skin. Something was off. I wanted my skin to burst and for my muscles to find a new place to rest-settle.

Standing in front of the bathroom mirror between technique class and pointe class, I had to take my skirt and leotard off to be able to pull my tights down and pee. I looked at my breasts in the mirror and felt disgust. I would distort and press them down, imagining being a more desirable figure for ballet if I had perfectly flat chest. I was 15 years old. There was nothing I could imagine more physically satisfying than if one day these budding fat deposits evaporated. Here I was again obsessing over the perfect dancer's body—the body of a girl child who never hit puberty. I wanted a body that was genderless—which in actuality at this point in time meant a body that did not show its Blackness through its figure. I did not know what I was asking for. There was a child's body that had already left me and, despite my attempts at physical deprivation, was never going to return.

My body started to get me in trouble. My desires for its radical change and its inadequacy were confirmed by those who had the power to choose my future. If I had a body whose shape appeased the desires of White hegemony in the ballet world, I perhaps could have made a serious career. Somehow, even once the prospect of a professional dance career was off the table, some of these feeling lingered. Internal dialogues constructed over a long period of time do not evaporate just because you rid yourself of the external source. These corporeal memories, desires, and sensations of muscles dripping with perspiration had roots that sedimented deeper than the trauma of Eurocentric physical training. However, it would be over a decade later that I would begin to untangle the concentric circles that formed a very complex relationship to my physical-spiritual body. There was a lack of rootedness and a discomfort in my skin and myself that would remain unsettled and that, without the easy and explainable scapegoat of the dance world to assuage my discomfort, I was at a loss. Why would these feelings of masculinity and the inadequacy of my Black woman's body not leave me?

Poetics of Black Transness

Returning a final time to Spiller's formulation of Black masculinity that can only be birthed in relation to a full embrace of Black femininity, it is my fundamental belief that Black trans identity can be birthed from and in a profoundly rigorous feminist process of history-hailing and worldmaking. In an ancestral gesture, myself a descendant of blood ancestors who were enslaved, I find myself birthing and continuing to birth myself into my trans identity, walking in the legacies of Black men and women who found their humanity through fugitive resistances. Following the work of Spillers and Snorton, Black masculinity gains a particular historical agency by honoring a legacy of Black femininity as its center.[24] I create a third identity not born in negation, but rather as a synthesis of the tension of binary dualities as they intersect Black descendance of formerly-enslaved folks—what is perhaps more precisely wielded in *excess* of this very synthesis. The same sweat that pours down my loins draws the boundaries of a gender-beyond-colonial discourse—gender as a fugitive future child of the discourse that birthed it. The attempt to name this gender as "transmasculine" only exists in fragile relation to discourse and society's need to name because of the blackness of its core. Echoing Spillers's "yes," then, I/we can find one possible entrance into Black transmasculinity by truly saying "yes" to my/our feminine power.

Saying "yes" to a deep feminine self within Black transmasculinity is *one of* multiple possibilities for our erotic becomings. It is a struggle that so many Black masculine of center folks contend with on our paths to refusing patriarchal norms that surround us. May holding these multiplicities all at once get the space they need to be as complex as they are, as we are. Becoming *spills* beyond normative, hegemonic, and White supremacist rationalizations of embodiment, history, and knowing, rejecting linearity and rationality, and instead relying upon poetry and ancestrality. We require a fugitive stance against hegemonic and toxic masculinity so as to not erase racialized histories of subjugation and robbery of all of our children and child selves and to invite and create the material conditions for Black feminist spiritual becoming—coming home to ourselves and reuniting our people in the process, across our very flesh. What is Black transmasculinity without femininity and Black feminism? It is my contention that without these elements, Black transmasculinity runs the risk of being consumed by a vacuous hole of masculine fragility and/or hyper-preciousness, ahistorical in shape, losing itself to world that already refuses to value its life.

We must want and choose to be other otherwise. To become historical agents of our people's collective liberation.

Ancestral Spirituality: las olas del mar

Walking the seashore where sand meets desert and where enormous crabs scour the sand as the sun begins to go down, my hair is once again free and flying in the wind. I feel masculinity and femininity fully alive within me and I have no need to name them in binary opposition or in perfectly synchronous twoness. I hum and sense the sand beneath my toes and this is enough. I root myself and ground. There is warmth in the air and softness in the water. This place remains uncontaminated by major corporations and chemical toxicity. I have come to work on the preservation of sea turtles. This is the first time in my life I have felt an ancestral sense of home seep into my flesh. I am 17.

Turtles showed me the path. As I worked with colleagues and marine biologists to tend to their wounds and to nurse them back to health in their refuge from poachers, I learned from their eyes and from the labor of carrying their enormous and beautiful bodies back to sea. Their strength and their beauty astound me. I walk the shore in profound contemplation, with no regard for who might be watching. I feel the outlines of my face and the features I share with my father, my skin darkening in the daily sun, my eyes the color of my ancestors' skin, my curly crown and I bear witness to all that I am. Lingering in this state of acknowledgment of them in me and me in them, I am free. I harness all the sequestered moments of erotic power I had felt up until this point and find a center—a place from which I can reside.

At this point, I had left most of my dancer self behind me and had embraced a new erotic engagement. In my mind's eye, I am a turtle and a creature of my ancestors. I am a child and a birther of stories and of wonderment. I feel Blacker than I ever have, and my womb carries histories that I am meant to continue creatively birthing throughout the remainder of my sojourn in this form. I am masculine only insofar as I can be deeply feminine, while continually destabilizing an essential nature of either. I will never arrive, I will only ask for guidance along the way at different posts and thresholds.

Trans Fugitivity

What if I told you that Black transmasculinity is fugitivity in flight? That it is a reclamation of ancestral longings for true escape that never saw the light. That when I cry, I feel the pain of generations crying through me and that part of the life work they have chosen for me is to mourn hundreds of years of pain and reach the other side of it. That transmasculinity is part of Black womanhood that survived and that without femininity there would be no strength. What if

I told you that being trans is spiritual journey that chooses us? That there are lifetimes living through us that we can resist but we cannot ignore. That all of the attempts at the contrary are much more painful than living this resistance.

The erotic power of trans is bleeding and not dying.[25] It is the force of the sand that withstands the storm and the cactus that withholds the drought. It is Yemaya's waves crashing onto the shores of our skin, clearing us of ill will, and reviving us from within. It is resting at night and choosing to awake each day and face a world that would rather have us waste away. It is agency when we are expected to succumb to victimhood. It is the softness of holding and being held at the same time, carrying the weight of any who needs physical levity, while also giving your weight over. There are no bootstraps or start-ups. There *is* the delivery of our bodies to what was already in our soul. In the Eros of the most profound of our fears, we become. In the deep waters of our becoming, we are undone. When we come undone, we know we have come home. Here. We. Are.

Notes

1 Alexis Pauline Gumbs, "M/other ourselves: A Black Queer Feminist Genealogy for Radical Mothering," in *Revolutionary Mothering: Love on the Front Lines*, eds. Alexis Pauline Gumbs, China Martens, and Mai'a Williams (Oakland, CA: PM Press, 2016), 19–31.

2 Nayyirah Waheed. *salt* (CreateSpace Independent Publishing, 2013), 251.

3 I understand fugitive from Alexis Pauline Gumbs's latest work on Black feminist fugitivity, which I understand to mean all the ways Black women have survived over time through necessary escape, particularly when leaving relations of violence and patriarchy. Harnessing the power of their stories and therefore their examples, we find ways to remain alive. I borrow "disidentification" from the late José Estéban Muñoz who offered this term as an-other space that rejects the binary of positioning oneself either with their identity (hegemonically) or against it and instead looks for resistance strategies that are border identities, aligning with some aspects of identity and altering or moving away from others. See Alexis Pauline Gumbs. *Spill: Scenes of Black Feminist Fugitivity* (Durham, NC: Duke University Press, 2017). See also José Esteban Muñoz. *Disidentifications: Queers of Color and the Performance of Politics* (Minneapolis, MN: University of Minnesota Press, 1999).

4 Hortense Spillers. "Mama's Maybe, Papa's Maybe: An American Grammar Book." *Diacritics* 17, no. 2 (1987): 65–81, https://www.jstor.org/stable/464747. In using Spillers' work here, am following the work of C. Riley Snorton as he carefully considers the very trans nature of Spillers' germinal text in his book *Black on Both Sides: A Racial History of Trans Identity*. More on this later. It is my desire to consider the spiritual and erotic echoes of Riley's complex and brilliant historical and theoretical work. Riley makes a close analysis of "how ungendered Blackness provided the grounds for trans performances of freedom." See C. Riley Snorton. *Black on Both Sides: A Racial History of Trans Identity* (Minneapolis, MN: University of Minnesota Press, 2017), 58.

5 Macarena Gómez-Barris. *Extractive Zone: Social Ecologies and Decolonial Perspectives* (Durham, NC: Duke University Press, 2017), 1.

6 There never seems to be a time where I do not turn back to Audre Lorde. Lorde's erotic moves in diametrical opposition to the pornographic and instead remembers the erotic as fullness of being—wrestling it away from patriarchy's demonization. See Audre Lorde.

"Uses of the Erotic: The Erotic as Power," in *Sister Outsider*, ed. Audre Lorde (Berkeley, CA: Crossing Press, 1984), 53–59.

7 I used the phrase, "Hay una gran parte de mí que siempre será una mujer negra" or "There is a large part of me that will always be a Black woman" in a public intervention for the International Day of Afro-diasporic Women in 2016. I wish to honor having lived most of my life as a woman of color and holding this as a sacred part of my being as a transmasculine person.

8 Lorde, 54.

9 While the "we" I signal here for the purposes of this chapter more specifically deals with trans and GNC lives and bodies, I intend to also signal a larger "we" that implicates other multiply marginalized subject positions under processes of racialization and coloniality. With this, I continue to ask what erotic fullness could be for this larger we.

10 Gumbs, *Spill.*

11 Spillers.

12 Gumbs, "m/other."

13 Spillers.

14 Gumbs's, "m/other," 20.

15 Spillers, 75.

16 Spillers, 103.

17 Gumbs's, "m/other."

18 Riley, 77.

19 Spillers, 80.

20 Floetry, vocalist, "Say Yes," by Marsha Ambrosius and Andre Harris, recorded 2002, Universal Music Publishing Group, track 8 on *Floetic*, 2002, digital.

21 In reimaging a re-birthing of ourselves, I am in close study of Christina Sharpe's remarkable work *In the Wake: On Blackness and Being*. She discusses the Black woman's birth canal as the hold. She says,

> Reading together the Middle Passage, the coffle, and I add to the argument, the birth canal, we can see how each has functioned separately and collectively over time to dis/figure Black maternity, to turn the womb into a factory producing Blackness as abjection much like the slave ship's hold and the prison, and turning the birth canal into another domestic Middle Passage with Black mothers, after the end of legal hypodescent, still ushering their children into their condition; their non/status, their non/being-ness (74).

In creatively imaging a re-birthing of ourselves for Black transmasculine folks, I am committed to inventing new grammars for transness where our resignifying practices do not rely on the abjection of Blackness and transness, even as they reckon with historical legacy. In this read, then, I want to imagine a re-birthing of ourselves that can both honor a desire to live into the fullness of our transits while refusing to relegate the role of the Black women in our lines and the Black women in ourselves/histories as factories of abjection. See Christina Sharpe. *In the Wake: On Blackness and Being* (Durham, NC: Duke University Press, 2016).

22 Spillers, 66.

23 I would be remiss if I did not also cite the work of Cheryl Clarke who said, "While the Black man may consider racism his primary oppression, he is hard-put to recognize that sexism is inextricably bound up with the racism the Black woman must suffer, nor can he see that no women (or men for that matter) will be liberated from the original 'master-slave' relationship, viz. that between men and women until we are all liberated from the false premise of heterosexual superiority" (p. 132). Clarke, writing in the 1980s, also signalled some of the psychic remnants of enslavement for the Black man, one of them being a form of compulsory heterosexuality lathered in sexism. See Cheryl Clarke.

"Lesbianism: An Act of Resistance," in *This Bridge Called My Back: Writings by Radical Women of Color*, eds. Cherríe Moraga and Gloria Anzaldúa (New York, NY: Kitchen Table Women of Color Press, 1981), 128–137.

24 Snorton, making a distinction between Fanon's work and Spillers' work in relation to this "yes" says, "Whereas power remains a tacit–and normative (read: patriarchal)– context for Fanon's expression, Spillers' construction–the power of 'yes to the 'female' within'–articulates how the political praxis of accessing the Black mother requires a reading of her as the onto-epistemological framework for Black personhood" (p. 108). Here, Snorton is considering the trans in transatlantic as movements through blackness where the figure of the mother in through and beyond enslavement as the figure of the progenitor of race and therefor of gendered constructions in blackness. The Black mother as a figure is the site of the birth of being and knowing blackness and gender.

25 Nayyirah Waheed. "the lie," in *salt*, ed. Nayyirah Waheed (CreateSpace Independent Publishing, 2016), 27.

Bibliography

Clarke, Cheryl. "Lesbianism: An Act of Resistance." In *This Bridge Called My Back: Writings by Radical Women of Color*, 128–137. Edited by Cherríe Moraga and Gloria Anzalduúa. New York, NY: Kitchen Table Women of Color Press, 1981.

Gómez-Barris, Macarena. *Extractive Zone: Social Ecologies and Decolonial Perspectives*. Durham, NC: Duke University Press, 2017.

Gumbs, Alexis Pauline. "M/other Ourselves: A Black Queer Feminist Genealogy for Radical Mothering." In *Revolutionary Mothering: Love on the Front Lines*, 19–31. Edited by Alexis Pauline Gumbs, China Martens, and Mai'a Williams. Oakland, CA: PM Press, 2016.

Gumbs, Alexis Pauline. *Spill: Scenes of Black Feminist Fugitivity*. Durham, NC: Duke University Press, 2017.

Lorde, Audre. "Uses of the Erotic: The Erotic as Power," In *Sister Outsider*. Edited by Audre Lorde. Berkeley, CA: Crossing Press, 1984, 53–59.

Muñoz, José Esteban. *Disidentifications: Queers of Color and the Performance of Politics*. Minneapolis, MN: University of Minnesota Press, 1999.

Sharpe, Christina. *In the Wake: On Blackness and Being*. Durham, NC: Duke University Press, 2016.

Snorton, C. Riley. *Black on Both Sides: A Racial History of Trans Identity*. Minneapolis, MN: University of Minnesota Press, 2017.

Spillers, Hortense. "Mama's Maybe, Papa's Maybe: An American Grammar Book." *Diacritics* 17, no. 2 (1987): 65–81, https://www.jstor.org/stable/464747.

Waheed, Nayyirah. *Salt*. Scotts Valley, CA: CreateSpace Independent Publishing, 2013.

IN DEFENSE OF
THE TRANNY CHASER

Billy Huff

Ever since I became aware of myself as a sexual being, I yearned for gay masculinity. It was not only the bodies of men I desired, but I was also attracted to
a culture of casual and anonymous promiscuity that I perceived to exist among
some gay men. My sexual fantasies were populated by masked men in leather
who would tie me up and call me their boy. I craved the stories I heard from
gay friends who recounted experiences of having their cocks sucked by strangers
through glory holes and having their bodies assaulted by anonymous hands in
dark groping rooms in leather bars. I imagined making eye contact with a stranger at the baths and following him into the showers.

Although I was diagnosed[1] female at birth, my early adult thoughts never
entertained marriage, having babies, or even being in love. Disney did not make
films for me. More than anything I wanted a particular type of sex that I was
doomed to be denied because of my "female" body. I was not invited to gay
leather spaces, and glory holes only existed in my imagination. I wasted my early
adulthood in a series of unfulfilling relationships. I was forced to dwell within
a world of "straight" sex if I expected to get any at all, and easy access to the
"straight" world required that I cover myself in the trappings of femininity. I
never dared to disclose what I had to imagine in order to get off.

When I neared 40, I finally admitted to myself that maybe I could have
access to the gay sex I imagined in my dreams. Battling the discourses of sex
negativity that surrounded me in activist, academic, and social spaces, I made a
conscious decision to valorize sex and pleasure above all else. It was, after all, all
that I ever wanted. This was not an easy decision, and it is one that I suspect was
only conceived as a possibility by virtue of my positionality as a White, middle-
class, masculine-identified person with a body that is not often disabled by my

environment and with no religious affiliation. That is to say that I truly believe it is quite a privilege to be able to think my transness and queerness as a choice at all, not to mention my own privileging of sexual pleasure as fundamentally central to my fulfillment. My whiteness allows me to restrict my movements to spaces that are not marked by homophobia. My masculinity buys me some freedom to unproblematically seek and enjoy sex without apology. My lack of religious commitment frees me from experiencing a large degree of sexual shame. I do not have to struggle against ableist discourses that refuse me a sexuality at all. Finally, I can afford to transition without undue financial burden. I feel it is important not to underestimate the ways that our unique positionalities delimit the horizon of what is even thinkable.

It remains true, however, that I had never heard of anyone deciding to transition for wholly sexual reasons. Even the academic literature I read maintained a strict separation between sexual identity and gender identity and expression. I understand where the temptation to entirely disconnect sex and gender originates. It seems like a given that the best way to convince a patriarchal and heterosexist society that biology does not equal destiny is to rhetorically disconnect that gendered destiny from the flesh of the body. Also, as trans people experience the erasures and problematic assumptions that result from being included in a seemingly ill-fitting acronym (LGBT), many trans people find it necessary to differentiate their identities from notions of sexual orientation. Likewise, as cis LGB populations won their own struggle against pathologization with the removal of "homosexuality" from the *Diagnostic and Statistical Manual of Mental Disorders II (DSM-II)* in 1973, the desire to separate themselves from the still intact pathologization of people who are trans makes sense. The separations between gender and the body and between gender and sexual pleasure are ubiquitous in almost every feminist and trans space I have encountered, including in academic literature. These are also separations that have to be maintained by trans people in order to secure a diagnosis of gender dysphoria. I certainly knew that I could never admit my motivations to the therapist on whom I depended for access to testosterone. I wondered if I was the only one who could not think my gender aspirations and desire as separate aspects of my being. I experience my gender and sexual identities as one.

I searched everywhere for representations of queer trans boys like me taking up residence in the sexual spaces I longed to inhabit. My apprehensions were quelled when I discovered Buck Angel, the self-identified "man with a pussy." Buck Angel is a trans man who stars in gay porn. It was among the hottest porn I had ever seen, and given my largely virtual sexual satisfaction to that point, I had seen a lot of porn. I was overcome with my attraction to Buck's trans body, and I couldn't wait for my own secondary sex characteristics to catch up with my fantasies. More than anything, Buck Angel made it okay to enjoy and find pleasure in my trans masculine body. I learned from watching his porn how available the surface of the body is for resignification. He gave me hope that there might be gay men out there who are attracted to trans masculine bodies. His videos are profitable, so someone else out there is also getting off to them. It's hard to know if these other people experience their own affirmation as inextricable from their sexual pleasure in the same way that I do or if they might see themselves as "tranny chasers," those on whom I depend for recognition. My experience has made me acutely aware of the ways that sexual pleasure and social recognition can be tightly bound together. Is the success of Buck Angel's films proof that I'm not alone? In retrospect, the fact that I found myself reflected in pornography and not on the YouTube channels that so many of my peers turned to for support should have foreshadowed what was to come.

I patiently injected testosterone for a couple years, and then I downloaded every queer dating/hookup app I could find. I can't express in words the over-whelming excitement I felt when I sat in my apartment alone and made my first Grindr profile. I named my profile "Peter Pan" gesturing toward the youthful boy who will never grow up to be a man. I selected a picture from the previous Halloween. I dressed as a Cub Scout. They didn't make Cub Scout uniforms for adults, so I chose the "husky" size for larger boys. I remember marveling at myself in the mirror when I first put on the navy-blue pressed shirt with the words "Boy Scouts of America" emblazoned in yellow above the pocket. I had to be a Girl Scout when I was younger. Instead of camp fires, we earned our merit badges in pound cake baking contests. I pulled up the Cub Scout yellow socks, the navy shorts with an elastic waistband, and as I fastened the yellow bandana, I imagined an older troop leader tightening it around my neck. This was one of the first times I remember enjoying my own image in the mirror. My image finally matched the boy I dreamed myself to be in my deepest masturbatory fantasies. Now I just needed another to make them come true. I always somehow knew that I would need the recognition of another to make me real.

I assigned myself to the "Trans Tribe" in Grindr, reveling in the fact that for one of the first times I had the agency to assign myself to a particular destiny. These rare moments of self-definition for me are not insignificant. At least Grindr doesn't require diagnoses or "proof." I don't have to submit a letter or submit myself to their authoritative gaze. I not only wanted people to know I was a trans boy, but I also wanted them to desire my trans boy body. I was disappointed that Grindr lumped trans men, trans women, and those looking for trans men or trans women onto the same page. I wondered how anyone would ever find me. I published my profile, and I waited, and waited, and waited. It's not that I didn't receive responses. In fact, I received quite a few. The responses I received, however, did not match my eager expectations. I received messages from "straight" married men who were attracted to masculinity but terrified to be gay. "I'm not gay, but I appreciate a hairy woman," one man ventured. "I'm into trans women, but if you're femme enough, it could work," a few offered.

More than anything though, I grew tired of those who assured me they were not "tranny chasers." They commented on everything except for my transness—my smile, my eyes, and my somehow obvious sense of humor. The initial excitement and hope I felt every time my phone indicated a new Grindr notification soon wore off. I can barely bring myself to even check it anymore.

What's wrong with wanting to desire and fuck my trans masculine body? What's wrong with desiring to be someone's object? When I search representations of trans men, I am plagued by the idea that I must resign myself to being always subject, never object. The worst part for me is that it seems the policing is coming primarily from my own "community." The mainstreaming of people who are trans is experienced as a giant step toward progress for many trans people. "Trans" is now a topic of a number of national conversations. Trans characters appear in media, and people who are trans are often the subjects of "public interest" news stories. My story, along with many others, however, is entirely absent. In "Transnormativity: A New Concept and Its Validation through Documentary Film about Transgender Men," Austin H. Johnson defines transnormativity as the "specific ideological accountability structure to which transgender people's presentations and experiences of gender are held accountable."[2] Johnson finds that this ideology "circulates in media depictions of transgender people in ways that eclipse alternative explanations and experiences of gender non-conformity, especially those who do not conform to a medical model."[3] Johnson places discourses of transnormativity alongside discourses of heteronormativity and homonormativity, as these discourses similarly work to affirm those who least trouble institutionally and socially sanctioned gender and sexual relations and embodiments. Johnson's article brings attention to the ways that these normative discourses of accountability empower those who are closest to embodying norms of sex and gender while they simultaneously cause others to be "marginalized, subordinated, or rendered invisible."[4]

The tension between those who seek acceptance into normative structures and those, like myself, who aim to dismantle these same structures is one I have spent most of my adult life studying. I know these positions are ultimately incompatible, and this ubiquitous tension is irresolvable. I also know that we need both. It is the push and pull between these two positions, the times when they violently clash, and the times that they exist in rare moments of balance that make movements move. This is a part of what powers the engines of change. I also know that a large part of the pleasure produced by my queerness comes from it not becoming normalized. My pleasure paradoxically depends on the same normative structures I attempt here to challenge. This paradoxical structure of change leaves me riddled with questions for which I have no easy answers. I am stuck between my own desires and the weight of an entire community— between my steadfast political commitments to equity and justice and my own particular pleasure. It's difficult to know where to place blame or who might be on the losing end of my narrative were it to become publicly accessible and normalized. Is it okay for me to feel marginalized and hurt by the very same people who are merely trying not to offend? It's not their fault that they don't have access to my story, or is it? What might be the consequences for others if my desire to be treated as an object is granted? What about trans masculine people of color who already find themselves too unproblematically hypersexualized and objectified? Is it even ethical for me to consider my pleasure at the expense of those who have the most to lose in our common fight for equity? What kind of person does my defense of the "tranny chaser" make me? I know that these words might affect others in ways that are wholly unthinkable to me from my own privileged position. I welcome the critiques that are sure to come, but I am compelled to proceed anyway.

According to the Urban Dictionary, the website most often cited in blog definitions of the term, a "tranny chaser" is a negative term most often attributed by trans people to "straight" cismen who fetishize trans women. While the term might have originated to describe a problematic phenomenon targeting primarily trans women that is clearly rooted in misogyny and heterosexism, it has come to circulate in trans communities as a term that refers to any person (including other trans people) whose sexual desire is restricted to trans bodies. Many trans people, especially trans people like me who live in small towns, turn to the Internet to find community and validation. My online search reveals a multitude of either cis people defending themselves against the term or trans people discussing how to spot a "tranny chaser" in order to avoid them. In her blog, *Acceptance Revolution*, for example, Kristin Despina defends her position:

> So while, yes, I do happen to like – as Jess put it – "what kind of equipment they're packing," in regard to transguys, I don't fetishize them, and I'm not going to date someone solely based on that. I'm not just about what they're "packing," and in fact, even their trans-ness has only ever been a tiny portion of the equation for me; while, granted, they often have amazing and unique experiences to share because of their trans factor, there's A LOT more to it for me than that. I'm all about viewing whoever I date as the total package, and it just so happens that, in the past, I've found my personal definition of that in a few transguys. Sure, I dug their "equipment," and we had our fun in that department, but what really got me hooked and held my interest was so much bigger and so far beyond all that…"[5]

Despina, like so many others, feels compelled to distance herself from the accusation of "tranny chaser" by referring to what she desires beyond the transness of her partner. On the blog, *Transmuseplanet*, Sabrina Samone ventures that "heterosexual transwomen and gay trans-men may suffer the most because of their direct contact to men, who are often viewed with doing and saying whatever it takes to get laid."[6] She offers a "beware list" of ten ways to spot a "tranny chaser" in order to avoid the devastation they bring. I hesitate to quote her warnings here because of the possibility that it will educate others in how to avoid my desiring gaze. Or, maybe instead of a "beware list" it could be thought of as a blueprint for how to spot the men who might fuck me exactly the way I want.

I thought I might find a hookup or at least a community in support of my position on Fetlife. Fetlife is described as a social media site like Facebook for those interested in fetish, kink, and BDSM. I naively thought that given "fet" is part of the name, Fetlife might offer a celebration or at least a more nuanced understanding of fetishization and objectification than other online spaces. I was wrong. I joined a group called, "FTM Gay Boys," and I searched through thousands of posts for any sign of a "chaser." I finally found a post by a self-proclaimed "ftm chaser." Could this be my Mister Right Now? Apparently "ftm chaser" didn't get the memo about the negative perception of "tranny chasers" in the trans community. His post reads, "I'm a cismale that is very attracted to gay ftms, my second bf was a ftm and I think that's why I'm so attracted to you guys. The problem is that so many find my advances to be more a kink or curiosity thing. Any advice on what I can do to get a ftm bf?" To my dismay, even one who calls himself "ftm chaser" distances himself from the perception that his attraction to a trans person might be based in kink. He is looking for a boyfriend. Putting aside his obvious ignorance of the connotations that accompany his chosen screen name, "ftm chaser" proceeds to be thoroughly critiqued for his error. One responder says, "99% of trans people will not talk to you if you say you're a chaser. We don't want people who only fetishize us." Another offers, "You can start by not identifying yourself as chaser probably. It doesn't inspire confidence for most people I know." There are many other responses like these. I desperately wanted to offer a challenge to these responses, but fear of ostracism stopped me. I want sex, and I know that the validation of my identity as a queer trans boy depends upon realizing the hot, anonymous sex that so fundamentally directs my desires, but I also need community. I already feel so alone. I am always brought back to the push and pull of normalizing discourses and the impossibility of choosing between my particular desires and the nurturing home of a community that seems to require me to play a normative character in someone else's story.

I came to an understanding about my own evolving gender and sexuality within an academic context. I often wonder if I would have chosen to transition at all if not for academic literature in Queer Theory and Trans Studies that allowed me the privilege of unlearning all that I knew about what it means to be a gendered and sexed being in a social world. In fact, I often joke that "academic" is an integral component of my gender identity. I have at times experienced academic literature as a site of freedom, so I regularly turn there to help me think through the very real material conditions I face.

Although there is only a small body of academic literature that focuses on trans masculine desire, there appears to be an absence of work that questions whether fetishization and objectification are always bad. I was hopeful when I read "'There's No Chasing Involved'; Cis/Trans Relationships, 'Tranny Chasers,' and the Future of a Sex-Positive Trans Politics." Avery Brooks Tompkins argues that "a sex-positive trans politics cannot emerge in trans and trans-allied communities if the rhetoric of the 'tranny chaser' continues to inform discourses of desire and attraction to trans people."[7] Tompkins' research reveals exactly my own experience. It is the fear of being labeled as a "tranny chaser" that prevents many from expressing desire for trans bodies, and it is the fear of losing community that prevents trans people from challenging the limits of the term. In the end, however, Tompkins articulates a specifically "trans erotics" that is divorced from the objectification and fetishization that are associated with the "tranny chaser" label. Instead of arguing that the "tranny chaser" only represents a portion, albeit an acceptable portion, of those who pursue sexual encounters with trans people, and we need to expand the language available to talk about the intersections of trans and desire, Tompkins concludes that we should avoid using the rhetoric of the "tranny chaser" in our communities so we might have "conversations around safer sex practices and healthy relationships within our communities."[8] Implicit in Tompkin's definition of "healthy relationships" is the disavowal of objectification that I so desperately want. Perhaps we might consider that a "sex-positive trans politics" might also include those who desire to be the objects of someone else's fetish. Why must we deny gay trans men the kinds of sex that gay cismen can access?

As a young budding feminist, I immersed myself in arguments that critiqued the objectification of women. I understand the potentially dire consequences of objectification and the legacy of those who have fought against it. As someone who was socialized and lived for 40 years as a woman in a patriarchal society, the seriousness of violence against women who are always reduced to objects does not escape me. I understand the objectification of women, including trans women, as a manifestation of misogyny. I also understand that a number of feminists have fought among themselves for decades for their right to consent to objectification and fetishization, but does the negativity of objectification also apply to men's bodies? What about the bodies of men who are also gay? Can I belong to this category?

My bodily experience as a trans boy in this society tells me that my transition from a "female" body that was recognized as "woman" to a trans body recognized as trans masculine was also accompanied by a transition from only object to wholly subject. I have been, in Leslie Green's words, "subjectified."[9] While Green is interested in defending objectification in pornography for gay men who are rarely figured as objects of desire in a heterosexist society, I find that his argument echoes my experiences on Grindr and in most public discourse concerning trans masculine subjects. In the words of Green:

> Gay pornography contributes to gay life what is everywhere else denied – that gay sexualities exist, that gay men are sexual beings, and that men may be objects of male desire. How highly we value all that surely depends on the baseline from which we start. For some objectivity comes easily, subjectivity must be won. For others, including many gay men, subjectivity is fairly secure; it is objectivity that feels precarious and fragile.[10]

One can easily substitute "trans" for "gay" in this quotation. Trans masculine people are featured everywhere as only subjects. Trans masculine subjects who are also sexual beings and objects of male desire are almost absent. We are singers, artists, athletes, activists, and academics. Although most of us certainly experienced the oppression of what it is like to be treated as not more than a piece of meat before transition, we are now resigned to the opposite. Even Tompkins acknowledges that in current public discourse "the acceptable attraction to trans people cannot be sexual; it must go beyond the sexual."[11] I understand that this situation is not only acceptable, but it is even celebrated by most trans masculine folks. I understand that I might actually be alone, but I must at last come to the defense of the "tranny chaser." My existence and my pleasure depend on it.

Epilogue

I just found out about a new fetish hookup site for gay men called Recon. I begrudgingly set up a profile. I realize now that I will likely be treated as other. Men will be afraid to treat me the same way they treat the cismen on the site. Men who are cruising for nothing more than a piece of ass will avoid me. It doesn't help that I live in a small, southern town, so there are few options anyway. It doesn't matter that my participation on a gay fetish site should signal my consent. It doesn't matter that my profile includes that I identify as one hundred percent passive in my sexual role.

But this time it does matter. He calls himself "Exploring Boundaries," and his message says, "I hope you're having a good day, boy. My name is Jack. I'm into domination, leather, and discipline. You should meet me on Monday." He doesn't "reassure" me that he wants me for more than my trans body. He doesn't feel the need to get to know me better. He treats me like the gay boy I have imagined myself to be for at least three decades. If this goes as planned it will be the first time I get to experience what it's truly like to be recognized as a gay boy by a hot gay leather bear. I hope it won't be the last.

Notes

1 I strategically use the language of diagnosis here in place of the more commonly accepted language of assignment to indicate not only that it was under the authority of a doctor that I was assigned to the category "female" in the first place, but it was also only a diagnosis of "gender dysphoria" that allowed me to escape the original diagnosis. The language of assignment does the work of opposing the "born that way" argument in favor of social construction, however, it does not seem to adequately communicate the pathologizing weight of the medical diagnoses we are required to negotiate in order to take agency over our gender/sex.
2 Austin H. Johnson, "Transnormativity: A New Concept and Its Validation through Documentary Film about Transgender Men." *Sociological Inquiry* 86, no. 4 (2016): 466, doi: 10.1111/soin.12127.
3 Johnson, 466.
4 Johnson, 467.
5 Kristin Despina, "Human Connection: 'Straight,' No Chaser," *Acceptance Revolution* (blog), Jan. 22, 2012, https://acceptancerevolution.com/tag/tranny-chasers/.
6 Sabrina Samone, "Ten things a 'Tranny Chaser' says and what it Really Means," *Transmuseplanet* (blog), July 15, 2016, http://transmuseplanet.blogspot.com/2013/07/ten-things-trans-chaser-says-and-what.html.
7 Avery Brooks Tompkins, "'There's No Chasing Involved': Cis/trans Relationships, 'Tranny Chasers,' and the Future of a Sex-positive Trans Politics." *Journal of Homosexuality* 61, no. 5 (2014): 766, doi: 10.1080/00918369.2014.870448.
8 Tompkins, 776.
9 L. Green, "Pornographies." *Journal of Political Philosophy* 8, no. 1 (2000): 46, doi: 10.1111/1467-9760.00091.
10 Green, 48.
11 Tompkins, 771.

Bibliography

Despina, Kristin, "Human Connection: 'Straight,' No Chaser," *Acceptance Revolution* (blog), Jan 22, 2012, https://acceptancerevolution.com/tag/tranny-chasers/.

Green, L. "Pornographies." *Journal of Political Philosophy* 8, no. 1 (2000): 27–52, doi: 10.1111/1467-9760.00091.

Johnson, Austin H. "Transnormativity: A New Concept and Its Validation through Documentary Film about Transgender Men." *Sociological Inquiry* 86, no. 4 (2016): 465–491, doi: 10.1111/soin.12127.

Samone, Sabrina, "Ten Things a 'Tranny Chaser' Says and What It Really Means," *Transmuseplanet* (blog), July 15, 2016, http://transmuseplanet.blogspot.com/2013/07/ten-things-trans-chaser-says-and-what.html.

Tompkins, Avery Brooks. "'There's No Chasing Involved': Cis/trans Relationships, 'Tranny Chasers,' and the Future of a Sex-positive Trans Politics." *Journal of Homosexuality* 61, no. 5 (2014): 766–780, doi: 10.1080/00918369.2014.870448.

GENDER FUCKED

Stories on Love and Lust or How We Released Expectation and Found Ourselves in Trans Sexual Relation

Benny LeMaster and S. Donald Bellamy

A teacher who confesses or professes desire can no longer be scandalous except to those who still believe that the so-called life of the mind has nothing to do with the rest of the body.[1]

To put it bluntly: This essay centers trans people fucking. Respectability politics implores us to offer a content warning of sorts. Though the impetus for such a warning is hard to discern. In respectable terms a content warning might read accordingly: *This chapter contains explicit sexual content including sexually charged and derogatory language and imagery.* However, as folks who embody multiply marginalized locations, narratives of trans sexualities and desires in bodies like our own are anything but explicit nor are they derogatory. They are revolutionary precisely because they are life sustaining; extraordinary and anything but explicit.

> I (Benny) identify as a mixed-race Asian and White non-binary trans person who enacts queer sexualities and who navigates life with both chronic body pain and chronic cycles of anxiety and depression.
>
> I (Donny) identify as a Black transmasculine artist and academic. I spend most of my time trying to make the shift from surviving to thriving.

This chapter flirts with what we term "critical erotica." It includes narratives that meld fiction with nonfiction in order to ponder gender through trans sexualities derived of lived and desired intersectional experience(s). Critical erotica opens the epistemic terrain to envision and realize gender potentiality and affirmation in relational terms that engage and challenge the hegemony of oppressive representations through lived and desired erotic experience. Said more succinctly, critical erotica explores gender identity through erotic experiences that are both experienced and imagined. In this regard, critical erotica theorizes queer means of relating across what Yep terms "spheres of intimacy" and "spheres of desire." Spheres of intimacy include "closeness, deep knowing, mutual attunement, sensuality, and eroticism that could range from fleeting to enduring" while spheres of desire include "wishes, longings, needs, affinities, and yearnings that could range from internally held to externally articulated."[2] These spheres implore us to nuance the relational ties that bind self and/as other; moreover, they empower us to engage and affirm non-normative means of relating and connecting to self as well as to other.

Theorizing the queer relationalities of lived and desired erotic experience as trans folks, we seek to narrate in and through what trans theorist Stone referred to as the "gray area" that often constitutes trans folks' "erotic sense of their[/our] own bodies."[3] Our larger goal then is to complicate the gray areas that constitute our trans gender and sexual bodies through critical erotica in order to "bring 'trans' into a sex-positive arena of language, practice, and erotics that celebrate trans identities and bodies and makes it acceptable to speak the erotics of trans in sex-positive and affirming ways."[4] Sex positive in this sense that critical erotica emerges in response and as an alternative to hegemonic representations of marginalized bodies having *and* enjoying sex on our terms. In this way, critical erotica offers an alternative to what Lorde terms the "pornographic," which "emphasizes sensation without feeling."[5] Conversely, the erotic—especially for women in Lorde's estimation—"is a measure between our sense of self and the chaos of our strongest feelings."[6] Critical erotica engages the relational ties that bind self to/and with other in the context of sexualities unmapped as of yet.

Trans artist Diamond provides an important discursive anchor focusing our critical erotic labor:

> Transgender people maneuver in a world that seemingly offers little hope of finding love … or even good sex. If they aren't ignored and rendered invisible by mainstream narratives of romance, trans and gender-variant folks are consistently portrayed as deviants unsuitable to love. Prostitutes, imposters, freaks: these roles assigned to mainstream transgender characters help reinforce the normative gender binary that destroys any option for true gender fluidity in the world.[7]

Narratives of trans sexualities derived of lived and desired erotic experience serve as a source of empowerment in the agential act of authoring self outside of cisheteronormative logics.[8] Trans scholars have long theorized trans sexual potentialities. For instance, Hale turns to queer leather communities writing sex "practices that decouple genital sexuality from bodily pleasure provide the backdrop for … remapping" or "resignify[ing] sexed bodily zones."[9] Developing Hale, Steinbock theorizes: "The usefulness of sex for trans people (or entities) is that, regardless of surgical or hormonal transformations the body has undergone, sexual practices are an available means to differentiate (and regrow, perhaps) otherwise 'off-limits' body parts."[10] In turn, trans sexualities destabilize cisheteronormative logics in two steps: (1) trans sexualities belie "mimetic gender/sex categories" and in so doing (2) generate subjectivities that emerge relationally.[11]

With Diamond's words we rearticulate a content warning as an invitation. We invite you into a world of gender becoming relationally animated through trans sexualities of which you may already be intimately acquainted. We invite you into a world of explicit affirmation of self and/as other in and through and around a cacophony of erotics defined in terms that can evade, bend, and/or reinforce normativity. We invite you to release expectation and embrace the uncertainty of trans erotics for as Bochner reminds us more generally, "[W]e have to work to overcome our conditioned fears of erotic knowledge."[12] In so doing, we invite you to join us in (un)learning and (re)signifying the "discursive materialization" of gender through trans sexualities.[13] As a result of our lived and desired experiences, our critical erotica traces tales of gender becoming across intersectional lines of flight that resist and challenge—and sometimes reinforce—whiteness, cisheterosexism, ableism, and sizism, specifically. To be certain, this chapter serves less as an ideal for we are not so cavalier as to suggest our sexy ruminations here provide the framework from which all critical erotica should emerge. Rather, we intend to champion a dialogue that refutes the use of sexuality as grounds for gendered ridicule, dismissal, violence, and too often death of trans folks. In this regard, we turn to sex so as to materialize the complexity of gender as an always and already intersectionally constituted embodied structure.

(Un)Knowing Pleasure: Intersectional Flirtations

In this section, we offer three stories of critical erotica that seek to de-center normative gender understanding across embodied intersectional lines of flight. Thereafter, we close our chapter with a collaboratively written piece of critical erotica derived of our lived experiences both as individuals and as trans folks in love and lust with and without one another.

Flirtation 1: De-Transitioning Desire

The first time a gay man asked if I was gay, while sitting in a gay bar, I was confused. Now, I'm just bored.

The bar is busy enough to entice a drink but not busy enough to stay. Three stools sit empty at the bar; I choose the one to the left and sit gesturing toward the bartender. *He's cute,* I think to myself, *though I can't recall his name. Where is my wife, she's much better with names.* A salmon colored tank top, black booty shorts, and sandals accentuate his chubby Brown body. He approaches and asks, "What can I get you, love?" He winks unraveling my cognition.

I blink and look away resetting my mind. "Gin martini. Dry. Three olives." I order confidently, quietly. Routinely.

"Usual." He infers a scripted question as his gaze shifts from my eyes to the shaker.

"Hendricks," I respond. He nods while focused on making my drink. I loosen the top button of my untucked black button-up collared shirt revealing a tuft of light brown chest hair lining the base of my smooth, apple-less neck. Long black denim jeans coupled with black boots fastened with neon pink laces complete my look. I stand six-foot-one and weigh approximately 250 pounds; I am bulky. I wear a well-manicured medium-length beard populated with black, brown, red, silver, and white hairs. Scars dot my face where I once wore facial piercings; a few piercings remain. A fresh razor fade reveals three brightly colored pansies tattooed on the right side of my head, a public reclamation of a term once used to inflict discursive harm on my feminine performance of self. I am a pansy. A large pansy.

"Here you go, love." The bartender smiles placing the martini glass in front of me and atop a cardboard coaster. "Thirteen."

I hand him a ten and a five as I recall his name, "Thanks, Carlos." He smiles as he takes the cash and moves on to the Man who has taken up residency two stools to my right. The Man is older than me by at least a decade; or not. Age is increasingly difficult to discern the closer to forty I find myself. The Man orders a Bud Light as I focus in on my martini. I cradle the base of the martini glass with grace while my pinky stands erect with queer etiquette. I close my eyes and bring the rim of the glass to my lips. I sip, slurping slightly so as to fill my mouth with the tangy punch of chilled gin. It's perfect. My eyes remain closed as I take a deep breathe in followed by a slow warm exhalation. I feel the anxiety flirting with my joints and muscles melt away, releasing the chronic pain in my back. I broke my back nearly a year ago moving something: *Hey you're a man, help lift this.* Well, to be specific, it was a compression fracture in the mid area of my back that exacerbated a degenerative issue in the spine. And it sucked. Well, it sucks. The pain does not go away; it simply abides through deep rhythmic breathing in fleeting moments. Relief is as mythical as it is a state of mind.

About roughly the same time that I broke my back I admitted something of relational importance to myself:

My partner and I are
    not
        sexually
            compatible.

I did not believe sexual compatibility to be a "thing" until I lost it. To be clear, we have been polyamorous for as long as we have dated. In many ways we were never compatible; not in any normative sense.

> My masculine presentation draws her in
> as my feminine performance
> pulls her away. As
> her feminine presentation
> pulls me in
> as her feminine performance
> draws me in
> Closer.

Enbies do not have a "same" or "opposite" sex from which to leverage an "accurate" sexual orientation. Interpolated as "husband" by the State and she "wife" by the State, we are cisheterosexually constituted through Law; a binarized sham that dismisses the complexity of nuance.

> A lifelong of cisheterosexist exclusion alchemically transfigures my gaze as
> His pectorals become her breasts her legs her cock
> Becomes
> His cock his legs his breasts
> My gaze
> De-transitions   My wife.

And so I am here. Sipping my martini. To ease the pain. And to minimize the chasm of loneliness that is result of re-learning relationality in terms that are romantic and asexual. What was once polyamory as a result of desiring liberatory sexuality has become polyamory as a means of securing a queer futurity of our own romantic asexual making.

Muffled sounds draw me back to the stool in the bar as the pain in my back slowly ebbs and flows to the point of usual. I blink my eyes and look down at the martini glass sitting in my right hand, pinky still standing erect. I look to the Man sitting two barstools to my right who is awaiting my eye contact. I ask as I bring the martini glass to my lips, "Excuse me?"

The Man responds with the conspicuously loaded: "Can I ask you a question?" He moves to the stool between us leaning his head in closer to my own.

I can smell his beer breath; it isn't sexy. I wonder what his cock tastes like. I respond, "Sure."

"Are you gay?"

"What do you mean?" I ask genuinely confused.

"You look like some kind of biker dude but you're drinking a *fag* drink" he gestures at my erect pinky and martini glass emphasizing "fag" with vitriol. His demeanor suddenly shifts; we've been here before—claim the term before the homophobe. "I don't know whether you'll kick my ass or fuck it." He seems accomplished by his discursive work as he drowns a guttural chortle with a swig of beer. A simple gesture of sexual tension imbued with power dynamics that would drive some cis gays into a sexualized fantasy-induced frenzy places me on defense. His question—*are you gay*—is complicated. He presses, "So. Are you? Gay."

I don't lie, "Sorta."

"So, you're new?" He dismisses two decades of queer and trans becoming preferring to read me as a closeted gay man touring the gayborhood for an "authentic" gay experience. Or as simply straight.

"Not quite."

"Where are you from?"

"I live two blocks down the street. My wife and I moved here a few years ago."

Ah turns to apathy

> Falls from his lips
> As W-I-F-E renders me:
>   Cheating husband
> Never bi   nor pan   nor queer
> Not enbie[14]   nor trans   nor poly
> Limp wrist, loose lisp

Closet case

Ex-gay

Self-hating; denial

Straight/bent

"So, are you gonna show me how to be gay or what?" I ask acquiescing to a framework of cishomo[15] legibility. After all, I am in pain and lonely. And I want a man to touch me; or fuck me. I commit to boundaries of my own intrapersonal design:

> Sure, you can be my "first"; I wink
>   So long as I cum *first*
> I think to myself, his fat cock filling my throat
>   He craves the thing
>   She awaits
>   (presumed) cisheterosexuality
>   Projected. Again.
> What's your name again, Man?

Flirtation 2: No Choreography, Just Dancing

It is the first time we are meeting. The room is dark. Candles are lit, flickering in the breeze of a small box fan.

I take a seat on the far-left side of the small couch that looks like it would fit better in a dorm room than apartment. She slides down on to the floor. We stare at each other—I'm uncertain for how long. We don't have many other options in this small space.

The apartment is no more than 500 square feet and between the two of us there isn't room to move around. Or to think.

The air is sticky and still—the box fan provides minimal relief.

We stare. I can't actually see her face. Instead, the candles provide glimpses of her jawline. A basic outline of her physique. I see where she curves. I see her curves. Where she dips in and out. Where her body falls in on itself and doubles back out again. I obsess over my body being straight lines, hollow crevices; unimpressive plateaus—the candle light produces shadow that project masculine possibilities.

She collapses to her hands and knees and crawls gently toward me kissing me on the lips. It is short, shorter than I want for our first kiss but pleasant. We hold an intense stare between us before she quickly withdraws back to her corner of the small room. I am intrigued by her forwardness but remain completely still. Her actions confound me. I remain completely still even as I want more.

"Come lay with me," she whispers. I follow her technique, slide down to the floor, and lay next to her. The humidity dissipates, the air lightens, and my ability to breathe returns. She places her head on my bare shoulder and I wrap my arm around her back. The flickering candle highlights our cradling bodies.

"The apartments close to the beach like this didn't need air conditioning when they were built. You could just open the windows and let the breeze cool everything off" she explains.

"Hmm… that makes sense" I respond. Our small talk focuses my attention, which is drawn away as her hand starts to rub the patch of hair below my naval. As tingles spread throughout my body, I understand why they call it a happy trail.

> Up and down.
> Back and forth.
> Back and forth.
> Up and down.
>> Long soothing strokes.
>> Her strokes turn to squeezes.

Up and down.

A grab of the thigh.

Back and forth.

A squeeze on the shoulder.

Up and down.

A pinch on the ass.

Back and forth.

The clasping of hands.

"Is this okay?" I whisper through touches.

"Yes" she responds with confidence and slight annoyance.

My need for Consent. Clarification. Certainty. Interrupt our flow. Or is that our flow is predicated on their absence. That my flow needs recalibration. Rethinking.

There is no more room for words. We are only here to dance.

I give in. I trust. I consent with clear certainty.

Her yes is my yes; I kiss her. She kisses me back with her whole mouth.

Her tongue is wide.

Up and down.

Her lips are full.

Back and forth.

Her lips form a perfect circle around my mouth.

Back and forth.

Her tongue licks my teeth.

Up and down.

Our hearts race. Our breathing is heavy. Her exhale is my inhale; my exhale is her inhale.

Her arm wraps around my

neck and she rubs my face as we kiss. And kiss. And kiss.

No choreography, just dancing.

Clothing that once covered our bodies now decorate the small apartment.

There is pressure in her warm and soft touch. She climbs on top of my boxer covered thighs and places both of her knees parallel to my hips. She lines up our centers and we stare into one another. I am nervous and ready.

Leaning down she slowly kisses me using more air than lips. The weight of her body presses against me and I feel a slight pain in my lower back. I try to ignore it and focus on the way she kisses me slowly.

"Mmm" she moans. Her lips encircle mine again and I strain my neck to eagerly lean into her touch. I have never felt this way before. It's the feeling of anticipation before a roller-coaster takes off. The nervousness when a thunderstorm is near. The recognition of kinfolk after years apart. I feel all of this...and I also feel small.

Her body consumes mine and I start to think about how my bones stick out in places that are soft on others. How my hips are too wide from puberty; my hands and feet not wide enough, not big enough. I fixate on being four inches shorter than her and I forget our rules of no choreography. I count my steps to keep up with her confidence in an effort to evade the quicksand of dysphoric dissociation attempting to pull me in.

Her hand lowers to greet my shoulder.
One-two-three.
My shoulder shifts up to meet her hand.
Four-five-six.
She pushes me down.
One-two-three.
Arms around arms.
Four-five-six.
Frantically, as much as possible, I try to entangle my body with hers. I want some type of control. I feel out of control. Lost in another's dance.
One-two- … four, was it?.
My neck lifts to kiss her. She darts back to deny me access.
Four - five ---
"What's wrong?" I ask slightly panicked.
My sexual engagements are so limited.
Silence.
Do I know what I'm doing?
Only stares.
I've never had sex with someone who identifies as "super-fat." She's never had sex with someone who identifies as "trans."
"Nothing's wrong." She answers. Rubbing my face, "relax, it's just us." she reminds me.
Relax, I think, it's us… and all of my internalized transphobia that I hold in my small Black trans masculine body.
I take a deep breath trying to internalize her words and assuredness. More silence. More stares. Everything around me fades away as we find our way back to one another and we become only present for each other.
My lips press into hers and as hard as I can, almost as if I'm trying to push her away with my mouth. She pushes back.
I realize
There is no control to gain.
No choreography, just dancing.
We improvise rhythms of *kissing* and *moaning* and *breathing*.
Sucking lips.

Back and forth
    Tongues fighting.
Up and down
    Heavy gasps.
Up and down
    Wetness. Everywhere.
Back and forth

Moving past her silk nightgown, my hands find the moment where her hips become her thighs and they melt into her. I slowly thrust my hips up toward her body. My ass clenches to maintain my pelvic thrust. My entire body erupts in pure happiness as I enter her. Her eyes close as her body flinches and stiffens up.

"Can you feel that?" I ask. The way she slides down to meet my body lets me know she feels my phallus, too; together our bodies refuse cissexist interpellation in favor of a queer sexual formation.

We stare at each other and her only affirmative is in the form of a nod.

Her nod is enough.
No further communication needed.
Bodies are (ir)relevant when we decolonize our minds.
We are a flowing electric current.
Dancing without choreography.
She shifts back and forth.
    I thrust my hips into her.
Up and down.
    She pushes her body down to meet me.
Back and forth.
    I can feel her around my dick.
Back and forth.
    Warm.
        Wet.
    Soft like velvet.
Up and down.
    The air is sticky and still. The small box fan whirring endlessly.

My body is tingly and warm. With every thrust a small bolt of energy ignites in my stomach. Emotionally, I am overwhelmed. We are a magnetic field multiplying at an unprecedented rate. Every nerve ending in my body fires. Our connection is spiritual. It is my body, but I have let go of feudalistic control; embraced that The Holy Spirit has entered and we are now both speaking in tongues. No choreography, just dancing.

I feel a frisson of the unknown run through me.

> Up and down.
>> Scared.
> Back and forth.
>> Viscerally aware I've never fucked//like this before.
> Up and down.
>> Never even thought about doing.
> Back and forth.
>> My body and her body aren't shown together. We aren't in any imagination but of our own improvised design.
>> Bodies like ours are not seen dancing across the stage of the cultural imaginary.
>> Her darkness, curves, softness don't get displayed against my Black boney frame.
>> Black trans dicks don't get ridden.
>> Short and skinny bodies are held but never hold.
>> Fat Black girls don't get held; they are supposed to be undesirable. Ignored. Never seen.
> The world around me hasn't prepared me for my own pleasure!
> There is no choreography, just dancing.

Eventually she re-positions herself so that her face is in-between my legs, her hands clasp the outside of my thighs, and her ass stands straight up consuming my view. I feel her warm breath through my boxers as she begins to give me head. Her mouth and face run along the entirety of my crotch.

Back and forth.

Her exploration continues for some time and I am nervous from the vulnerability and anticipation of what she will do next. My body stiffens. The electricity shuts off. Darkness; stillness are left.

Sensing my hesitation, she looks toward me and waits before continuing. Her face flickers in the candlelight and it guides me back through the darkness. We stare at each other and my only affirmative is in the form of a nod. No further communication needed.

> Bodies are (ir)relevant.
> We are a flowing electric current once again.
> My yes is her yes and her mouth opens to perform fellatio through my shorts.
>> Her tongue is wide.
> Up and down.
>> Her lips are full.

Back and forth.
>Lips encircle.

Back and forth.
>Tongue massages.

Up and down.
>My Black trans dick.

Our bodies exist in ways the normative world wishes were impossible—in pleasure.

We enter and exit, kiss and contort, lick and slobber. No body part is spared. Elbows, necks, the backs of knees, pussies, dicks, feet…If it feels good, we do it.

Her yes is my yes.
>We dance without choreography until the sun comes up.

Up and down.

Back and forth.

Back and forth.

Up and down.

Flirtation 3: FEMME's Dystopic Euphoria

To be frank, I am bored. Turned on and bored. We are sitting on either side of his sectional couch. His bare back slouches against one couch end. His hairless, broad, bare chest reveals his bodybuilding labor. Two dark brown areolas the size of nickels dots either of his pectorals. His arms are large, masculine, protective, and scary: his right arm rests across his toned abdomen as he rests his left hand behind his head revealing his armpit; I lick my lips as I envision burying my face in his hairy pits but pretend not to stare—it's their game, not mine: Look, don't look. Finely detailed musculature traces his left leg, which extends out and toward the corner sectional where I sit. I feel the warmth radiating from his foot ride along my right outer thigh; his toenails are long and unattended. I overlook this as a biologically deterministic limitation: Men are gross. His right leg is curled tucking his foot in near his groin. His scrotum is purple-reddish and dangles down between his legs covering the fold of his ass cheeks and hole. I smile as I visually take in his unassuming flaccid cock, which is a shade sexier than his rough skin. The precum riding the tip of his foreskin glistens in the blue glow of the television. I lick my lips, hungry. A tuft of dark brown unkempt pubic hair hugs his cock and balls—the same thick, dark brown hair covers his ass cheeks and legs. He is sexy. And his masculine body terrifies me. I act cool; as if this is ordinary.

I sit on the complimentary side of the sectional couch, my clothed back sitting upright against the cushion. I face the small plasma television sitting atop a black bookshelf populated with video games, digital music equipment, paperback science fiction and fantasy novels, and empty bottles of liquor. I wear a button-up shirt, black denim, and a pair of boots. He sits to my right as I pretend to play on my cell phone waiting for the moment when the straightness of heterosexuality bends. We've been here before; both of us, in different contexts and with different people—and with one another.

Neither of us are "gay."

Both of us desire—no, crave—Touch.

"My favorite part is coming up," he says excitedly as he turns the volume up. We're watching *Mad Max: Fury Road*. Whether it includes tossing a ball, playing a video game, or watching a filmic and epic fight scene: the price I often pay to fuck cishet[16] men includes engaging in cultural performances of hyper-masculinity that provide balance for what they perceive as a less masculine performance: being fucked by a fat and hairy enbie who presents masculine and performs feminine. In essence, we share the same "favorite part": We fuck as we re-assert in our respective ways how *not gay* this really is. While I do not identify as a man, I do desire men. And in this large, hairy, fat body that often means meeting gay men, whose preconceived notions of "gay" and "man" exclude enbie and queer embodiments like my own. And so I often turn to cisheterosexual men who are able to perceive my femininity, my queerness, and my transness on its own terms.

Behind closed doors.

He presses pause and stands up, stretching his beautiful masculine body as he arches his back. He walks toward me pushing the coffee table away from the couch. He stands naked to my right as I look toward the paused image on the monitor. He extends his left hand out and places it atop my head, gently turning my head so that I can face him. I look up at him as he looks down at me smiling as he asks, "Can I get you anything?" The fingers of his left hand cradle the back of my head as his thumb gently grazes my cheek and into my beard. I'm blushing. "How about some water?" I nod. He walks to the kitchen, his hairy ass entices. I'm turned on and harder than I have been in a long time. He returns to the living room and places the glass of water on the coffee table. He stretches once more arching his back and inching his groin closer to my face; I can smell the musk emanating from his body drawing me in; I am intoxicated. "I'm gonna take a piss. When I get out you had better be naked. I can't be the only one naked in here." He smiles as he closes the door. I swear he winked.

My heart races; we're at a crossroads. Again. My mind shifts to dissociation as my clothes fall to the ground. I'm nude sitting in the same place on the couch as he exits the bathroom. He pauses taking in my round, pasty, hairy, soft body. "You're beautiful." I exhale with relief feeling grounded as he uses words that feminize my body; I lie to myself: *You do not need his validation.*

I want him in me;
to fuck me into affirmation.

In ways that concurrently affirm his cishetero masculinity and my queer enbie femininity; to perform a queer hetero sexuality. A queer hetero sexuality that does not limit "sex" in terms that define but envisions what sex can do in terms that imagine. A queer hetero sexuality that allows for fluidity through normative discursive constraints.

He presses play and the infamous chase scene ensues across the dystopian desert. I grab his ankles as he slides onto his back; his gaze shifts from me to Imperator Furiosa and back to me as I toss his knees to his chest. His muscle succumbs to my fatness as the weight of my body presses down and onto the back of his thighs revealing a hint of pink just below thick dark brown hair. My manicured nails feature a glittery blue polish that compliments my tattooed knuckles: my left knuckles read "BUTCH" and my right read "FEMME." BUTCH grasps the underside of his right thigh as FEMME clasps the underside of his left thigh and I lower the weight of my body onto his thighs. As he winces for breath my tongue traces the rim of his hole—his breathing will not find a steady rhythm for a while. Heavy, long yet short, slow breathes punctuate the mediated apocalyptic fight ensuing in the background.

I press my tongue against his pink anus, taking him in. Slowly, FEMME shifts focus as my middle finger begins to wrestle my tongue. In time, fingers and tongue dance in suit as I slowly enter him. One finger. Two fingers. In and out. More tongue. Grunt. Breathe. Tongue switches to lube. Three fingers. Four. All but the "F" in FEMME are inside of him. BUTCH continues pressing weight against the back of his thighs.

As he exhales I lean up and in lowering my face toward his. The four fingers of my left hand slowly enter and exit his hole as our lips connect and breathe one another in and out. He tilts his head up and presses his lips against mine sealing our mouths as his tongue slowly rides the inside of my mouth. Our tongues touch and ripple to singularity as I continue slowly finger-fucking him. He releases his lips as he whispers through exacerbated and sweaty breathes: "I'm getting close." I take his cue as my fingers speed up fucking him harder, deeper, and faster. Shallow breaths pick up pace as the quiver in his legs reverberate up and into his core and chest. He grabs my arm and thrusts it toward him demanding "ALL OF IT!" My fist enters him as he arches his back and releases an orgasm through clenched teeth; sweat flings from the tips of his now wet hair that land on my face and chest. I slowly fist him as he rides a wave of euphoria. This will be the first anal induced orgasm for the night.

The film credits have long ended as I withdraw my hand smiling down at him. He sits up scoots over and onto my lap resting his head on my sweaty chest. He runs his fingers through the hair on my chest as he looks up at me smiling, "Thank you." His lips meet my pink areolas as the tip of his tongue tickles my right nipple. He whispers, "And now it's your turn, lady." He shifts his weight

and slowly lays me down onto the couch; my fatness gives way to his musculature as the relational dynamics transform: I am his bottom. And the way he bites
his lip tells me he sees me; wants me.

Finding Self in (Trans Sexual) Relation: An Arousing

Critical erotica provides a narrative platform in which to theorize intersectional and relational becoming in sexual contexts derived of lived and
desired experience. This work is indebted to the profound trailblazing work
of organic intellectuals making sense of our lives as trans people who are
sexual, too.[17] At the same, critical erotica is informed by work theorized
within the academy. Pensoneau-Conway calls for a "pedagogy of the erotic"
that "makes the experiencing body matter" by focusing on the ways "desire,
passion, and curiosity are wrapped up in the body; they are bodily experiences."[18] If, as Pensoneau-Conway remarks, sexuality is a "communicative
relationship," then critical erotica provides narrative grounds on which to
sustain an intellectual and poetic pursuit of embodied knowing through critical eroticism. Moreover, critical erotica daringly challenges what Greteman
theorizes as "intimatphobia" or the fear and hatred of "acts and individuals that disrupt the status quo or proper manners of relating to others."[19]
Informed by Sedgwick, Greteman understands intimaphobia as reflecting
a paranoid reading of intimacy in education contexts that is exacerbated by
"education's emphasis on the law and legislation to deal with classroom relationships and dynamics that 'cross the line.'"[20]

Critical erotica no doubt *crosses the line* and in turn implicates each of us differently based on our respective intersectional embodiments. The implication
nonetheless reveals less about the trans sexual relationalities here and more about
the intersectional structures discursively and performatively constituting non-
normative formations as *crossing the line* while others accomplish the same to
different—often congratulatory—ends. And so we end where we began: With
a content warning of sorts: The material you just read was intended to unravel
you. For the profound learning to be had is not located in seeking to authenticate
gender with some farcical certainty claiming material realness but in recognizing and releasing the violent normative sexual expectations we thrust onto bodies as a result of the gender(s) we would rather someone performed for our own
relational and erotic becoming.

Flirtation 4: Willfully Loving

"Is this okay?" He asks. His teeth peek through a smile that cracks at the corners
of his plump lips. I like the way he smiles when we're alone.

"Yes." They respond nervously. Excited. Their coy meets my brazen.

We meet at affirmation as olive oil melds fingers to clit and balls. Our eyes fuse as our breath cycles to one. They grunt quietly; their pelvis rotates slowly as their bear ass massages my worn out couch cushions.

"Can I touch you there?" He whispers while spreading my thighs to tickle my balls just beyond my clit. His right hand meets my form as his grasp tightens slightly, moving up and down, back and forth. "When's the last time you fucked and it felt good?" He inquires.

"Good in every way?" They ask clarifying. Sweat gathers across the brow they resent.

"Good in every way," He answers in kind, his deep voice penetrates as he bites his lip; his gaze focuses his handy work. My clit is hard, ready to give.

"I'm still waiting." Their breath
                    misses a beat as my pace quickens.
                    They are ready to give.

"You deserve orgasms." He remarks. His hands slip and slide, our skin glazed with oil.

"And so do you." They respond leaning forward, slowing my hand. Our lips meet and their legs quiver.

                I toss a leg across their lap my dick hovering as their clit explodes
                                                    into a chain reaction
                                                            Improvised
                                                    Panting and holding
                                            As we collapse into one/another

His/their dick/clit
F(r)ictions materialized.
            You deserve orgasms.   Your body deserves orgasms.
            And love.
And touch.

Notes

1 Steven Ungar, "The Professor of Desire." *Yale French Studies* 63 (1982): 82, doi: 10.2307/2929833.
2 Gust A. Yep. "Further Notes on Healing from 'The Violence of Heteronormativity in Communication Studies.'" *QED* 4, no. 2 (2017): 120, doi: 10.14321/qed.4.2.0115.
3 Sandy Stone. "The *Empire* Strikes Back: A Posttranssexual Manifesto," in *The Transgender Studies Reader*, eds. Susan Stryker and Steven Whittle (New York, NY: Routledge, 2006), 228.
4 Avery B. Tompkins. "'There's no Chasing Involved': Cis/trans Relationships, 'Tranny Chasers,' and the Future of a Sex-Positive Trans Politics." *Journal of Homosexuality* 61, no. 5 (2014): 774, doi: 10.1080/00918369.2014.870448.
5 Audre Lorde. *Sister Outsider* (New York, NY: Ten Speed Press, 1984/2007), 54.
6 Lorde, 54.

7 Morty Diamond, editor. *Trans/love: Radical Sex, Love, and Relationships Beyond the Gender Binary* (San Francisco, CA: Manic D Press, 2011), 7.
8 Frederick C. Corey and Thomas K. Nakayama, "Sextext." *Text and Performance Quarterly* 17, no. 1, (1997): 58–68, doi: 10.1080/10462939709366169.
9 C. Jacob Hale, "Leatherdyke Boys and Their Daddies: How to Have Sex without Women or Men." *Social Text* 15, no. 3–4 (1997): 230, https://www.jstor.org/stable/466741.
10 Eliza Steinbock, "On the Affective Force of 'Nasty Love.'" *Journal of Homosexuality* 61, no. 5 (2014): 761–762, doi: 10.1080/00918369.2014.870446.
11 Steinbock, 758.
12 Arthur P. Bochner, "Criteria against Ourselves." *Qualitative Inquiry* 6, no. 2 (2000): 271, doi: 10.1177/107780040000600209.
13 Eva Hayward, "Spider City Sex." *Women and Performance* 20, no. 3 (2010): 227, doi: 10.1080/0740770X.2010.529244.
14 "Enbie" is a broad identity marker used to reference non-binary gender identities.
15 "Cishomo" is shorthand for cishomosexual, which combines cisgender with homosexual.
16 "Cishet" is shorthand for cisheterosexual, which combines cisgender with heterosexual.
17 Patrick Califia. *Boy in the Middle: Erotic Fiction* (San Francisco, CA: Cleis Press, 2005); *Trans Entities: The Nasty Love of Papí and Wil*, directed by Morty Diamond (2007; United States: Self distributed, digital; Diamond, *Trans/love*; Tobi Hill-Meyer. *Nerve Endings: The New Trans Erotic* (http://www.instarbooks.com/, 2007); Tristan Taormino, editor. *Take me There: Trans and Genderqueer Erotica* (Jersey City, NJ: Cleis Press, 2011).
18 Sandra L. Pensoneau-Conway, "Desire and Passion as Foundations for Teaching and Learning: A Pedagogy of the Erotic." *Basic Communication Course Annual* 21 (2009): 185, http://ecommons.udayton.edu/bcca/vol21/iss1/12.
19 Adam Joseph Greteman, "Beyond Intimaphobia: Object Lessons from Foucault and Sade." *Educational Philosophy and Theory* 46, no. 7 (2014): 750, doi: 10.1080/00131857.2013.792724.
20 Greteman, 749.

Bibliography

Bochner, Arthur P. "Criteria against Ourselves." *Qualitative Inquiry* 6, no. 2 (2000): 266–272, doi: 10.1177/107780040000600209.

Califia, Patrick. *Boy in the Middle: Erotic Fiction*. San Francisco, CA: Cleis Press, 2005.

Corey, Frederick C. and Thomas K. Nakayama. "Sextext." *Text and Performance Quarterly* 17, no. 1 (1997): 58–68, doi: 10.1080/10462939709366169.

Diamond, Morty, editor. *Trans/love: Radical Sex, Love, and Relationships Beyond the Gender Binary*. San Francisco, CA: Manic D Press, 2011.

Greteman, Adam Joseph. "Beyond Intimaphobia: Object Lessons from Foucault and Sade." *Educational Philosophy and Theory* 46, no. 7 (2014): 748–763, doi: 10.1080/00131857.2013.792724.

Hale, C. Jacob. "Leatherdyke Boys and their Daddies: How to Have Sex without Women or Men." *Social Text* 15, no. 3–4 (1997): 223–236, https://www.jstor.org/stable/466741.

Hayward, Eva. "Spider City Sex." *Women and Performance* 20, no. 3 (2010): 225–251, doi: 10.1080/0740770X.2010.529244.

Hill-Meyer, Tobi. *Nerve Endings: The New Trans Erotic*. Instar Books: http://www.instarbooks.com/, 2007).

Lorde, Audre. *Sister Outsider*. New York, NY: Ten Speed Press, 1984/2007.

Pensoneau-Conway, Sandra L. "Desire and Passion as Foundations for Teaching and Learning: A Pedagogy of the Erotic." *Basic Communication Course Annual* 21 (2009): 173–206, http://ecommons.udayton.edu/bcca/vol21/iss1/12.

Steinbock, Eliza. "On the Affective Force of 'Nasty Love.'" *Journal of Homosexuality* 61, no. 5 (2014): 749–765, doi: 10.1080/00918369.2014.870446.

Stone, Sandy. "The *Empire* Strikes Back: A Posttranssexual Manifesto." In *The Transgender Studies Reader*, 1st ed., 221–235. Edited by Susan Stryker and Steven Whittle. New York, NY: Routledge, 2006.

Taormino, Tristan, editor. *Take Me There: Trans and Genderqueer Erotica.* Jersey City, NJ: Cleis Press, 2011.

Tompkins, Avery B. "'There's No Chasing Involved': Cis/Trans Relationships, 'Tranny Chasers,' and the Future of a Sex-Positive Trans Politics." *Journal of Homosexuality* 61, no. 5 (2014): 766–780, doi: 10.1080/00918369.2014.870448.

Ungar, Steven. "The Professor of Desire." *Yale French Studies* 63 (1982): 80–97, doi: 10.2307/2929833.

Yep, Gust A. "Further Notes on Healing from 'The Violence of Heteronormativity in Communication Studies.'" *QED* 4, no. 2 (2017): 115–122, doi: 10.14321/qed.4.2.0115.

Untitled

Danny Shultz

Dysphoria is
Not about
A discrepancy
Between my
Genitals and
My gender;
It is
About a
Discrepancy between
My existence
And
Cultural ideology.

Untitled 2

Danny Shultz

> Gender is the solution
> To problems
> Without questions.

SECTION IV

Queering History, Imagining Futures

The term "futurity" signals a shift in research praxis to focus on advancing liberation and creating a future environment free from oppression, trauma, violence, and discrimination. It is a political future that assumes humans have done the work to rid their communities of physical, discursive, and legislative violence. It is also a fictional future that strives to offer hope for those most marginalized. Thus, futurity studies exist beyond the horizons of our current constraints, center on the nuanced connections between the political present and the hopeful future, and thus require radical imagination to resist the idea that marginalized bodies are always already doomed.[1]

"Radical imagination," as defined by Max Haiven and Alex Khasnabish, is the "socio-political possibility... of dynamic and shared visions animated by individuals and collectives as they struggle."[2] Imagination helps us to define what *could be* in the future. In the pursuit of social justice, imagination plays an important role in the fundamentally political labor of redefining the social world. The word "radical" is concerned with deeper meanings, implying that we must look beyond answers on the surface and strive to uncover the reasons for our present realities. "The radical imagination [then] is not just about dreaming of different futures. It's about bringing those possibilities back from the future to work on the present."[3] Or in bell hooks' words, radical politics work to "eradicate domination and transform society."[4]

In his groundbreaking text *Freedom Dreams: The Black Radical Imagination,* Robin D. G. Kelley offers a historical outline of Black radical imagination in the United States that follows how Black intellectuals and freedom fighters envisioned freedom.[5] He wanted to understand how radical thinkers imagined their life after revolution and where their ideas came from. He posed the question,

"What kind of world [do] we want to struggle for?"[6] Khasnabish and Haiven stated, "Imagination is a collective process rather than an individualized thing and emerges not from unique geniuses in their romanticized autonomy, but from communities and collectivities as they work their way through their world."[7] With this in mind, radical imagination is not the task of one person. It is something we do collectively to reimagine and build the future. As institutions and those in power change, so does the radical imagination. It is not constant; therefore, it cannot be singularly defined. Social movements, however, implicitly convoke radical imagination. To fight for change in the future that is unknown is to radically imagine the possible outcomes based on prior knowledge and learned experiences. Struggling for the world we want to live in is an exercise in both invoking the radical imagination and futurity, while also rebelling against determinacy.[8]

My (Amber) entrance into futurity and the Black radical imagination stems from Afrofuturism. Birthed from a nexus of social movement, technology, transnational capital, and artistic expression, Afrofuturism is an aesthetic manifestation of storytelling critically aware of possibility.[9] Designed to project the mind and body into a future free from colonialism, Afrofuturistic artists, activists, and scholars look toward the critical embodiment of Afrocentric imagination in art forms such as film, music, visual art, fashion, and literature as a means of replacing presumed whiteness as authority. Afrofuturists argue that "a person's Black state of consciousness, released from the confining and crippling slave or colonial mentality, becomes aware of the multitude and varied possibilities and probabilities within the universe."[10] Within the refrain is a nod to history, institutional and political memory, the present, and the future. Afrofuturists rely on memory and history to inform the present in order to critically reimagine alternative futures.

While the language of Afrofuturism creates a level of unification that renders the critical imagination of blackness visible, the ways in which androgyny has been employed as a technological future create tension. Genderless and androgynous android narratives create a particular kind of gender freedom, or freedom from gender in futuristic imaginings, but not all bodies want to be genderless, and not all bodies can transgress into genderless embodiment due to various aesthetic, genetic, capitalistic, and/or cultural reasons. So what does a futurity that embraces non-normative sexualities and genders offer the radical imagination? Queer futurity pushes us to think through what it means for bodies to be free from the constraints of binary gender and heteronormativity, while also wrestling with the roles that memory, the present, and history play in the liberated future.

My (Benny) entrance into futurity is through queer futurity, which serves as an alternative and complimentary entrance point that tends to non-normative racialized sexual and gender identities with intention while wrestling with the future/present dichotomy. José Esteban Muñoz defines queer futurity as "a temporal arrangement in which the past is a field of possibility in which subjects can act in the present in the service of a new futurity."[11] Writing against the whiteness organizing dominant queer culture (i.e., "homonormativity"), including individualized articulations of "freedom," Muñoz argued queer modes of relating (e.g., family of choice versus family of origin; other non-normative means of relating) serves as the ground for cultural transformation or worldmaking. This focus on the relational continues to serve as an important point of departure for critical communication research, particularly as it pertains to the embodied and mundane performance of survival as queer and trans subjects of color.[12] More specifically, queer futurities desire a queer relational ethic in the present that was never realized in the past. Though, Muñoz warns us of the false future/present dichotomy, arguing "against disappearing wholly into since 'one cannot afford' to simply 'turn away from the present.'"[13] Muñoz argues that the present demands our ethical considerations. The goal is not to recuse history or the present, but rather to use it a vantage point to understand intersectional power before and after catastrophe. Critics of campaigns like "It Gets Better" argue that focusing on the future too heavily diminishes the struggles of the current moment and reduces liberation to a time pinpointed to a horizon that, in reality for many queer and gender non-conforming people of color, may never be reached.[14] However, Dustin Goltz's investigation into the "It Gets Better" campaign found that it offers a semblance of Muñozian perspective. Goltz argued that the campaign was successful at highlighting memory, the past, and the present by mapping queer futures through multivocality, internal contradiction, and a reimagining of what *better* might be for varying bodies within systems of intersectional power.[15]

Another campaign that reflects Muñoz's desire to be considerate of past and present while forging futures is ACT UP. Upon reflecting on ACT UP's 25th anniversary, Pascal Emmer calls for a "critical nostalgia," or what James Clifford, interpreting Raymond William's, called "a way to break with the hegemonic present by asserting the reality of a radical alternative."[16] Emmer asks us to be critically nostalgic "regarding not just what histories we tell but how this very telling structures the rules of engagement between queer leftist generations."[17] Emmer argues for a "meta-generational approach to connecting ACT UP's past with the current AIDS movement, and the potential of a queer future, by recognizing the multiple histories and presents available as political resources."[18] Emmer goes on to suggest that "metagenerational work is urgently important because it constitutes an active and archival process; it interfaces past and present activist knowledges."[19]

Both queer futurity and Afrofuturism rely on historical and personal memory to forge into potential. By replaying the constraints of the past but flipping them, memory becomes a source of resistance and possibility.[20] Utilizing memory is not a function of forgiving the colonial and cisheteronormative past, but rather a flipping of the past and present to provide an alternative future that glimmers in hope and potential realities, albeit far fetched feeling or not. By locating future in the past and present, we alter our present.

The chapters in this section use memory and hope to distill through the nuance of being present and future queers. They also offer up a lived experience full of contradiction, nihilism, and hope for a future that doesn't diminish pain for a broken ideology of "it gets better," but rather a full recognition of the political, cultural, and systemic constraints that contextualize our past, present, and future. Kai M. Green opens the section with a poem about childhood mothering and the radical potential of the push and pull of straightening hair as a metaphor for the tenuous relationship many trans children face when negotiating their gender identities with authoritative adults. In "The Burgundy Coat," Craig Gingrich-Phillbrook reflects on the enduring effect of being asked, as a child, to choose a sports coat for his father's funeral, but then being told he chose a color that "boys don't wear." His writing style attempts to track and represent the vagaries of memory, but also their importance, despite their uncertainty. In "A Present, Past, Future Negotiation of Queer Femme Identity," Kathryn Hobson writes through "FemMe-mories," or memories interspliced with a performance about her femme gender identity in the academy. She recalls how she negotiated her femme gender identity throughout life, both in present and past, and suggests that the future is femme. In "Narrative Embodiment of Queer Futurity: Pause for Dramatic Affect," Shane T. Moreman offers masculine Latinx intersectionality as considerations toward queer futurity by peering into his life growing up as a child juxtaposed to the shooting at Pulse nightclub in Florida. He demonstrates how queer futurity is created by performing queer memory. As queer memories are re-told, they say less about the moment remembered and more about the queer present moment lived. If read through a trans framework, Moreman argues that his memories offer insights into a queer future to be imagined. The poem "Pulse," by Amber L. Johnson follows as a memorial and space of grieving for the victims of the Pulse night Club shooting.

In "Writing a Hard and Passing Rain: Auto-Theory, Autoethnography, and Queer Futures," Stacy Holman Jones experiments with "auto-critical" writing that puts together ideas about intersectional critique, feminism and queer utopias in a dance of identities, stories, and lists. Finally, in "Pay It No Mind," Vin Olefer considers what happens when we embody the wise words of Marsha P. Houston who said the "P" in her name stands for "Pay It No Mind!" What do we free up in our own lives when we stop paying mind to the ideologies, theories, standards, and normative notions that attempt to control our bodies and spirits? This section does just that by attending to the notions we should pay no mind via intentional disruption and evolution. Each author points to a moment in time and/or memory that fosters senses of self while also serving as departure points for future selves. In order to imagine radical futures, we must be attentive to the past and present, but not be constrained by them. The chapters in this section grapple with historical and personal memory, their connections to the present, and plausible departures for the future.

Discussion Questions

1. Each author argues for queer gender and queer sexualities through memory and often metaphor. How do you make sense of your gender identity through to memory, metaphor, and masculine/feminine ideals?
2. Re-read the narratives and find examples of intersectionality. What are some strong examples of intersectionality? Where could the authors have done better? Where is the author out-of-date with intersectionality from the time in which you are reading them? Where might the authors be ahead of the time in which you are reading them?
3. If you could create a future community where gender freedom and liberation exist, what would that community look like? How would it function? What would make it hard to imagine that future or alternative?
4. List at least three primary identities that are not your gender directly, but inform your gender. What are the structural constraints that allow these different identities to work with and against each other as they inform your gender? Place your list in conversation with your peers. Where are the overlaps and tensions that take place? How do you understand your genders as unique and relational at the same time?
5. If you could perform gender in any way you want, what would it look like? How would your performance of gender change the way the people see you or interact with you?

Notes

1 Dustin Goltz. "It Gets Better: Queer Futures, Critical Frustrations, and Radical Potentials." *Critical Studies in Media Communication* 30, no. 2 (2013): 135–151, doi: 10.1080/15295036.2012.701012.; Jeffrey McCune. "The Queerness of Blackness." *QED: A Journal in GLBTQ Worldmaking* 2, no. 2 (2015): 173–176, https://www.muse.jhu.edu/article/585660.
2 Max Haiven and Alex Khasnabish. "What Is the Radical Imagination?" *Affinities: A Journal of Radical Theory, Culture, and Action* 4, no. 2 (2010): iii, https://ojs.library.queensu.ca/index.php/affinities/article/view/6128.
3 Haiven and Khasnabish, iii.
4 bell hooks. *Feminist Theory: From Margin to Center* (New York, NY: Routledge, 2014), 20.
5 Robin D. G. Kelley. *The Black Radical Imagination* (Boston, MA: Beacon Press, 2002).
6 Kelley, 7.
7 Alex Khasnabish and Max Haiven. "Convoking the Radical Imagination." *Cultural Studies ↔ Critical Methodologies* 12, no. 5 (2012): 419, doi: 10.1177/1532708612453126.

8 Christian De Cock, Alf Rehn, and David Berry. "For a Critical Creativity: The Radical Imagination of Cornelius Castoriadis," in *Handbook of Research on Creativity*, eds. Kerry Thomas and Janet Chan (Northampton, MA; Edward Elgar, 2009), 150–161.

9 Reynaldo Anderson and John Jennings. "Afrofuturism: The Digital Turn and the Visual Art of Kanye West," in *The Cultural Impact of Kanye West*, ed. Julius Bailey (New York, NY: Palgrave Macmillan, 2014), 35.

10 Andrew Rollins. "Afrofuturism and Our Old Ship of Zion: The Black Church in Post Modernity," in *Afrofuturism 2.0: The Rise of Astro-Blackness,* eds. Reynaldo Anderson and Charles Jones (Lanham, MD: Lexington Books, 2015), 127.

11 José Esteban Muñoz. *Cruising Utopia: The Then and There of Queer Futurity* (Durham, NC: Duke University Press, 2009), 16.

12 Robert Gutierrez-Perez and Luis Andrade. "Queer of Color Worldmaking." *Text and Performance Quarterly* 38, no. 1–2 (2018): 1–18, doi: 10.1080/10462937.2018.1435130; Benny LeMaster. "Unlearning the Violence of the Normative." *QED* 4, no. 2 (2017): 123–130, doi: 10.14321/qed.4.2.0123; Benny LeMaster, Danny Shultz, J. Nyla, Gray Bowers, and Rusty Rust. "Unlearning Cisheteronormativity at the Intersections of Difference: Performing Queer Worldmaking through Collaged Relational Autoethnography." *Text and Performance Quarterly* 39, no. 4 (2019): 341–370, doi: 10.1080/10462937.2019.1672885; Shane T. Moreman and Stephanie R. Briones. "Deaf Queer World-making." *Journal of International and Intercultural Communication* 11, no. 3 (2018): 216–232, doi: 10.1080/17513057.2018.1456557; Gust A Yep. "Further Notes on Healing from 'The Violence of Heteronormativity in Communication Studies.'" *QED* 4, no. 2 (2017): 115–122, doi: 10.14321/qed.4.2.0115.

13 Joshua Chambers-Letson, Tavia Nyong'o, and Ann Pellegrini. "Foreword," in *Cruising Utopia: The Then and There of Queer Futurity*, ed. José Esteban Muñoz (Durham, NC: Duke University Press, 2009), 16.

14 Tina Majkowski. "The 'It Gets Better Campaign': An Unfortunate use of Queer Futurity." *Women and Performance* 21, no. 1 (2011): 163–165, doi: 10.1080/0740770X.2011.563048.

15 Goltz, 139.

16 James Clifford and George E. Marcus, editors. *The Poetics and Politics of Ethnography* (Berkeley, CA: University of California Press, 1986), 114.

17 Pascal Emmer. "Talkin' 'Bout Meta-Generation: ACT UP History and Queer Futurity." *Quarterly Journal of Speech* 98, no. 1 (2012): 93, doi: 10.1080/00335630.2011.638664.

18 Emmer, 93.

19 Emmer, 94.

20 Amber Johnson. "Confessions of a Video Vixen: My Autocritography of Sexuality, Desire, and Memory." *Text and Performance Quarterly* 34, no. 2 (2014): 182–200, doi: 10.1080/10462937.2013.879991.

Bibliography

Anderson, Reynaldo and John Jennings. "Afrofuturism: The Digital Turn and the Visual Art of Kanye West." In *The Cultural Impact of Kanye West*, 29–44. Edited by Julius Bailey. New York, NY: Palgrave Macmillan, 2014.

Chambers-Letson, Joshua, Tavia Nyong'o, and Ann Pellegrini. "Foreword." In *Cruising Utopia: The Then and There of Queer Futurity*, ix–xvi. Edited by José Esteban Muñoz. Durham, NC: Duke University Press, 2009.

Clifford, James and George E. Marcus, editors. *The Poetics and Politics of Ethnography*. Berkeley, CA: University of California Press, 1986.

De Cock, Christian, Alf Rehn, and David Berry. "For a Critical Creativity: The Radical Imagination of Cornelius Castoriadis." In *Handbook of Research on Creativity*, 150–161. Edited by Kerry Thomas and Janet Chan. Northampton, MA; Edward Elgar, 2009.

Emmer, Pascal. "Talkin' 'Bout Meta-Generation: ACT UP History and Queer Futurity." *Quarterly Journal of Speech* 98, no. 1 (2012): 89–96, doi: 10.1080/00335630.2011.638664.

Goltz, Dustin. "It Gets Better: Queer Futures, Critical Frustrations, and Radical Potentials." *Critical Studies in Media Communication* 30, no. 2 (2013): 135–151, doi: 10.1080/15295036.2012.701012.

Gutierrez-Perez, Robert and Luis Andrade. "Queer of Color Worldmaking: <Marriage> in the Rhetorical Archive and the Embodied Repertoire." *Text and Performance Quarterly* 38, no. 1–2 (2018): 1–18, doi: 10.1080/10462937.2018.1435130.

Haiven, Max and Alex Khasnabish. "What Is the Radical Imagination?" *Affinities: A Journal of Radical Theory, Culture, and Action* 4, no. 2 (2010): i–xxxvii, https://ojs.library.queensu.ca/index.php/affinities/article/view/6128.

hooks, bell. *Feminist Theory: From Margin to Center*. New York, NY: Routledge, 2014.

Johnson, Amber. "Confessions of a Video Vixen: My Autocritography of Sexuality, Desire, and Memory." *Text and Performance Quarterly* 34, no. 2 (2014): 182–200, doi: 10.1080/10462937.2013.879991.

Kelley, Robin D. G. *The Black Radical Imagination*. Boston, MA: Beacon Press, 2002.

Khasnabish, Alex and Max Haiven. "Convoking the Radical Imagination." *Cultural Studies ↔ Critical Methodologies* 12, no. 5 (2012): 408–421, doi: 10.1177/1532708612453126.

LeMaster, Benny. "Unlearning the Violence of the Normative." *QED* 4, no. 2 (2017): 123–130, doi: 10.14321/qed.4.2.0123.

LeMaster, Benny, Danny Shultz, J. Nyla, Gray Bowers, and Rusty Rust. "Unlearning Cisheteronormativity at the Intersections of Difference: Performing Queer Worldmaking through Collaged Relational Autoethnography." *Text and Performance Quarterly* 39, no. 4 (2019): 341–370, doi: 10.1080/10462937.2019.1672885.

Majkowski, Tina. "The 'It Gets Better Campaign': An Unfortunate use of Queer Futurity." *Women and Performance* 21, no. 1 (2011): 163–165, doi: 10.1080/0740770X.2011.563048.

McCune, Jeffrey. "The Queerness of Blackness." *QED: A Journal in GLBTQ Worldmaking* 2, no. 2 (2015): 173–176, https://www.muse.jhu.edu/article/585660.

Moreman, Shane T. and Stephanie R. Briones. "Deaf Queer World-making: A Thick Intersectional Analysis of the Mediated Cultural Body." *Journal of International and Intercultural Communication* 11, no. 3 (2018): 216–232, doi: 10.1080/17513057.2018.1456557.

Muñoz, José Esteban. *Cruising Utopia: The Then and There of Queer Futurity*. Durham, NC: Duke University Press, 2009.

Rollins, Andrew. "Afrofuturism and Our Old Ship of Zion: The Black Church in Post Modernity." In *Afrofuturism 2.0: The Rise of Astro-Blackness*, 127–148. Edited by Reynaldo Anderson and Charles Jones. Lanham, MD: Lexington Books, 2015.

Yep, Gust A. "Further Notes on Healing from 'The Violence of Heteronormativity in Communication Studies.'" *QED* 4, no. 2 (2017): 115–122, doi: 10.14321/qed.4.2.0115.

Black Girl Memory

Kai M. Green

A poem for the little Black girl who couldn't sit still as Mama pressed
Comb to stove to hand to head
And back again.
Mama pressed and pushed and prettied little Black girl because she loved her.
Little Black girl learned Black love in that kitchen, in between Mama's legs
Head pulled left, turned right, and back again.
Little Black girl wasn't so good at following directions, both tender and
hard headed,
She jerked away from Mama sometimes.
She got burned sometimes.

THE BURGUNDY COAT

Craig Gingrich-Philbrook

1.

How do we remember the various ways people have said we cannot depend on memory? Can we trust ourselves to correct for biases we believe we have learned about in this or that article? Or was it a book? A lecture? A conversation? A dream? How can we trust our memory for critiques of memory? Is the memory of those critiques somehow separate from the memory those critiques of memory besmirch? Should we resort to flash cards, perhaps? Repetitive citations?

What were we talking about?

2.

Every few years I remember it, in the midst of doing something else. It doesn't help that the colors of the university where I teach are maroon and white. Maroon is so close to that shade of burgundy, at least as I remember it, and there are maroon things everywhere, here. It's a sea of triggers, with me on a raft of fingers.

Sometimes, it doesn't take much: I see a maroon coat, I think about the burgundy coat in the boy's department at some Sears or JC Penny's, and I begin to kind of feel the weight of it on its hanger, hooked on my hand. I feel flush with embarrassment and anger and that sensation that adults are not to be trusted are incoherent and are just plain broken by the privilege they like to deny, by saying how magic childhood is and other nonsense that is and is not nonsense. I might be trying not to cry, or crying, or entirely dry-eyed. The issue isn't any one thing happening or not happening. The issue is the gestalt, the rejection, sort of like a betrayal of trust. Whatever it is, I'm at a standstill, speechless, shaking in the student center or the mall or wherever I happen to actually be; it all seems so arbitrary. And my thinking kind of goes dark, which is less about the absence of light than the absence of agency.

And I feel all that, even though I'm shut down in the present.

I realize that I don't know what city the boy's department in either the JC Penny's or the Sears is even in. *Was* even in. It depends on how far my mother and Aunt Ginger were thinking ahead, because those first few days after my father died involved a lot of travel up and down California. We could have been in Burney, or Redding, or Chico, or San Dimas, or who knows?

And so I ask myself: *Where are you now? What is in the room with you? What were we talking about? What am I doing in class today? What am I at the grocery store to buy? Oh, that's right—something about the evidence of experience and extra-large tortillas. Or who knows, maybe I'm just driving.*

3.

Some facts are pretty much unassailable:

I am 12.

My father has died.

My mother, sister, Aunt Ginger, and I are shopping for something to wear at the funeral. My mother has expressly forbidden black, because it's too macabre, in her mind, too morose. She has given me one instruction apropos the coat, and it is something like: *No black. Get a color that makes you happy.* This instruction occurs in a familiar register that valorizes repression of feeling. It's almost all she can muster in those days. I recognize it as the same way of speaking she used when she said *Pretend it's a movie, Honey; that's what I'm doing* and *We don't cry at the funeral; we don't make a spectacle.* These are not direct quotations, memory research tells us. Whatever. It's all upside down, anyway. You know. Figuratively. I am entirely aware that things were not actually upside down.

Although they might as well have been.

So I'm looking for a coat that makes me happy.

I am probably not entertaining any meta-theoretical questions about what color even is, anyway, that some of its incarnations might, in certain circumstances, have the power to make one happy. Even at 12, the proposition that color can make one happy has already been firmly integrated into my worldview. Color has already begun to save me. For example, consider the red plaid on the square little lunchbox that I carry with me in the car on all of those trips up and down California from where we live to where my father will be buried, then back up to pack so we can move back down later. The lunchbox has some of my pencils and little containers for collecting rocks and copies of *Ripley's Believe It or Not* and a notebook. Although it is likely that some of those containers were empty pill bottles from my mother's Valium and Darvon, I do not know this to be the case, so I offer the detail speculatively.

I carry the lunchbox with me from house to house as we work our way south toward the funeral, because mom and dad have plots at Rose Hills. That's where our people are buried. While Mom and Aunt Ginger talk about this or that arrangement or stare out the window and talk about absolutely nothing, I pack and repack the lunchbox in the back seat, trying to find ways of getting more and more inside it and still be able to close the latch.

What were we talking about?

The boy's department. I see. I'm looking for color, for a color that will make me happy, that would look interesting in the pretend movie, that would decrease the likelihood of crying and making a spectacle. Or, no, I'm just 12, and it's all very simple: I'm looking for a sports coat that I like, and I find one that I like, and the one that I like is burgundy, and it feels like I've completed my mission, who'd have thought, but there it is, burgundy, hanging on its hanger and weighing on my fingers as I take it to them and they look at me, and then look very disappointed, and Aunt Ginger says, *Honey, go pick another one; that's not a color boys wear.* Which makes no sense to me, as I have a robe and slippers that color, plus, and this is the most important thing, *we are standing in the boy's department.*

And what does my mother do?

I have no idea, but it amounts to agreeing.

Perhaps she is tranquilized fairly heavily. Perhaps she is having her own difficult time thinking or doing anything more than going with the flow of her best friend, the kind of best friend who goes shopping with you and your children to buy clothes for your husband's funeral. The kind of best friend my mother will die a few days after, with the clothes she planned to wear to Aunt Ginger's funeral laid out, on the back of the sofa, for her funeral as will happen to my mother, oh, let's say 35 years after this day in the boy's department.

Some other facts are unassailable:

It is clear to me that I have to pick another coat, and either I give up and pick an ugly brown one or they pick an ugly brown one out for me because I am inconsolable. I have no memory after they say no to the burgundy coat.

This is approximately four months after I've been bashed in the hallway at school and told to admit I'm queer. Four months after my feet are stomped over and over again and my parents don't take me to the doctor because they are ashamed that I didn't fight back. Never mind that there were more of them, they were older, and fighting back would have accomplished nothing.

And if I felt similarly sick to my stomach in the boy's department of the Sears or JC Penny's in Burney or Redding or Chico or San Dimas, who could blame me? There were more of them, they were older, and fighting back would have accomplished nothing. My body felt hot and wrong, damp with rage, and buzzing with futility.

Pick a color that will make you happy.

We don't cry at the funeral; we don't make a spectacle.

Pretend it's a movie, Honey; that's what I'm doing.

4.

Whenever I see a plaid lunchbox, I think about *Ripley's Believe It or Not.* I think about what I thought I needed to carry a hole-punch or a magnifying glass for, what notes I took, which rocks I carried with me or hoped to find. I think about the way I had of taking everything out and putting everything back in over and over and what doing that did to my sense of selection and arrangement, paradigm and syntagm, this next to that in poems, performances, sentences. I think about the rising faith I had in that latch, keeping all that in, a little private universe that opened and unfolded and retreated and closed like the breath carrying an idea out into the world and then being pulled back inside. Here are a few more unassailable facts for good measure:

1. The proto-disco song "Love's Theme" was popular on the radio after my father died. When it was playing in the car, I would look out the window and imagine it was the soundtrack to the opening or closing credits to the movie I was pretending all of this to be. When I hear the song, to this day, I'm looking out the window of our station wagon at the fields up and down Interstate 5.

2. When I packed for my mother's funeral, I considered wearing the burgundy coat I had bought for myself as a professor, because boys do, in fact, wear that color, or this boy does, and fuck them and their god-damned "boys don't wear that color" in the boy's damned department in Burney or Chico or Redding or San Dimas. But thinking all of that, in that foul, if righteous, register, when I touched my burgundy coat on its hanger, I felt more anger and sorrow and all of that than I could bear. Than I could wear on my shoulders in the sunshine on that family slope at Rose Hills, beside my mother's open grave. I did, however, wear black. And I made a spectacle of myself at the end, sitting on the grass, the last one to leave, leaning my head against the casket, telling her I'd do it all again.

And I kind of do; I kind of do it all again. Memory by memory works itself up in and then out of my body, like storms on a California highway. One learns that there will always be another.

And if you added them up and put them side by side, all the minutes in which the weight of that coat on its hanger hooked on my hand and all the shame *was not* registering, *was not* present, would amount to years and years and years. However summonable that day in the boy's department remains, however exhausting it is to recall, it does not exhaust me.

But it matters.

Believe it or not.

A PRESENT, PAST, FUTURE NEGOTIATION OF QUEER FEMME IDENTITY

Kathryn Hobson

In the following chapter, I experimentally write through poetry, "FemMe-mories," or memories about my queer femme identity, juxtaposed with a performance I did about my femme gender identity in the academy. I recall how I have negotiated my femme gender identity throughout my life, both in present and past, and suggest that the future is queer femme.

FemMe-mory: 2007

How do you read my body? My tall White cisgender body. My hips, my stomach, my breasts—eyeliner, lipstick, and earrings. My skirt? Don't lift it up you might be scared by my hairy legs—I do not always shave them. Is this the femme part of me? My aesthetics?

When you see me do you see those who came before me; those who are still with me? Like Joan Nestle; Amber Hollibaugh; Minnie Bruce Pratt; Carmelita Tropicana; Leah Lakshmi Piepzna-Samarasinha; Bevin Branlandingham; Alok Vaid-Menon; and the many friends and enemies I have acquired over the years. Their spirits teach me how to live in my imperfect body that I often try to make perfect. Is this the femme part of me? My lineage.

When you see me do you see my great grandmother's hands living around my heart. I do nothing without thinking about her—I am nothing without her. I hear her bellow in the night, "Kathy," "Kathryn," "Kathryn Dora." Dora, the name of my great great grandmother. They are both long gone. I channel their spirits into my goddess necklace, and I rub it as I walk. Is this the femme part of me? My matriarchy.

When you read me do you see that I live in a constant state of pain—that my ovaries and uterus will be removed? Is this too much information for you? Is this the femme part of me?

The removal.

The removable.

When you see my body—my tall, white, slender, queer, female body—my hips, eyeliner, and breasts juxtaposed with another body, a body that looks like a male body and sometimes is, and sometimes is not. My bisexuality. Is this the femme part of me? Our juxtaposition?

When you read my body do you see my skepticism about Myself? Do you see my whiteness? I'm sure you do even if you do not assess the meanings of privilege it deserves. Do you acknowledge my privilege? I always try to. Is this the femme part of me? My attempts?

When you read my body do you see the fragments—the parts that don't know anything? The parts that question everything from the aesthetics, the lineage, the matriarchy, the removal, the juxtaposition, the attempts? The beginnings and the endings that go on that never begin and never end.

These are all the femme parts of me.

FemMe-mory: 2005–2015

In 2007, when I wrote the above poem, I had been searching for the meaning of my queer femme identity for years. As any definition of identity, even in the most fluid of senses, defining queer femme identity is potentially problematic. This is why queer femme must be broadened to include more than just feminine looking lesbians with their butch partners. Femme needs to expand to include trans femmes, gender fluid, and non-binary folks who embrace femininity as strength and empowerment. In that vein, we need to embrace and continue to push Brushwood and Camilleri's definition of femme:

> Femme might be described as "femininity gone wrong"—bitch, slut, nag, whore, cougar, dyke, or brazen hussy. Femme is the trappings of feminin-ity gone awry, gone to town, gone to the dogs… We want to push things further…to experiences of femme also complicated by maleness, by racist queers, and racism, by transsexuality, by the politics of fat, by class, by age, and institutionalization. Many femmes are lesbian, but femmes are also drag queens, straight sex workers, nelly fags, all strong women and sassy men.[1]

This was before many of the writings like *Femme Shark Manifesto*,[2] performances like *The Femme Show*,[3] *In the Street Productions: Heels on Wheels Glitter Roadshow*,[4] *Femme Dagger's: Femmes Want Revolution*,[5] and gatherings for femmes like FemmeCon were widely accessible to a naïve college femme in small-town Iowa.

Instead, a few years earlier I learned about femme identity from the now-defunct Michigan Womyn's Music Festival (MichFest), a music festival that systematically excluded trans women until the founder shut it down in 2015 rather than allow trans women to attend.

While at MichFest[6] in 2005, I marched in the "Femme Parade" wearing loosely attached black and pink eyelashes, a matching black and pink tulle dress and combat boots, and had short bright red hair and makeup to try and cover my acne-scarred face. I had no idea what I was doing, but I knew wearing that outfit and meeting up with other femmes felt like nothing else ever had. I was shrouded in both incredible self and community love and also femme competition/jealousy. I was jealous of the short, small-breasted, long-haired, and incredibly thin New York femmes with their group of fawning masculine-of-center suitors trailing them. I wanted their bodies and I wanted their boifriends.

I did not look a thing like those femmes, and I measured myself against them and their aesthetics. Why didn't I look like that? Why didn't their boifriends, or those types of queer masculine-of-center folks think I was attractive or want to date me (all this despite I had a girlfriend at the time). My idea about what made a good femme, the right kind of femme, was constrained, rather than open, despite my poem's allusion to femme's indeterminacy.

As I live my life, I continue to try and make sense of what it means for my gender and sexuality to be queer femme. What I've come to understand is that femme is a much broader identity—a more intersectional identity then I ever knew it could be over ten years ago. In the rest of this chapter, I trace my femme identity through experimental genres, including performance and FemMemory recollection.

Performance: Coming out Queer-femme 2014

This performance originated for the panel, "Coming out queer-femme in a masculine-centered academy," held at the 2014 Eastern Communication Association conference.

Stage directions are indicated in italics and parenthesis with narrative in plain text. The setting is simple, with chairs to the right and left with an aisle down the center. Conference floor carpet is under my feet. A table with a chair is set up like a vanity with a small mirror, a tube of lipstick, and an empty bottle of perfume.

Scene 1: Intertextual Intersections

(Performer begins stage right. She is wearing a green button-up dress, seamed beige hose, and heels. Bright red lipstick adorns her mouth with lots of eyeliner and mascara. Her hair is up in a tight bun.)

(The performer raises head and makes eye contact with the audience and begins to walk stage right saying the following.)

"I walk down the halls of my department, red lips, painted eyes."[7]

(The performer pauses center stage and begins the following rant in the center of the stage. It begins slowly and the pace increases as she speaks.)

I could never lose the desire to wear lipstick. Good feminine arguments against the cultural objectification of women and about the cultural compunction that urges women to fill the coffers of the cosmetic industry, and for taking action against the cultural war on women, could not dissuade me from coloring my mouth. Colored lips, colorful words. My mouth demands your attention. Look here! My mouth asserts my presence; I enunciate and articulate my being here, with my mouth. I dab the color on the fleshy cushions of my mouth. I smack with color. Pillow lips, yes, but what comes out between them is often biting, occasionally sharp, sometimes flawed, sometimes intelligent. The rouge is only a ruse. The ruse is perhaps only rouge. Do not be lulled into traditional assumptions about femininity, about women. If wearing lipstick invites objectification, then I object. There are as many nuances in this scenario as there are shades of red in Revlon's lipstick display case at the local Wal-Mart.[8]

(The performer turns and walks stage right saying the following):

"I walk down the halls of my department, red lips, painted eyes, a woman whose brand of feminism is suspect."[9]

(The performer pauses, as though remembering something and she shuffles backward toward center stage.)

Wait!

(The performer shouts!)

Hold up.

(The performer says more quietly).

That's Lisa Lockford's story, not mine! Sometimes when I read Lockford's performance on femininity, I get so engrossed that I forget where her narrative of femininity ends and my narrative of queer femme begins. Her story is my story, but it is also her story, and my story is mine.

(The performer rips off the green dress to reveal a short, bright, sequined, red dress underneath, and her beige hose have bright red bows at the tops, which peek out at the audience when the performer turns her back.)

(The performer takes a deep breath and says)
There now
(deep breath)
that's better. Now I fit.
(She turns and sits on the table behind her, ankles crossed).

FemMe-mory: 2008

"I do not see the connection between gender, sexuality, and power," a graduate school colleague once says during a heated debate around queer theory. Ouch! My history, my narrative has been erased and made insignificant. "Lesbians and gay men experience the same kind of oppression—there's no difference," she says. "What about femmes," I say. "Well, then you just pass for straight," she says.

This is not an uncommon assumption. As Martin explains, cross-gender identification—butchness—is seen as a real lesbian transgression, whereas femininity and femme are seen as a "capitulation, a swamp, something maternal and ensnared, and ensnaring."[10] Thus, femmes fail to defy heteronormative and homonormative ideals of femininity and sexuality according to both those within and outside the community, while those people view butches and masculine of center cis women as the "real" queers.[11]

Performance

Scene 2: Femme Privilege and Passing

"But you can pass," a former work colleague says. "You can blend in as straight and no one has to know you're queer."
(The performer points down to red sparkling dress and gestures confusedly.)
Does it look like I can just blend in with my surroundings? There is no such thing as passing privilege for femmes—femme is behavior *and* identity.

Until you've made your way into my bedroom, you have no idea just how queer I need to be. How queer I am.
(The performer says with a sly and feisty grin.)
(The performer uncrosses her ankles and moves to the chair behind the table, and in a matter-of-fact tone leans forward and says)
"You wear your queer femme identity on your sleeve," another colleague tells me.
(The performer leans back and crosses her arms.)
She is right, except I think I wear it on my face and my feet.

I appreciate my colleague's sentiment because in a world where I am told that I pass, I often want to scream: "Pass for what?" According to Johnson:

> Central to femme invisibility (which should be called femme erasure, in my opinion) is the allegation that femmes are not "gay looking." Ok, then who is and why? Who gets the privilege to set the tone of the conversation of what it means to look queer or gay? Clearly not femmes or we would have at least included ourselves.[12]

It is not passing to not be seen. If people don't see me, they are not looking hard enough. Queer femme invisibility? More like queer femme erasure. Queer femme denial. Go away, queer-femme, there is no room in the alphabet soup for you.

BUT!

There certainly are other types of privilege that I benefit from.

(The performer stands and mimics holding up a clipboard and pen.)

White privilege? Check

(The performer exaggerates making check marks on the clipboard.)

Cisgender privilege? Check. Sort of? In normative spaces? Yes. In queer spaces? That's more complex.

In many queer communities it is more hip and cool to be gender non-conforming, and/or trans masculine, than being feminine, woman, and trans feminine.[13] Thus, queer femmes performing femininity, are often marginalized in queer communities because we are supposedly less queer because of our aesthetics, even when it is the people who desire us most that deny our existence. Then, in mainstream culture, I am assumed to be straight because of my commitment to femininity as strength.

(The performer erases the whole check mark and then writes half of one on the clipboard.)

Attractiveness privilege? I struggle with this one

(The performer hesitates)

but it seems to be what others have told me, sooooooo—Check.

(The performer makes a smaller check mark on the invisible clipboard).

Size privilege? Depends on the year, but generally—Check.

There are many other intersections wrapped up in my gender identity of queer femme. As Anzaldúa states, "Identity is not a bunch of little cubbyholes stuffed respectively with intellect, race, sex, class, vocation, gender. Identity flows between, over, aspects of a person. Identity is a river."[14]

Gender privilege—NOPE. Last time I checked being a woman was not a privilege.

Heterosexual privilege—Queer, bisexual, and femme with a trans man. It's complicated, but generally, NOPE.

Able-bodied privilege—Definitely not.

(The performer hesitates and sets down the mimed clipboard.)
Identity is a river. I am a river. I. Am. A.
River.
(The performer moves hands outwards and inwards slowly moving hands further apart and ends the scene with arms spread wide, hands gently undulating in and out and she looks side-to-side.)

FemMe-mory: 2019

Ruminating on my past performance, I think, what a simplistic way to represent queer femme identity and privilege—as though it is just a laundry list of identities without context or history. This has to partly be the reason for so many tensions within the queer femme community. There I went, I had gone and done the thing queer femmes of color had attempted to educate me on what NOT to do, separate identities into small compartments and I had done it. If I'm being honest, intersectionality is complicated to write about, and complicated to perform.

If I could do it again, I would problematize privilege, starting with White privilege because yes, I do have it. My whiteness roots into all of my privileges—my cisgender privilege, pretty-girl privilege, and size privilege, which are contextually specific. I am a curvy, White woman, with long highlighted brunette hair, I have a symmetrical face, and large green, semi-hooded eyes—good hair, good eyes. Juxtaposed with those who are gender non-binary and trans, in mainstream culture, as well as my daily life, my gender as a woman is never challenged nor is it under suspicion, but instead it is often touted with praise. However, juxtaposed with White cisgender men, my gender as a White cis woman is not privileged.

My weight flux has changed the curviness of my body over time, the compliments and concerns about my weight loss have turned to silence when I have gained it back. But thinness is not valued the same in every community or culture. My whiteness frames my hourglass body as "curvy" instead of "thick." Thick, sometimes thicc, is a term rooted in Black culture to celebrate and simultaneously sexualize Black women's bodies. Since my body occupies space outside of Black culture, it does not accrue thick body privilege. In some communities and cultures, fat bodies have positivity and privilege attached to them, so there is no one way to dictate body and size privilege.

And my sexuality? Who knows? My mother has tried to explain to me that I am pansexual, attracted to people not parts, but it just was not a term that was used when I was coming out as a baby queer in the early 2000s. Bisexual fits my behavior but feels limiting, even as activists-scholars are trying to redefine it to not be about a gender binary.[15] So queer, bisexual, pansexual might all apply in different contexts. But heterosexual? Never. Being assumed to be straight because of my femininity provides me with some privilege, although it erases so much of my identity as queer, bisexual, and femme.

FemMe-mory: 2015

I used to wear a lot of dresses. Cute ones that fell off shoulders and exposed pink lace bras, and were short enough that my panties poked out. Heels, mostly wedges, but heels. It's different now. Since the two moves, the quitting smoking, the gaining weight. It used to be endometriosis. My ovaries and uterus were removed to mitigate the pain. It didn't work. Could I be femme without my woman parts? I never identified with my reproductive organs to begin with; having them removed was a sigh of relief. Then it was interstitial cystitis—painful bladder syndrome. They put an implant in my backside to help with the pain. It didn't work. Then it was Irritable Bowel Syndrome, maybe Celiac disease, but to know for sure I would have to eat gluten for a month. I didn't risk it. Then it was degenerative disk disease, a pinched nerve, muscle spasms. Never any answers, just fire in muscles and joints. Pain in my whole body, and sensitivity to the cold. No more cute short dresses and lacy bras. Never heels. Never heals.

For now, the diagnosis is fibromyalgia—living in a constant state of pain, unable to differentiate the environment from my body, the external from the internal. Surprisingly, the word "fibromyalgia" still gives me hope. I never had the words to describe what my body was going through when other folks didn't live in consistent pain like me. Kind of like "femme". I never had the word to describe what I was going through when other girls and women in my life weren't doing their gender like me. For some, femme is dysphoric. For many, femme is dissonance. For no one is femme simplistic.

Performance

Scene 3: Beyond Aesthetics

(The performer stands center stage and walks down the center aisle of the performance space.)

"I walk down the halls of my department, red lips, painted eyes, a [femme] woman whose brand of [queerness] is suspect."[16]

(The performer runs back down the aisle to center-stage.)

Queer femmes are in a precarious position in queer communities, in scholarly communities, and society at large.

(The performer mimics walking a tightrope, teetering one way and then the other outstretched.) Femmes are only fantasy, not reality.

"Straight girls are really hard to read," my butch ex tells me.

(The performer halts and bends down slightly on the tightrope.)

"Straight girls?"

"Yeah, you know, lipstick lesbians, femmes, straight or "bi" girls who end up being not totally straight? They are tricksters. One minute they are queer and the next minute they're out the door with a dude," she tells me. This echoes Califia's observation, "Butches think of femmes as straight girls taking a Sapphic vacation from serving the patriarchy."[17]

(The performer crouches down behind the table, an obvious challenge to get down on all fours.)

Like we femmes are the ones waiting behind bushes just waiting to spring out.

(The performer gently leans forward hands up in a claw-like position)

and tell our lovers, our partners, and our friends, "I was just kidding all along; I'm straight. No big deal. The lipstick and heels finally got to me and turned me into a heterosexual cis woman." Because that's a thing?

(The performer says sarcastically while peeking out from behind the table.)

Hello, femme-misogyny (disliking femmes and femininity), queer femme and bisexual erasure (pretending queer feminine women and bisexuality are not real gender or sexual orientations), and femme and bi-phobia (the fear of femme and bisexual folks' power, especially the power to "turn the straight into the queer"), it is terrible to meet all of you. Yet, here you are, embodied by queer people telling femmes that their queerness is not transgressive enough, and embodied by straight and queer communities telling queer bisexual femmes that they simply are confused and will eventually figure it all out. These may be platitudes that people are tired of hearing, but until folks stop saying them, I am going to keep pointing them out, writing about them, and advocating for myself and others who encounter such hateful remarks every day.

Tell me to cut my hair. **I dare you.**

(Using the table to get up, the performer moves from the floor to standing next to the table.)

As Miller has observed:

> The fix for femme invisibility on a large scale isn't for all the ladylike lady lovers to trade in our lipstick for crew cuts and our seamed stockings for Chuck Taylors…we need a world where appearance isn't automatically linked to orientation—where everyone agrees that feminine women might be gay and masculine women might be straight [and that anyone might be bisexual or queer].[18]

I wear my queer femme identity on my face and on my feet no doubt, but I also express it in my relational style, my pedagogy, my research, and my politics. And sometimes my ignorance, and my privilege.

(The performer kicks off her heels close to the audience and applies more lipstick in a hurried fashion. The lipstick is not in lip lines and there is some on her teeth.)

FemMe-mory: 2012

"How many of you tried to be scent-free" the queer femme keynote speaker asks the audience? Several hands, including mine, raise up. At the Femme Conference, held in Baltimore, MD, in August 2012, a problem arose that most attendees and organizers were not expecting: people with multiple chemical sensitivities[19] were angered by not having a more explicit "No scented products" community guideline.

Conference attendees, who while not unsympathetic, felt they had a right to bring and use their choice of products, proclaiming that they helped them to express their queer femme identity, which is tantamount at a conference for queer femmes. Much of this response came from femmes of color and working-class femmes for reasons of availability and financial access. The cultural politics of smell have often deemed some bodies as pleasant smelling and others as stinking.[20]

How queer femmes express our feminine aesthetics is complex. There is no one way to perform queer femme identity, and it was never more evident than at the Femme Conference where there were so many different outfits, hairstyles, makeup, shoes, body sizes, mobility aids, and so many more aesthetic choices. Many of these aesthetics are culturally constructed, or necessitated by other intersectional identities, like class, ability, gender identity, and race and ethnicity.

There were femmes similarly dressed to me, although my slightly tomboyish style set me slightly apart. My thin but curvy White, cisgender body wore a tight thrift store blue dress with a pink bra hanging out, ankle boots, with an athletic style jacket and bright yellow purse, with tall short hair did not garner much praise or adoration at the conference. Additionally, there were popular, White, curvaceous high femmes, wearing short sparkly dresses, seamed fishnet stockings with garters, and tall stiletto heels taking sexy pictures in the lobby. However, there were also femmes of color in glittery miniskirts, colorful tights, and tall boots, in addition to gender non-binary femmes, specifically a trans masculine femme, wearing a tutu, wings, and glitter eye makeup, all who were consistently praised for their dramatic interpretation of queer femme identity.

As a scent-sensitive queer femme, I am always conscious of chemical sensitivities, as I have had many a reaction to hotel bed sheets, fragranced air, and essential oils touching my skin, but I also know that in asserting my sensitivities to others, I potentially infringe upon others' personal expressions, especially those from ethnic and racial backgrounds other than my own, those with different class standings, and those with different access to scent-free products. I realize that at once I am both marginalized in my aesthetics by my sensitivities and privileged in my access to the resources to provide me with scent-free products. Aesthetics, as part of femme identity, are very complicated, not only in how queer femmes perform them but also in how they are interpreted by queer communities and mainstream communities.

No story is ever as simple—there are always other vectors, other shoots of identities, writhing their way to the surface, wanting to be recognized as part of femme identity.

Performance

Scene 4: Queer Femme Agitators

(The performer stands in front of the audience trying to fix the lipstick on her face and says very seriously.)

I've been known as an agitator. I directly attribute this to my queer femme identity. Agitators are described as people who stir up public feelings in order to change an oppressive social system.[21] I'm an agitator; I talk about whiteness and racism when it is too much for people to handle. I talk about queerness, safe(r) sex, fluid bonding, and polyamory. I lead privilege workshops and I talk about my experiences as a queer femme with a queer partner.

(The performer begins to set the table with placemats and then mimes setting down three plates, napkins, and forks. Then she sits at the table and picks up the large silver serving spoon.)

These are not the kind of things most "respectable" people talk about at their dinner tables; however, my working-class roots get off on discussing challenging topics loudly at the dining-room table.

(The performer mimics dishing up food to each place setting, her talking getting faster as she goes around serving.)

"You are too confrontational."

(The performer spoons a large helping of food on the first plate.)

"You're too much."

(The performer spoons a large helping of food on the second plate.)

"You make people feel uncomfortable."

(The performer spoons a large helping of food on the third plate.)

"You are intimidating."

(The performer spoons a large helping of food on the fourth plate.)

"You are way too much."

(The performer slams a large helping of food on the first plate.)

"You wear too much makeup"

(The performer slams a large helping of food on the second plate.)

"You don't have good boundaries."

(The performer slams a large helping of food on the second plate spilling over to the third plate.)

"You are waaaaaaaaaaaaaaayyyyyyyyy tooooooooooooo much!"

(The performer slams several large helpings of food on the fourth plate shaking her hand to get rid of as much food as possible.)

(The performer throws the large spoon to the ground, close to the kicked off shoes.)

I have been called an agitator; one of those queers who talks about racial and economic justice, disability, and socio-economic status, instead of just being a sexual deviant wanting marriage equality, the ability to adopt a child, and "the right" to be in the military, to die for one's country that cares little about our histories, communities, and identities.

I'm an agitator and this is what agitators do.

(The performer removes the lipstick from her face, takes out a pair of leggings, a cardigan, tall brown boots, and a scarf. She carefully puts on the clothes and takes the tube of pinkish lipgloss and applies it to her lips. She puts her hair in a low ponytail.)

I'm a professor now, an agitator still, but I am not sure what femme professors should do? Can do?

(The performer bows her head signaling the closing of the performance.)

FemMe-mory: 2018

"Dr. Hobson, I see you. I like what you're doin' with that top. Can I have it when you are done?" says JayLynn one day when I wear a sparkling gold top to teach. It is a moment of connection between a student who is African American and their professor, me. Most days, when I walk in the classroom, they start like this...

"I like your nails, Dr. Hobson."

Thank you. I think yours are better, much more sparkly.

"You always look so cute, Dr. H, is that awkward to say?"

No, I think it's fine, especially because it's true, I joke.

"Dr. Hobson, how do you get your hair to curl like that?"

I use a curling wand with no clamp. It's pretty easy, but I had to watch some YouTube tutorials.

"Those are great boots. The buckles, adorable."

Thanks, they are very warm, which is why I love them.

"Your eyeliner looks like Beyonce's today."

Well, your makeup looks like Beyonce's every day.

"You look like Jess from New Girl. Do you know who that is?"

Yes, I know. If I didn't have bangs I don't think we would look that much alike.

"I keep telling all my friends they need to take your class."

"Everyone needs to take your class."

"You're a gangbanger. You tell it like it is and do not worry about White students feeling uncomfortable."

"It's great because you all make it great. I am a facilitator, but you are the ones making the magic happen."

As Lockford, suggests, "Increasingly I think that taste and ideology are so interconnected that they can no longer be separated."[22] Our tastes, our sense of appropriateness, our affinities, repulsions, and tolerances are ideological, and have a larger social meaning and implications that cannot be separated from the systems of oppression in which they operate.

Queer femme is not just my aesthetics, and expression, but it is the intentional way I relate and find community with people of contentious identities, including my friends, my partners, my colleagues, and my students. As Moraga writes, "I have come to believe that the only reason women of a privileged class will dare to look at how it is that they oppress, is when they've come to know the meaning of their own oppression. And understand that the oppression of others hurts them personally."[23]

Femme is a political style because building communities among oppression is the only way we are going to tear the system down that is set up to discipline and punish people who embody femininity while they agitate. And even though my experience is not the same as anyone else's, and I experience a lot of privilege for being cisgender, White, Ph.D. educated, and a US citizen, finding places of connection, support, and alliance is a significant gesture in a place like the academy where people have labeled this as inappropriate, having bad boundaries, uncouth, and being waaaaaaayyyyyy tooooooooooo much.

I'm a femme agitator and when I walk anywhere my being is suspect. "Why are you wearing bright green nail polish with a bright pink, soft cotton dress, a full-face of glittery makeup, your head held high, making eye contact with everyone, including the creepy guys that stare and catcall you?" Because that is how I do my femme now. It is a combination of soft fabrics and harsh edges. It is neither only feminine nor only masculine; it is both and something else entirely. It is constrained by social and cultural expectations, but I have hope and faith in resistance. Maybe that's my queer femme optimism. The world could always be worse, right? I don't know about that, but it certainly could be better.

Toward a Queer Femme Futurity: 2019

Being queer femme is rooted in privilege, marginalization, trauma, and often insecurity. I wish my relationship to femme was an easier one; less fraught with contention and anxiety, jealousy, criticism, and shame. Living in a small community where the queer people in general are hard to find, let alone femmes specifically, I negotiate what my queer femme is going to be every day. It is about a look, and makeup is my art form, but it's also about creating safer spaces for students, finding ways to talk about complex social injustices, and showing up for community protests against the abuse against minors in a Juvenile Detention Center in your area, or KKK and White supremacist rallies in Charlottesville, VA. It could be displaying a "Black Lives Matter" sign in your front window, which the Black garbage men tell me they appreciate every week, or a "But the Name Hurts" in response to a movement to "Save the Name" aka, keeping our small, Southern town's high school named Robert E. Lee High, who was a great oppressor of Black folks in our segregated town. Queer femmes must embrace political positions aimed at collective liberation.

My queer femme gender identity helps me to make sense of my feminine self in relation to others. There is no one femme identity, aesthetic, or behavior. My story can never represent all femmes' journeys, and I would never suggest that we share a collective story of oppression. Femmes are different from one another in so many ways, including how our femme-ness has come to be tied up with our race, class, gender identity, sexuality, abilities, nationhood, language, and also our aesthetic choices, affectations, and desires to build and relate in different communities. These differences can connect us and can keep us apart. We are more complex than one or two words can encapsulate. Yet, at the same time, I know how amazing femmes can be, and more importantly, I know how important embracing femininity is, especially because it is devalued in many spaces.

Femmes, including myself, have to recognize the ways that our identities are imperfect. I am still working, still trying to make sense of what femininity means in terms of my identities, my tastes, my privileges and marginalization, trauma, consumption, beauty, and how all of these discourses intersect and inform my femme identity. My identity, it isn't singular; it is multiple and always expanding as it flows. As small streams flow creating the river, it expands. This river femme cannot be contained to one identity, to a simplistic binary, or just to me. Embracing femme has the potential to shift the ways in which we experience the world, changing the ways we care for each other, express ourselves, and agitate for social change.

These are all the femme parts of me.

Notes

1 Chloë Brushwood Rose and Anna Camilleri. *Brazen Femme: Queering Femininity* (Vancouver, BC: Arsenal Pulp, 2002), 13.
2 Leah Lakshmi Piepzna-Samarashina and Zuleikha Mahmood. *Femme Shark Manifesto*. (Femme Sharks, 2008), http://www.qzap.org/v5/gallery/main.php?g2_view=core. DownloadItem&g2_itemId=799
3 *The Femme Show*, founded by Maggie Cee, prod. In the Streets Productions, 2007, http://www.thefemmeshow.com/the-femme-show.html.
4 *Glitter and Grit*, prod. Heels on Wheels Glitter Roadshow, 2010, http://www.heelson-wheelsroadshow.com/bios/about/.

5 *Femmes want Revolution*, prod. FemmeDagger Production, 2012, https://www.youtube.com/watch?v=MPSMvHYs8_w.
6 The Michigan Womyn's Music Festival (MichFest) is a now defunct feminist music festival started in 1976 by Lisa Vogel, a radical, lesbian feminist. MichFest featured women's music, primarily radical and lesbian music. It was a week-long festival in which only "womyn-born womyn" were allowed to attend, meaning that you had to be a cisgender woman to attend the festival, and transgender women could not attend the festival. Camp Trans was created as a response to MichFest's Trans-Exclusion policy. In 2015, under immense pressure from queer communities to open up the festival to all women who identify as women, Vogel instead closed the festival rather than change the policy.
7 Lesa Lockford. *Performing Femininity: Rewriting Gender Identity* (Walnut Creek, CA: AltaMira, 2004), 126.
8 Lockford, 126.
9 Lockford, 126.
10 Biddy Martin. "Sexualities without Genders and Other Queer Utopias." *Diacretics* 24, no. 2–3 (1994): 105, doi: 10.2307/465167.
11 Sally R. Munt. *Heroic Desire: Lesbian Identity and Cultural Space* (New York, NY: New York University Press, 1998).
12 Cyree Jarelle Johnson. "Femme Privilege Does Not Exist." *Feministing*, 2013, http://feministing.com/2013/01/07/guest-post-femme-privilege-does-not-exist/.
13 J. Halberstam. "Between Butches," in *Butch/Femme: Inside Lesbian Gender*, ed. Sally R. Munt (Washington DC: Cassell, 1998), 57–66.
14 Gloria Anzaldúa and AnaLouise Keating. *The Gloria Anzaldúa Reader* (Durham, NC: Duke University Press, 2009), 166.
15 Shiri Eisner. *Bi: Notes for a Bisexual Revolution* (Berkeley, CA: Seal Press, 2013).
16 Lockford, 126.
17 P. Califia. "Clit Culture: Cherchez la Femme…" *On Our Backs* 8, no. 4 (1992): 10.
18 Lindsay King-Miller. "My Life as an Invisible Queer Cosmopolitan." *Cosmopolitan*, April 9, 2014, https://www.cosmopolitan.com/lifestyle/advice/a6323/invisible-queer-femme/.
19 Multiple chemical sensitivities (MCS) is a disorder in which some individuals experience stronger reactions to chemicals in the environment than other individuals; may occur from a lot or a little exposure to common irritants like pesticides, perfumes, and cleansers.
20 Constance Classen, David Howes, and Anthony Synnott. *Aroma: The Cultural History of Smell* (London: Routledge, 1994).
21 Nick Crossley. *Making Sense of Social Movements* (Philadelphia, PA: Open University Press, 2002).
22 Lockford, 141.
23 Cherríe Moraga. *Loving in the War Years: Lo Que Nunca Pasó Por Sus Labios* (Cambridge, MA: South End Press, 2000), 49.

Bibliography

Anzaldúa, Gloria and AnaLouise Keating. *The Gloria Anzaldúa Reader*. Durham, NC: Duke University Press, 2009.
Califia, P. "Clit Culture: Cherchez la Femme…" *On Our Backs* 8, no. 4 (1992): 10.
Classen, Constance, David Howes, and Anthony Synnott. *Aroma: The Cultural History of Smell*. London, UK: Routledge, 1994.
Crossley, Nick. *Making Sense of Social Movements*. Philadelphia, PA: Open University Press, 2002.
Eisner, Shiri. *Bi: Notes for a Bisexual Revolution*. Berkeley, CA: Seal Press, 2013.

Halberstam, J. "Between Butches." In *Butch/Femme: Inside Lesbian Gender*, 57–66. Edited by Sally R. Munt. Washington DC: Cassell, 1998.

Lockford, Lesa. *Performing Femininity: Rewriting Gender Identity.* Walnut Creek, CA: AltaMira, 2004.

Martin, Biddy. "Sexualities without Genders and Other Queer Utopias." *Diacritics* 24, no. 2–3 (1994): 104–121, doi: 10.2307/465167.

Moraga, Cherríe. *Loving in the War Years: Lo Que Nunca Pasó Por Sus Labios.* Cambridge, MA: South End Press, 2000.

Munt, Sally R. *Heroic Desire: Lesbian Identity and Cultural Space.* New York, NY: New York University Press, 1998.

Rose, Chloë Brushwood and Anna Camilleri. *Brazen Femme: Queering Femininity.* Vancouver, BC: Arsenal Pulp, 2002.

NARRATIVE EMBODIMENT OF LATINX QUEER FUTURITY

Pause for Dramatic Affect

Shane T. Moreman

As a scholar who helped to establish Critical Race Theory (CRT), Crenshaw[1] has been a part of an intellectual movement that has explained how the practice of everyday life is specifically shaped by the policies of cultural institutions which are symbiotic with local, state, national, and international laws. Crenshaw's specific contribution to CRT—intersectionality—has now been applied, developed, and adapted for over three decades. Concurrent to intersectionality's presence in academic knowledge production has been the rise, wane, and roam of identity politics. These identity politics have been borne out of differing generations' identificatory trajectories, but also, as CRT explains, these identity politics have been in reaction to and under the jurisdiction of the interlock of legal decisions and public discourse. For example, in my lifetime, US Supreme Court rulings have directed laws that have determined how I could perceive of myself, how others could be in relationship with me, and how communities could form with or without me. Like a table of contents, these Supreme Court of the United States rulings become a list of titles that are both just words on a page but also are meanings through a body: Hernandez v. Texas (1954), Loving v. Virginia (1967), Roe v. Wade (1973), Regents of the University of California Berkeley v. Bakke (1978), Plyler v. Doe (1982), Reno v. Flores (1993), Gratz v. Bollinger (2003), Grutter v Bollinger (2003), Obergefell v. Hodges (2015), and Janus v. AFSCME (2018). Also, during my lifetime, neoliberalism has taken hold of meaning-making. As such, the practice of everyday life continues to be in a renegotiation with the mutating politics of public life and private life.

Specific to my life, the concept of subjectivity has been of central concern to my academic work. At the intersections of queer and Latinx, my work continues to center upon the languaging and the embodiment of a subjectivity toward meaningful relationships with others but also meaningful relationships to my history/present/future. Complicating and nuancing these intersections have been gender and sexuality (i.e., a/o/x), somatics (i.e., skin color), language (i.e., Spanish), and citizenship (i.e., documentation). My intellectual work has been self-referentially heuristic while also seeking to offer narratives that others can use to generalize to and theorize about the idiosyncrasies of their own existences. As my academic work continues to transmute and modulate, adjusting to the changing times but also to my own changing experiences, the concept of subjectivity is changing. I understand subjectivity through a performance studies paradigm that manifests itself as embodied discourse. These embodied discourses are framed and shared as narratives. As *homo narrans*, we have multiple stories to live but also multiple ways to tell the stories that frame and reframe the discourses we live. However, narrative, as a logical structure, carries a delimiting particular pattern: exposition, initial conflict, rising action, climax, falling action. The critiques of this structure are abundant and appropriate, from the narrative structure's Western-bias (i.e., many cultures do not follow this structure) to its heteropatriarchal sexual design (i.e., it follows the one-shot male orgasm).

While intersectionality provides a theoretical framework for comprehending that our subjectivity is situated within multiple discursive valences of norms and aberrations, narrative method offers us a workshopping space to reflect upon how those valences are dynamically lived within ubiquitous cultural discourses. Taking it one step further, autoethnography grants us a way to avoid narrating our lives as hagiographies but rather to deconstruct our lives as they are lived in order to reconstitute the storied data of our lives with reparations of hope and optimism. As an approach to ethnography, autoethnography requires the researcher to coordinate the story of one's life with all the possible emergent meanings of those stories. Those meanings are contextualized both within the time lived and within the time the story is told. Putting lived stories in print does, as autoethnography intends, allow one to read his/her/their own life as a text and then to make multiple interpretations of that text. While most of us know that narrative can be interpreted in multiple ways, we often fail to re-interpret our own life narratives. However, there are exceptions among us. For example, Johnson recasts their practice-of-everyday-life choices and in turn enacts a self-empowerment over their intersectional positionality as a queer Black non-binary person.[2] Once a story is arrested in memory and even printed in fonts, it is not necessarily sealed in time. Those stories are never finished. Further, our stories should be read for the future tense they imply rather than the present tense they portend. "Through self-reflexively embodying and enacting messages that are meaningful despite being outside of normative discourse, we in turn, alter our queer future."[3] Therefore, resisting the trappings of memory and of academic publishing, I encourage you to read my following autoethnographies for futurity, specifically their queer futurity. Consider them to be oral texts more than written records. They are publicly told stories of queer futurity released out of a queer present and a queer past.

Academia is an institution that mandates knowledge development and distribution. And as academia continues to diversify, the people who make up academia continue to request and implement differing ways of theorizing and researching our realities. For example, *QED: A Journal in GLBTQ Worldmaking* offers a publication space for differing ways of theorizing and researching non-normative gender and sex positionalities, all inspired by Berlant's and Warner's classic essay, "Sex in Public."[4] This queer worldmaking becomes a project for survival that is both material and conjectural.[5] Within a trans understanding, LeMaster deepens the offerings of queer worldmaking, shifting it from an individual identity project to a relational endeavor. "Trans relational bonds become evident when we recognize the queer world as comprised of individual subjects in community who, as a result of institutional constraints and affordances, participate in queer worldmaking that respond to those impositions."[6] Importantly, queer worldmaking allows for theorizing and researching positionalities to expand our sexuality options, to challenge gender assumptions, and to note meaningful moments of all positionality types. I am adopting a trans methodological approach to autoethnography to embrace queer futurity as a coalitional endeavor. However, I do so with trepidation in that I do not want to appropriate trans people's identities as my own, nor do I want to trivialize trans communities' struggles. As Courvant explains, "To be trans in modern U.S. society is to be misunderstood."[7] She goes on to explain that there is sometimes more hurt in non-trans persons seeking to speak for trans communities from narrow examples that become generalizable for all trans persons. Clarkson confirms that the terminology about and from trans persons quickly and continually shifts and the best source for explaining ways that trans people self-name is to be invitational and aware of multiple perspectives from multiple persons.[8] Further, as confirmed by LeMaster and Johnson, naive and insensitive cultural discourse on trans communities adds to confusions on trans positionalities.[9] To mitigate those confusions, Drabinski[10] adopts Stryker's[11] approach to center the discursive practice of gender and sex rather than the identities.

Approaching trans as a phenomenon rather than a person generates critique and explanation of the institutionally sanctioned discourses that contour trans lives. The approach also makes way for multiple and myriad ways to enact trans identity. Chu and Drager explain that trans can be considered as a method in motion, as "transing."[12] However, they warn against transing being a panacea for the world's discursive ills. With a campy and provocative tone, Chu asserts, "Verbing does not a theory make. But if we hang onto it, transing should be a methodology that would start with the premise that everyone's gender is a political disaster and refuse to fix it."[13] Balancing the stories (disasters?) of my life between the institutional and individual, the following autoethnographic texts are stories that I tell about myself and/or speeches I have given. They are oral texts that are contextualized in the time they were lived but also within the time that I tell them. However, they are always meant to offer a vision for a time that will be. Although they are issued together here in a particular order, they are not meant to be stories that move in chronological order. To trans my stories, you may read them in any order. Importantly, they are not meant to be stories that result in self-actualization. Indeed, if queer futurity offers us anything, it offers us an approach to a life beyond self-actualizing or self-materializing and more toward relationality. As such, queer futurity provokes from us aspirations toward diffusing ourselves across one another so that we can connect and commune for a better forthcoming. That urge for what is next is queer futurity, and queer futurity concerns what is trans identity; that is, what is across, beyond, and through. A trans reading is a queer futurity reading that allows readers to actively adapt these narratives for themselves or even against themselves so that they can relate the meanings to themselves in all their present and forthcoming trans ways.

Baby

Sometimes the subject comes up. It usually arises when there's nothing else to talk about. Like during late-night drives, on autumn hikes, or when you've been lying on a beach too long. "What's your earliest memory?" The answers vary, but there are themes. A parallax view of a dinner table that only a toddler would see. A birthday party with cake and a few candles. A blanketed, premie brother being brought home for the first time.

"My earliest memory is of my mother stabbing me."

That's how I introduce the memory, often pausing for effect.

An eighteen-wheeler passes with a Doppler roar. Dry branches snap under heavy feet. A wing-spread seagull lands.

Then I continue.

"I was lying in a crib and my mother was leaning over the side rail, changing my cloth diaper. She was speaking to me in sweet tones as she cleaned my body. The talcum powder perfume masked the shit stench.

She opened a diaper pin with a yellow duck-head clasp. Fastening the cloth diaper, she misjudged and stabbed me in the left hip. My body tensed and I screamed. Her sweet tones became panicked. First, she checked my hip. Then she picked me up and held me close, with my diaper half hanging. As I wailed a red-faced, tearful, trembling cry—so did she."

I pause.

"I know it seems impossible but that's my earliest memory."

Somewhere in My 20s

During my MA program, I was awarded a modest summer research grant. I used it to enroll in Dr. Amira de la Garza's "Postcolonial Ethnography" course in Mexico City. Once the course concluded, I stayed in Mexico City (or DF ['de efe'] as it's colloquially called) and lived out the rest of the summer at the apartment of Pancho, an artist boyfriend. During the day, I volunteered at Mexico City's first HIV/AIDS clinic helping them translate and finesse grant applications into English. At night, without Pancho, I took full advantage of the gay scene in one of the world's largest cities. Pancho was bored with DF's club scene. I loved it.

Putos

Under disco lights of a Mexico City gay bar, "Clandestine," a stranger dances in tight-tight jeans and a navy blue t-shirt—his ass round and firm, his skin smooth and sweaty. His eyes, hair, and height—brown, black, and short. From the edge of the dance floor, I objectify him. It is the type of stare used when you've had four beers (two free with the cost of admission, two I purchased for 20 pesos apiece).

I leave the roving lights and wander to a dim restroom. Not much of a room at all, it is a narrow hallway with a urinal, sink, and a wet, seatless toilet. Finishing up, I shake my dick and zip my pants. I turn to see him walking toward me, sloshing through floor fluids. He smiles up at me with a leer like he knows he is taking a risk, and he relishes it. We kiss as someone else pisses. I smell the salty urine as I taste his cigarette tongue.

On the second floor of the disco is a dark room with banquette seats lined along the walls. Holding hands, lapping lips, and stumbling on the stairs, he and I swagger toward the darkness. Once there, we pant and rasp and grab. I see no one, but I hear their moaning and slurping. I smell their writhing bodies.

A big-bellied, thick-necked, mustachioed ogre stands in the doorframe. His slightly swaying silhouette looms large. He takes out his cigarette lighter and flicks, creating a strobe effect. Squint-eyed figures cast ephemeral shadows. In stop motion, we are all cowering from the light, grimacing at the ogre.

"Puuuuuuutos," he bellows. With both shame and approval, he sputters "¡Putos!" as he shuffles away.

In moments when I can catch my breath, I get the details.

In his chilango accent, he says, "My name is Charlie."

In my pocho accent, I respond, "Me llamo Chango."

To locate me, he holds my face with both his hands and stage whispers. "I love you forever."

"Pues," I propose. "¿Nos vemos mañana?"

Nada.

Augie

Two weeks later it's Pride in Mexico City, and I am marching with thousands of people to the Zócalo, Mexico City's center square. It is a balmy summer night, and along with the throng, I carry a slender white candle that lights up my face. With glowing, solemn expression, all of us are moving in silence, winding along Spanish colonial facades and Mexican modern storefronts. Our purpose is to publicly present a human mass who remembers the victims of AIDS and who condemns the government policies that have catalyzed these deaths. My coworker (and now friend) Kenya runs among me and my colleagues to relight snuffed wicks.

As we herd past Clandestine, I spy the bar's doorman. With a lit cigarette and a scowl, he harrumphs in the doorframe and seems impatient for us to pass. This march is a motley collection, but as we pass, I learn from people near me that Clandestine is opposed by DF's gay community. The club refuses to protect its patrons from gay bashing crimes on its perimeter; also, the club does not have condoms readily available on its bar tops or in its bathrooms. Until Clandestine improves its offerings, most gay patrons choose to go somewhere else. Only tourists and corporate types from out of town are foolish enough to go there. I glance at the doorman with a countenance of shame. For him. For me.

Under a full moon and beneath a wilted Mexico flag, the names of hundreds and hundreds of dead are read in remembrance. On the stage, a determined-looking woman takes care to bring the next reader up as she directs the last reader off. With grace and without losing any time, she adjusts the height of the microphone, shows the reader the list of names for which they are responsible, and then she looks out at the crowd with hard swallows. "Eusebio Esteban Morales de Martínez, María Tomasa González, José Enrique…" Like the people who continue to stream into the Zócalo, the names keep coming.

It's a staging of remembering, though the audience does not know them all. But we know a few. And if not, we know the names of those not spoken aloud. And we fear to know others who may one day die from this, perhaps even ourselves. Despite being among thousands, I feel myself to be standing alone. Squinting at my candle's flame, I try to remember a past boyfriend's full name. What was his middle name? We were a serodiscordant couple. My first and—to my knowledge—my last. "Augie." "Augustino." "Augustino Leal." I also struggle to remember stories of him and me. How'd we meet? What'd we do the last time we saw each other? It's only been two years since he was buried, and I've forgotten so much already. I shout out his name, "¡Augustino Leal!" From the stage, the names keep coming.

Somewhere in My 30s

As an untenured assistant professor, I was asked to present at my campus's Take Back the Night rally. An annual event, this rally is to recognize and condemn the socially sanctioned violence against women. It offers a platform for survivors and their allies to acknowledge the violence and to practice public, vocal resistance to the violence. A female undergraduate student—a favorite of mine as I was of hers—invited me to speak at the event. I declined. I understood the event's woman-focused importance and did not want my male-privileged voice to subvert or distract. However, she wanted a queer voice to be heard and no one else would agree. After multiple requests from her, I relented. The following is my speech.

¡Cállate Joto!

The US Department of Health and Human Services estimates that suicide attempts and suicide ideation is higher among LGBTQ youth than straight youth. Lesbians, gays, bisexual, transgender, the queer in all of you... They taught you to hate yourself. What, then, are our afflictions?

- Disproportionately higher rates of depression
- Disproportionately higher rates of suicide attempts
- Disproportionately higher rates of self-mutilation
- And a loss of voice

You had a voice once. You have a voice now. They silenced you and now you must take it back.

Cállate joto—¡NO CÁLLAME!

¡Apaciguate Maricón!

Domestic violence in straight relationships is a serious issue. Shamefully, this violence is tolerated and encouraged by our rape culture. We have heard and we will hear important experts and survivors of this violence. Their message is clear: we have to do better. In developing my speech, I hastily sought to find statistics on domestic violence against men by men in romantic relationships. The search functions were too complicated: "gay marriage," "lesbian marriage," "domestic partnership," "lovers," "queer," "transgender," "homosexual," "queer of color," "same sex." I cheated myself and I cheated you by not giving myself more time.

So, rather than speaking about what's in print, I decided to speak about what's lived out. I turned to the main battered women's shelter here in Fresno. Previously, I had heard that they do not accept battered gay men and do not accept battered lesbians. So I called them myself.

A volunteer answered the phone and I said, "Hi, this is Shane. I have a question. Do you accept gays and/or lesbians if they are victims of domestic violence?"

> Not using the word lesbian, she answered, "We will accept women, not men."
> Then I asked, "Where do you advise the gay male victims of domestic violence to go?"
> She answered, "I don't know. Please hold."
> Then she came back. "Gay men are advised to go to L— on M—."
> I asked, "What is L— on M—?"
> She answers, "I don't know. Please hold."
> She comes back, "I still don't know what L— on M— is but I've got a number and I can call them for you."

I thanked her for what her center does and I thanked her for having an option for battered lesbians (although she never confirmed they accepted lesbians) and for having an alternative for battered gay men. Then I hung up to dial the new number.

When I called L— on M—, I found out it is a transitional living facility. It has been set up to house second-strike high-control parolees who have just gotten out of prison and are transitioning back into society. Battered gay men are accepted there, also, to live with these men who have just been released from prison.

We have to do better.

Apaciguate maricón—¡NO APACIGUAME!

¡Quítate Puto!

At least once a semester, this campus invites participants in the promotion of an organization that openly discriminates against gay men.

I began my employment here at this university in fall 2003. On September 10 of that year, I attended my first campus blood drive to "give the gift of life." During the pre-screening session, a screening nurse asked me if I was a man who has had or has sex with other men. The answer is yes, so she denied me the opportunity to give blood. But, the screening nurse did provide me with a coupon for a free pint of Baskin Robbins ice cream, usually reserved only for blood donors.

In September of this current semester, a blood mobile was on this campus. While walking to my classroom to go teach, I was approached by a screening nurse who asked if I would like to donate blood. I said, "Sure." When he asked if I was a man who has had or currently has sex with other men, I said, "Yes." So, he denied me the opportunity to give blood.

I reminded this nurse and all the other staff working the blood drive that HIV is not a gay male disease. HIV is a virus that can be passed on via anyone's blood or other body fluids. Angrily I told him that every time he and his co-workers are at my place of work, I am reminded that being gay is a stigma and that there are still government institutions that tell me that I am a pariah due to my gay identity. There are university-affiliated institutions that tell me that I am a pariah due to my gay identity.

Quítate puto—¡NO QUÍTAME!

¡Siéntate Fresa!

Similar to violence directed toward those for ethnic, religious, or for any reasons found inherent in the victim's inner-self, anti-gay, anti-lesbian, anti-bisexual, and anti-transgender violence may pit victims against other victims and against themselves. Feelings of vulnerability due to socially sanctioned discrimination can lead to self-dehumanization.

Queers who view themselves as perpetually vulnerable, or that their existence is the cause of the violence, are caught in a view that is self-destructive and wrong. It is important not to fall into the trap of self-blame. It is important to recognize that your positionality does not cause the attacks on you. However, sadly, these attacks are not random or coincidental either. They are premeditated. They are purposeful. They are intended.

A community that accepts higher rates of suicide, depression, and self-mutilation supports premeditated, purposeful, and intended attacks.

A community that accepts programs for battered gay men that possibly place them in more harm supports premeditated, purposeful, and intended attacks.

A community that accepts institutions who discriminate against same-sex loving supports premeditated, purposeful, and intended attacks.

A community that accepts these things needs to hear your voice.

Siéntate fresa—¡NO SIÉNTAME!
¿Cállate? ¡No cállaME!
¿Apaciguate? ¡No apaciguaME!
¿Quítate? ¡No quítaME!
¿Siéntate? ¡No siéntaME!

Somewhere in My 40s

As a full professor, I was invited to be a part of a large panel at the convention of the National Communication Association. This panel would address the mass killings of queer patrons of the Orlando nightclub, Pulse. The afternoon before the early-evening panel, I landed, disembarked from my plane, and immediately took a taxi to a downtown liquor store. I purchased the largest bottle of the best añejo tequila the store offered. I then taxied to the conference with 15 minutes to spare. Using the water glass provided by the hotel, I seated myself on a raised dais and poured myself a shot. My colleagues on the panel—high-profile, established, tenured scholars, and highly ambitious, tenure-seeking new scholars, began to seat themselves around me. I offered shots to everyone on the panel. They all happily accepted. Some sat with their neat shot, nursing it throughout the 90 minutes of presentations. Others, like myself, took as many shots as they desired. When it was my turn to present, I approached the podium with my glass and my almost-empty bottle. By the end of my individual presentation, there was no more tequila. Fifteen minutes after the end of the panel session, I was in a taxi on my way back to the airport to catch my flight home. The following is a transcript of my presentation.

TRIGGER WARNING

[Shot of tequila]

This performance is dedicated to Luis Alfaro, Latinx Mejicanx Chicanx performance artist extraordinaire.

Take a moment right now and think. Think about your favorite food. What is your favorite food dish? What food do you eat when you want to feel better? What food do you treat yourself with on your birthday or at celebrations? What's the dish that has to be there during Thanksgiving or it's not Thanksgiving? During Hanukkah? During Ramadan? During an anniversary? Perhaps even in honor of a death?

As most of you know, Día de los Muertos just came and went. Each Día de los Muertos I buy marigolds and place them on a makeshift altar in my house, and I light candles around the flowers. Some Latinxs in my family and in my community place pictures of loved ones on their altars. They also place trinkets and mementos to remember these loved ones. I don't. I'm minimalist and my altar is minimalist.

TRIGGER WARNING

[Shot of tequila]

But the one way I do celebrate is through food. I have a hot dog for my grandmother; I make arroz con pollo for my Tía (her recipe); and I drink a beer, ANY beer, for my Tío Panchito. Next year's Día de los Muertos will be particularly exciting because marijuana will be legal in California. Although

I'm not a smoker, I plan to spark up a joint for my Tía, and THEN eat the arroz con pollo. She'll be proud.

And for you? For you, I would eat the food that you imagined at the beginning of this presentation, the food that you thought about as your favorite dish, the food that nourishes you when you're sad or rewards you when you're happy. When I am dead, I am making this request of all of you right now: remember me with tequila.

TRIGGER WARNING

[Shot of tequila]

I bring up the food and drink of Día de Los Muertos because I am choosing to remember the dead of the Pulse Nightclub with tequila. Of all the news articles I read and of all the news videos I watched about the horrible nightclub, there was a dearth of information about the alcohol, about the scent of weed in the air, about the ways that those bodies were moved into the ecstatic as they danced on the dance floor in altered states of reality. I honor their memory through a tradition of Día de los Muertos. I honor their memory by bringing into my body the alcohol that they were savoring at the time that Omar Mateen ended their lives.

Think of the current trends of the communication field… narrative, autoethnography, performativity, intersectionality, neoliberalism, and especially the turn to affect. I read article after article of scholars scrounging to make affect what saves their publication, indeed what makes it publishable. Our field loves our trends. What I consistently struggle with is how the affect of the scholars is so often rational—a rational being within a context that generally fails his/her/their logic. With his/her/their affect, there is no passion—only professionalism. But perhaps affect can best be understood when "external tactics" like alcohol or drugs are involved.

TRIGGER WARNING

[Shot of tequila]

As a Christmas gift, I received a DNA test kit from my half-Mexican mother-in-law. Before I could even show the kit to my family members, I had spit into the test tube and packaged it up for mailing. A month later, I got the results: 35% Iberian Peninsula, 20% Great Britain, 25% Native American, 6% Middle Eastern, 3% North African, 2% Senegal, 2% Mali, and the rest were 1% like Finland, Italy, Greece, Eastern Europe, and South Asia.

I can see from my DNA that my ancestors were travelers. No doubt we moved from seaport to seaport, sharing our stories—we love to tell stories—sharing ourselves. And sharing our liquor.

In 711 AD, the Moors crossed the Strait of Gibraltar to conquer the Visigoths and most of Iberia. Many of us adopted the Arabic language and converted to Islam. Most didn't. For 800 years, the Muslims ruled the south of the Iberian peninsula, until 1492. That's when the European and African and Asian parts of my DNA "discovered" the Native American parts. Assholes!

So where do I find this Muslim inside of me? Or the Jew? Or the Christian? The Aztec? The Karankawa? I find them all in language. In Spanish, we use "ojalá" when we are in the subjunctive mood. The word is rooted in Arabic and comes from the 800 years of Arabic spoken in what is now Spain. "Ojalá" means "hopefully"… related to "Allah," "if God wills"… It's about what might happen if it all turns out right…

Ojalá we've learned a lesson from Pulse. One lesson is that Omar Mateen was not irrational—instead he was hyper-rational and was railing against a context that did not make sense to him and therefore failed him. Ojalá we've learned a lesson from Pulse. Another lesson is that emotion and affect are never the same. My emotions about this horrible tragedy are the same as yours. Each time I return to it, though, my affect changes.

Each Día de los Muertos, I celebrate dying and I age just a little bit more. My grandmother, my Tía, my Tío—remembering them gives me a chance to emote. And in return, each offers an affective experience related to who I am now, but also who I will hopefully be one day.

TRIGGER WARNING

Arriba. Abajo. Al centro. Pa' dentro.
  Ojalá.

[Shot of tequila.]

[Pause for dramatic effect, for dramatic affect. Walk away.]

Notes

1 Kimberlé Crenshaw. "Demarginalizing the Intersection of Race and Sex: A Black Feminist Critique of Antidiscrimination Doctrine, Feminist Theory and Antiracist Politics." *The University of Chicago Legal Forum* 1989, no. 1 (1989): 130–167, https://chicagounbound.uchicago.edu/uclf/vol1989/iss1/8; Kimberlé Crenshaw. "Mapping the Margins: Intersectionality, Identity Politics, and Violence against Women of Color." *Stanford Law Review* 43, no. 6 (1991): 1241–1299, doi: 10.2307/1229039; Kimberlé Crenshaw, Neil Goranda, Gary Peller, and Kendall Thomas, editors. *Critical Race Theory: The Key Writings that Formed the Movement* (New York, NY: The New Press, 1995).
2 Amber Johnson. "Confessions of a Video Vixen: My Autocritography of Sexuality, Desire, and Memory." *Text & Performance Quarterly* 34, no. 2 (2014): 182–200, doi: doi:10.1080/10462937.2013.879991; Amber Johnson. "From Academe, to the Theatre, to the Streets:

My Autocritography of Aesthetic Cleansing and Canonical Exception in the Wake of Ferguson." *Qualitative Inquiry* 24, no. 2 (2017): 88–100, doi:10.1177/1077800416684869.

3 Shane T. Moreman. "A Queer Futurity Autofantasía: Contouring Discourses of Latinx through Memory and Queer Youth Literature." *Text & Performance Quarterly* 39, no. 3 (2019): 187, doi: 10.1080/104629937.2019.1620959.

4 Lauren Berlant and Michael Warner. "Sex in Public." *Critical Inquiry* 24, no. 2 (1998): 547–566, https://www.jstor.org/stable/1344178.

5 Shane T. Moreman and Stephanie R. Briones. "Deaf Queer World-making: A Thick Intersectional Analysis of the Cultural Body." *Journal of International & Intercultural Communication* 11, no. 3 (2018): 216–232, doi:10.1080/17513057.2018.1456557.

6 Benny LeMaster. "Notes on Trans Relationality." *QED* 4, no. 2 (2017): 89, doi: 10.14321/qed.4.2.0084.

7 Diana Courvant. "Strip!" *Radical Teacher* 92 (2011): 26, doi: 10.5406/radicalteacher.92.0026.

8 Nicholas L. Clarkson. "Teaching Trans Students, Teaching Trans Studies." *Feminist Teacher* 27, no. 2–3 (2017): 233–252, doi:10.5406/femteacher.27.2-3.0233.

9 Benny LeMaster and Amber Johnson. "Unlearning Gender: Toward a Critical Communication Trans Pedagogy." *Communication Teacher* 33, no. 3 (2019): 189–198, doi:10.1080/17404622.2018.1467566.

10 Kate Drabinski. "Identity Matters: Teaching Transgender in the Women's Studies Classroom." *Radical Teacher* 92 (2011): 10–20, doi: 10.5406/radicalteacher.92.0010.

11 Susan Stryker. "Transgender Feminism: Queering the Woman Question," in *Feminist Frontiers*, 10th ed., eds. Verta Taylor, Nancy Whittier, and Leila J. Rupp (Lanham, MD: Rowman & Littlefield, 2019), 83–88.

12 Andrea Long Chu and Emmett Harsin Drager. "After Trans Studies." *Transgender Studies Quarterly* 6, no. 1 (2019): 103–116, doi:10.1215/23289252-7253524.

13 Chu and Drager, 112.

Bibliography

Berlant, Lauren and Michael Warner. "Sex in Public." *Critical Inquiry* 24, no. 2 (1998): 547–566, https://www.jstor.org/stable/1344178.

Chu, Andrea Long and Emmett Harsin Drager. "After Trans Studies." *Transgender Studies Quarterly* 6, no. 1 (2019): 103–116, doi:10.1215/23289252-7253524.

Clarkson, Nicholas L. "Teaching Trans Students, Teaching Trans Studies." *Feminist Teacher* 27, no. 2–3 (2017): 233–252, doi:10.5406/femteacher.27.2-3.0233.

Courvant, Diana. "Strip!" *Radical Teacher* 92 (2011): 26–34, doi: 10.5406/radicalteacher.92.0026.

Crenshaw, Kimberlé. "Demarginalizing the Intersection of Race and Sex: A Black Feminist Critique of Antidiscrimination Doctrine, Feminist Theory and Antiracist Politics." *The University of Chicago Legal Forum* 1989, no. 1 (1989): 130–167, https://chicagounbound.uchicago.edu/uclf/vol1989/iss1/8.

Crenshaw, Kimberlé. "Mapping the Margins: Intersectionality, Identity Politics, and Violence against Women of Color." *Stanford Law Review* 43, no. 6 (1991): 1241–1299, doi: 10.2307/1229039.

Crenshaw, Kimberlé, Neil Goranda, Gary Peller, and Kendall Thomas, editors. *Critical Race Theory: The Key Writings That Formed the Movement.* New York, NY: The New Press, 1995.

Drabinski, Kate. "Identity Matters: Teaching Transgender in the Women's Studies Classroom." *Radical Teacher* 92 (2011): 10–20, doi: 10.5406/radicalteacher.92.0010.

Johnson, Amber. "Confessions of a Video Vixen: My Autocritography of Sexuality, Desire, and Memory." *Text & Performance Quarterly* 34, no. 2 (2014): 182–200, doi: doi:10.1080/10462937.2013.879991.

Johnson, Amber. "From Academe, to the Theatre, to the Streets: My Autocritography of Aesthetic Cleansing and Canonical Exception in the Wake of Ferguson." *Qualitative Inquiry* 24, no. 2 (2017): 88–100, doi:10.1177/1077800416684869.

LeMaster, Benny. "Notes on Trans Relationality." *QED* 4, no. 2 (2017): 84–92, doi: 10.14321/qed.4.2.0084.

LeMaster, Benny and Amber Johnson. "Unlearning Gender: Toward a Critical Communication Trans Pedagogy." *Communication Teacher* 33, no. 3 (2019): 189–198, doi: 10.1080/17404622.2018.1467566.

Moreman, Shane T. "A Queer Futurity Autofantasía: Contouring Discourses of Latinx through Memory and Queer Youth Literature." *Text & Performance Quarterly* 39, no. 3 (2019): 185–202, doi: 10.1080/104629937.2019.1620959.

Moreman, Shane T. and Stephanie R. Briones. "Deaf Queer World-Making: A Thick Intersectional Analysis of the Cultural Body." *Journal of International & Intercultural Communication* 11, no. 3 (2018): 216–232, doi:10.1080/17513057.2018.1456557.

Stryker, Susan. "Transgender Feminism: Queering the Woman Question." In *Feminist Frontiers*, 10th ed., 83–88. Edited by Verta Taylor, Nancy Whittier, and Leila J. Rupp. Lanham, MD: Rowman & Littlefield, 2019.

Pulse

Amber L. Johnson

After the pulse of a rhythm enters your body,
Your body is never the same.
It memorizes the rhythmic changes, and adapts.
It begins to feel the way the muscles react
and interact in an exchange of growth and longing.
        A longing for a place,
           or time,
                or memory,
                    or body.
                        A longing for a life
                          or a second chance.

It is nostalgia in the making, the pulse of a rhythm.
Nostalgia for what?
I can't remember a time when things were good for us.
When sacred spaces didn't have to exist
hidden in gay club like identities hidden in a closet.
Where bathroom conversations didn't include
transphobic remarks about little children, sodomy, creeps, and rape.

How fitting that queer persons of color would die in a bathroom?
The very same bathrooms that the world is yelling for queers to
                  STAY OUT.
If only he had listened.
To the world.
To his friend who thought
        "this feels like death."
Would he still be alive to hold his mother one last time?
Text his mother one last time?

Instead his blood pooled next to a public toilet searching for a drain to freedom.
We are dying in bathrooms that we want to enter.
We are dying outside of bathrooms we cannot enter.
We are dying in clubs that act as sanctuaries because sanctuaries aren't
sanctified enough to know
        the difference between love and hate.
We are dying in the streets, in our relationships, at home, on the corners.
                WE ARE DYING.
Breaking News.
20 deaths.
        30 deaths.
                40 deaths.

The number keeps growing.
Like bpms getting faster and faster.
Eventually I concede.
I cannot keep up with that rhythm.
It moves too fast, the death toll.
Up.
Up.
Up.
Then still,
resting at 49.
But even in death, the pulse of rhythm still lingers.
The pulse lingers in the heartbeats that mourn your absence.
The pulse lingers in the spirituals sung loudly at your funeral.
It lingers in the messages you left
with your voice quivering
as you begged
for someone to call the police.
It lingers in the clicks of a keyboard
as we share your name,
now as a hashtag.
The pulse lingers.

49 hearts no longer beating.
98 feet no longer dancing.
490 fingers no longer clapping.
A week later the victims names and stories are beginning to circulate.
Black bois.
Brown bois.
Black womyn.
Brown womyn.
Puerto Ricans.
Floridians.
Students.
Friends.
Lovers.
Their names are familiar.
Names I have spoken.
Names I know.
Names I feel.
Names that roll
off my tongue
like heavy chocolate
and red wine.
They are mine to grieve this time.

WRITING A HARD AND PASSING RAIN

Autotheory, Autoethnography, and Queer Futures

Stacy Holman Jones

Manning Up on International Women's Day

I arrive at the International Women's Day breakfast and take a seat at a table populated by women who keep the university machine running—office managers, executive assistants, professional staff. Over mini croissants and veggie frittata cubes, I ask these women about their work and thank them for making things so efficient. So possible.

I have not chosen to sit at the table populated by the powerful academics; or more probably I have not been invited to sit there, but I don't think of this, at least not right away.

I pour a second cup of coffee and settle in for the speeches. Women complement other women on their stamina, their outspokenness, and their "take no prisoners" attitudes. On International Women's Day, we are advised by these women speakers to "man up" in response to the ever-increasing demands on our time and our lives. We are told to stop whining and "grow a pair." We are asked to believe that we must do and say such things because we are smart and hardworking and have so much to offer.

Because we are feminists.

Because we are the privileged women invited to breakfast at the faculty club on International Women's Day.

Because sometimes you need to know what makes it hard to stay.[1]

"To live a feminist life is to be a feminist at work."

Universities are institutions that are structured by power relations all the way down.

To work as a feminist means trying to transform the organizations that employ us—or house us.

This rather obvious fact has some telling consequences.

When we try to shake the walls of the house, we are also shaking the foundations of our own existence."[2]

"This is my story. It is personal. *The personal is institutional*."[3]

Vegetarian Frittata

2 tbs. Melted butter
1 sweet potato
2 eggplants
3 zucchinis
¼ cup olive oil
1 cup grated cheese
6 eggs
2 tbs. finely chopped parsley
Salt and pepper to taste

Preheat/
steam/
chargrill/
arrange/
whisk/
season/
pour/
bake/
set out to cool/
cut into cubes.

Serve.

Cells of Desire

To get the most accurate information on how to arrange—and pay—for a breast augmentation or a bilateral mastectomy or a vaginoplasty or phalloplasty or other body- and being-altering surgeries, you must call the receptionist. She is the person with the power of information—the cluster of promises that a bunch of cells (or their removal or their transformation) might make to a person you love. Might make possible for them, and us. To get this information, all we need to do is ring. And wait, pen in hand, as the receptionist tells us which doctor, which private hospital, which insurance cover will get you there. Will get you into the body you want to be. Where we ask questions in hushed tones, the receptionist speaks with confidence and clarity, saying, "Of course!" and, "Why wouldn't you?" She says, "No dramas" and "Too easy" and we wish that were true. She says, "Be sure to call us back once the mandatory waiting period of 12 months" has come and gone and we say we will. We will call back when the future we have imagined becomes possible. When that far-away tomorrow becomes the future in the present.[4]

Public health insurance exclusions:

- Plastic and reconstructive surgery
- Gender reassignment services
- Rehabilitation and psychiatric services
- Assisted reproductive services
- Pregnancy and birth services
- Hip and knee replacement services
- Cardiac and cardiac-related services
- Physiotherapy services
- Optical services
- Dental services
- Osteopathy services
- Chiropractic services
- Acupuncture
- Weight loss services
- Yoga

"When we are talking about an object of desire, we are really talking about a cluster of promises we want someone or something to make to us and make possible for us. This cluster of promises could be embedded in a person, a thing, an institution, a text, a norm, a bunch of cells, smells, a good idea—whatever."[5]

José Esteban Muñoz writes that queerness is performative—it is not simply a mode of being, but instead "a doing for and toward the future."[6] If queerness is about "the rejection of a here and now and an insistence on potentiality or concrete possibility for another world," what happens to queerness once that potentiality and possibility comes to be?[7] What happens to queerness "as a belonging in particularity" once you get the bunch of cells you desire?[8] Can we animate the "crushing force. . . of the here and now" [and] desire differently, and more and better once we get into the bodies we want to be?[9] What do we do about the future, then?

Beating Blue

"I remember that day very clearly; I had received a phone call. A friend had been in an accident. Perhaps she would not live … When I walked into my friend's hospital room, her eyes were a piercing, pale blue and the only part of her body that could move. I was scared. So was she. The blue was beating."[10]

I remember that day very clearly; my mother had called in the middle of the night. My grandmother had collapsed and wouldn't live to see the week out. I caught the first flight out, and when I walked into her hospital room late the next day, her eyes were closed. She was soft and round, her body bloated by fluids. Her white hair stood up around her head. I stood by her bed with my father for a long, long time. Neither of us spoke. I finally felt the courage to touch her hand and speak her name. Her eyelids fluttered open then. Her eyes—blue stars against a white, white sky, the only part of her body that could move—took hold of me. Touched me. I spoke then, a rush of words, trying to say something—anything—everything—about what she meant to me.

I remember that day very clearly; I have written sentences about blue and missing and hope,[11] not hoping for her return or for some different kind of ending, but out of a belief in the idea that it's "worth it to keep one's eyes open," worth writing of this moment, again and again.[12] It's worth returning to because it keeps my eyes open to how things can change in a matter of hours or minutes, a rush of words, in the beating of blue against a white, white sky.

Objects retrieved from my grandmother's apartment following her death:

1. Replica of Edvard Eriksen's Little Mermaid statue, which has perched waterside at Langelinie Promenade for nearly 100 years. The tiny reproduction statue, purchased in a Danish souvenir shop, sat perched on my grandmother's dressing table for as long as I can remember.

2. Trivet featuring a black and white whale painted on white ceramic tile and framed in bamboo; another souvenir from my grandmother's trip to Denmark. An excellent example of mid-century Danish design, which I have loved for as long as I can remember.

3. Watch on a gold fill chain, a piece of costume jewelry she wore all through the 1970s, the watch long stopped.

4. Fabric scroll featuring appliqued apples, persimmons and pears in autumnal velvet stitched onto nubby gold fabric. The scroll hung in every kitchen in every house my grandmother lived in, at least in my memory.

5. Pack of UNO cards nested in a brown and orange needle-pointed box inscribed with a single-word label: UNO. Product of my grandmother's crafty and nervous hands, as were many of the projects she cross-stitched, knitted, or crocheted after she quit smoking, also in the 1970s. Proof that my grandmother was an iconoclast.

6. Pair of thick, blue oven mitts, crocheted with the same fervor for the same reasons.

Sword Mountain

I go to see a therapist in California, someone recommended by a friend, who is also a therapist. I'm seeing someone new, someone who blurs all of the boundaries I thought we had around gender, all the boundaries I thought I had around myself. Someone who blurs all the boundaries I had around what love and relationships and sex could be. I am fiercely, deeply in love and I am terrified.

The therapist's office is in her home in Valley Village, a suburban neighborhood nestled in the 2-mile square bordered by Studio City, Sherman Oaks, North Hollywood and the 170 in Los Angeles. A place with a White, White population living inside condominiums that rise like stucco mountains in the center of a neighborhood originally filled with ranch- and mission-style houses.[14]

I enter through the side entrance meant for patients and wait in a cold living room filled with couches, pillows, and chairs.

When the therapist comes into the room, she turns up the heat and invites me to sit.

I choose a cushion and sit on the floor.

She sits, cross-legged in front of me, and places a tray filled with sand between us. She asks me to tell her why I'm there.

I say that I am seeing someone new, someone who blurs all of the boundaries I thought we—I—had around gender, around myself, around what love and relationships and sex could be. I tell her I am fiercely, deeply in love, and I am terrified.

The therapist nods and places a box of objects next to the sand tray. She asks me to choose an object to represent myself, represent this new love, and to place them in relation to one another in sand.

I choose two iridescent shells and place us in the upper left, a small island positioned to receive the rays of an imaginary rising sun.

She asks me to tell her about my extended family—my child, my ex-partners, my parents, my grandmother—and to choose objects for them.

I choose objects for these family members and place them on the sand in radiating clusters. Some form a shoal of shells that buffer us, others huddle together in pebble hills.

I place one object—the only object that isn't a stone or a shell or a piece of wood, but instead a small metal ikebana frog—at the far edge of the scene, just where light would slip into darkness as an imagined sun sets.

The therapist asks me about the small, spiky object.

I tell her I recognize it as an object that populated a home I shared with a woman years ago, a woman I loved but not in any recognizable way. I tell her I chose it as a symbol of something—someone—meant to hold and sustain beauty, but that, instead, terrifies me. I recall the woman showing me how she used the frogs to hold the flowers she arranged every Thursday night in her ikebana[13] course. Suddenly I remember that she taught me the name of that frog: *kensan*, a sword mountain. The *kensan* is something or someone meant to hold beauty, but here, on its own, it is a field of spiky pins not-quite buried in the sand.

The therapist asks me who I've chosen the *kensan* to represent.

I begin to cry.

She asks if I'd like her to move the spiky object out of the box.

I say yes.

She asks me where I'd like her to put it.

I look at her, unable to answer.

She asks if I'd like her to take it out of the room.

I nod and begin to sob.

She asks if I'd like her to take it out of the house.

I say yes.

She stands and leaves.

I hear the door meant for clients open and shut once, then open and shut again.

The therapist returns to the room and sits across from me. She asks me how I feel.

I tell her I am still afraid but no longer terrified.

She tells me our time is up.

I say yes.

She asks my permission to take a photo of the sandbox so we can return to this scene the next time we meet.

I stand and retrieve my wallet from my bag.

She takes the photos while I pay.

Sandplay objects in the therapist's office:

- Shells
- Pieces of driftwood
- Tiny starfish
- Marbles of all shapes, sizes, and colors—black, clear, yellow, blue, red, and orange
- Pieces of obsidian, lapis, malachite, and jade
- Clear, rose and smoky quartz crystals
- Fossils
- Pieces of amber with sticks and insects caught inside
- Animals carved from natural stone—tiny lions, snakes, birds, butterflies, horses, and frogs
- Pine cones and dried flowers
- Polished stone stars, hearts, moons, and suns
- Small metal tools—thimbles, scissors, teapots, and trowels
- Ikebana *kenzans* and *shippos* (metal holders with partitions)

Sandplay therapy was developed and elaborated by psychologists Margaret Lowenfeld and Dora Kalff, little-mentioned contemporaries of Melanie Klein and Anna Freud. Lowenfeld was moved by the trauma inflicted on children during the world wars and inspired by H.G.Well's book *Floor Games*, in which he recounts his son's imaginative play using wooden blocks, miniature figures, and objects found at home and in the garden. Dora Kalff, who studied psychotherapy with Emma and Carl Jung but was denied certification for not having traditional university training, saw this method as a performative embodiment of the exchange between the conscious and unconscious parts of ourselves. Both women were dedicated to helping others make pictures of their worlds when talking does not work and when identities are multiple and shifting.[15] The sandbox is a stage for bringing "what was heretofore unknown into being."[16]

The Unifying Force of Color

Some of the 127 colors available in PowerPoint by RGB (Red, Green Blue) Value and Name:[17]

0	0	0	Black
250	240	190	Blond
42	82	190	Cerulean Blue
222	93	131	Blush
150	75	0	Brown
140	146	172	Cool Gray
220	20	60	Crimson
237	201	175	Desert Sand
133	187	101	Dollar Bill
240	248	255	Ghost White
0	47	167	International Klein Blue
138	121	93	Shadow
255	250	0	Snow
226	230	0	Terra Cotta
91	146	229	United Nations Blue
255	255	255	White

A meeting. A PowerPoint presentation on how to turn university fundraising into a culture of philanthropy.

A series of questions.

And answers.

Question: How do we turn ideas—theirs and ours—into a shared and collaborative vision?

Answer: By telling a compelling *story*.

Question: What is a compelling story?

A compelling story is one that makes *a* difference while highlighting points *of* difference; one that focuses on the coherence and stability of expertise while championing change.

It's a story that changes how we make change.

One that turns the whole enterprise around, as though looking down is, now, looking up.

A meeting. An occasion for thinking of other things, for example, Rebecca Solnit's essay "The Blue of Distance," a series of associations. She writes, "In 1957, Yves Klein painted a globe his deep electric blue, and with this gesture it became a world without divisions between countries, between land and water, as though the earth itself had become sky, as though looking down was looking up. In 1961, he began painting relief maps this same trademark blue, so that the topography remained but the other distinctions vanished."[18] Klein's quest was to "erase the many for the sake of one,"—symphonies composed using only one note, paintings forged from one brilliant blue pigment, maps of the world that joined land and water in one continuous ocean-sky.[19] Where Klein's work might offer us a blueprint of moving from the material to the immaterial, the dissolution of difference for the sake of one does not, today, turn looking down into looking up. Instead, the "unifying force of color" is on display in all the most predictable ways.[20] The folders and the conference room table and the people around it and the people missing in this scene map the relation between the known world and the "Terra Incognita" of difference inside the academy. And out.

A writing session. An occasion for connecting a story of turning one thing (the eliding of difference, tokenism) into something else (critique, accountability). If intersectionality calls attention to how oppressive institutions, attitudes and actions in cultures including racism, xenophobia, sexism, heteronormativity, classism, religious and spiritual fundamentalism, ageism, and ableism do not function independently but instead are connected and mutually influencing, how does this story about the unifying force of color work? How could it "capture the complexities of intersecting power relations that produce multiple identities and distinctive perspectives on social phenomena"?[21] As Tami Spry puts it, "One of the things we do best in autoethnography is critical reflection upon the effects of hegemonic power structures even, and especially when, we may be the arbiters of such structures."[22] Here, around the conference table, we are arbiters of such structures. In this story, the nearly all-White committee members, including me, pass around promotional materials featuring the students of color poised to change the world for the better. Slick cardstock folders float atop the conference table like so many islands—or boats of asylum seekers dotting the sea.

And between the words of this—my—story is "silence, around ink whiteness, behind every map's information is what's left out, the unmapped and unmappable."[23]

The meeting ends and the fundraisers-turned philanthropists, including me, file out of the room. I save the folder full of promotional material for later; when I sit down to write about it.

Coming Out as Dragging Back

We are discussing queerness and recognition in the performance studies classroom. We are discussing how recognizing someone as part of a context or a culture or a scene depends on the other. This is, we say, something we recognize about performance, about being on stage. We stage a reading of theory, because getting the words into our bodies tells us things we need to know, because we are trying to feel into how "theory can do more the closer it gets to the skin."[24] Not theory as abstraction, but rather, theory that is "in touch with a world" and our own experience.[25]

Scene 1:

ACTOR 1: "The question most central to recognition is a direct one, and it is addressed to the other:"

ACTOR 2: "'Who are you?'"

ACTOR 1: "This question assumes that there is another whom we do not know and cannot fully apprehend. . ."

ACTOR 2: "Who are you?"

ACTOR 1: "What kind of action does this speech act perform?"

ACTOR 2: To speak and to act, we must, "answer to the question asked to every newcomer: 'who are you'?"[27]

The scene ends and someone says, "We're theatre kids. We know all about the stranger, the 'now you see me, now you don't.' The 'who are you'."

Someone asks, "If we know all about the newcomer and the 'who are you,' why is it so hard to do that at home? Why is it so hard to get the people who are supposed to love you to *see* you?"

Someone says, "I think I came out to my parents last night. And all my mother could think to say was, 'It's all those parts you're playing. I bet if you played a straight part, instead of all the lesbians and bisexuals, you'd feel differently."

Someone asks, "Why does anyone have to come out anymore? How can something so fundamental to who you are be invisible? And anyway, coming out isn't the scary thing it used to be. Is it?"

Half the room breathes in.

The other half breathes out.

Someone says, "My family doesn't know I'm transitioning, and I'm not going to tell them."

Someone says, "People are so much more accepting than they used to be."

Someone says, "I'm asexual. Do you know what it's like to have people say, 'Is that even a thing' to me? About me?"

Someone says, "NO ONE reads me as queer. I have to come out about 10 times a day. More. It's exhausting, dragging yourself out of the closet every time someone else drags you back in."

We return to the scene of theory, trying to work out what we know in our bodies.

Scene 2:
ACTOR 1: "The personal is theoretical. [ACTOR 2:] Theory itself is often assumed to be abstract: something is more theoretical the more abstract it is, the more it is abstracted from everyday life.
[ACTOR 1:] To abstract is to drag away, detach, pull away, or divert.
[ACTOR 2:] We might then have to drag theory back, to bring theory back to life."[28]

"Performance Exercise: The Gaze, or, Discovering the Other 'Others'

Duration: 5–7 minutes

Level: Foundational

Comments: Prolonged intense eye contact between two people has different connotations for different cultures. Be aware of the cultural implications for your group and explain the exercise accordingly.

Begin walking randomly around the space . . . Keep your eyes open, and make eye contact as an act of acknowledgment as you pass one another.

Continue to walk and think of someone you would like to get to know better. Ideally this should be someone you don't know very well and, if possible, someone who is as "different" as possible in obvious ways (race, gender, age, body type. . .)

The goal is very simple: to be present and open, to express a basic existential message with your gaze that goes something like, 'We happen to be here today, to coincide on this strange planet and it's OK. We are here together sharing a moment in life and art. It's a pleasure to be here with you.'"[26]

Gravitate toward that person and intuitively assess if your desire to partner is reciprocated. If not, don't take it personally and continue walking around until you find someone. . .Find your own space in the room and stand two feet apart facing each other. Now, look into each other's eyes without blinking. . .

A Hard and Passing Rain

"Perhaps this is why writing all day, even when the work feels arduous, never feels to me like 'a hard day's work.' Often it feels more like balancing two sides of an equation— occasionally quite satisfying, but essentially a hard and passing rain."[29]

A work is an object overflowing its frame. . . . A work works when it becomes human. This becoming occurs when we realize it. Specifically, it occurs when we realize where it occurs. It occurs inside. We do not need to find a way into a work, since the work is already inside. Instead we realize a work and its harmony with our point of view. Then it and we begin to work, and the play of work begins.[30]

The equation of when and where queer work works:

On one side: experience— my own and that of others I am in relation with and to.

On the other side: critical theory—a way of not only explaining the inside working of relations but also a means for imagining how those relations might work differently, otherwise.

I have been writing all day, and my work has not felt arduous. It has felt like a balancing act in which I am attempting to work both sides of multiple equations—narrative and theory, fragment and through-line, personal and political, queer and ?—all at the same time. I'm not sure they all add up, though I have never taken to mathematics. Or, I should say, I have somehow seemed to invent my own ways of working through such equations, if not to find the answer, then to find something that works for me. One thing I have discovered is that when I feel the quite satisfying sensation of writing that comes together like a hard and passing rain, it feels very much like what Matthew Goulish describes as being inside the work as it *works*.[36]

When I'm writing, though, it doesn't quite work the way Goulish describes it, probably because there's so much in the world that doesn't feel inside to me. So much in the world that doesn't harmonize with my point of view. This is when it feels like the work of queering things is *hard work*. Hard because what's inside, what's now, isn't a future that's "already" here.[37] Instead, it's that illusive but oh-so-satisfying hard and passing rain and when we smell it on the air, we just have to stay with it, future-bound in our desires and designs.[38]

Queer grocery lists and other notes

July 25, 2018, 11:27 am
Baking soda
Ramen
Milk
Sliced cheese
Granola bars
Cucumber
Avocado
Bananas
Strawberries
Lettuce
Feta cheese
Veggies for stir fry
Tofu
Coffee
Icy poles
Jam
Mustard
Yogurt
Red wine
Kalamata olives
Post-it notes
Chapstick

February 27, 2018, 11:49 am
A body must be touched

I want to learn by heart

What is the other side of humility?

November 16, 2017, 2:34 pm
Shampoo and conditioner
Ketchup and mustard
Orange juice
Milk
Cereal
Salmon
Asparagus
Potatoes
Onion
Vitamin C
Buns

I have called this way of working critical autoethnography, a writing practice that works as a "living body of thought."[31] I love doing this kind of writing because it allows me to work both sides of several equations—specific and concrete, what holds us together and what holds us apart, the here and now and what might be possible—all at the same time. Others have called this kind of work "autotheory" (as in the case of Maggie Nelson's *The Argonauts*, along with many other books)[32]—a "combination of autobiography and critical theory."[33] Though as Monica Pearl observes, the categories we are working on either side of that equation *change* as they come into contact. When we're using critical theory in autobiographic accounts we "stretch" the categories/genres of both autobiography and critical theory.[34] In the collision and commingling of the personal and the theoretical, we queerly transform the "parts" and possibly the purposes of each. In such writing, the form and content—memoir or monograph or grocery list; family or gender or sexuality—might look the same (as other works) but "is not the same thing, depending on who is doing it, who is doing it with whom, and how they are thinking about it. It has new parts."[35]

Queerness in autotheory and other forms of auto/critical writing is not simply a category or genre, but instead a set of practices that accomplishes an "undoing," a "fluctuation of parts."[39] If this kind of work works to "capture something shifting and subversive and untamed, then it does the work of what naming (and taming) an affect—or feeling—might do: it harnesses something wild, something that only truculently obeys boundaries and borders."[40]

July 9, 2017, 9:22 pm
If you give acceptance messages, change is likely to come (later).

Demand messages don't lead to change but instead to resistance.

A life of learning/unlearning

19 February 2016, 6:58 am
Flowers
Eggs
Peppermint tea
Butter
Cucumbers
Paper towels

May 23, 2015, 4:17 am
A wound needs a witness.

Notes

1 Sara Ahmed. "Resignation Is a Feminist Issue." *Feminist Killjoys*, August 27, 2016, https://feministkilljoys.com/2016/08/27/resignation-is-a-feminist-issue/.

2 Ahmed, "Resignation."

3 Ahmed, "Resignation."

4 José Esteban Muñoz. *Cruising Utopia: The Then and There of Queer Futurity* (New York, NY: New York University Press, 2009), 49.

5 Lauren Berlant. "Cruel Optimism." *differences* 17, no. 3 (2006): 20.

6 Muñoz, 1.

7 Muñoz, 1; Muñoz's project is to write and theorize a "concrete utopianism" through the lens of performance studies by enacting a critical and associative methodology that "can best be described as a backward glance that enacts a future vision" (4). In doing so, Muñoz draws on Ernst Bloch's writing about utopias, particularly his distinction between "abstract" utopias, which fuel "a critical and potentially transformative political imagination [but] falter . . . because they are untethered from any historical consciousness," and "concrete" utopias, which are "relational and historically situated struggles, a collectivity that is actualized or potential" (3). Here, getting into the body you want to be might untether "you" (and "us") from collective political struggles. Or, as Benny and Amber put it, "achieving institutionally derived 'goals' (including 'passing' based on particular morphological expectations of gendered bodies) [might] render abstract utopias whose goals are uncertain or foggy at best." At the same time, it's worth asking whether and how a concrete utopia—an animation of the "hopes of a collective" for a different future (3)—*materializes* the moment any one of us gets into the body we want to be, even if we have no certain or clear answer to that question.

8 Muñoz, 28.

9 Muñoz, 189.

10 Maggie Nelson. *Bluets* (Seattle, WA: Wave Press, 2009), 9.

11 Stacy Holman Jones. "Lost and Found." *Text and Performance Quarterly* 31, no. 4 (2011): 322–341, doi: 10.1080/10462937.2011.602709; Anne Harris and Stacy Holman Jones. *The Queer Life of Things: Performance, Affect and the More-than-Human* (Lanham, MD: Lexington Books, 2019).

12 Nelson, *Bluets*, 13.

13 Ikebana is the classical art of Japanese flower arranging introduced in the sixth century by Chinese Buddhist missionaries seeking to formalize and teach the ritual practice of offering flowers to the Buddha. See Editors of Encyclopedia Britannica, *Encyclopedia Britannica*, "Ikebana." Encyclopedia Britannica, 2008. https://www.britannica.com/art/ikebana.

14 Valley Village is a predominately White suburb in Los Angeles County, with White people making up nearly 67% of the population. It's rumored that the move to separate Valley Village from North Hollywood was motivated by racial prejudices regarding the Latino population there and the predictable effects of such prejudices on property values. The move to separate was part of a campaign to stem construction of high-density apartments and office buildings in the area, what residents termed "stucco mountains" created parking and traffic congestion and spoiled the views of the Spanish- and ranch-style homes on large residential lots in the neighborhood. See "Valley Village, Los Angeles." *Wikipedia*, last modified October 23, 2019, https://en.wikipedia.org/wiki/Valley_Village,_Los_Angeles.

15 Barbara A. Turner. "Introduction: What Is Sandplay Therapy," in *The Routledge International Handbook of Sandplay Therapy*, ed. Barbara A. Turner (New York, NY: Routledge, 2018), 1–3; Rosalind Heiko. *A Therapist's Guide to Mapping the Girl Heroine's Journey in Sandplay* (Lanham, MD: Rowman & Littlefield, 2018), 32.

16 Turner, 10.

17 WorkWithColor. "Color Chart One-Page View." WorkWithColor, 2018, http://www. workwithcolor.com/color-chart-full-01.htm.

18 Rebecca Solnit. "The Blue of Distance," in *A Field Guide to Getting Lost*, ed. Rebecca Solnit (New York, NY: Penguin, 2006), 168–169.

19 Solnit, "The Blue," 169.

20 Solnit, "The Blue," 169.

21 Patricia Hill Collins. "Black Feminist Thought as Oppositional Knowledge." *Departures in Critical Qualitative Research* 5, no. 3 (2016): 135, doi: X.10.1525/dcqr.2016.5.3.133.

22 Tami Spry. *Autoethnography and the Other: Unsettling Power through Utopian Performatives* (New York, NY: Routledge, 2016), 37.

23 Solnit, "The blue," 161–162.

24 Sara Ahmed. *Living a Feminist Life* (Durham, NC: Duke University Press, 2017), 10.

25 Ahmed, *Living*, 10.

26 Guillermo Gómez Peña and Roberto Sifuentes. *Exercises for Rebel Artists: Radical Performance Pedagogy* (New York, NY: Routledge, 2013), 57–59.

27 Judith Butler. *Giving an Account of Oneself* (New York, NY: Fordham University Press, 2005), 31.

28 Ahmed, *Living*, 10.

29 Nelson, *Bluets*, 74–75.

30 Matthew Goulish. *39 Microlectures: In Proximity of Performance* (New York, NY: Routledge, 2000), 102.

31 Stacy Holman Jones. "Living Bodies of Thought: The Critical in Critical Autoethnography." *Qualitative Inquiry* 22, no. 4 (2016): 228–237, doi: 10.1177/1077800415622509; See also Della Pollock. "Part I Introduction: Performance Trouble," in *The SAGE Handbook of Performance Studies*, eds. D. Soyini Madison and Judith Hamera (Thousand Oaks, CA: Sage, 2006), 1–8.

32 Maggie Nelson. *The Argonauts* (Melbourne, Australia: Text Publishing, 2016). There are too many examples of "autotheory" to list. A personal and therefore idiosyncratic list: Roland Barthes. *A Lover's Discourse*, trans. Richard Howard (New York, NY: Random House, 1977/2002); Beatriz Preciado. *Testo Junkie: Sex, Drugs and Biopolitics in the Pharmacopornographic Era* (New York, NY: The Feminist Press at the City University of New York, 2008); Kathleen Stewart. *Ordinary Affects* (Durham, NC: Duke University Press, 2007); Ali Smith. *Artful* (London, UK: Penguin, 2012); Rebecca Solnit. *The Faraway Nearby* (London, UK: Granta, 2013); Solnit, "The Blue," 155–174; Lesley Stern. *The Smoking Book* (Chicago, IL: University of Chicago Press, 1990); Julie Taylor. *Paper Tangos* (Durham, NC: Duke University Press, 1998).

33 Monica B. Pearl. "Theory and the Everyday." *Angelaki: Journal of the Theoretical Humanities* 23, no. 1 (2018): 200, doi: 10.1080/0969725X.2018.1435401. Preciado is said to have coined this term in *Testo Junkie*, writing: "The philosophy of the pharmacopornographic regime has been reduced to an enormous, dripping butt-plug camera. In such circumstances, the philosophy of such high-punk modernity can only be autotheory, autoexperimentation, auto-techno-penetration, pornology" (347). Fournier views autotheory as a "trans-medial, feminist and queer feminist practice that manifests across function, critical writing, sound, film, video, art writing and criticism, and performance art," noting that in autotheory "theorized personal anecdotes or embodied actions constellate with fragments from the history of philosophy to form potent analyses of gender, politics, academia, and contemporary art. Embodied experience becomes the primary material for generating theory, foregrounding disclosure and ambivalence as that which enhances critical rigour and relevance; this some is fundamentally feminist, even as many of these writers and artists openly problematize the feminist position." See Lauren Fournier. "Auto-theory as an Emerging Mode of Feminist Practice across

Media," Unpublished doctoral dissertation (University of York, Canada, 2017). The writing of queer autoethnographers brings the feminist and queer autotheory project to writing about identities, relationships, performance, activism, affect, new materialism, and the more-than-human (see, for example, Tony E. Adams. *Narrating the Closet: An Autoethnography of Same-sex Attraction* [Walnut Creek, CA: Left Coast Press, 2011]; Bryant Keith Alexander. *Performing Black Masculinity: Race, Culture and Queer Identity* [Lanham MD: AltaMira, 2006]; Ragan Fox. "'Homo-work': Queering Academic Communication and Communicating Queer in Academia." *Text and Performance Quarterly* 33, no. 1 [2013]: 58–76, doi: 10.1080/10462937.2012.744462; Craig Gingrich-Philbrook. "Autoethnography's Family Values: Easy Access to Compulsory Experiences." *Text and Performance Quarterly* 25, no. 4 [2005]: 297–314, doi: 10.1080/10462930500362445; Stacy Holman Jones and Tony E. Adams. "Undoing the Alphabet: A Queer Fugue on Grief and Forgiveness." *Cultural Studies↔Critical Methodologies* 14, no. 2 [2014]: 102–110, doi: 10.1177/1532708613512260; Stacy Holman Jones and Tony E. Adams. "Autoethnography and Queer Theory: Making Possibilities," in *Qualitative Inquiry and Human Rights*, eds. Norman K. Denzin and Michael D. Giardina [Walnut Creek, CA: Left Coast Press, 2010], 136–157; Stacy Holman Jones and Anne Harris. *Queering Autoethnography* (New York, NY: Routledge, 2018); Harris and Holman Jones. *The Queer Life*; Amber Johnson. "Doing It: A Rhetorical Autoethnography of Religious Masturbation and Identity Negotiation." *Departures in Critical Qualitative Research* 3, no. 4 [2014]: 366–388; Amber Johnson. "Confessions of a Video Vixen: My Autocritography of Sexuality, Desire and Memory." *Text and Performance Quarterly* 34, no. 2 [2014]: 182–200; Benny LeMaster. "Telling Multiracial Tales: An Autoethnography of Coming out Home." *Qualitative Inquiry* 20, no. 1 [2014]: 51–60.

34 Pearl, 200.
35 Pearl, 200.
36 Goulish, 39.
37 Muñoz, 185.
38 I am riffing (and revising a bit) on Muñoz on queer futurity when he writes: "We must vacate the here and now for a then and there … queerness is not yet here; thus, we must always be future bound in our desires and designs …. What we need to know is that queerness is not yet here but it approaches like a crashing wave of potentiality. And we must give in to its propulsion, its status as a destination" (Muñoz, 185).
39 Pearl, 201.
40 Pearl, 201.

Bibliography

Adams, Tony E. *Narrating the Closet: An Autoethnography of Same-Sex Attraction*. Walnut Creek, CA: Left Coast Press, 2011.

Ahmed, Sara. *Living a Feminist Life*. Durham, NC: Duke University Press, 2017.

Ahmed, Sara. "Resignation Is a Feminist Issue." *Feminist Killjoys*, August 27, 2016, https://feministkilljoys.com/2016/08/27/resignation-is-a-feminist-issue/.

Alexander, Bryant Keith. *Performing Black Masculinity: Race, Culture and Queer Identity*. Lanham, MD: AltaMira, 2006.

Barthes, Roland. *A Lover's Discourse*, trans. Richard Howard. New York, NY: Random House, 1977/2002.

Berlant, Lauren. "Cruel Optimism." *differences* 17, no. 3 (2006): 20–36, doi: 10.1215/10407391-2006-009.

Butler, Judith. *Giving an Account of Oneself*. New York, NY: Fordham University Press, 2005.

Collins, Patricia Hill. "Black Feminist Thought as Oppositional Knowledge." *Departures in Critical Qualitative Research* 5, no. 3 (2016): 133–144, doi: 10.1525/dcqr.2016.5.3.133.

Fournier, Lauren. "Auto-theory as an Emerging Mode of Feminist Practice across Media." Unpublished doctoral dissertation. University of York, Canada, 2017.

Fox, Ragan. "'Homo-work': Queering Academic Communication and Communicating Queer in Academia." *Text and Performance Quarterly* 33, no. 1 (2013): 58–76, doi: 10.1080/10462937.2012.744462.

Gingrich-Philbrook, Craig. "Autoethnography's Family Values: Easy Access to Compulsory Experiences." *Text and Performance Quarterly* 25, no. 4 (2005): 297–314, doi: 10.1080/10462930500362445.

Gómez Peña, Guillermo and Roberto Sifuentes. *Exercises for Rebel Artists: Radical Performance Pedagogy.* New York, NY: Routledge, 2013.

Goulish, Matthew. *39 Microlectures: In Proximity of Performance.* New York, NY: Routledge, 2000.

Harris, Anne and Stacy Holman Jones. *The Queer Life of Things: Performance, Affect and the More-than-Human.* Lanham, MD: Lexington Books, 2019.

Heiko, Rosalind. *A Therapist's Guide to Mapping the Girl Heroine's Journey in Sandplay.* Lanham, MD: Rowman & Littlefield, 2018.

Holman Jones, Stacy. "Living Bodies of Thought: The Critical in Critical Autoethnography." *Qualitative Inquiry* 22, no. 4 (2016): 228–237, doi: 10.1177/1077800415622509.

Holman Jones, Stacy. "Lost and Found" *Text and Performance Quarterly* 31, no. 4 (2011): 322–341, doi: 10.1080/10462937.2011.602709.

Holman Jones, Stacy and Anne Harris. *Queering Autoethnography.* New York, NY: Routledge, 2018.

Holman Jones, Stacy and Tony E. Adams. "Undoing the Alphabet: A Queer Fugue on Grief and Forgiveness." *Cultural Studies ⇔ Critical Methodologies* 14, no. 2 (2014): 102–110, doi: 10.1177/1532708613512260.

Holman Jones, Stacy and Tony E. Adams. "Autoethnography and Queer Theory: Making Possibilities." In *Qualitative Inquiry and Human Rights,* 136–157. Edited by Norman K. Denzin and Michael D. Giardina. Walnut Creek, CA: Left Coast Press, 2010.

Johnson, Amber. "Confessions of a Video Vixen: My Autocritography of Sexuality, Desire and Memory." *Text and· Performance Quarterly* 34, no. 2 (2014): 182–200, doi: 10.1080/10462937.2013.879991.

Johnson, Amber. "Doing It: A Rhetorical Autoethnography of Religious Masturbation and Identity Negotiation." *Departures in Critical Qualitative Research* 3, no. 4 (2014): 366–388, doi: 10.1525/dcqr.2014.3.4.366.

LeMaster, Benny. "Telling Multiracial Tales: An Autoethnography of Coming out Home." *Qualitative Inquiry* 20, no. 1 (2014): 51–60, doi: 10.1177/1077800413508532.

Muñoz, José Esteban. *Cruising Utopia: The Then and There of Queer Futurity.* New York, NY: New York University Press, 2009.

Nelson, Maggie. *Bluets.* Seattle, WA: Wave Press, 2009.

Nelson, Maggie. *The Argonauts.* Melbourne, Australia: Text Publishing, 2016.

Pearl, Monica B. "Theory and the Everyday." *Angelaki: Journal of the Theoretical Humanities* 23, no. 1 (2018): 199–203, doi: 10.1080/0969725X.2018.1435401.

Pollock, Della. "Part I Introduction: Performance Trouble." In *The SAGE Handbook of Performance Studies,* 1–8. Edited by D. Soyini Madison and Judith Hamera. Thousand Oaks, CA: Sage, 2006.

Preciado, Beatriz. *Testo Junkie: Sex, Drugs and Biopolitics in the Pharmacopornographic Era*. New York, NY: The Feminist Press at the City University of New York, 2008.

Solnit, Rebecca. "The Blue of Distance." In *A Field Guide to Getting Lost*, 153–176. Edited by Rebecca Solnit. New York, NY: Penguin, 2006.

Solnit, Rebecca. *The Faraway Nearby*. London, UK: Granta, 2013.

Smith, Ali. *Artful*. London, UK: Penguin, 2012.

Spry, Tami. *Autoethnography and the Other: Unsettling Power through Utopian Performatives*. New York, NY: Routledge, 2016.

Stern, Lesley. *The Smoking Book*. Chicago, IL: University of Chicago Press, 1990.

Stewart, Kathleen. *Ordinary Affects*. Durham, NC: Duke University Press, 2007.

Taylor, Julie. *Paper Tangos*. Durham, NC: Duke University Press, 1998.

Turner, Barbara A. "Introduction: What Is Sandplay Therapy." In *The Routledge International Handbook of Sandplay Therapy*, 1–32. Edited by Barbara A. Turner. New York, NY: Routledge, 2018.

Pay It No Mind

Vin Olefer

I would believe she grew those flowers herself,
Sprouted from her rich, dark skin, and woven
Into the crown on top of her tight curls.

She is still a queen.
Mother gave life to everything she touched,
She did not bear her children,
but she Brought us to life,
nurtured our spirits
So we could become.

That red-satin smile of hers, I swear
It's etched on the walls of my heart
So bright and big, it distracts the eye from
The target on her back.

Mother, I wish I could tell you,
We don't believe the cops
For a face as warm as yours does not
Become a case so cold.

Mother Marsha, you might want to know
Your children are still legendary, we
Bear your smile and your pride,
And yes, mother,
We still don't pay it no mind.

GENDER FUTURITY

A Plea for Pleasure

When we set out to write a conclusion for this volume on gender futurity, as a site of potential liberation and possibility, we were focused on what was missing from the research on gender non-normativity: pleasure. Gender research that focused on the dysphoria, pain, shame, and terrifying experiences of trans and non-binary people saturated the literature until recently when scholars began to focus on shifting narratives of gender to what was possible when we choose to unapologetically live in our bodies. As we bring this volume to a close, we want to theorize from a place deep within our own pleasure centers, unattached to scholarship and rigid notions of what is, but rather what could be, if we hone in on our intuitive needs to feel good, free, and purpose-filled in our pleasure. In this final conversation, we conceptualize gender futurity from a place of pleasure and freedom. We begin with a question. Who would you be if you were invited to express your identities in ways that please you?

Amber: When I began thinking about this question and entering this conversation, my imagination automatically went to Billy Porter, the famous queer fashion icon who was rendered a household name following his role as Pray Tell in the amazing FX series *Pose* about 1980s ballroom culture. His Instagram feed is a carefully curated expression of unapologetic gender expression @theebillyporter way. His style has been all the rage for so many warranted reasons. But the reason that draws me in is that his looks are always rooted in fun, pleasure, and extreme joy. From the colors, to the textures, gender-fluidity, grandeur, and sparkle, he embodies a person who chooses to feel good. He echoes my own reading of feeling good in an interview about his style. When he was asked "where does your sense of style come from," Billy Porter answered, "I choose joy. If you're not having fun, you may as well hang it up."[1] This is where I enter this question. If I was invited to express my identities in ways that please me, I would be a walking expression of joy and fun. I would have found the joy in colorful collar clips, freshly pressed pocket squares, leather wing tip Oxfords, and a good fitting pair of chinos long before someone told me, "Girls can't wear that." To which I would have never had to respond, "I am not a girl." When adrienne marie brown theorized that pleasure is a measure of freedom,[2] I squealed. Had I been invited to express my gender identity in ways that please me, I would be free. Every day I inch closer and closer to freedom.

Most people assimilate to gender norms and roles unconsciously and mindlessly. We are taught from birth to perform certain roles and many never question those roles. I questioned those roles, but not from a place of possibility. Operating from an ethic of pleasure means constantly questioning anything that makes us feel less than pleased within our bodies versus questioning our bodies. Gender as pleasure means never questioning my body, just the institutions that ask me to question my body.

Benny: In short, I would be me. But let me explain. See, norms don't exist though they structure life. As Andrea Long Chu and Emmett Harsin Drager remind me, "the desire for the norm consists, in terms of its lived content, in *nonnormative* attempts at normativity."[3] Said differently, my various and relative attachments to norms, and the paths I have taken in relation to those norms, whether compelled "by desire, by habit, [and/or] by survival," reveal I have always already arrived.[4] Please allow me to explain otherwise. That I desire to be seen and affirmed by my family isn't normative, that I use(d) the institution of marriage to do so is. That I habitually mask my gender differences to survive particular contexts, including academe, isn't normative; that I might turn to my institutional role as "professor" to justify a refusal to intervene in moments where others are targets of cisheterosexist domination is. That I draw on and use my intersectional privileges to survive everyday life isn't what's normative; that I do so without reflexively recognizing the ways in which said privileges hinge on the domination of others is. I would be me to the degree that where I am reflects my pasts making due with the materiality of my present always focused on tomorrow today.

And, we end with a question. What is gender futurity to you?

Amber: Gender futurity is an intervention of sorts. It is an imaginative space of reinventing the gendered alternative toward freedom. If we think about that question in terms of the four sections of this book, the first section focused on compulsory identity categories that push us to express ourselves in rigid, binary ways. What if it was compulsory to please the body by adorning it and expressing it in ways that make us feel good? Compulsion in public has been cast as inappropriate, offensive, and out of control. So the body that gives into the compulsion to feel joy publicly is the disruptive body because pleasure is not an appropriate public act. If my existence is disruptive and I am going to have to disrupt some shit, I might as well enjoy it. The second section focused on identity negotiation and internal struggles. By moving gender beyond a social category to something that is felt, expressed, embodied, avowed, and mapped into/onto the body via pleasure, we eliminate the need to negotiate and we eliminate internal struggles because gender is no longer dictated by social norms, but rather by what pleases us. The third section requires that gender be a source of the erotic, meaning it must bring pleasure instead of pain, fear, or shame. It requires us to live out loud in our bodies in ways that pleasure us. Finally, it is imaginative in that it cultivates the opportunity to always be reinventing itself.

When I think about my processes of shifting away from compulsion and moving into revisioning my history to write my new future, I think of my childhood traumas less as permanent stains on my gender journey and more as departure points that I no longer grant the power to define me. I think of my gender fluid child and the way their unapologetic becoming taught me to be embrace my body. It is this line of thinking that I choose my closing poem, inspired by and dedicated to Audre Lorde.

> All the while I am happy
> My childhood self fails to understand that
> Because she was never taught that Black trans love is Black wealth
>
> I really hope they ALL write about me
> And piece together different parts of our truth
> Because it was never
> Just
> My mother's cisness
> Or my father's absence
> Or the boy at 6
> Then 15
> Then 20
>
> It wasn't just the sorrow
> It wasn't just the pain or the trauma
>
> It was the water
> And the purple bike with rainbow streamers
> It was the bedazzled turtleneck and snaggletooth portraits
>
> It was the blood
> And the ancestry
> And the lineage

It was their suckling
And their first bath
And the moment my
        gender fluid
            child joined me
                 in the water
                    for the first time
Even though I followed them.

Benny: I write where I am, in the future. And in this future, I choose reconstruction and bodily recovery over academe's deconstructive edge.[5] I choose to live (in) my genders, as a felt sensation, affirmed by the few who relationally matter (to) me. Like Chu and Drager, I understand everyone's gender to be a "political disaster," and I "refuse to fix it."[6] As such, in this future, I invest in the relational forces that sustain a core sense of self. For, in this future, in the present, the State will/does not save us.

We do.

For survival is relational.

And what I choose to fix, if anything, in this future, are relational bonds that exceed, reject, develop, and sometimes parallel normative means of relating— Not the State or its institutional tendrils. What I choose to nourish are both the subversive and the mundane relational means by which we navigate said tendrils using everything we got—even when what we got looks and feels an awful lot like that which mirrors the State. For it is in relational forces that we can sustain gender possibilities. And with that, I end with a plutonic love note.

We've known one another since the mid-1990s
    my bestie and I.
When Bradley sang of weed and Snoop Dogg reigned supreme.
We went to different schools in different districts.

    He, a lesbian at the time.
    Me, a gay boy at the time.
        We did what we did to survive.
        We do what we do to survive
            tomorrow today.
We meet once a week to walk and to talk.
About the usual: transitions
        of mind, of body, and of relational intimacies.
His words a gesture of love,
      You've helped so many of us
      to find peace with our genders and transitions.
      When will you affirm your own?

A plutonic love letter filled with words that stick.
Like fibers animating our relational force.
He has always seen me on my terms as I've always seen him on his.
    But sometimes touching tomorrow today takes time.
And so we wait, and nourish. Recover and reconstruct.
    That which was ripped from us.

And while our paths may often look and feel regressive or backwards, they are always working in service of futurities, potentialities, bound and constrained by the materialities of yesterday today.

Notes

1 Billy Porter. (@theebillyporter), "Honored to Be Part of @people Magazine's Exclusive 'The Greatest Stars on Earth' #emmys2019 Portfolio Shot by the Iconic @ruvenafanador." Instagram, August 24, 2019, https://www.instagram.com/p/B1kGamPFiwo/?igshid=1i1dgaezei44g.
2 adrienne maree brown. *Pleasure Activism: The Politics of Feeling Good* (Oakland, CA: AK Press, 2019), 1.
3 Andrea Long Chu and Emmett Harsin Drager. "After Trans Studies." *Transgender Studies Quarterly* 6, no. 1 (2019): 107, doi: 10.1215/23289252-7253524.
4 Chu and Drager, 108.
5 Cáel Keegan. "Getting Disciplined: What's Trans★ About Queer Studies Now?" *Journal of Homosexuality*, 9–10, doi: 10.1080/00918369.2018.1530885.
6 Chu and Drager, 112.

Bibliography

brown, adrienne maree. *Pleasure Activism: The Politics of Feeling Good*. Oakland, CA: AK Press, 2019.

Chu, Andrea Long and Emmett Harsin Drager. "After Trans Studies." *Transgender Studies Quarterly* 6, no. 1 (2019): 103–116, doi: 10.1215/23289252-7253524.

Keegan, Cáel. "Getting Disciplined: What's Trans★ about Queer Studies Now?" *Journal of Homosexuality*, 1–14, doi: 10.1080/00918369.2018.1530885.

Porter, Billy (@theebillyporter). "Honored to Be Part of @people Magazine's Exclusive 'The Greatest Stars on Earth' #emmys2019 Portfolio Shot by the Iconic @ruvenafanador." Instagram, August 24, 2019, https://www.instagram.com/p/B1kGamPFiwo/?igshid=1i1dgaezei44g.

INDEX